THE BIRTH OF THE CHRISTIAN RELIGION

Alfred Loisy

Translated from the French by

L. P. Jacks

THE BOOK TREE
San Diego, California

This English edition originally published
1948
George Allen & Unwin, Ltd.
London

New material & revision
© The Book Tree 2018

ISBN 978-1-58509-390-8

Cover art
Sunrise on Great Arber Mountain,
Bavaria, Germany
© Nemo 1963

Cover layout
Paul Tice

Published by
The Book Tree
P O Box 16476
San Diego, CA 92176
www.thebooktree.com

We provide fascinating and educational products to help awaken the public to new ideas and
information that would not be available otherwise.
Call 1 (800) 700-8733 for our FREE BOOK TREE CATALOG.

CONTENTS

Preface, by Gilbert Murray..5

Author's Introduction..10

The Sources...17

The Gospel of Jesus...61

Birth of the Belief in Jesus as the Christ................................89

The Birth of Apostolic Propaganda......................................121

The Apostle Paul..151

Persecution Begins...181

Birth of the Christian Mystery and of Its Rites....................219

Earliest Theories of the Christian Mystery..........................253

The Gnostic Crisis..295

Birth of the Catholic Church..325

Notes...361

Index...411

PREFACE

by

GILBERT MURRAY

DR. JACKS has rendered a great service to religious thought by his translation of this very remarkable book, which sums up the main conclusions of M. Loisy's elaborate studies of early Christian literature. It represents the latest, and, in my judgment, the most masterly of all the attempts to understand and describe according to the normal canons of human history, without prejudice and without miracle, a movement which has shaped the whole subsequent religion of the Western World. Previous historians of Christianity have generally been theologians, convinced of the miraculous nature of their subject and consequently, however learned, compelled to be uncritical. Only a few have deliberately rejected the miraculous, and many of them, in their anxiety to be freed from a false mythology, have been betrayed into a polemical attitude and failed to appreciate the grandeur of their theme. But, apart from these considerations, the subject itself is curiously difficult and obscure. The actual Christian literature proves on examination to be so different from what it seems. The Gospels, which look at first sight like simple lives of Jesus, prove on analysis to have had quite a different purpose and also to have been exposed to varied and incalculable influences in the interests of different doctrines and communities. It is only of recent years that scholars have begun to understand how different from a modern book, printed off in a thousand or so uniform copies, was the nature of an ancient book written out copy by copy; how different again the book which, although written, is still in the main merely an instrument for oral recitation, liable to be improved or altered according to circumstances or the taste of the reciter; different again the book of devotion or edification meant to enforce or correct the rites and beliefs of a community. M. Loisy's analysis of the books of the New Testament and other early Christian literature surpasses, in my opinion, any previous analysis known to me. He writes with an intimate understanding of the problems before him which seems to me to shed a new, and I would almost add a convincing, light on one of the most important movements in human history. I only hesitate to use the word "convincing" because, as he himself emphatically warns us, the evidence itself often leads only to a doubt or at most to a strong probability.

There is another advance of knowledge in recent years which explains much in the rise of Christianity and its acceptance by the Greco-Roman world which must have seemed inexplicable a generation ago. To one who, like myself, approaches the problem from the Greek side it is very significant that the language of the New Testament is Greek. The crude contrast between "Christian" and "Pagan" is really a false one. The idea of a son of God born to save the world is essentially a Greek idea. All the Greek-speaking populations of the Levant were permeated by the old agricultural worship of the Renewal of Life in the New Year after the dead winter. The Renewal was of course conceived as a person. He was the fruit of the marriage of earth with Heaven through the spring Sun and Rain; a son of God and an earthly *Kore* or maiden; a babe who will become King and make all things new, shaking off the dead impurities of the past. This theme is the subject of countless myths and rituals and forms a specially large element in the Drama and the ritual of Dionysus. From early times onward, and increasingly in the Hellenistic Age, these myths and rites were allegorized. The $T\rho\acute{\iota}\tau o\varsigma\ \Sigma\acute{\omega}\tau\eta\rho$, the "Saviour" who comes "Third," after the death of the Vegetation-King and of that king's slayer, became something much more than the saviour of the seed sown and the life of the ploughed field; he was to save the life of the world, and above all to save man's soul. All the philosophy of the Hellenistic age is tinged with a mysticism which comes chiefly from a sublimation of this agricultural New Life, combined with the desire for *Gnôsis*, Knowledge of God or union with God, of which there were germs in Plato and intense developments in the Egyptian and Oriental mystery-cults. There was also a wide-spread groping towards monotheism, attained not by denying any of the gods—that would have seemed impious —but by explaining them as emanations, or interpreters, or merely other names, of the One; and lastly in almost all the religious or philosophical movements one finds a tendency towards asceticism or at least a strong protest against the lusts of the flesh.

On Greek minds affected by these ideas contact with the Jews seems to have had almost the effect of a revelation. The very qualities which made that strange race so unpopular, their intolerance, their denial of the gods, their contemptuous hatred of idolatry and blood-sacrifice, had for thoughtful minds an extraordinary power of attraction. Here at last, in the phrase of one Greek writer, was a φιλόσοφον ἔθνος, "a philosopher nation," in which the whole people had risen above the turmoil of vulgar superstitions and incessant religious observances which beset the Pagan world, and moreover had a clear moral standard in sexual matters. The Jews stood altogether for a cleaner and less frightened world. Besides, in place of the confused mythical legends of the Greeks, this nation had an ancient and sacred Book, of uncontested authority, containing laws and prophecies which had stood the test of time. And they were all expecting a Messiah, a Saviour.

By the time of St. Paul these influences must have become more intense, more disturbing. A new sect of Jews was saying that the Messiah had actually come and that his kingdom was about to be proclaimed; only it seemed that he had failed. He was dead, condemned by law and crucified. As M. Loisy points out, that disaster would by no means be fatal to the survival of an ordinary sect, like that of the followers of John the Baptist, disciples of a human prophet. It was a much severer blow to worshippers of a Messiah announcing the arrival of a heavenly kingdom. One who failed, it seemed obvious, could not be the Messiah. But was this objection really valid? The common people of the Hellenistic world knew that the Saviour must die; to die and be re-born was the course of his normal history. And as for the condemnation and crucifixion, the more educated men were familiar with Plato's famous description of the righteous man in an unrighteous world, who must expect "to be thrown into prison, scourged and racked, and after every kind of torment . . . be impaled or crucified." It is not difficult to imagine speculations of this sort bearing fruit in the mind of Paul during his period of conversion.

Thus Hebrew ideas influenced the Greek mind, and in return ideas that were traditional among the populations of the great cities and country villages of Greek Asia not only gave a new inspiration to the Jewish followers of Jesus but inevitably invaded and shook the narrow Jewish orthodoxy. It was not a mere

Jewish Messiah that the world hungered for; it was a Saviour of mankind. And such a Saviour must, according to all Greek precedent, be the son of a God by a daughter of Earth, and she, on the analogy of many myths, a Virgin of royal birth, made fruitful by the divine Touch or Breath or Spirit. The Jews might indignantly protest. Greek philosophers might cry halt. But these ideas were too wide-spread and deep-rooted to be suppressed, and soon began to lead away from strict monotheism to something more emotional and more familiar; to the immemorial worship of the Mother Goddess, to the old Trinity of Father, Mother and Child in different forms, and to various rites for entering into communion with God by the mediation of minor deities or by the mystical partaking of the divine blood. No wonder there was bitter opposition between Christian and Jew. The Jews could not but feel that these Hellenizers were trying to drag them into a swamp of mere paganism.

It was a long time before these various streams of religious emotion could be shaped into one coherent Christian creed. At first, apparently, it was enough to have received the Good News that the Saviour had come and suffered and re-risen, and now the Kingdom of God was at hand. Even when that Good News proved to be not true in its literal sense, the intense longing which inspired that unhappy generation was too strong to let it die. It was preserved as at least an allegorical truth. In the early days it seems clear that there was no exact orthodoxy. Different teachers and different parts of the Hellenistic world followed their divergent ways of thought. I suspect, however, that one binding force among Christians was the conscious misery of the subject populations of the Roman Empire after the awful series of civil wars and proletarian rebellions whose effects still persisted even after the establishment of the Augustan Peace. The early Christian literature which accepts as obvious the wickedness of *publicani* and upper-class Pharisees and the extreme improbability of any rich man entering the Kingdom of Heaven, which cries that the foxes have holes and the birds of the air have nests but the son of man has not where to lay his head, was, as Arnold Toynbee has pointed out,[*] repeating an old "flying word" which had been familiar to unhappy populations from the time of Tiberius

[*] *Study of History*, vi, p. 414.

Gracchus onward. Such a movement brought union among the oppressed and at the same time roused terror in society generally. Again and again the writers of the New Testament repeat the command "Slaves, obey your masters,"* and explain that they use no violence and seek no earthly kingdom. Those who remembered with horror the risings of Mithridates, of the Heliopolites in Asia, Spartacus in Italy, the slave-king "Antiochus" in Sicily, were mistrustful of this mysterious current of emotion among the proletariates of the eastern cities, and its occasional outbursts of unconcealed fury against the Harlot seated upon Seven Hills and drunken with the blood of saints. When one reads of the horror inspired by the name of Christian and the monstrous persecutions to which Christians were exposed in a world which did not persecute other religions, I suspect that the explanation lies chiefly in two of the new religion's noblest qualities. It represented the cry of the poor in a suffering and harshly administered world, and it proclaimed a great, if temporary, liberation of the human mind by its wholesale denial of false gods and idolatrous pietisms.

* Eph. vi, 5; Col. iii, 22; Tit. ii, 9; 1 Pet. ii, 18.

AUTHOR'S INTRODUCTION

THE present study of the origin of the Christian religion comes in sequence to that which the author has recently published on the religion of Israel, the mention of which suffices to render another introduction unnecessary. A complete translation of the New Testament has also been edited[1] which, to some extent, supplies the documentation and critical discussion behind the present synthesis, while the synthesis completes that volume by placing the New Testament writings, and the other sources of primitive Christian history, in their original setting.

Needless to say, a synthesis of this kind can be no more than an essay, related as closely as possible to the present state of knowledge, but making no pretence to offer a definite solution of all the problems raised by the birth of the Christian religion; problems concerning the character of the evangelical writings and the Epistles attributed to the apostle Paul; problems concerning the evolution of the religion from its point of departure in Judaism until the time when the Church, in the last quarter of the second century, is seen building itself up, in opposition to a flood of gnostic systems, on the base of a tradition alleged to be apostolic, of which the New Testament is held to be the witness, and the episcopate called catholic claims to be the authorized interpreter or guardian.

The author of this book makes humble avowal of not having yet discovered that Jesus never existed. The conjectures by which some among us, in these latter days, would explain the Christian religion without him whom that religion regards as its founder have always seemed to him as fragile as they are vociferous. These conjectures come, for the most part, from persons who have arrived somewhat late at the problem of Jesus, and not all of whom have prepared for that problem by deep study of the history of Israel's religion or of the Christian. For them the non-existence of Jesus forms part of a philosophical system, except where it proceeds from polemical interests avowed or discreetly veiled. Long ago the Christ was discovered by Dupuis to be a solar myth; Bruno Bauer and the Dutch school (Van Manen excepted) make him out a pure creation of Alexandrian allego-

AUTHOR'S INTRODUCTION

rists, in which they are followed by W. B. Smith, Drews and Robertson. In France P. L–Couchoud (*Le mystère de Jésus*) and E. Dujardin (*Le Dieu Jésus*) have each struck out on a line of his own; Couchoud postulating a pre-Christian myth of a suffering Jahveh (!) which a vision of Simon Peter suddenly transformed into a living religion; Dujardin, a pre-Christian worship of Jesus with the fictitious crucifixion of an individual playing the part of a god, the Christian religion having its origin in the last exhibition of this pageant, which also gives the date of its birth.

These hypotheses all share in a common defect: they are air-drawn fabrics and they do not explain the birth of the Christian religion. For the part played by myth in the Christian tradition concerning Jesus is as undeniable as it was inevitable in the origins of the Christian movement; but the witness to the Christian fact does not entirely dissolve into a myth, and the fact itself is not a myth. The messianic myth supports Jesus, but Jesus together with the myth support the Christian religion; the distinctively Christian myth of Jesus–God did not exist before Christianity, but was formed inside that religion, and formed stage by stage, to the glory of Jesus. The Christian myth of salvation was, in a manner, called into being and set on foot by Jesus himself, to be afterwards elaborated in the first age of the Christian religion. The testimony and the facts being what they are, the mythical theory unduly simplifies the problem of Christian origins, which it does more to obscure than to illuminate. In the *Revue Critique*, 1925 (pp. 343–347) the present author wrote as follows: "the part played by myth in the birth of Christianity is more easily determined by the historian than is the part played by Jesus himself. While the Christian religion was not created by myth alone, so, certainly, it was not created by Jesus alone; its creator was neither Jesus without the myth, nor the myth without Jesus. Jesus the Nazorean is at once an historical person and a mythical being who, supporting the myth and supported by it, was finally made by it into the Christ, Lord and God, for the faith which so acknowledged him. To say this is not to reduce the part of Jesus to an occasional cause. On the other hand, to present, as the sole and total cause of Christianity, one human being who, considered as divine, was also the very object worshipped by that religion would only be to create another myth."

It is however true that the ancient testimonies do not permit us to reconstitute the human figure of Jesus, his personal doings, the meaning of his career and its chief circumstances, with full and unfaltering certitude.

That Jesus was one among a number of agitators and enthusiasts who appeared in Judea between the years 6 and 70 of our era; that his appearance is to be placed towards the middle of this period or the beginning of its third; that it had, in one form or another, a messianic character; that Jesus was crucified as a pretended Messiah by sentence of Pontius Pilate—all this has the highest degree of probability; to be more exact, the whole Christian movement becomes unintelligible if these beginnings are suppressed. No consistent argument authorizes their elimination and there is nothing to replace them. But what idea had Jesus of his mission, if even he had any precise idea? What did he hope for and aim at? What was his message and on what special charge was he condemmed to death? How were his followers grouped round him and on what grounds did they become convinced after his death that he was still alive, immortal, powerful and glorified at the right hand of God? How was Christ Jesus presently sublimated into Jesus the God-saviour? These are questions which the evidence does not permit us to answer with complete certitude and in detail. And the most brilliant hypotheses brought forward to answer them are not necessarily the best founded.

The Tradition which has preserved for us the memory of Jesus was at its origin entirely different from historical tradition. From the very beginning it was a tradition of *faith*, and almost immediately afterwards the tradition of a *cult* which grew continually more impassioned and developed until it attained complete deification of its object. Memory, in a word, was transfigured into faith and adoration. In all strictness the Gospels are not historical documents. They are catechisms for use in common worship, containing the cult-legend of the Lord Jesus Christ; that, and no other, is the content they announce; that, and no other, is the quality they claim. Even Luke, which assumes a high degree of editorial exactitude, set out to be, before all else, "sound instruction in the Word"—as we should say, "a good manual of Christian initiation" (i, 1–4). Even the teaching attributed to

AUTHOR'S INTRODUCTION

Jesus is constructed, for the most part, to meet the needs of Christian propaganda, for the edification of the earliest communities, or, yet again, especially in the fourth Gospel, to elaborate a mystical theory of salvation by Jesus Christ. We cannot complacently assume that we are able clearly to recognize, behind all these elaborations of faith, the real features of Jesus, his personal activities and the precise circumstances of his ministry and death. What the historian sees directly before him in all this is the faith of the first Christian generations and the intensity of their devotion to Jesus, the Saviour.

There is nothing to make good this insufficiency of the Gospel evidence. The Acts of the Apostles, supposed to narrate the history of the first Christian age, contain the legend and, in some respects, the myth rather than the history of it, insomuch that the general perspective of the book is, in its own way, as artificial as that of the Gospels, if not more so. The Epistles known as apostolic have been edited in the same spirit as the Gospels and with likelihood hardly greater of being the work of the authors to whom they are attributed. Little by little it has perforce been admitted that the Gospels are not the personal works of individual writers, and that the traditional attribution of these books to apostles or to apostolic men is contestable in every instance. It has also at length been recognized that a false authorship has been attributed to several Epistles and that their date is uncertain: cases in point are Hebrews, Ephesians, second Thessalonians and the Epistles known as catholic. Furthermore it has become impossible not to recognize traces of compilation in the two Epistles to the Corinthians, and the conclusion has followed that they were composed by amalgamating matter drawn from a much larger number of authentic letters. Even bolder conjectures, not only for the two Epistles in question, but for Romans, first Thessalonians and perhaps others, might be reasonably defended. The obvious doctrinal incoherence between the Epistles, and often in the same Epistle, would thus find a better explanation than that afforded by the restlessness of mind with a superabundant endowment of which the Apostle is usually credited. Thus the question arises of whether the theories of redemption brought forward in the Epistles called Pauline are really those of the Apostle. Or do they represent flights of gnostic speculation later than Paul but earlier than the chief systems of heretical gnosticism?

In the next chapter we shall see how limited are the resources which other Christian documents anterior to the year 180 offer to the critical historian. We feel therefore entitled to remark, in terminating this preamble, that while every history of Christian origins rests, admittedly or not, on more or less shaky foundations, the fault is not necessarily attributable to the historian who tries to write that history, but to the condition of the evidence on which he has to base it. For that reason we here make no pretence to give a finished and balanced picture of the birth of the Christian religion. Our aim will be to show forth with simplicity what seem the most probable conclusions in this delicate matter, as they offer and prove themselves to our own mind.

CONTENTS

CHAPTER		PAGE
	PREFACE BY GILBERT MURRAY O.M.	5
	AUTHOR'S INTRODUCTION	10
I.	*The Sources*	17
II.	*The Gospel of Jesus*	61
III.	*Birth of the Belief in Jesus as the Christ*	89
IV.	*The Birth of Apostolic Propaganda*	121
V.	*The Apostle Paul*	151
VI.	*Persecution Begins*	181
VII.	*Birth of the Christian Mystery and of its Rites*	219
VIII.	*Earliest Theories of the Christian Mystery*	253
IX.	*The Gnostic Crisis*	295
X.	*Birth of the Catholic Church*	325
	NOTES	361

Chapter I

THE SOURCES

ALL indications point to the conclusion that the Christian religion, though an offspring of Judaism, did not issue from any of the great currents then dominant in Jewish thought and known under the name of Pharisee, Sadducee and Essene. It sprang from small eccentric circles and stood out so little in the history of Palestinian Judaism before the year 70 that Josephus thought himself dispensed from mentioning it in his writings.[1] Christianity was not a contagious movement of organized asceticism, still less a form of legalist pietism and least of all a school of traditional conservatism. It was distinctly a Messianist movement, carried on in conditions peculiar to itself and without the sanguinary fanaticism of the Zealots. It invoked as its head a Christ who, after dying on earth, was living at the right hand of God; his return would proceed from the higher world, that is, from his own being and nature, and in this sense it soon became a salvation-mystery of which the Christ was life and soul, the coming of this Christ progressively shifting its position to a new point and becoming realized, so to speak, in the faith of his Church. A mystery of this nature could not fail to get defined in a theology. In the beginning, however, Christianity was a religion of humble folk. Men of learning, dogmatizing theologians, contemplative dreamers were not its originators.

The Christian religion was not founded on doctrine formulated in a book. It formed its own doctrine as it grew, and the books distinctively its own, known among us as the literature of primitive Christianity, are the products and the historic witnesses of its doctrinal elaboration as this was achieved during the first hundred or hundred and fifty years in the life of the new religion. It may be said with confidence that Christianity, at its point of departure, had no other literature than that of the Judaism from which it sprang. This literature it began to interpret in a manner all its own, with reference to its Christ and in the interests of Christian propaganda, while reserving till later the creation of its own literature in answer to the needs which arose in the course of its experience. This specifically Christian literature is the principal and almost the only source at our disposal for understanding Christianity in the first age of its evolution. The direct evidence of Jewish writers is relatively late, scanty, of mediocre scope and value, while that of pagan writers concerns only the outside of Christian propaganda and informs us chiefly of the impression it made on the "enlightened" opinion of that age.

In a sense very true, the history of primitive Christianity is a kind of pre-history which has to be reconstructed—one might almost say to be guessed—from documents which reflect it but were not originally conceived, nor later edited, for the purpose of putting it on record. The labours of criticism are therefore indispensable, and so much the more in need of cautious handling as the scientific examination of these documents is far from having spoken its last word.

From about the year 180 onwards the history of the Christian religion is no longer beset by great obscurity. With the writings before us of Irenaeus, Tertullian, Clement of Alexandria and Hippolytus we have enough daylight to make visible the interior organization, the exterior relations and the characteristic doctrines of the new religion. As for the earlier period, we are bound to admit that information is far from complete, indeed almost fragmentary, and too often untrustworthy and difficult to interpret. The present chapter will offer a kind of inventory of the documents in question. The chapters to follow will unfold the meaning we find in them for reconstructing the history of the Christian religion in the earliest period of its life.

1. The New Testament

To the books comprised in what is known as the New Testament, which forms a pendant to the collection of the Old, inherited from the Synagogue and from hellenizing Judaism, tradition assigns a place of their own as books divinely authorized and the work of apostles. In reality the apostolic elements in these books are not very numerous. They were canonized by and for their employment in the Christian communities for public reading in preference to others of similar character which the Church thought well, as occasion called for it, to set aside or to condemn. We may recall that the collection of the Old Testament was also fixed in Jewish tradition, derived from synagogal usage, to the depreciation of a literature, apocalyptic or otherwise, and partly more recent, of which the disqualification was judged desirable. In both cases, Old and New, the authenticity of the canonized writings, relative to those excluded from the canon, is artificial and based on theological convention; in both cases the authorship of books is falsely assigned, or partly falsified, for the purpose of guaranteeing the exceptional credit claimed for all parts alike of a collection of books thenceforth to be regarded as sacred.

Although the writings comprised in the New Testament constitute our chief source for the history of primitive Christianity, they carry no privilege in the eyes of the scientific historian, save what may be derived from their relative value as evidence, when compared with non-canonical writings. All the documents of ancient Christianity, canonical and non-canonical, will be classed in this chapter according to their kind, though not according to their literary kind precisely, since the greater number do not fall into any of the accepted classes of literature. We shall deal first with those documents which affect, more or less distinctly, the form of epistles; second, with those in the form of apocalypse; third, with those, known as Gospels, which present the sacred legend of Jesus and the apostles; fourth and last, with the sharply defined group of second century apologists. Had the writings of the second century gnostics come down to us, them also we should have to consider; but little more is known of them than what can be gathered from ecclesiastical authors who placed these writings on their list of heresies or laboured to refute them.

Pauline Epistles

Fourteen Epistles appear in the New Testament under the name of Paul. Few critics have had the hardihood to class them all as literary forgeries, and those who have done so, Bruno Bauer and the Dutch school of Van Manen, seem to have taken insufficient account of the great variety of elements which have found their way into the two Epistles to the Corinthians and the Epistle to the Romans.

To begin with, the Epistle to the Hebrews stands apart as one whose origin was matter of debate in the ancient Church. The Roman Church, while not ignoring it, long refused to recognize it as Paul's and attributed to him thirteen Epistles only. The heretic Marcion (140–150) knew, or recognized, only ten, not knowing, or rejecting, the two Epistles to Timothy and the Epistle to Titus; he accepted the so-called Epistle to the Ephesians under the name of the Epistle to the Laodiceans, a name he can have had no reason to invent. This, however, does not prove the complete authenticity of the ten. That Marcion put much of his own into them is neither proved nor even probable; he did not force his system into them any more than he put it into his Gospel; contenting himself with cutting down or retouching in the Gospel of Luke whatever was in conflict with his system, he would do the same in the Epistles with passages that displeased him. The fact remains that the ten, the thirteen, or the fourteen, whatever their connexion with Paul, were not preserved for themselves as epistles, but as providing catechetical matter and passages to be read in public for the instruction and edifying of congregations. If some of them are fictitious, as seems certain, it cannot be *a priori* improbable that compilations like the Epistles to the Romans and the Corinthians contain considerable additions to their authentic elements.

Thessalonians

The First to the Thessalonians, if authentic, as it seems to be, would date from the year 51, the oldest document of Christian literature to which an approximate date can be assigned. It is not free from editorial surcharges[2] and the long passage on the ressurrection (iv, 13–v, 11) must be a late insertion.[3]

Imitated from the First Epistle and specially co-ordinated with the insertion on the resurrection of the dead, the Second to Thessalonians is, for the most part, a theological dissertation on the conditions of the Second Advent. It is not written for the instruction of a particular community but aims rather to dissipate the general uneasiness of Christian thought in regard to the Parousia, impatiently expected and continually postponed. The author enlarges on the apocalyptic theme of the Antichrist, perhaps identified with Nero risen from the dead, whose manifestation was to cause the ruin of the Roman Empire. The document is conceived in the spirit of the synoptic Gospels and is probably not earlier than the first quarter of the second century. Since Marcion accepted it as authentic, we can hardly place it as late as 130–135. The pains taken by the author at the end (iii, 17) to declare his signature genuine render it the more suspect.

Corinthians

The two Epistles contain elements bearing on the relations of Paul with the community of Corinth, during the years 50–56 approximately, which cannot be explained on any other hypothesis than that of their authenticity. But the two Epistles in their traditional form are not pieces of written correspondence. They are two discourses made up of letters and instructions of various kinds at a date considerably later than the years in which epistolary relations existed between Paul and his Corinthian converts.

We gather from the first Epistle that Paul, while at Ephesus in 54 or 55, wrote to these converts with the aim of healing divisions of whose existence in the community he had been informed (i, 1–16);[4] the final recommendations (xvi) are co-ordinated with this opening and the interval between them filled with ill-assorted matter of various kinds. We begin with an eloquent outburst on the mystery of the Cross, hidden from the heavenly powers appointed to govern the world, who crucified the Lord in their ignorance (i, 17–ii, 8);[5] of this mystery, Paul, taught by the Spirit, is the herald (ii, 10–16); if he has not spoken to the Corinthians as spiritual, that is because they are carnal, as they are proved to be by their quarrels (iii, 1–4); following this, a sublime conception of the apostolate and the consideration of Paul's unique relation to the Corinthians. All of which is pitched on so high a level that we cannot but ask whether the point of view may not be that of polemical theory rather than that of the modest reality. To the latter belongs what we go on to read about Timothy's preliminary errand, of Paul's impending visit to Corinth and the incestuous man whose excommunication he decrees. Moral lessons come next, grouped by a certain analogy of subject, but without real cohesion. Then follow a mystic couplet about the old leaven, the Christian azyme and Christ the pascal victim of the faithful (v, 6–8); a remark on keeping bad company awkwardly adjusted to what has been said about the incestuous man, which again is disastrously cut up and surcharged in a passage against lawsuits between believers; and then a moral lesson against impurity (vi, 12–20). From this point the document before us ceases to be a letter and becomes an assemblage of miscellaneous instructions: further rules of discipline later in origin than the beginning of apostolic preaching; rules on marriage and virginity (vii);[6] on the eating of meat that comes from pagan sacrifices, the passage cut in two by an editor (viii; x, 23–xi, i)[7] and doubled by mystic instruction on the same subject (x, 1–22) which contradicts the disciplinary rule first given; in the space between, an apology, mainly retrospective, for the action Paul has taken to avoid being a charge to his converts, especially to the Corinthians (ix);[8] further on (xi, 3–16) two rulings on the holding of assemblies; the first, enjoining the women to keep veiled when they prophesy in course of the meeting, inserted into the framework of the second which has to do with the good order and especially the high signification of the Eucharist (xi, 2, 17–34);[9] another instruction on spiritual gifts divided into two parts, the theory of the *charismata*, their rôle in the life of the community, and rules for speaking with tongues and prophesying in the assembly of the faithful (xii, xiv),[10] with the Song of Love (xiii, 1–12) intercalated between the two parts and coming in as a corrective to the foregoing decree;[11] followed up by a dissertation on the bodily resurrection of the Christ, type of a general resurrection of the dead and especially of believers (xv), in which there is revealed a certain development of the evangelical tradition and of the Christian gnosis. The conclusion of the original letter (xvi) then follows without further preparation.

The Second to the Corinthians was written from Macedonia in the autumn of the year 55; but this Epistle, though less complicated than the first by editorial treatment, also contains elements of various date and origin. The opening (i–ii, 13) appears to belong to a letter of reconciliation or of consolation written by Paul after experiencing a great affliction while in Asia, from which he had been delivered by the good news that Titus had brought him of better conditions in Corinth. The affliction in question was less probably persecution undergone at Ephesus than the anguish of mind into which Paul had fallen after making a visit to Corinth, which had rather aggravated the difficulties between him and the community, difficulties which the intervention of Titus had subsequently smoothed over. But even in this part of the letter certain additions tinged with mystical gnosis may have been made (i, 3–7; 12–14, 21, 22). Suddenly the flow of the original is arrested to make room for a long dithyramb in praise of the true apostleship which belongs solely to Paul, herald of the new convenant in the spirit, triumphant in weakness and suffering while waiting for eternal glory, knowing no man after the flesh, not even Christ, and announcing with unwearied zeal the message of the reconciliation of the world to God by faith in Christ risen from the dead; at this point he beseeches the Corinthians to be faithful to the grace of God and to enlarge their heart towards him, now straitened on his account (ii, 14–vi, 13). Then comes a new insertion into the flow of this fine utterance, which resumes its course a little later on (vii, 2–3) but only to lose itself immediately in a forced transition to the letter of reconciliation (vii, 4). The inserted passage is an instruction about keeping company with pagans (vi, 14–vii, 1) which connects with nothing in the Second to the Corinthians and must be a quotation from elsewhere. What follows (vii, 5–16) concerns the happy issue of the mission to the Corinthians undertaken by Titus: it forms the original conclusion of the letter. The two pieces about the collection for the saints in Jerusalem (viii, ix) hang loose from the context and cannot have been written at the same time; the older of the two (ix) has been placed second by the compiler.[12] The greater part of the last chapter is conceived in the same spirit and tone as the earlier eulogium of Paul's apostleship, except for several passages of a distinctly personal character which seem to come from the severe letter, written after Paul's second stay in Corinth, to which the letter of reconciliation makes allusion (vii, 8). The most important of these personal passages is a fighting apology against "the very chiefest of the apostles" (xi, 5)[13]—who are the elder apostles of Jerusalem and not any kind of missionaries—

to whom Paul boasts of being inferior in nothing. Here is another insertion about the disinterested conditions of Paul's Corinthian mission (xi, 6b–12a).[14] Whereupon the denunciation of the super-apostles is resumed with increased vigour, Paul sounding his own praises in abundance by recalling his labours and tribulations, nay even his visions, especially the most important which carried him up to the third heaven;[15] "a thorn in the flesh" warns him not to be overproud; but for all that he will yield in nothing to the highest of them; and his apostleship has been made plain by many a prodigy. Then, suddenly, the tone changes and the question turns to the disinterestedness Paul has shown among the Corinthians; he will not change that attitude; if he now seems to be defending himself that is because he is on the point of coming to Corinth for the third time and is unwilling to find himself in the midst of their quarrels and disorders; let them mend their ways that he may not have to employ severity. But the grandiloquent apology preceding, which shows a very precise knowledge of Paul's career, would perhaps be better understood as coming from a distance in time and from the pen of an empassioned disciple. It flows in the same current of thought and style as the praise of the apostolate in the first part of the Epistle.

Galatians

There is a question whether this Epistle, written towards the end of the year 55, before the Second to the Corinthians and the Epistle to the Romans, was addressed to the communities of Pisidia and Lycaonia[16] or rather to those of Galatia proper. Perhaps it concerned all of them. But the capital question is that of its authenticity. Paul would seem to have written to justify his apostleship against Judaizing propaganda which was meeting with success in the communities. Fundamentally, the issue concerned a matter quite other than the uselessness of the Jewish observances. Paul presents himself as an apostle sent direct from God and from Christ the redeemer (i, 1–7) and anathematizes those who would turn the Galatians from the true Gospel (i, 5–9); describes the conditions in which the revelation of this Gospel was directly imparted to him (i, 10–12); how he fulfilled his vocation of apostle to the Gentiles up to the moment when he got his doctrine and practice recognized by the Jerusalem apostles and the admission made that he was to preach to the Gentiles while the other apostles occupied themselves with the Jews; which form of the compact Peter is said to have broken at Antioch (i, 13–ii, 14).[17] But the rebuke which Paul boasts of having administered to Peter face to face is lost sight of in a formal announcement of the thesis of salvation by faith in the Christ without the works of the law (ii, 15–20). To the demonstration of this thesis by diverse arguments, all inspired by the mystic gnosis already met in certain parts of Corinthians and methodically developed in Romans, the rest of the Epistle is thenceforward devoted. Entangled with these arguments are speculations about the faith of Abraham, type of the justified man, who received the saving benediction due to faith on behalf of all believers, Jews and Gentiles (iv, 21–31). Throughout all this there is only one small fragment that bears a genuinely personal accent (iv, 11–20), where Paul describes his present anxiety and the special circumstances in which he had preached the Gospel to the Galatians. The moral counsels of the last two chapters are, for the most part, in the customary vein of mystical gnosis.[18] It is in conformity with this gnosis that the origin of Paul's career is here interpreted, a mode of interpretation under which his conversion and apostolic activity become almost unintelligible to the historian, and the authenticity of the Epistle, taken as a whole, is gravely compromised. There cannot be a doubt that Paul, in becoming converted, adhered to a gospel preached before he took it up. As a matter of fact the conversion of Paul was not the absolute beginning of hellenic Christianity, and the division of the world to be converted, Jews to Peter and Gentiles to Paul, was not realized. Whence we may infer that the division was never agreed on.

Romans

The document called the Epistle to the Romans, so far as it comes from Paul's hand, probably dates from the year 56, having been written at Corinth a little before Paul left that city to carry to Jerusalem the collection made in the communities. Whatever value we may assign to it, the Epistle, like the two to the Corinthians, is a compilation. In the preamble (i, 1–17) Paul announces an explanatory apology for his ministry to pagans. Connected with this explanation is the discussion of Abraham's righteousness realized in his faith (iii, 28-iv), a line of thought already encountered in Galatians, and here completed by the discussion of prophetical texts which the author interprets as foretelling the conversion of the Gentiles and the reprobation, at least temporary, of the Jews. The passages at the end of the Gospel, describing the projects of Paul (xv, 8–38), are equally authentic.[19] But the theory of sin and grace, of salvation by the death of Christ, which is expounded at great length (v–viii) is clearly detached from these passages, has a style peculiar to itself and makes no attempt to support the argument in detail by scriptural texts.[20] On the other hand, certain developments[21] seem to have been inserted to soften the rigour of this theory (i, 18–iii, 20) and to prevent its abuse in practice by conclusions that might be drawn from it. The moral part of the Epistle must in like manner be secondary, since it was not for Paul to offer such lessons to a community of which he had no personal knowledge; these lessons moreover were not all inserted at the same time (xii–xv, 7).[22] The formulas of conclusion, which multiply towards the end (xv, 13, 33; xvi, 16, 25), bear witness to surcharges and retouchings.

Colossians, Ephesians and Philippians

The Epistles to the Colossians and Philippians, which some critics would attach to a hypothetical captivity at Ephesus, seem rather to have been written while Paul was a prisoner in Rome between 59 and 61. But the authenticity of Colossians is contestable. In it there is developed a mystical gnosis in affinity with that in Romans, though sensibly different in its formulas,[23] and akin to the Epistle to the Hebrews (cf. Hebrews i, 1–4). This gnosis has the appearance of being affirmed in opposition to another of Judaizing tendency which may possibly be the cult of Zeus Sabazios (ii, 16–23). Certain incoherences in the editing of the Epistle lead us to think that a document of Christian gnosis was attributed to Paul, as an afterthought, by means of the additions concerning his captivity, an authentic letter being utilized at the end for establishing a close relation between the Epistle to the Colossians and that to Philemon, as we now have them (iv, 7–11, 14). The authenticity of the latter, as a whole, presents no great difficulty. But the Epistle to the Colossians should rather be referred to the beginning of the second century.

The Epistle to the Ephesians figures in Marcion's collection as the Epistle to the Laodiceans. Imitated, though in a manner more servile, from the Epistle to the Colossians, as the Second to Thessalonians was imitated from the First, it was probably presented originally as the letter to the Laodiceans mentioned in Colossians (iv, 16).[24] The style of this spurious Epistle is turbid and obscure. As to the foundation of it, the author replaces the cosmological and soteriological gnosis of Colossians by a gnosis which might be called mainly ecclesiological, integrating the myth of salvation by the Christ into his own myth of the Church. Since it was known to Marcion the composition goes back to the first third of the second century.[25]

Though of mediocre compass, the Epistle to the Philippians has the appearance of being a compilation of two letters. Towards the middle we find a clean cut, following on a vehement outburst against Judaism which recalls the fiery apology of Paul in Second Corinthians (iii, 1–iv, 1, 8–9). Moreover in the first part of the Epistle (ii, 25–30) we read that Epaphroditus, Paul's messenger to the Philippians, has just left the Apostle after being long at his side, while in the second part (iv, 18) we are told that this same Epaphroditus is just come to him, bringing the help for which Paul thanks the Philippians. Plain proof that the Epistle is a compilation made up of two short letters placed in inverted order, the first belonging approximately to 59, the second to 60. To the two letters thus brought together were added, about the beginning of the second century, certain elements of Christian gnosis and anti-Jewish polemic.[26]

Pastoral Epistles

The term "pastoral" is commonly applied to the two Epistles to Timothy and the Epistle to Titus on the ground that they are chiefly concerned with the institution of pastors and with church discipline. Conceived with the purpose of checking the growth of gnosticism, they are much later than the apostolic age. It may well be that these apocryphal compositions were not divulged in the communities till after the explosion of Marcion's heresy: Timothy vi, 20 seems aimed directly at his *Antitheses*. As to their place of origin, the Roman souvenirs apparently contained in the Second to Timothy are not decisive for preferring Rome to the East. The hypothesis of short authentic letters embedded in a later commentary applies only to the Second (iv, 10–20) and is not exempt from question. Moreover the First does not seem to have been written continuously.[27] It is possible that a body of rules claiming to be apostolic has been drawn upon by the editor of our two Epistles, which probably have a common origin.

Hebrews

The Epistle "to the Hebrews" known in Rome at an early date, is earlier than the Epistle of Clement to the Corinthians which stands to it in a relation of dependence.[28] The attribution of the authorship to Paul, long unknown at Rome, seems to have been first made in Alexandria. Keeping the date commonly assigned to the letter of Clement (about 95) the Epistle to the Hebrews could not be later than 80. If the dates be postponed to the second century it would have to be admitted that the last two verses (xiii, 23–25) are a fictitious addition intended to support the attribution of the Epistle to Paul. In the same way the title "to the Hebrews" is no more than an ancient conjecture, perhaps originally connected with the said attribution. The attribution of authorship to Barnabas professed by Tertullian (*De Pudicitia*, 20), and perhaps current at Rome in his time, cannot be sustained, since the author places himself outside the apostolic age (ii, 3, 4).[29] A treatise rather than a letter, consisting of doctrinal and moral instruction, the document is addressed to a community of converted pagans nourished on the Old Testament as the only authorized scripture.[30] But the display of quotations serves only to support a Christian gnosis of salvation by the mediation of Christ, unique priest and victim, distinguished in express terms from the elementary catechesis in which the common teaching of Christianity was summed up (vi, 1–2). The conclusions which the author draws from the

Mosaic ritual are derived from texts, not from observances then flourishing, while the moral teaching is addressed to believers already tried by persecution and liable to lose their confidence in the mystery of salvation here presented as the true fulfilment of Jewish scripture. Earlier than the explosion of the gnostic crisis and the canonization of the Gospel, the Epistle is probably of Alexandrian origin.

Incidentally, this Epistle affords a striking example of the freedom with which primitive gnosis developed the conception of the Christ, and of its independence of what is commonly called the Gospel tradition. We find it especially in the parallel instituted in chapter vii between Melchisedec and Jesus, in which the Christ, without father or mother, without beginning or end of life in this world, "rose up," like a star—allusion to the star of Numbers xxiv, 17—"from Judah," whose descendant he certainly was not in the Gospel tradition.

Peter and Jude

The first of the Epistles named after Peter would be placed under the patronage of that apostle at a time when he had become recognized as the founder of the Roman community: it is a catechism or homily in which baptism is made much of, but with a theme of wider range than baptismal instruction. Rome is here spoken of under its mystic name of Babylon (v, 13) and perhaps the mention of Mark (v, 13) is intended to promote his claim to the authorship of the second Gospel. But this writing contains little sign of influence by Gospel tradition, the sole feature, on which the writer insists complacently, as though it were well known, being the descent of the Christ into hell (iii, 19-20; iv, 6), a feature hardly hinted at in the canonical Gospels. The document is almost contemporary with the Epistle to the Hebrews, but of Roman origin, at least in its canonical edition.

The second Epistle attributed to the same apostle is perceptibly of a later date. The central part of it (ii, iii) which corresponds with the Epistle of Jude, is an attack on the gnostic movement then in full life and vigour. In the preamble[31] it refers not, as commonly supposed, to the Gospel story of transfiguration, but to the Apocalypse of Peter—which we shall discuss later on. In the conclusion (iii, 15, 16) it mentions a collection of Paul's Epistles of which certain heretics are making abusive employment; this doubtless is the collection of the ten Epistles known to Marcion. The Epistle therefore must be later than the birth of Marcionism and was most probably composed in the East, about 150 at the earliest.

Apart from its superscription (1-2) and doxology (24-25), the Epistle named after Jude embodies, in a form at least relatively primitive, the anti-gnostic writing, or fragment, which is paraphrased in Second Peter. The original writing may be dated as far on as about 130, and its working up into an Epistle to 150. The relative antiquity of this composition appears in the quotations from the Apocrypha, Enoch and the Assumption of Moses (14, 15 and 9), which Second Peter has not retained.

James

The so-called Epistle of James is a piece of simple moral instruction drawing its inspiration from a catechism rather Jewish than Christian. It makes a lively attack on the idea of faith without works which suggests that its editing took place before the time when the four Gospels, and the writings attributed to Paul, were advanced to canonical authority, that is, before 150.[32] The fictitious address to the Twelve Tribes, which transforms a collection of moral maxims into an Epistle, is symbolic, like that of 1 Peter to the "dispersed" Jews of Asia Minor. A certain affinity in tone with the Pastor of Hermas suggests that its place of origin was Rome.

John

Of the three Epistles attributed to the apostle John, the first, like the Epistle to the Hebrews, does not affect the form of a letter. It consists of instruction, dogmatic and moral, perhaps originally founded on a rhythmical discourse like those found in the Fourth Gospel. The successive editions of the Epistle seem to have been co-ordinate with those of the Gospel itself; whence it would follow that the last edition, directed against gnosticism, cannot be earlier than the middle of the second century.33 This would also be the date of the two smaller Epistles, which have only the appearance of letters, the designation of the author being deliberately vague, as well as that of the recipients. The two were intended to act as convoy to the first in its final form, the second condemning the Docetic Christology, perhaps especially that of Marcion, while the third blasts those leaders of the community who oppose the Johannine writings. All three Epistles, like the fourth Gospel, were worked into their present form in Ephesian surroundings.

Barnabas

The Epistle "of Barnabas,'" also anonymous in itself, presents a certain analogy to the Epistle to the Hebrews, and must belong to nearly the same period, to a time, that is, when the Gospel legend was in process of formation.34 The Epistle of Barnabas has no dependence on any of the canonical Epistles. In the moral part it reproduces instruction about the "two ways," the way of light and the way of darkness, a kind of Jewish catechism also made use of in the *Didache*. It was probably composed, therefore, at Alexandria in the first third of the second century.

Clement

Addressed in the name of "the community of God living in Rome to the community of God living in Corinth," the Epistle attributed to Clement is a long piece of moral teaching composed on the occasion of troubles which had broken out in the Corinthian community and intended for their remedy. The document itself is one of the most authentic, but the date commonly assigned to it, about 95, seems open to question. Although it quotes the First to the Corinthians it is more indebted for its Christology to the Epistle to Hebrews than to Paul. It speaks of Peter and Paul as founders of the Roman Church, but seemingly more on the strength of the legend to that effect than of recent memories,35 and conceives the organization of the communities after the pattern common to the Pastoral Epistles. An elder of the Roman community writing in 95, only some thirty years after the persecution of Nero, could hardly have said that the disciples of Christ set out to preach everywhere immediately after the resurrection, instituting bishops and deacons and even laying down rules for their succession and life-long tenure of office. The indications rather are that the author of the letter is the Clement mentioned by Hermas and that he wrote towards 130–135.

Of different origin and less ancient date is the homily named in tradition as the second Epistle of Clement. This composition presupposes a great development of the Gospel literature; some of its quotations appear to come from the so-called Gospel of the Egyptians. In all probability the homily is of Alexandrian origin and belongs to the second half, if not to the end, of the second century.

Ignatius and Polycarp

The authenticity of the letters attributed to Ignatius of Antioch martyred under Trajan (98–117), was at one time strongly denied, then recognized, but has recently become the object of a new attack. The fact is that these letters lose their historical background if placed in the time of Trajan, since the seven in question inculcate a system of belief and discipline which correspond to the conditions of the later period when the gnostic crisis was at its height. Moreover the Epistle of Polycarp to the Philippians seems to have been interpolated into the collection of the Ignatian letters, by their author or editor, for the purpose of recommending them; this alone would seem to prove them apocryphal and later, at least in publication, than the death of Polycarp. Irenaeus quotes the Ignatian letter to the Romans, which we must suppose in existence about 170, but without naming the author whom he seems not to know as a quasi-apostolic person connected with Polycarp. Neither can Polycarp's Epistle, when freed from its artificial attachment to the Ignatian letters, be dated in the reign of Trajan; it belongs to the last years of its author's life.[36] In this way we can explain this author's apparent knowledge of the collection of the thirteen Epistles of Paul, the Acts of the Apostles, First Peter, the synoptic tradition of Jesus' discourses, the Epistles of John and his reproval, without theological reasoning, of Marcion's Docetic gnosis by utilizing 1 John iv, 2–3. The Johannine writings, whose existence we find him attesting, have but a very slight influence on his thought and style, which would be extremely surprising if the fourth Gospel were the work of an apostle or of an apostolic person of whom Polycarp himself is said to have been the disciple.

The Didache

Here it will be in place to call attention to the type of catechesis which has come down to us under the name of *Doctrine* (*Didache*) *of the Twelve Apostles*, a work of moral and disciplinary instruction highly esteemed in the first Christian age, which seems to have been composed in Syria or in Egypt at the beginning of the second century. As already pointed out, the moral part reproduces a body of Jewish teaching on "the two ways," eternal life and eternal death, intermingled with Gospel sentences corresponding to the tradition in Matthew. The second part has to do with baptism and the communion, the good order of assemblies and the choice of ministers, overseers (bishops) and deacons. The baptismal formula and the Lord's Prayer are identical with the canonical text of Matthew (vii, 1; viii, 2). In the ordering of the communion the prophets have liberty to render thanks in their own terms (10), as an exercise outside the indicated formulas. From this we are led to assign a rather early date to the rule, seeing that, in the time of Justin, the Supper has a president who alone may pronounce the eucharistic prayers. The prayers of the *Didache*, moreover, do not give the impression that the Supper, as understood by the author, is the mystic commemoration of the death of Christ indicated in First Corinthians and in the Gospels.

2. THE CHRISTIAN APOCALYPSE

The imminent return of Christ Jesus to the earth had been proclaimed for many years before the story was told, in oral preaching and in evangelical writings, of what in detail Jesus had done, taught and suffered before ascending into heaven to prepare the day of God. The Gospel was the announcement of this coming Day before it became an account of the Christ's teaching and of his saving death. For that reason the documents of Christian apocalyptic will here be considered before we come to those of the literature known as "the Gospels."

Reference has already been made to the more or less considerable elements of apocalyptic to be found in the epistolary, or rather catechical, literature we have just been considering, such as chapter xv of First Corinthians, the dissertation on the resurrection of the dead included in First Thessalonians (iv, 13–v, 11), and the central passage in Second (ii, 1–12). The *Didache*, the Doctrine of the Twelve Apostles, while containing no summary of the Gospel story, terminates in a short apocalypse closely related to the discourse on the end of the world common to the three Synoptics (16). And this discourse is itself the Christian adaptation of a Jewish apocalypse contemporary with the siege of Jerusalem by Titus. All that Christian apologetic did was to co-ordinate and interpret the elements of the Jewish apocalypse in application to the second coming of Jesus, impatiently expected and always postponed, and this it did not only with the apocalypse current before the preaching of the Gospel but with that of later date, which uttered its last cries of anguish and hope amid the death throes of nationalist Judaism.37

Thus it was that apocalyptic found its way into the Gospel tradition, which originally had no more of it than is contained in its general idea of the speedy coming of the Reign of God. But the Great Coming seeming ever to be further off, the delay was explained as a providential ordering of events prophesied as due to happen first. Jewish eschatology and Jewish apocalyptic contained a rich mine of allusions, no better understood, and of predictions not yet fulfilled. All this was now regarded as due to happen before the Day of God and his Christ, "the sorrows" naturally preceding the "coming." The synoptic apocalypse accordingly marks out three stages, the beginning of the sorrows, the climax of the sorrows, and then the "end." They are expressly distinguished in Mark xiii, 8, 14, 24.

The Apocalypse of John has the appearance of a methodical exposition of Jewish hopes interpreted in a Christian sense, and is conceived on the model of the Jewish apocalypses then current, which in turn professed to interpret ancient prophecies. In its groundwork the Johannine Apocalypse would seem to be a compilation, but there is an almost mathematical regularity in its logical structure and literary arrangement. The traditional date of it is probably correct; it saw the light among the communities of Asia to which it was originally addressed, most likely at Ephesus towards the end of the first Christian century. The author was probably a Jewish Christian who had fled from Palestine during the Jewish war; certainly not the apostle John; nor can he have been "John the elder" known to Papias as a witness to the Gospel tradition. To that tradition the Apocalypse pays scant attention, knowing only that Christ, as the first to be raised up, is "the firstborn of the dead" (i, 5, 18); incidentally it mentions that he was crucified at Jerusalem (xi, 8). Some time must have elapsed between the publication of the Apocalypse in the Asiatic communities by the act of the prophet himself and what may be called the final edition of it for general circulation throughout all the communities as an apostolic work by the same author as the fourth Gospel and the three Epistles. This identification and the constitution of the Johannine collection of books took place towards the middle of the second century.

The Apocalypse of Peter and the Pastor of Hermas are also books of Christian prophecy, which failed however to get admission into the collection of the New Testament. But mention must first be made of other writings more closely related to the Johannine Apocalypse. These are the Christian parts of the Ascension of Isaiah, the Christian oracles annexed to the Jewish Apocalypse called the Fourth Book of Esdras and the Christian elements in the Sibylline Books.

In the Ascension of Isaiah we can recognize three writings originally distinct, of which the oldest is the Jewish legend of the prophet's martyrdom under Manasseh. The other two are Christian. The longer of these is an ecstatic vision of the Ascension of Isaiah to the seventh heaven in which he sees God and the Christ, "the Lord of all Glory," and hears the Most High dictate to the Christ the programme of his earthly manifestation and of his return.[38] The third piece, inserted into the legend of martyrdom, is a vision concerning the coming of Christ and of Antichrist, in which the resurrection of Jesus is described as in the Gospel of Peter and allusion made to Peter's martyrdom in the persecution by Nero, who is Antichrist. The two Christian fragments are relatively old, probably of the second century, the part attributed by both to the earthly life of Jesus being in harmony with the development of the Gospel literature. The author of the Ascension, who knew the substance of Matthew's Gospel, may have been a Syrian and must have written between 130 and 150: the author of the other fragment is more recent and, in virtue of its almost certain dependence on the Gospel of Peter, cannot have been written before 170–175.

Almost of the same date is the fragment of apocalypse represented by the first two chapters of the Fourth Book of Esdras in editions of the Latin Bible, a self-contained prophecy originally in Greek, but, like the book of Hermas, composed in the West when Greek was still the liturgical and literary language of the Christian communities. It consists of an indictment of the Jews and a vision of the eternal Jerusalem. The prophecy contained in the last two chapters of the same Book of Esdras is more recent and may have been originally conceived as an appendix to the book to which we find it annexed. It contains an exhortation to persecuted Christians which tells us almost nothing about the evolution of apocalyptic beliefs in the early Christian age.

The third of the Sibylline Books contains a Christian interpolation set in a Jewish context. In this interpolation Beliar, or Satan-Antichrist, appears to be identified with Simon Magus. The eighth book, wholly Christian, was composed in the last years of Marcus Aurelius; like the Johannine Apocalypse, it centres round the Antichrist Nero. The Jewish Sibyl, in the fourth of the Books, written shortly after the eruption of Vesuvius in 79, exhibits Nero, "the fugitive from Rome," crossing the Euphrates with a great army and goes on to speak of him in the fifth book. But in that book Nero is introduced as still a living man and in hiding among Parthians, whereas, in the Christian apocalyptic, Nero, still supported by the Parthians, and in the character of Antichrist, appears as a ghost or as risen from the dead.

Less ancient than these, the Apocalypse of Peter is also less preoccupied with revelation about the end of the world, and seems to aim rather at instructing believers as to the respective fates that will fall after the judgment on the wicked and on the righteous. In its treatment of that topic it comes near not only to the Ascension of Isaiah and the first two chapters of Fourth Esdras but also to the Egyptian mysteries and to the Orphic tradition. It is connected with the Gospel of Peter by the place it assigns to the cross in the second coming of the Lord. (In the Gospel the cross comes forth from the tomb behind the Christ as he rises from the dead; in the Apocalypse Jesus says that the cross will go before him when he comes in his glory.) In the Second Epistle of Peter formal reference is made to the Apocalypse in the opening chapter. It is therefore earlier than 150, and perhaps was written about 135. A Greek fragment of the apocalypse, with a passage from Enoch and a part of the Gospel of Peter, was found at Akhmim in Egypt, while the whole text, perhaps a little touched up and interpolated, has been preserved in an Ethiopian version.[39]

The scene depicted in this apocalypse presents the critic of the New Testament with a problem that demands the most careful handling. Jesus, having risen from the dead, is on the Mount of Olives with his disciples who question him about his second coming and the end of the world; Jesus answers by a short discourse which corresponds to the synoptic apocalypse, especially to Luke xvii, 20–27, and to the preliminaries of the Ascension as told in Acts; the discourse finishes with an allegorical declaration connected with the fig tree; on the request of Peter, Jesus comments on what he has just said by a paraphrase, not of the comparison with a fig tree in the synoptic apocalypse (Mark xiii, 28; Luke xxi, 29–30), but of the parable of the barren fig tree in Luke xiii, 6–9; the tree which must be cut down is Judaism with a false Jewish Messiah, a persecutor of Christians—probably Barkochba—whom the two messengers of God, Enoch and Elias, will unmask; follows a description of the Second Coming and the Last Judgment; the Christ then reveals to Peter in great detail how the wicked will be punished after the judgment;[40] the elect will be witnesses of their chastisements and will be able to obtain from the Lord pardon for those among the damned whom they have known;[41] Peter is then warned of the fate that awaits him in the capital of the West; finally Jesus and his disciples repair to the holy mountain[42] where two luminous beings, Moses and Elias, make their appearance; on Peter asking where the patriarchs are, Jesus causes him to behold the dwelling place of the blessed; Peter then declares his intention to set up three tents, for Jesus,

Moses and Elias, for which the Christ rebukes him severely (in terms corresponding to Mark viii, 33); whereupon the voice of the Father is heard saying "this is my beloved son in whom I am well pleased"; a bright cloud envelopes Jesus, Moses and Elias, who are carried to heaven in the cloud; the heavens open to receive them, and then close; the disciples descend the mountain "praising God who has written the names of the righteous in the book of life in heaven."

Here then we have gathered into one picture the transfiguration of Jesus and the apocalyptic discourse reported in the first three Gospels (Mark xiii; Matthew xxiv; Luke xxi), together with the scene of the Ascension described in Acts, not to mention the prediction of Peter's martyrdom found in the Fourth Gospel. The problem to be solved by the critic is this; how was pseudo-Peter able to dispose, apparently at his own will, of elements utilized in a manner so different by the Gospel tradition and the Acts of the Apostles? Perhaps we may answer that the arrangement of elements in the Apocalypse of Peter is no more arbitrary than that to be found in the canonical writings. The apocalyptic discourse in Mark is an extract brought in from elsewhere and substituted for another conclusion to the Jerusalem ministry—the parable of the Wicked Husbandmen, originally conceived as the end of Jesus' teaching in Jerusalem. The discourse itself may very well have been drawn up at first in the form of a revelation made by the Christ after rising from the dead, a hypothesis supported by the preamble to the Ascension in Acts (i, 6–8). In the same way it has long been suspected that the transfiguration of Jesus was originally a manifestation of the risen Christ which Mark has thrown back into the Galilean ministry.[43] What may be taken as certain is that, before the canonization of the New Testament, a great liberty was used in the dealings of tradition with the manifold material at its disposal for constructing the legend of Jesus and his ministry—material messianic, eschatological, apocalyptic and theosophic. The Apocalypse of Peter belongs to this precanonical age when the literature of the Christian religion had no stereotyped form, the religion itself being still amorphous; Marcion had not yet become active and the reaction against him and against gnosticism in general had yet to come. It is moreover evident that the second Epistle of Peter, in all it says about the revelation made to Peter on the mountain about the glory of the Christ (i, 12–19), is not based on the story of the transfiguration as told in the Synoptics, nor on Acts for what it says of the Ascension, nor on the Fourth Gospel for the prediction of the apostle's death, but entirely and exclusively on our apocryphal book. This book seems to have been written at Alexandria and Clement was making great use of it in 135, citing it largely in his *Hypolyposes*. Be it noted that Alexandria, towards 135, was using its Gospel of the Egyptians. Our pseudo-Peter in writing his apocalypse would therefore be unrestrained in breaking up and arranging at his pleasure a mass of material which the canonical Gospels and Acts arranged in a different pattern. We can well understand why in the process of definitely canonizing the Gospels and Acts, there would be no long delay in excluding a document which doubled their stories and contradicted them too plainly. We may note, however, that towards the year 200 Rome still kept the Apocalypse of Peter in its collection of the Scriptures, although there were some who contested it, along with the Apocalypse of John (Canon of Muratori).

Hermas

Hermas lived at Rome during the first half and wrote in the second quarter of the second century.[44] The tradition of the Roman community made him a brother of the bishop Pius; the rest of our knowledge of him is derived from what he says of himself in his book. He was not without learning, but is generally not regarded as a man of genius. Like the Apocalypse of John, but with fewer repetitions and incoherences, his book has an almost mathematical arrangement. It is divided into three: visions, to the number of four; commandments, to the number of twelve; similitudes or parables, to the number of eight—the ninth being a summary of what has been said in the visions, and the tenth serving for conclusions. The whole book has the character of a vision, both the precepts and the parables being dictated or shown to Hermas by an angel garbed as a shepherd. The significance of the book of Hermas lies chiefly in its relation to the history of Christian discipline.

To the Epistles attributed to Paul, the Epistle to the Hebrews and the first Epistle of John, the idea of the Christian as a sinner is repugnant; they regard baptism as a final regeneration by means of which the saints acquire at once the sinlessness of the redeemed. But as the parousia came not and the Church continued its life, the question of the Christian sinner began to present itself and became urgent. Hermas, inspired to declare that God will give pardon, once but no more, to the Christian who has sinned gravely after his baptism, was the first to administer a corrective to the notion that the believer became the unconditional heir of immortality on undergoing the rite of Christian initiation. What we encounter in Hermas is no longer a vision of the Eternal Jerusalem ready to come down to earth, but the church in process of organizing itself on earth. The prophet, confronted with growing abuses, here sets out to bring them remedy by giving utterance first to the angel of the Church itself, and then to the mystical Shepherd changed into an angel of penitence.45

In his knowledge of the Gospel tradition Hermas seems little better informed than the author of the Johannine Apocalypse or Clement of Rome who, as mentioned above, was probably a contemporary of Hermas and identical with the person named in his *Vision* (ii, 4). With some of the Gospel writings he was certainly acquainted; on occasion he is inspired by their sayings and he consciously imitates the parables. But it cannot be said that the Gospel legend was his favourite theme of meditation. The salvation-myth he reduces to its simplest form of expression. All the evidence points to the conclusion that the outbreak of the gnostic crisis, with its lawless flood of speculation and fiction, compelled the church to go back on its steps, to sift its archives, to catalogue and guarantee them and to define the right faith. Hermas brings us to the eve of that decision, which he did not foresee and which finally was to turn against him.

About half a century after Hermas the author of the Canon of Muratori expounded and defended the New Testament catalogue of the Roman Church. Having closed the list with the Apocalypses of John and of Peter, and before mentioning the works of the heretics reproved by the Church, he wrote as follows: "As to the Pastor, it was written recently in our time at Rome by Hermas, his brother the bishop then occupying the chair of the Roman community. Therefore we ought indeed to read it"—for private edification—"but it may not be publicly read to the people in the church"—because it would be held of no account—"nor among the prophets, of which the number is complete"—the prophets of the Old Testament of whom the full list was long since established—"nor among the apostles, to the end of the ages"— Hermas not having been an apostle nor one of their disciples as the author believed the New Testament writers to have been. We may read between the lines that the Pastor had for some time figured on the margin of the apostolic collection and that the reaction against the Montanists may have done him as much harm in Rome as did the definition of the Canon in opposition to the gnostics. In the fourth century the book was still used for public reading by congregations in the East, but only for the instruction of catechumens and without decisive authority in matters of faith.

3. Gospels and Acts

The four Gospels and the Acts of the Apostles are traditionally regarded as the most important part of the New Testament. On first inspection they would seem to contain the history of the very beginnings of the Christian religion. Nevertheless they are far from being books of history proper, far from having been originally conceived by their authors as history, or selected by the Church, from among many other writings of similar character, on account of their historical value.

A distinction has to be made between *the* Gospel and the Gospel*s*. The word "Gospel" in the New Testament is not a name given to *books* about the life and death of Jesus; it signifies "the good news," that is, the message of salvation won by the Christ. Even in our canonical Gospels the word is applied to this salvation, as made real by Jesus, and not to what seems to have been the theme of his preaching, the theme, namely, of the imminent coming of the Reign of God and the need of repentance for those who would share in its blessedness. In the end "Gospel" came to refer to the life and teachings of Jesus, but only so far as the life and the teachings were integral parts of the saving work which reached its climax, so to say, in the death and resurrection of the Christ. Moreover, when the word came to be applied to a plurality of books, the fact that only *one* Gospel was involved, or had ever existed, was indicated in the titles used to denote their authors, which titles ran, not the Gospel *of* Matthew or *of* Mark, but *according to* Matthew and *according to* Mark. This "according to" implied no doubt or attenuation of the authorship attributed to the book. As expressly stated by Irenaeus (*Heresies*, iii, 1) it was intended to emphasize the *oneness* of *the* Gospel under the four authorized forms of its text. Each of the communities began the use of books with one short book only; this, for the community using it, was "*the* Gospel." Many of the gnostic sects, Marcion's for example, did the same.

Justin is the oldest author to employ the word "Gospels" in the plural, to designate the books of the Good News;[46] their use in liturgical reading would lead to them being so named. The oldest author to affirm that there were four, and only four books so authorized, is Irenaeus.[47] The tone he assumes leaves no doubt as to the unique and exclusive authority of these writings; but the insistence displayed both by him and by the author of the Canon of Muratori in defending their authority rouses a suspicion that the fixing of the fourfold collection was not so primitive nor so natural as their tone of assurance might suggest to the incautious reader.

From our examination of the epistolary and apocalyptic literature it seems that the Gospel literature did not acquire importance till after the close of the first century. It is evident, moreover, that the legend of Jesus and the tradition of his teaching were not fixed at the outset of the Christian movement, and that for a long time the writings to which they were consigned continued to be produced without much restraint and without being authorized or commended otherwise than by their content. It is also certain that the practice began at an early date of putting forward, under the name of the Christ, teaching about the end of the world which had been borrowed from the apocalyptic tradition of Judaism; and, further, that many a lesson reflecting the needs of the infant communities or their propaganda was ascribed to him, together with revelations about his own transcendent personality and mission. By the visionary and fervid temper of the first generations acquisitions of all kinds were made easy. The imagination of the believer was constantly in search of anything which would exalt the Christ beyond comparison with the pagan gods and leave no doubt as to his relations to Judaism, whose sacred books it turned into witnesses to Jesus. There is no difficulty in perceiving, in the documents of primitive Christianity, how theories of salvation, mystical interpretations of the messianic rôle attributed from the first to Jesus, though not logically deduced from the Scriptures, were artificially supported by them, and how even the legend of the Christ was similarly constructed by attaching it to messianic texts, real or supposed, in the Old Testament. We can understand how, under these conditions, Gospel writings began to multiply from an early date. They would have continued to multiply indefinitely had not the Church laid down a rule in the matter.

It is, however, important to remark that the use of these books by congregations in meetings for worship tended to fix their theme and give authority to certain writings. The Gospels when closely examined are far less the echoes of a tradition zealous to keep intact the memories of Jesus than a didactic instrument, we might even say, a catechism of the worship rendered to the Lord Christ. Those which the Church decided to retain are small books, very sober in style, not overcharged with matter but made up of selected elements, of stories brief and full of meaning, of teachings concise and sententious. Two cycles, or centres, are discernible, the cycle of the preaching in Galilee and the cycle of the passion in Jerusalem; the instruction of catechumens and the revelation of a mystery; the baptismal catechism and the eucharistic. The whole is thus brought into co-ordination with the great rites of Christian initiation and with the Christian mystery. It is no effect of chance that the Fourth Gospel, in the story of the passion as given in its source document, is found to justify the Easter observance of the "quartodeciman" congregations of Asia, while the first three conform to the common practice of Sunday observance ordained by the Roman Church. Our Gospels were originally conceived as ritual books for both observances, and were subsequently corrected at a few points to cover up the difference between them on this. Their literary form, their liturgical and oracular style, are in keeping with the purpose they are intended to serve. The question of the New Testament style is still under examination. It is certain that the discourses in the Gospels, even those in the fourth, were originally short writings composed in the rhythmic form peculiar to the poetic writings of the Old Testament, Psalms, Proverbs and the discourses in Job. It is equally certain that some parts at least of the Epistles and the entire Apocalypse were put out at first in rhythmic form. The same may well be true of the Gospel stories.

Both the history and the fortunes of the Gospels are thus explained. Originally they were anonymous writings belonging to the communities which used them. The third Gospel seems an exception, offering itself to the reader as a personal work and with a dedicatory preface in the form then customary with profane writers. But this laicization of the Gospel theme hardly goes beyond the preface; moreover the editorial elaboration of Luke and Acts reduces them to the common level of biblical historiography. At the height of the gnostic crisis Marcion, opposing the common Christianity with a Gospel which, according to him, was the one Gospel and the only true, depersonalized Luke and further lightened it of everything that he found of Judaizing tendency. Then it was that the Church replied by canonizing the Gospels most in honour among the chief communities, disdaining the others and setting them aside, especially those which the gnostic themselves had fabricated or arranged. The reason why the Church did not limit its choice to one Gospel and only one, as Marcion had done, probably lay in the fact that the canon of the four Gospels resulted from a compromise between the influential communities. These came more easily to agreement in mutual recognition of the texts they were severally familiar with than they would have done in elaborating a single Gospel and securing its acceptance by them all.

As to what followed, there can be little doubt that the canonization of the four Gospels as traditional provided the occasion for some retouchings of their already edited text. It may well have had the further effect of giving consistency to the attribution of authorship, by means of which it was hoped to render indisputable a number of books which, in reality, did not come directly from any apostle, and in which the faith, aspirations and prophetic genius of the first Christian generations chiefly found utterance. The statements of John the Elder, reported by Papias of Hierapolis, in regard to Mark and Matthew, were put into words, at the very time when the canonization of the

Gospels was under consideration, with the object of guaranteeing the application of the apostolic names to writings for whose authority that form of recommendation was judged to be indispensable. The situation these statements were intended to justify was one of fact and of right; of fact, in respect of the credit already acquired by the writings in question; of right, in respect of the eminent authority that had to be given to books about whose origin little was known, or whose real origin would not have sustained their prestige at a sufficient height. The fiction of apostolic origin was a necessity for Christian apologetic when at grips with gnosticism. The fixation of the canon, to which the apostolic fiction was linked, was itself a necessity for the same reason—as the argument of the Canon of Muratori in regard to Hermas has already shown us. The fiction is without bearing on the history of the composition of the Gospels, except at the final stage of that history and in regard to the revision of their text in the process of forming them into a canonized group.

The Gospel attributed to Mark, generally regarded as the oldest of the Four,[48] is a shortened manual of Christian catechesis, not all of one piece and not exempt from retouchings. The last of these consisted in the adding of a conclusion (xvi, 9–20) perhaps as recent as the middle of the second century.[49] The basis of Mark seems to have been a document which agreed with John in the date of the passion, that is to say, in implying the coincidence of the Christian with the Jewish Passover.[50] This document has been worked over and surcharged, one part of the alterations betraying the influence of Pauline tendencies and doctrines while others[51] reveal the knowledge of didactic elements expanded in Matthew and Luke and readjustment of the passion stories to adapt them to the practice of the Sunday Easter. The date of the fundamental document may be earlier than the year 70; the subsequent editorial revision is later than the fall of Jerusalem. The final editings of Luke and of Matthew are founded on Mark as it stands, minus the deuterocanonical conclusion. After the discovery of the empty tomb, which these Gospels take from Mark, their editors artificially introduce completely divergent stories of apparitions of the risen Jesus. Both of them agree in loosening the tongues of the women whom the editor of Mark (xvi, 8) expressly makes silent, because he was aware that his story of the empty tomb had been unheard of till he told it. This compromising feature in Mark is redressed in Matthew xxviii, 8 and in Luke xxiv, 10–11; but what the two evangelists go on to relate on their own responsibility is no less freely invented and put together than the story of the empty tomb.

Mark seems to have been a Roman Gospel of ancient date.[52] Its attribution to Mark possibly coincides with the final revision of the book and the introduction of the Sunday Easter, when the Roman community ceased to celebrate the festival of salvation on the same day as the Jews. This would be some time before 150–160, when Pope Anicetus was able to cite the tradition of his predecessors in opposing Polycarp on the question of Easter Day.[53] Disparaging references to the Galilean apostles found in Mark are the following: Peter's lack of intelligence, viii, 32, 33; his ridiculous remark, ix, 5–6; ill-judged demand of the sons of Zebedee, x, 35–40; Peter's boasting and denial, xiv, 29–31, 54, 66–72; pitiful attitude of Peter, James and John at Gethsemane. On this we may remark, but only by way of a probable hypothesis, that the revision of Mark thus characterized by ill will to these apostles was the work of parties in Rome devoted to the memory of Paul, and was finally adopted, with the observance of the Sunday Easter, when the Roman community became united towards the beginning of the second century. But the dependence of the other Gospel writings, notably Matthew, revised in the East, on a document of this nature, is enough to prove the original poverty of what we are accustomed to call the Gospel tradition.

The first of our canonical Gospels seems to have circulated to begin with among the hellenic-christian congregations in Syria and Palestine. The narrative parts are mainly founded on Mark, what is added to them being secondary fiction with apologetic bearings and sometimes romantically conceived, as in the rôle attributed to Pilate's wife in the story of the passion (xxvii, 19). The birth-stories belong to the order of mythical fictions and are studiously elaborated in connexion with texts from the prophets (i, ii). The idea of conception by the Holy Spirit, notwithstanding its superficial resemblance to Isaiah vii, 14, is thoroughly pagan; if it first saw the light in Jewish-Christian circles, they must have been considerably paganized. These birth-stories, however, seem to have come into the text at the last revision of the Gospel, and in any case proclaim themselves clearly enough to be adventitious. The special interest of the Gospel, to which it owed its high credit among the early communities, lies in the place it gives to discourses attributed to Jesus, a mass of teachings not without Jewish-Christian features and bearing, in the total, the mark of their Jewish origin, but adapted under revision to the spirit of universal Christianity. As the greater part of these teachings are repeated in the third Gospel, with variations which affect only their literary form, critics generally admit the dependence of Matthew and Luke, for the discourses, on a common source, but in two different versions both derived from a Semitic original of relatively ancient date. But the evangelical matter in Matthew, so far as it consists of teachings, does not represent a single collection of memories faithfully preserved from the apostolic age, any more than its narratives represent the legend of Jesus preserved in the same way. It contains rather a series of acquisitions successively taken over under the pressure of circumstance, of the progressive needs of Christian propaganda, and as required by the organization of Christian teaching in the communities. The original document was a *Didache* (a "teaching") afterwards worked up into a Gospel of the canonical type by amalgamation with Mark. The importance attached to the person of Peter, notably in xvi, 13–20, derives from the fact that this Gospel took form in Jewish-Christian circles with a turn for universalism. The same is true of the Peter-legend developed in the first part of Acts.

In the traditional form it now has, the first Gospel cannot be much earlier than the year 125, a date somewhat movable, like all those here indicated for the Gospels, since retouches were always possible up to the final canonization of the books and of their official text. There is no doubt that it existed before Justin and was known in Asia, as Mark also was, in the time of Papias. We are much in the dark as to the reasons for its being attributed to the apostle Matthew; we may recall what has been said above of the originally anonymous character of the Gospel revisions. The substitution of the name Matthew for Levi in the story of the calling of the publican (ix, 9) must be connected with this attribution; but, if the intention is clear, the motive is not. By a forced interpretation of the evidence of Papias, often adopted since Schleiermacher, but open to question at every point, it has been supposed that the Gospel was judged to be the work of Matthew because this apostle had composed the collection of discourses which is one of its chief sources. But that collection was an impersonal work and not apostolic.[54] Some apostolic name had to be chosen to give authority to the Gospel: the reason for the choice of Matthew the publican lying perhaps in some legend about him which made him a reciter of the Gospel.

The writings of Luke present another enigma. The preface to the third Gospel and that of Acts[55] show that the two books were originally the first and second parts of one work which professed to be composed under conditions common to the issue of books in that time, with a dedication to some eminent personage. But the preface to Acts has been mutilated, the first stage in a process of alteration which seems to have been extended to the whole of the original document; the first part, or Gospel, was apparently recast and completed in a similar manner. It seems impossible to admit the view that the author of this, the original, document was the person who writes "we" in certain narratives in Acts, and who is to be identified with Luke the companion of Paul, and that this man, arriving in Rome with Paul about the year 60, wrote the story of Christian origins about the year 80. The author of the general preface (Luke i, 1-4) does not place himself among the companions and disciples of the apostles; the underlying idea of his preface is that of an apostolic tradition transmitted in good order down to the time of those, who, like himself, have undertaken to describe the institution of the Christian faith. And the writings said to be Luke's, taken in the form in which they have come down to us, cannot go back to the apostolic age, nor even to the end of the first century; they are the prelude to the age of Christian apologetic as practised by Athenagoras and Justin. This Gospel, moreover, is no longer the mixed catechesis of Mark and Matthew, nor is it the gnosis of John. But Luke and Acts are earlier than 140, since Marcion, excommunicated from the Roman church about 144, furnished his sect with our third Gospel as an authorized version, with the matter omitted that conflicted with the heresiarch's system. The contrary hypothesis, which makes Marcion's Luke the original and our canonical Gospel the derivative, is indefensible. Marcion took the Gospel used by the Roman Church and adapted it in conformity with the needs of his doctrine. In this procedure he took no greater liberty, in principle, than the editors of our Gospel texts were wont to allow themselves.

Luke is a compilation analogous to Mark and Matthew and like them intended for reading aloud in the assemblies. Here again Mark has furnished most of the stories in the body of the book; what does not come from Mark is legendary fiction or mythical construction; examples of these are the preaching of Jesus at Nazareth (iv, 16–30), the mission of the seventy-two disciples (x, 1–12),[56] the ascension of the risen Christ (xxiv, 50–53).[57] The birth-stories, though not constructed all at once, are better put together than in Matthew, but with as little basis in tradition; though not independent of ancient prophecy they are not constructed on texts for the purpose of showing their fulfilment. The idea of virgin conception (i, 34–35) is adventitious; it is only in their source that the stories are of earlier date than Matthew's. The evangelical teachings are as abundant as in Matthew but more dispersed. Certain parables, of deeply moving character—the Rich Man and Lazarus, the Prodigal Son, the Pharisee and the Publican and others—are peculiar to Luke, where they represent an original development of tradition. By an almost mechanical device of editing the greater part of the discourses attributed to Jesus are lodged between the departure of the Christ for Jerusalem and his arrival in Judea (ix, 51–xviii, 14). The explanation is that the sayings and parables having no attachment to time and place in the traditional souvenirs, the evangelists inserted them as best they could in the course of the narratives, Matthew preferring an arrangement in long discourses and Luke in distributed pieces.

The Acts of the Apostles

This book, in the form it now has, is an amalgamation of primitive data concerning the beginnings of Christian preaching and the missions of Paul with mythical and legendary fictions, and discourses artificially composed in the manner of ancient historiography. Anti-Jewish polemic, perceptible in all the Gospels, is here outstandingly tendentious, the author having set himself the task of proving that Christianity is the most authentic form of Judaism and has the right, in that capacity, to the same tolerance by Roman authority as that enjoyed by official Judaism. Peter and Paul are in the forefront of evangelical activity, and it would seem that the author has taxed his wits to furnish them with the same miracles; each brings a dead person to life, cures a paralytic and performs miscellaneous miracles, the one with his shadow, the other with aprons snatched from his body. But, in all this, Paul is given second place to the elder apostles, especially to Peter whom we find taking the lead in preaching to the Gentiles (x–xi, 18); while every trace of old disputes and rivalries between them is carefully obliterated, and the presentation of the primitive history dominated throughout by the fictitious idea of an apostolic tradition originally guarded by the Twelve.

Both the Gospels and Acts acquired their final form in the first half of the second century—a conclusion which may be taken as guaranteed by the proceedings of Marcion and by the apologist Justin's employment of the third Gospel. The first book "to Theophilus" became, in revision, a cult-book impersonalized and enriched with the latest acquisitions of the faith, while the passion and resurrection stories were retouched and augmented, not only for the demonstration of the Christian message, but to adapt the stories to the Easter usage of the Roman congregation. On the latter point the revision of the third Gospel, like that of the first, was conformed to the revision of the second and then brought to the point by stories of the resurrection which bring the Sunday Easter into plain relief.[58] While the systematic preoccupation with prophecy betrays a development of Christian belief and apologetic in presence of Judaism and in opposition to it, it is not impossible that the ardour for the Old Testament apparent in Luke and Acts attest a reaction against those gnostics who, like Marcion and Basilides before him, repudiated the Old Testament and the God of the Jews. We have still stronger grounds for supposing that the materialization of the apparitions of the risen Christ, both in the Gospel and in Acts, is aimed at destroying the influence of the Docetism which denied his material existence, but of which Marcion was not the initiator. It should not be overlooked that, alone among the New Testament writers, the editor of Luke and Acts has had the hardihood to represent the risen Christ as eating material food (Luke xxiv, 42; Acts x, 41) and as remaining among his followers for a longish period afterwards, as some of the gnostics also did. It remains to be said that the dependence of certain passages in Luke and Acts on the so-called Johannine tradition and on the fourth Gospel,[59] in the revision of which the aim at Docetic gnosticism is equally apparent, invites us to place the canonical revision of our two books near the time when the group of four Gospels was canonized as a whole.

Wherever they were composed, the third Gospel and Acts reflect the development of Christian faith and institution between the years 125 and 150. The two books were prepared and revised in a great centre of Christianity which also undertook their general diffusion. The Roman Church itself had perhaps promoted their last revision for the purpose of admitting them into its collection of the Scriptures, and therefore knew what it was about in admitting them. We can easily understand how this Church found the Gospel of Mark, which it already had, inadequate for Christian instruction; and how the original work of Luke failed to make good the inadequacy. For neither Mark, nor, probably, Luke's original related the birth of the Christ; moreover, they lacked the greater part of the sayings which were circulating among the communities at the opening of the second century as discourses of Jesus.

The Fourth Gospel

In the matter forming its groundwork the Fourth Gospel is of later date than the three Synoptics and would seem to have been conceived in another setting and on a different pattern. Perhaps, however, in its original form, the frame was not very different, though the Gospel was wholly unlike the others in spirit and doctrine. Towards the end of the first century there appeared at Ephesus, perhaps from Syria, a mystical prophet, a master of Christian gnosis rather than a preacher of the Gospel, who conceived and gave form to the sublime discourses and the symbolic visions on which the Gospel was finally built up—the style of the discourses being rhythmic, like that of the sayings and sentences in the Synoptics, but the development of the thought more spacious and the themes perceptibly different.[60] But the mystic Christ of our prophet not being born of the flesh, and his gift to those who were his being simply that of immortal life, it soon became necessary to conform his figure to the Christ of the common tradition in whom the Jewish prophecies were fulfilled and who was soon to appear in his Kingdom and raise the dead from their graves. Had not the Apocalypse, conceived in that strain, just been published at this same Ephesus? Two chief stages can be distinguished in the literary formation of this Gospel: a first official edition, about 135–140, ended by the present conclusion of chapter xx, and characterized by the greater part of the borrowings from the Synoptic tradition and by passages specially conceived to effect the adjustment, probably also by the fixation of the chronological framework and distribution of the material in accordance with it;[61] then a second edition, the canonical, about 150–160, almost contemporary with the last editions of Matthew and Luke.[62] In this second edition chapter xxi is the piece most easily recognizable as a newcomer; but various retouchings and further additions may have been made in the body of the book, notably in regard to the beloved disciple, who is given a prominence of his own as author of the book at the same time as he was being proclaimed the author of the Apocalypse and an apostle of the Lord Jesus. The object aimed at in this edition seems to have been precisely that of procuring the inclusion of the book in the authorized group of Gospels by making it acceptable to the community which apparently had the leading part in fixing the New Testament Canon, to wit, the Roman. It may be said, for example, that chapter xxi was added to make good the legend of Peter as chief shepherd of Christ's sheep, by harmonizing it, as well as might be, with the fiction of the beloved disciple. But it is important to note that during the Montanist crisis towards the end of the second century, in the time of Irenaeus, the canonization of the fourth Gospel had opponents. Not only does Irenaeus mention them in *Heresies* (iii, 11, 9) but finds it necessary to condemn them at the end of his *Exposition of Apostolic Preaching*.

The fourth Gospel agrees with the Easter usage of the "Quartodecimans" who celebrated Passover on the same day as the Jews. Their Passover was the festival of a beneficial death, the Christ being thought to have died at the hour when the lamb of the Jewish festival was sacrificed. This being certainly the primitive custom, and implied in the foundation documents of Mark and Luke, we are bound to conclude that our Gospel supplanted one of the others, Luke probably, in Ephesian usage, and in a form not yet adapted to the Sunday observance of Easter, though doubtless the adaptation had by this time already been made in Rome. When the Easter controversy broke out about the year 190 the Roman party did not perceive, or pretended not to perceive, that while the Synoptics, in their last edition, were now supporting the common Sunday observance, the fourth Gospel fully authorized the other, the Asiatic observance. In what followed the discord on this point was at last covered up under borrowings made by the editors of John from the last edition of the Synoptics, notably those taken from the narrative which fix the passion on Friday and the resurrection on the following Sunday. The discord remains none the less, and the ill-disguised contradiction would be enough to prove that the Gospels are, before all else, a catechism of Christian initiation. It shows that even in their most important part, and the part historically the best guaranteed in the essential datum, namely the crucifixion of Jesus, we have clearly the wording of a liturgical drama, rather than a record of accurate memories of the facts commemorated in the liturgy.

The Non-Canonical Literature

In the period when effort was being made to fix the canon of the New Testament, other Gospels and even other Acts of the Apostles, less recommended by church usage, if not positively disqualified by heretical origin or flavour, were offered for the edification of the communities. A certain number of these writings are known to us only by their titles or in fragments, catholic tradition having either neglected or suppressed them.

Some nevertheless exercised an appreciable influence on the evolution of Christianity of which they were also a product.

As the Gospel tradition was more or less Jewish-Christian at its point of departure, it is a disaster that the Jewish-Christian Gospels have not come down to us. The most important of these, if not the oldest, seems to have been the Gospel of the Nazareans (a Jewish-Christian sect), the Gospel of which Jerome says he translated the Aramean text,[63] wrongly making it the original of canonical Matthew. It is at least true that the Gospel in question was somewhat nearly related to Matthew and, as it had a history of its own, may have been earlier than Matthew at some points and dependent on it at others. It was preserved in Jewish-Christian groups which accepted the virgin conception and were still in existence at the end of the fourth century. According to Eusebius (iii, 39, 16) it contained the incident of the woman taken in adultery, a fragment belonging to the synoptic tradition which, passed by in the first three Gospels, fell in time, and as though by chance, into John. According to Jerome (*de viris*, 2) the first apparition of the risen Christ was accorded by this Gospel to James,[64] which is not surprising in a Jewish-Christian book: after the apparition, Jesus administers the holy sacrament to James who is said to have eaten nothing since the last supper; a trait conforming to the customs of fasting at the Passover, which shows that this Jewish-Christian Gospel, like the four canonicals, was intimately connected with Easter observance.[65] The question is still discussed as to whether the Gospel according to the Hebrews, which seems to have been used by Jewish Christians in Egypt at a very early date, is to be distinguished from the Gospel of the Nazareans, or is only another name for it.

The Gospel according to the Twelve, known as the Gospel of the Ebionites, belonged to Christian groups existing in Transjordania at the time of Epiphanius; the genuine fragments of it are those given by him (*Heresies*, 30). Denying the virgin birth and professing that Jesus was made Son of God by his baptism, these Jewish-Christians were regarded as heretics; but, Jewish as its colour was, their Gospel prescribed the abolition of the sacrifices, baptism taking its place. The Christ is made to say "if you cease not your sacrifices, wrath will not cease to smite you." In general pattern the Ebionite Gospel resembles Mark; as to the contents, its affinity is with Matthew, and it professed to have been revised by that apostle. It was originally written in Greek and depended on earlier Gospels, but only on those in the synoptic tradition, chiefly Matthew and Luke. That it owes nothing to John does not prove it earlier and there seems no compelling reason to place it further back than the last quarter of the second century.[66]

The Gospel according to the Egyptians, of which it is to be regretted that we possess only a few fragments,[67] must have been more ancient and more gnostic in character. The Naasseenes quoted it; but Clement of Alexandria cites it after "the four transmitted to us"; so too, and with equal respect, does the homily known as the Second Epistle of Clement. Origen pays it no other honour than to place it at the head of the non-inspired Gospels and supposes that the prologue to Luke refers to this book and to the Gospel according to the Twelve as "attempts" preceding his own. The Gospel according to the Egyptians, so named in Egypt itself, must have been the one in use among Christians of Egyptian origin, the Gospel according to the Hebrews being that of Jewish-Alexandrian converts. The two, if as old as Origen makes them, would be of great value to the historian. It remains to add that the language of the Gospel of the Egyptians had a savour of gnosticism and that it taught a sex-mystery, an *encratism*, on which fuller information were much to be desired;[68] it is said to have been Sabellian which, however, does not diminish the interest of the problem raised by its existence. It was a Gospel parallel to the Synoptics, but edited independently of them.

The Gospel of Peter, known to us in a considerable fragment dealing with the passion and resurrection of the Christ, is an hellenic-christian Gospel of gnostic tendency on much the same line as the Gospel of the Ebionites in its relation to the canonical four, except that it depends on John as well as on the Synoptics.[69] Not without reason did Serapion, Bishop of Antioch, having found it used by a Syrian community towards the end of the second century, reject it as infected with Docetism.[70] It must have been composed about the middle of that century, perhaps in Syria, and is related to the apocryphal Apocalypse of Peter already discussed.

Basilides, a gnostic teaching in Alexandria, about 140 composed a Gospel on which he wrote a commentary. The Gospel was presented as based on the authority of Glaucias, a disciple of Peter—a case analogous to that of Mark—and in it we find the parable of the Rich Man and Lazarus. There is no reason to regard this Gospel as more freely composed than the others of which we have spoken, or that of Marcion. Like the Gospels of Valentinus and of Marcion, it was written for the use of the group of believers whom the author had gathered round him. As the church hierarchy was as yet but little organized, there was nothing abnormal in the literary experiments of these doctors and, apart from their particular tendencies in doctrine, they used no greater liberty in their method of composition than did the authors of the canonical Gospels.

Of the Gospel of Truth, used by the Valentinians, we know little more than the name. Valentinus appears to have put it out as derived from a certain Theodas, a disciple of Paul.[71] Marcion's Gospel, entitled simply *Evangelion*, with no recommending name, was presented by him as the only true, he himself having amended it in conformity to what he believed was the doctrine of Paul. (To Marcion, with his *Evangelion* and *Apostolicon* we shall return later.) Other gnostic Gospels made their appearance at the same time, such as the Gospel of Matthias, of Philip, of Judas, of Eve, of Mary, etc. It is easy to understand how, confronted with this inundation of Gospel literature, the leaders in the churches, beginning with the Roman, who had already repudiated Valentinus and Marcion, made up their minds to fix once and for all what Gospels, to the exclusion of all others, were to be retained as apostolic.

Mention must here be made of Tatian's *Diatessaron* which was in essence a Gospel remodelled by the method generally adopted from the beginning in Gospel literature. The *Diatessaron* was the first Gospel of the Church of Edessa and for long remained official among the Syrian congregations; an interesting fact as showing how little regardful these congregations were, about 170, of the canon which Irenaeus had just vaunted as fixed, and how they could arrange for themselves a Gospel not in liturgical use in the congregations of the Roman world. It is however certain that Tatian's work was a harmony of the four canonical Gospels with a small number of secondary features seemingly borrowed from the non-canonical. More significant are the omissions and retouches which reveal Tatian's encratism and anti-semitic bias.72

The work of the Christian imagination in dealing with the birth of Jesus was not limited to the stories in Matthew and Luke. Some of the gnostics took part in it, and the idea of the virgin birth, with its mixed savour of encratism and docetism, probably came from that source.73 Among the gospels of the infancy which have most influenced catholic tradition is the Protoevangel of James, a book written to establish the virginity of Mary *ante partum*, *in partu* and *post partum*, and in which the author has amplified both Luke and Matthew.74 Although Justin's dependence on it is not proved, the core of the book may be dated as far back as the middle of the second century. It was written outside of Palestine and by a writer ignorant of Jewish affairs.

Very different in character is the Gospel of Thomas which tells of the miracles performed by Jesus in his infancy. The catholic version which has come down to us is apparently based on a gnostic gospel in which the story of Jesus bears a strong resemblance to that of the youth of Krishna, if not really modelled on it. The catholic versions are not very old, but the gnostic Gospel at the base was known to Irenaeus and Hippolytus, and is mentioned by Eusebius. Here, too, the date may go back to the middle of the second century.

The Acts of Pilate (the Gospel of Nicodemus) are of the fourth or fifth century and have no interest for our subject. When Justin refers his readers to the acts of Pilate for information about the passion of the Christ he is not referring to a book any more than when he refers them, for information about the birth, to the registers of the census made by Quirinius. But Tertullian, in his *Apology* (21), mentions a story told by Pilate at Tiberias about the life, death and resurrection of Jesus which seems to have been preserved as an appendix to the Gospel of Nicodemus. This document, fictitious as it is, would thus be earlier than 197. It is based on canonical Matthew.

In the literary class called "Acts" or "Travels," widely known and circulated in Hellenic antiquity (πράξεις, περίοδοι) 75 canonical Christian literature has produced only the Acts of the Apostles—a book improperly named, since it comprises only the Acts of Peter, stopped short at his imprisonment by Agrippa I and his miraculous escape, and the Acts of Paul in his missions and captivity, but not continued to his martyrdom. Other Acts were written completing the canonical book in matters regarding Peter, Paul and John, or about other apostles less important in the tradition. Needless to say, the object aimed at in recounting the apostolic travels and miracles was to edify the reader in respect of the Christian propaganda and to shed lustre by one means or another on Christian teaching. But these apocryphal Acts, in contrast to the canonical book, do not rest upon a basis having the slightest claim to be historical and inform us only of the spirit and turn of mind of those who wrote them or found them to their taste.[76] They are pious romances more recent in date than the canonical Acts which they feebly imitate. Certain of their apostolic discourses are written in the style of rhythmical chanting, and occasionally we come upon veritable hymns—precious samples of the Christian manner of worship.

Among these apocrypha, the Acts of John, incompletely preserved, seem to be the oldest. They are saturated with Docetism. They contain the Ephesian legend of John fully formed and were probably composed in Asia; in their first form before the end of the second century. In no sense is the book Marcionite, but Docetic in the highest degree: the identification of Christ with God is absolute, his humanity and death mere appearance and the whole symbolic.

The Acts of Paul, known to Hippolytus and to Origen, were widely diffused in the East. Tertullian says that the author, a priest of Asia, was dismissed when his fraud was discovered (*De Baptismale*, 17). None the less the book, constructed on canonical Acts and starting with Paul's mission to Antioch of Pisidia, continued to be widely read. Only fragments of it have survived, the most considerable and the most in favour being the piece which bears the title Acts of Paul and of Thecla. The mention of it by Tertullian places the composition towards 160–180. The author appears to belong to the region chosen for the scene of his romance and may have exploited a local tradition along with Acts and the thirteen Epistles attributed to Paul.

The Acts of Peter, which it has been possible to reconstruct from the Clementine apocrypha,[77] and the Catholic Acts, in which the legend of Peter's martyrdom is developed, probably go no further back than the beginning of the third century, but they reflect some traditions and doubtless incorporate older documents.

Of all these unorthodox lucubrations the strangest is the Acts of Thomas, a Syrian work apparently composed in Syriac. It is made up of marvellous stories and liturgical hymns, all strongly impregnated with gnosis and encratism. The Greek version, if it is a version, is hardly less ancient than its Syriac original of which the date may be given about 200, without excluding the possibility of an earlier date for some of its elements.

The vogue enjoyed by all these writings of suspect origin is a point worthy of attention as proof that ancient Christianity was endowed with a singular capacity to receive what was offered to it, and even at a time when it was engaged in the war with Gnosticism.

With the apocryphal Acts we pass beyond the limit of direct witness to the Christian movement before the year 180. It remains to mention those of the Christian apologies which have come down to us from the second century, chiefly the writings of Justin, his *Apologies* and *Dialogue with Trypho*. Here we have a Christian teacher not without culture but with a mediocre range of mind, a Hermas but better versed in the Scriptures and with a tinge of philosophy. He was a moral philosopher inclined to take Christianity as moral philosophy and to make it acceptable as such to pagans. His writings enable us to grasp the position of Christianity, about 150–160, surrounded by Judaism, paganism, gnostic heresy, and the first approach of that theory of the Logos which soon, at the hands of Irenaeus, Tertullian, Clement of Alexandria, Hippolytus, in preparation for Origen, was to fix the direction of the Christian gnosis. From these doctors themselves, or by inference from their writings, we cannot fail to learn how, during the middle part of the second century, there was forged the mighty power which the Church invoked at the time, and was to evoke thenceforward, against all innovators, namely the power of *tradition*, embodied in the collection or canon of scripture, in the symbols of faith (creeds), in the episcopal magistracy—the whole, scripture, symbols and magistracy being held of apostolic origin, or rather as going back, through the apostles, to Jesus himself and his Gospel.

We shall find the testimony of profane writers valuable at certain points, but they cannot make good the insufficiency and clear up the obscurities of the Christian witness to Christian history. At least they convey to us the impression made by the new religion on the men of letters, the statesmen and the philosophers of the time. Thus Celsus, though known to us solely through Origen, gives us the impression made by Christianity on enlightened people in the time of Marcus Aurelius, and shows us how the apparently irreconcilable conflict between Christianity and paganism might have ended by the incorporation of Christianity in the imperial religion, into which all religions were admitted, if hellenized Christianity had not been strong enough to compel its final acceptance as the one religion of the Empire. The genesis of the gnostic sects, of which the Great Church disencumbered itself by condemning them, is in like manner not accessible to us in the original writings of the doctors who founded them; the men and their writings we know only from those who refuted them when the sects had already lost some of their primitive force. Thus we are less well informed about dissenting Christianity than about dominant Christianity. More strictly speaking, the general history of the Christian movement, from its point of departure to the year 180, has to be deduced from documents distinctly non-historical in the proper sense of history, but intended to serve in some way the movement which produced them, and not as a faithful record for posterity of its stages and fortunes. To sum the matter up in a sentence, all the difficulties and gropings in the dark which the interpretation of these documents imposes on the impartial historian proceed from the fact that the documents he is interpreting are something other than history.

Chapter II

THE GOSPEL OF JESUS

WHEN Tacitus, in his account of the burning of Rome in the year 64, comes to the point where mention has to be made of the Christians, he writes of them as follows:—

"The founder of this sect, Christ, was condemned to death in the reign of Tiberius by the procurator Pontius Pilate, but the disastrous superstition, repressed for a time, spread not only throughout Judea, where the evil was born, but also through the City, the place of confluence from everywhere of all sorts of abominable and shameful things, and the scene where they are practised."[1]

Tacitus has no more information to give about the career of Jesus. He conceives it as an outbreak of propaganda arrested by the death of its author, but afterwards renewed and with such vigour that, passing the frontiers of Judea, it reached Rome almost immediately. In the same way Tacitus is repeating a current opinion when he writes of Judaism, *Histories*, v, 3: "Moses, quo sibi in posterum gentem formaret, novos ritus contrariosque ceteris mortalibus indidit."

At the time when Tacitus thus evaluated the Christian religion and its founder, Pliny the Younger wrote on similar lines to Trajan that the Christians "in their meetings sing praises to Christ as to a god."[2]

From these statements we may gather the official opinion of high functionaries and educated persons, at the beginning of the second century, in regard to the Christian religion. It was to the effect that this new religion, sprung from Judaism in the time of Tiberius, had been founded by an agitator to whom Pilate had put an end and whom his followers had quickly turned into an object of worship. Neither Tacitus nor Pliny had read the Gospels. Their opinion is that which was formed by the administrative personnel of the Roman Empire after the judicial interrogation of the Christians. To be more exact, since Tacitus reflects the opinion of the time of Nero, it must be conceded that this opinion was formed as much on the basis of official information received from Judea as from the statements of Christians themselves when on trial before the Roman tribunals, beginning with the trial of Paul and the martyrs of the year 64. The Christians, then, make their entry on historical ground as claiming to be under the leadership of Jesus called Christ, who had been condemned to crucifixion by Pontius Pilate, while those who were first opposed to their propaganda admitted his historical reality, just as the Christians did.

After all, then, the difficulty encountered by the historian who has no axe to grind is not that of ascertaining whether Jesus ever existed, but of discerning what his action and teaching really were, and how this action and teaching led on to the movement which began with him. Viewed in the light of the cult devoted to him, and in Christian tradition, the Christ would be incommensurable by any standard of human greatness. But, as facts of history, the appearance of Jesus as a figure on earth and the birth of the Christian religion are neither more nor less explicable than the appearance of Mahomet and the birth of Islam. Our task is to study the conditions of that appearance and of that birth, as they are furnished by the environment and by the times which produced them. In regard to Jesus the only environment with which we are concerned is that of Palestinian Judaism; and the time is the period, probably very short, within which the career of the Galilean reformer was confined.

1. JOHN THE BAPTIST

In an earlier volume (*La Religion d'Israel*, p. 308) we have shown how the Kingdom of Herod the Great was first divided between three of his sons and how a few years later the portion of Archelaus, that is to say Judea proper with Samaria, was placed directly under the government of Rome. From this point we may date the crisis which ended in the birth of the Christian religion and the destruction of Jewish nationalism. Further back in history preparation for the crisis had begun. It was during the Babylonian captivity that Jewish eschatology began to shape itself as a project of national restoration concurrent with the religious and moral regeneration of the chosen people.

Most of all, the way had been paved by the foolish policy of Antiochus Epiphanes, which had the effect of provoking a reaction of Jewish faith, in the form of a belief in the near and decisive intervention of God for the extermination of the imperial oppressor and the establishment of his own Kingdom—a fever-heat of enthusiasm rather inflamed than allayed by the temporary establishment of a national monarchy. But the reduction of Judea to the status of a Roman province caused a shock to the Jewish mind which was only appeased, and that only for a feeble minority of the Jews, by the progressive spiritualization of their hope under the influence of the Christian Gospel, and, on the other hand, for the mass of the people, by the overthrow of Jewish nationalism. It is, however, true that both the spiritualization of the Jewish hope and the overthrow of Jewish nationalism were realized only by stages. Christian hope was still violently revolutionary when the Apocalypse appeared towards the end of the first century, while Jewish nationalism, surviving the destruction of Jerusalem in the year 70, was not finally broken down until a new revolt had been suppressed in the time of Hadrian.

It is well to remember also that in this crisis Galilee was a hotbed of Jewish nationalism. Thence came that Judas whom Josephus represents as the founder of the school of uncompromising resistance which he compares to the schools of the Pharisees, the Sadducees and the Essenes. Judas the Galilean was certainly no master of religious philosophy or of ascetic living; historically little more than the leader of a band of brigands, he is yet a representative of that spirit of blind and unyielding faith which embraced the idea of the Kingdom of God in all its rigour. It was a principle of these zealots—and on this point we can trust Josephus[3]—that the Israelites, the people and children of God, had no master on earth save their Master in heaven. Hence the Roman government was a sacrilege, its exercise an impious usurpation, and there must be no paying tribute to Caesar.[4] Insurrection against the idolatrous emperor was, of all duties, the most sacred. But Roman power being what we know, this simplest of duties became the crowning folly.

We know that not all the Jews drew the same consequences from this principle, which became, in sum, the dominant motive of Jewish faith. The Sadducees tended to regard the Kingdom of God as essentially realized in observation of the Law; the Essenes believed it attained in their Mystery and, in an eternal future, by the ascension of souls to God. A considerable party of educated Pharisees, while cherishing the idea of a Kingdom of God on earth, and accepting the resurrection of the dead, denied that there was any need to lend the aid of human violence in founding an order of things which only the power of God was able to bring about. But the various forms of the national hope, of which it would be a mistake to deny the diversity, did not come into conflict on the field of practice. They subsisted in the inner life of Judaism, rather associated than antagonistic, loosely held together by common faith in the revelation which made Israel the privileged object of divine solicitude, and by the hope of a national future which their divine protector would clothe with glory. Fundamentally, foreign rule on the soil of Palestine was an offence to all these parties. When the great revolt broke out in the time of Nero, the number of sincere believers who understood the futility of that desperate attempt seems to have been small.[5]

Under the working of this faith, to which the course of events lent its aid, the popular imagination became more and more excited and the superheated atmosphere was created in which religious movements are likely to be born.[6] It was no effect of chance that the beginning of our era witnessed the appearance of a swarm of sects in Palestine and the region of the Jordan. John the Baptist, Simon the Magician and Elchasai are witnesses, each in his own way, to the religious ferment of which the Christian religion was also an issue.[7] The sects founded by them missed the great fortune in store for the Christian movement, though they are more or less related to it. But while we can clearly see their failure to win the same success, it is not so easy to explain why it so happened, the play of circumstances and the character of the men concerned being too little known to us. Of the three we have mentioned it is John the Baptist of whom exact information would be of most value to the historian, since it was to him that the Christian religion, up to a certain point, traced its origin, while Simon and Elchasai, who also depend on John,[8] stand rather in a relation of rival movements to the Christianity of the first age.

John appeared on the scene earlier than Jesus and founded a sect, slightly anterior to the Christian, which became a rival whose claims are combated in the Gospel literature.9 But what the Gospel tells us about John is a tendentious legend, while the notice bestowed upon him by Josephus,10 though commonly accepted by critics, is of doubtful authenticity, and vague enough in any event. The Gospels are more precise but not more trustworthy. Even if the stories in Luke about the birth of John have been borrowed, as Bultmann supposes, from the Johannite sect, they are none the less fictitious on that account. The testimony which John is made to render to Jesus, in giving himself out as the precursor of the Messiah, as in the synoptic tradition, or in expressly designating Jesus as the Messiah expected, as in the fourth Gospel which contradicts Matthew xi, 2, 6 and Luke vii, 18–20, is another fiction contrived by Christian apologetic for the purpose of attenuating or disguising the original dependence of the Christian sect on the Johannite. Even the account of the martyrdom of John in the first two Gospels has few marks of historicity. Herodias is a new Jezebel persecuting the new Elijah. All the legend leaves us is the fact that John was put to death by order of Antipas.

We may take it as certain that John proclaimed himself as the messenger of God, a prophet of the end of the age with a mission subordinate to that of no other prophet, and not even to that of the Messiah; a precursor of none save of God only in his coming to judge the world, unless he be subordinate to the Son of Man, the great Envoy; but it was not thus that his sectaries seem to have understood him. It was within the Baptist sect that John was first proclaimed as "a prophet and more than a prophet"; equally from within the sect came the application to John of the text from Malachi (iii, 1) "behold I send my messenger who shall prepare my way before me"; and it was within the sect that the saying was current "among them that are born of women there has not risen up a greater than John the Baptist."11 All this was marked for correction by the Gospel tradition; but there would have been no need to correct it if it had not been professed. In like manner it is incredible that John should in advance have discredited his own baptism in favour of Christian baptism by declaring that his own was a mere symbol and that the only true and efficacious baptism was that which the Christ would give in the Holy Spirit.[12] These sayings are put into the mouth of John in order to avoid the simple avowal that the baptismal rite had been borrowed by the Christian sect from the Johannite. All these petty frauds are significant, indeed more significant than would have been the simple avowal of the truth.

Mark and Matthew have a strange manner of introducing their account of the Baptist's death and burial by making Antipas declare, as an explanation of Jesus and his miracles, that "John is risen from the dead"; and it is not impossible that we have signs here of a set purpose to confuse and discredit the faith of the Baptist sect in the survival of the prophet martyr. Mark, in relating the burial of John (vi, 14, 16, 29), has an air of suggesting that it was not followed by his resurrection. In Matthew (xiv, 1–2, 12) even John's own disciples, who come to inform Jesus of their master's death, seem to imply that his ministry has come to an end. Not thus, assuredly, was his ministry understood in the Baptist sect.

John, then, was a preacher of the Kingdom of God some time in advance of Jesus. His ministry was carried on beside the Jordan in the territories of the tetrarch Antipas.[13] He was probably an ascetic after the manner of the Essenes, although, in all probability, he did not belong to their order. For John acted on his own account and founded his own sect, his activity resembling in certain respects that of the hermit Banus mentioned by Josephus. Needless to say he was not a Sadducee. Matthew, no doubt by way of conforming him to Jesus, makes him preach against the Pharisees, adding the Sadducees at a venture (iii, 7) while Luke (iii, 7) speaks only of "crowds." He proclaimed the imminence of the Great Kingdom which he expected to be brought in by God only. He was, moreover, detached from apocalyptic preoccupations, and being a stranger, like Jesus, to the science of the schools, he engaged in no speculations concerning the preliminaries of the coming End. He insisted on repentance in preparation for God's judgment of the world and, in prevision of its coming, it may be said that he instituted, if he did not adopt, a veritable sacrament of purification,[14] which became at the same time a guarantee of salvation. This was nothing more than baptism by immersion in the waters of the Jordan. In this practice he again comes near to the Essenes, with the difference that the Essenes required many ablutions and bathings. John seems to have attached essential importance to the one total immersion he imposed on his converts, regarding it as the symbol of conversion, the effectual sign of forgiveness and regeneration.

It is remarkable that neither sacrifice, nor the bare idea of sacrifice, finds any place in this scheme of salvation, and furthermore that the death of the prophet was not interpreted as providing vicarious satisfaction for the redemption of sinners. A rite of purification at once the most significant, and the simplest, commonest, and one may add the oldest and most universally practised by mankind was enough to put the man of goodwill in a condition to face the judgment of God. It may be that John, like the Essenes, passed no condemnation on the legal sacrifices, his doctrine of salvation simply leaving them on one side as having no meaning for the religious life as he conceived it. For the rest, we cannot be certain that John's baptism allowed of no repetition. But we can hardly doubt that, like Christian baptism, it operated once and for all on every individual receiving it. Had it been a repeatable ablution there would be no ground for comparing it with the Christian rite.

At first sight it would seem that there was no reason why political authority should consider John more disturbing than the Essenes. But the Essenes did not proclaim that the Judgment Day of God was at hand. The soul, according to them, when duly purified by continence, holy washings, holy feasts and prayers would be able, after death, to reascend to the heaven whence it came down, without interfering with the order established on earth. But the universal judgment which John announced as on the point of coming implied something more than the recompense due to the righteous and the punishment that would fall on the wicked: it implied an immediate and complete revolution in which the Kingdom of God would make a clean sweep of all human governments. An outlook such as this could not be regarded with an indifferent eye by the shepherds of the people, even though the eye were that of a sceptic. It was an expectation likely to agitate the public mind in a way not conducive to the tranquillity of the ruling powers. Accordingly,

Antipas made short work of the Baptist, by casting him into prison and cutting off his head. The particular circumstances of his imprisonment and death are unknown to us, but it is safe to say that the agitation provoked by John was judged by political authority to be dangerous. In point of fact it is hardly possible that it could be long restrained within purely moral limits and that the eager longing for divine judgment could have no effect in compromising obedience to established authority. It may very well be that the Tetrarch decided to take the prophet's life on finding that his imprisonment had failed to put a final stop to the agitation.

His death, however, was not enough to discourage his followers and here his case again deserves study for the analogy it affords to that of Jesus. The sect John left behind him was rendered inoffensive by the death of its founder, but none the less it continued to exist under his name. It was perpetuated especially in Transjordania, where the Essenes, the Jewish Christians and the Elchasaites also had a footing. The signs which some have thought to find of the sect's diffusion in Alexandria and Asia are more than fragile; for the author of Acts, when he speaks of Apollos and the twelve disciples of Ephesus as "knowing only the baptism of John,"[15] does not seem to have had in mind the followers of the Baptist; and the polemic of the Fourth Gospel, which aims, through John, at the whole religious economy of the Jews, does not necessarily imply that the Baptist's sect was represented at Ephesus. In like manner the place given to John by the Mandeans in their tradition does not go back to the source; it seems to have been invented in Islamic time to give importance to the Mandean sect and to ensure its conservation. But if John was not the precursor of Jesus in the sense in which Christian tradition makes him out to be, he and his sect were historically, and in a very true sense, precursors of the Christ and of the Christian religion.

2. JESUS

Though myth and legend have considerable place in evangelical tradition, our knowledge of Jesus is somewhat fuller than of John the Baptist. But all the mythical and legendary elaboration within the tradition bears testimony, in its own way, to him from whom the Christian movement had its beginning. Whatever may have been said to the contrary, there is not a single Christian document of the first age which does not imply the historicity of Jesus. The gnostic Docetists who denied the materiality of Christ's body and the physical reality of his Passion believed, with the mass of Christians, in the historicity of Jesus and of his appearance as a figure upon the earth; their Christ, immaterial but visible, was not for them an unreal phantom, a pure image of the mind, as our mythologues would sometimes make him out to have been. And pagan writers least favourable to the Christian religion, from Tacitus to Celsus and the Emperor Julian, always regarded Jesus as an historical figure, Christ being for them the name of a Galilean agitator who came to an evil end and whom his followers had absurdly made into a god. The criticism which attempts to replace this figure by a myth will find itself involved in endless subtleties and travelling on a road which leads to nowhere. None the less it is true that Jesus has lived on in myth, and been carried by myth to the highest peak of history.

Where exactly he was born is unknown to us; we know only that he came from Galilee. The oldest legend shows him at Capernaum and in the region north-west of the Lake of Tiberias; this probably is the region of his birth. The myth which assigns his birthplace to Bethlehem and makes him of the family of David is founded on an arbitrary interpretation of prophecy and contains nothing of primitive and historical tradition. The myth, moreover, is full of contradictions. In order to fix his birthplace at Bethlehem of Judea, Matthew domiciles his parents there; then, to bring him from Judea into Galilee he imagines that Joseph, after his flight into Egypt, not daring to re-install himself in his own country, established himself at Nazareth, whence Jesus came to Capernaum; all of it presented as a fulfilment of ancient prophecies on the strength of an exegesis carried to the extreme of phantasy.[16] Luke, quite differently, supposes that the parents of Jesus had their home in Nazareth and that Jesus was born at Bethlehem by accident, his parents having been brought there in consequence of the census presided over by Quirinius; though it is far from clear why Joseph, even if he was a descendant of David, should have had to report himself at a place which his ancestors had quitted a thousand years previously. This evangelist is equally unaware that he contradicts himself by dating the birth of Jesus both under the reign of Herod, who died in the year 4 before our era, and in the year of the census, which took place after the deposition of Archilaus ten years later.[17] In reality, evangelical tradition had no knowledge either of the village in Galilee or of the year in which Jesus was born. Nor was it any clearer on the point of his Davidic descent, since the two genealogies presented mutually contradict and annul each other.[18] Jesus was made a descendant of David because that was what the Messiah had to be.[19]

The assignment of Nazareth as the family home of Jesus was an attempt made by the same tradition after the event to explain the surname "Nazorean," which was originally added to the name of Jesus and remained the name for designating Christians in Rabbinic literature and in Eastern countries. This name, Nazorean, is quite clearly the name of a sect having no connexion with the town of Nazareth, unless it be that of a common etymology. Nor has it any closer connexion with the *nazirs*, "the men under vow," mentioned in the Old Testament. It may have been the name of the Baptist's sect, of which the Christian was originally an offshoot.[20] Jesus himself, before beginning an independent ministry of his own, was probably at first a member of the Johannite sect. But the story told in the Gospels about the relations of John and Jesus belongs to legend. The message sent to Jesus from prison by John is merely a frame within which considerations are introduced for exhibiting the superiority of Jesus and the Christian Gospel to John and his preaching.[21] The story of the baptism of Jesus by John is nothing else than the myth of the institution of Christian baptism.[22] It pretends to found the complete independence of the Christian scheme of salvation, in relation to other baptist sects and to Judaism, on a decree of divine providence. Implied in the story there is a consciousness of the independence of Christianity, in regard to Judaism, which cannot have been acquired before the year 70, our texts showing signs of having been incessantly retouched in the course of handing the story on.[23] The account of the temptation in the desert has the same mythical character and the documents of the New Testament bear their witness to its evolution. The reason is obvious why the Fourth Gospel omits the temptation, as it omits the cures of demoniacs and even the baptism of Jesus by John. A single trace of service rendered by angels to the Son of God is retained in John i, 51.

In the tradition common to all the Gospels, Jesus is a wandering preacher, as John the Baptist had been before him. The two preachers are not represented as teaching in the manner of contemporary rabbis, but rather as prophets, and both as prophets of a single oracle—"the Kingdom of God is at hand" (Matthew iii, 2; iv, 17). In the Synoptic tradition Jesus is also a wonder-working exorcist—nothing more natural in those times; but in the fourth Gospel, while the wonders increase in magnitude, the exorcisms disappear, as does the story of the temptation in the desert. There is, however, no reason, so far as the personal history of Jesus is concerned, to linger over a detailed discussion of the miracles attributed to him. They represent the appanage of "powers" or "virtues" with which, in the thought of the time, a ministry such as his would be endowed.[24] They are constructed in accordance with current types and are even presented as types, arranged in a series, and, at the same time, turned by all the Gospels, but especially by the fourth, into symbols of the spiritual work accomplished by the Christ. Just as the parables in the Gospels are mystical allegories, so the miracles are "signs," σημεῖα, not only marks of divine power, but symbols of salvation.[25] As spiritual symbols they foreshadow the formation of the Christian Mystery as a whole. But there is no room to doubt that the gift of healing was attributed to Jesus in his lifetime and that he himself deliberately exercised it. The first Christian missionaries were preaching exorcists, as Jesus had been before them, and in that were doing no more than following his example.[26] The Christian religion was not born in an atmosphere of transcendent mysticism and erudite theology.

It is very remarkable that tradition never represents Jesus as preaching in large towns, except when he came to Jerusalem to meet his end. We see him going from one to another of the townlets and straggling villages of Galilee and entering their small synagogues; but there is no evidence that he ever went to Tiberias, a profane town, ordinary residence of the Tetrarch, nor to any other of importance. We must conclude that towns did not provide him with an atmosphere favourable to his message. The people with whom he sought contact were fishermen round the Lake of Gennesaret, poor craftsmen and workers on the land in his neighbourhood. The geographical frame of his ministry did not enclose a large area. Nearly all the souvenirs, if souvenirs they be, are attached to Capernaum and the surrounding country.

It was, then, in a few villages, or at most in a few districts of Galilee, to the north-west of the Lake, that we must conceive him as teaching for some time and with some measure of success. A theatre so small and, moreover, so little known can hardly have been invented by tradition as the scene of a ministry to which it attached importance so great, the connexion of it with these humble localities by means of the text in Isaiah indicated by Matthew (iv, 12–16) being surely an afterthought. The journeys outside Galilee attributed to Jesus were not preaching tours. If they ever took place, it must have been towards the end of the Galilean ministry, and they would seem to have been undertaken by Jesus to escape from the pursuit of Antipas when the attention of the Tetrarch had been drawn to the movement excited by his preaching.[27] We are told, and it is probably true, that quite early in his career Jesus recruited a certain number of companions who followed him regularly from place to place—though the stories of their vocation that have come down to us are all typical and symbolic. What the Gospels have to tell us about the crowds which pressed upon the footsteps of the preacher, and the thousands who came from all Palestine and from Transjordania to hear the Sermon on the Mount, can only be regarded as the work of pious exaggeration.[28] The preaching of Jesus could not have reverberated far beyond Galilee, and the Sermon on the Mount, a collection of didactic fragments and sentences originally distinct, was never preached.

Of what the teaching of Jesus was in reality only an approximate idea can be formed from the teaching that has been attributed to him. It may be said without a trace of paradox that of the teaching he actually gave no collection was ever made. Neither the preacher nor his most faithful hearers dreamed of fixing the tenor of his preaching for the purpose of transmitting it to posterity; every purpose of that kind was thrust aside by the imminent prospect of the Kingdom of God, the near coming of which, with the Christ in glory, was continually announced by the first apostles after the death of Jesus. It was only after the lapse of a considerable time, when groups of believers had become organized in permanent confraternities, that the need for more complete instruction began to be felt, and the teaching *about* Jesus and the teaching *of* Jesus, the latter already greatly modified and augmented, were more and more fused together to form the books of liturgical catechesis for which the name "Gospel" was retained.

Our Gospels, even the Synoptics, are more truly understood as containing the elements of the primitive Christian catechism than as representing instructions really given by Jesus in Galilee and Jerusalem. Needless to say, the mystical gnosis of the fourth Gospel was wholly outside his ken. Just as a legend has been built up for him, so too there has been built up for him a body of teaching, and it has been done by borrowings from many quarters. One part of the sayings which constitute the synoptic tradition was taken from the teaching of the Rabbis, while the whole of it, even where the spirit is that of hellenic Christianity, has the tone of Jewish hellenism.[29] It is safe to say that the teaching of the first three Gospels is conceived after the manner of Jesus and directly penetrated by his spirit. But no attempt could be more futile than that which aims to-day at reconstituting the teaching of the Christ by arranging, in an order more or less logical, the discourses and sayings scattered throughout the first three Gospels. The thought of Jesus is not more directly reflected in such a synthesis than it is in the broken order of the discourses it seeks to arrange. These discourses are constructs designed for the Christian communities, with a view to their needs, their misgivings, their sufferings, their interior difficulties, their position in the pagan world and their controversies with the Jews. It may be that the general principles of this teaching were laid down by Jesus, or merely foreshadowed by him. But, in all strictness of language, the teaching of the discourses and sayings called evangelical are one thing, and the personal preaching of Jesus was another.

Some critics, notably Schmiedel[30] and Goguel more recently, have been forward in maintaining that clearly authentic sayings of Jesus are to be recognized in certain declarations which run counter, more or less, to the early Christologies and so create embarrassment for the apologists. Examples are the following: "Why callest thou me good: there is none good but God," which seems to make the Christ a man subject to imperfection; the despairing outcry of Jesus on the Cross, "My God, my God, why hast thou forsaken me?";[31] "some of them that stand here shall not be dead when the Son of Man comes in his Kingdom." Others again have found a unique savour of originality in sayings such as these: "The sabbath was made for man, not man for the sabbath";[32] "not that which goeth into a man defileth him, but that which cometh out," and such like invectives against the Pharisees. It is a risky kind of argument. The saying about "goodness" as an incommunicable attribute of God is a theological subtlety the credit for which may well belong, if not to an evangelist, to some pious rabbi, the taste of whose wisdom was familiar to the Marcan tradition. The dying outcry of Jesus marks the fulfilment of Psalm xxii by the Passion of the Christ. The saying about the near approach of the parousia expresses the faith of the first community of Christians, though in a form which had lost something of its original force. The sayings about the sabbath and about the cause of defilement are as much in the tone of Jewish wisdom as in that of the Gospel; they may be in harmony with the spirit of Jesus but there are no other grounds for asserting that he was the first to formulate them in his preaching and was not repeating them after others. As to the invectives against the Pharisees, they are just as likely to have come from a Christian prophet as from Jesus himself.

Let us be content with the knowledge that while Pontius Pilate was procurator of Judea, perhaps in 28 or 29 of our era, perhaps a year or two earlier, a prophet appeared in Galilee, in the region of Capernaum. He was called Jesus, a name so common among the Jews of that time that assuredly no reason can be found for conceding to the mythologues, as Guignebert does, that the name might have been given him after his death to mark the rôle of saviour early ascribed to him by his followers. This Jesus was a man of lowly origin. It is improbable that Joseph, the name of his father, and Mary, the name of his mother, were invented by the tradition. He had brothers[33] who played a part of some importance in the life of the earliest community of believers. Doubtless he was born in some townlet or village of the region where he began to teach. There are also reasons for believing, as indicated above, that he was for some time attached to John the Baptist, or affiliated to the sect called after him, before himself beginning to preach the near approach of the Kingdom.

The Gospels probably had reasons for defining his teaching and that of the Baptist by the same general formula: "Repent, for the kingdom of God is at hand."[34] This simple though widely comprehensive indication gives us our surest knowledge of his teaching. We may regard it as certain, first because it remained the fundamental element in the faith of his earliest followers who continued his work after his death in proclaiming him Christ: and second, because the earlier elaborations of the Christian tradition, always bound to this as their initial datum, consisted in retouchings or attenuations of the same idea—the coming of the Great Kingdom. We know moreover that the hopes of the Jewish people all came to a head precisely in that idea, and that Jesus was regarded as appointed to bring the realization of these hopes to his faithful followers.

There is no reason to doubt that Jesus, like John, presented the Kingdom unencumbered by the preliminaries in which apocalyptic literature was fond of indulging. The coming of the Kingdom would be immediate and sudden as was befitting, or seemed befitting, to the majesty and might of Him who was to bring it to pass, thereby replacing at a stroke all the kingdoms of flesh, which the powers of our lower world were upholding in unjust exercise of the mandate committed to them by the Master of the universe. What would be the conditions of his coming? How would his reign be carried on? There is no proof that the mind of Jesus dwelt on this subject, which he had not studied in books, as did the apocalyptic writers from Daniel onwards. But there is no sign that he or his first disciples were preoccupied by these fantastic speculations. They were men of the people and their conception of the Great Kingdom had the same simplicity as that of the Zealots, though entirely free from the violence of their fanaticism. We may conclude, then, that Jesus proclaimed, if not the end of the world—for we should have to ask whether he had an idea of the "world," and if so what—at least the end of the present age, the end that is of Satan's Kingdom and of the earthly powers set up by him, the coming of God, the reign of the just, the resurrection of the dead, and the Great Assize at which the wicked everywhere would be sentenced to extermination. With the view before him of judgment about to fall, let the wicked man repent and change his life!

Did Jesus, like John, baptize those who were converted by this message? The Synoptics do not affirm that he did, and critics are generally content to say that he required only the change of heart, thus making him the teacher of a pure religion entirely free from ritual magic. But Jesus had no intention of founding a religion; the idea never entered his mind. It is probable that his baptism by John, whether historical or not, figured at the head of the evangelical catechesis, but quite impossible to say exactly when, how, or why his disciples after him adopted a rite which, on the hypothesis favoured by the critics, Jesus himself neither recommended nor practised. Is not the silence of the Synoptics on this matter a simple consequence of the fact that the story they tell of his Galilean ministry does not aim at recording the historical actions of Jesus, but at instructing the believer about to undergo an initiation, of which the outward ritual is marked with sufficient clearness by the baptism of Jesus himself at the opening of the catechism? Strange as this idea may seem to those who insist on taking the arrangement of Gospel stories as representing the perspective of factual history, it is not impossible that adhesion or, one might say, conversion to the message of the Galilean Jesus was marked by the same rite of baptism as that which marked conversion to the message of John.[35] Nor is it impossible that even the meals taken in common by his regular followers were strongly coloured, as Renan supposes,[36] by a mystical element as prefiguring the banquets of the elect in the Kingdom of God.[37] Preconceptions are rife as to the conditions under which Jesus delivered his message, and it is a common assumption that these differed greatly from those which attended the ministry of John. But the plain truth is that we know very little about either, the Gospels giving us no information on the subject, or informing us inexactly, even in regard to Jesus. After all, a group of believers would not have been so easily formed after the death of Jesus had he not gathered around him during his lifetime a sort of confraternity analogous to that which we know was gathered round John and perpetuated in a sect after the Baptist's death.

Did Jesus claim for himself an eminent place in the coming Kingdom? In recent times many have deemed it possible to answer this question in the negative, but without suspecting that they might be bringing Jesus too near to their own mentality or to their own religious ideals. In their view Jesus was a mystical philanthropist, the Kingdom of Heaven was essentially inward and moral, the presence of God in the soul, the revelation and intimate awareness of the divine fatherhood and goodness, of the law of love, of the dignity of man. And this no doubt is what the Gospel may seem to those who try to find themselves in it and view it, from a great distance of time, sifted by the experience of nineteen centuries. But Christianity was not born in that transcendent atmosphere and our metaphysical universals were as remote from the mind of Jesus as were the sceptical smiles of Ernest Renan and the humanitarianism of Henri Barbusse. The dominating perspective of the Gospel, and the dominating thought of Jesus, is the concrete, real and even realistic conception of the Kingdom of God, involving the complete renovation of the human order both inward and outward. The value of the human soul—still less its absolute value, the autonomy of human personality in a transcendent individualism—is not presented in the Gospel independently of the individual's destiny in the coming Kingdom; the law of love is not laid down independently of the renunciations required by the coming revolution in earthly affairs; the relief of the poor man is not prescribed independently of his exaltation in the everlasting Kingdom. In sober truth, neither the revelation of Divine Goodness, nor the value of the soul, nor the law of love, nor the dignity of the poor has the eminent place in the primitive Gospel which many in our time would assign to it. These are the elements of the Gospel which, more or less magnified when seen from our point of view, happen to be for us the least worn out by time. But, for the historian, the sum and substance of the Gospel can always be found, and must always be found, in the eschatological idea of the Kingdom of God, all the rest being subordinate to that.

That being so, Jesus could hardly have overlooked himself as a figure destined to play a part in the coming Advent of God. To be sure he does not seem to have given much thought to the order that would be set up by the divine polity of the future. The saying about the thrones on which his principal disciples were to sit at his side does not go back to him, but was probably conceived by the earliest community in honour of the Twelve. There is at least an equal probability that the notion of the Son of Man, which holds so large a place in the Gospel tradition, was introduced into it for the purpose of glorifying Jesus after his death and linked to that event in order to bring out its providential significance. "The Son of Man" is a mythical conception, earlier than the Gospel tradition which so largely exploits it; earlier than the apocalypses of Daniel and Enoch, where use is made of it.[38] Its origin is pagan, probably Chaldeo-Iranian.[39] In the apocalyptic tradition it became a kind of definition for an idealized Messiah. Although the history of the myth is far from being clear, it is assuredly pre-Christian and was probably without influence on the Gospel at its point of departure, that is on Jesus and his first disciples. The idea, in short, is bound up with a redemption-gnosis which the Epistles present in a developed form but whose place in the Gospel is progressive and of secondary importance only.[40] We may agree further that Jesus never described himself in set terms as the future King of the Elect, and that even the confession of Peter at Caesarea Philippi anticipates a faith which, as so defined, was that of the first group of believers and only came into being after the catastrophe of Calvary. But it remains true that, before the final drama, this faith was in a manner existent, and to some extent explicit, among the first converts to Jesus' Gospel, and in Jesus himself as naturally involved in the initiative taken by him in proclaiming the Great Event and making preparation for its advent.

It was as an Envoy of God, not as a simple prophet, nor as a sage and a moralist, that Jesus presented himself to his contemporaries. He claimed a special and unique mission in regard to the Great Event, but did not define it with precision. "The Great Envoy" would be the equivalent in our language. So far as we can judge Zoroaster and the Buddha made similar claims; so, too, did Mani and Mahomet. There could be no question of his being the Messiah there and then, since the Messiah was the

Prince of the Great Kingdom and there could be no Messiah till the Kingdom came. Elsewhere the author of this book has argued for the view that Jesus was Messiah in expectation, Messiah presumptive, and some of his critics have condemned the idea as a theological subtilty. Perhaps it is neither as subtle nor as theological as they deem it to be. But let us keep only to this; Jesus, as the Great Herald of the coming Kingdom, certainly made claim, before the end of his life, to the rôle which would involve his becoming, after his death, the Messiah who was to come with the Kingdom. Nothing else is of import if his mortal career is to suffice as an explanation of his immortal destiny. The closer definitions of that destiny would never have come into being if the faith of Jesus and his disciples had not, in one way or another, contained their beginnings and their justification. This faith it is that also explains the culminating action of Jesus at Jerusalem; this faith it was that triumphed in his death.

3. Jesus Proclaims the Kingdom in Jerusalem

Believers, even the most liberal, and they perhaps most of all, are still loath to admit that the action of Jesus in carrying his message to Jerusalem was not, humanly speaking, more reasonable than that of the others who are commonly known as "false Messiahs": for example, Theudas who, fifteen years after the death of Jesus, recruited some thousands of followers in Perea and brought them to the side of Jordan in the belief that the river would open up its waters to facilitate their triumphal march on Jerusalem; or the Egyptian, of whom Acts also speaks (xxi, 38), who led a much more formidable body of partisans as far as the Mount of Olives, convinced in their simplicity that the walls of Jerusalem would fall down at the voice of their prophet.[41] These cases however are parallel to that of Jesus and their issue, so far as the immediate result was concerned, was much the same for him as for them.[42] But our liberal believers are not content with insisting that the personality of Jesus was loftier and purer than that of these men, who were only adventurers and visionaries; they will have it also that Jesus was less under illusion than they, or even—an absurd supposition both historically and psychologically—that he was under no illusion at all about the fate in store for him at Jerusalem, which, had illusion been absent, he would have had no motive to encounter. Jesus, they would have it, came to Jerusalem at the risk of his life to accomplish a great duty. As the interpretation of an act of faith, and, we must add, of religious illuminism, all this is too modern and rationalistic.

On this occasion Jesus was not visiting Jerusalem in the character of a simple pilgrim.43 It is possible that he had made several pilgrimages to the city before taking up the rôle of a prophet; but it is wholly improbable, not to say quite impossible, that he was there more than this once as announcer of the Kingdom of God. The synoptic tradition gives us to understand that he presented himself with this announcement on the occasion of a Passover which, in Luke's reckoning, would probably be that of the year 29. The artificial chronology and editorial arrangements of the Fourth Gospel need not be taken into account. Being what it was, the preaching of Jesus in Galilee must have been of short duration; to make it last a few months is to give it good measure. Whether the reason was that he had seen the speedy collapse of the credit accorded his message at its first announcement, or that he had reason to think that Antipas was about to put a violent stop to his preaching,44 or simply because Jerusalem was the appointed place for the publication of his message, as well as being the place predestined for the Great Coming, Jesus resolved to proclaim the word of the Kingdom in the Holy City.

No direct testimony has come down to us to throw light on the convictions which determined his action at this conjuncture. The Gospels present him to us as fully conscious of providential designs and as going to Jerusalem that he might there procure the fulfilment of divine intentions and ancient prophecies—a systematic and apologetic conception of which next to nothing can be retained for the psychology of Jesus. It cannot be repeated too often that the Gospel stories are the scenes of a ritual drama in which the actions of the characters, especially of the chief character, are governed by the faith which the drama is designed to represent, to fortify and, one might say, to realize. Most assuredly the young Galilean continued in Jerusalem to be animated by the faith and the hope which had led him in his own country to proclaim the speedy coming of the Great Kingdom. It was that same impulse of faith and hope, raised perhaps to a higher ardour by the obstacles already encountered, encouraged also by the measure of success already won and rendered more urgent by the necessity to proclaim the divine message to the Jewish people at the centre of the national life—that same impulse it was that drew Jesus on to his fate, but without giving him clear foreknowledge of what that fate would be.[45] Doubtless his hope was too masterful to permit him to envisage, with complete lucidity and calm, the likelihood, in reality a certainty, that death was awaiting him. What he did expect, and his followers expected with him, was the manifestation of divine power, the advent of the Kingdom foretold, the dawn of the Day of God. Neither in the messianic tradition of Judaism, nor in the message of the Kingdom as he had delivered it, was there anything to make him suppose that his own death was a necessary condition of the Great Event. He came to Jerusalem fully confident in the power of God, in the validity of the ancient promise to Israel, in the urgent need of divine intervention to establish the reign of justice on the earth.

We could not be worse informed than we are about the real events immediately preceding the tragic climax of this religious adventure. The affair of the Egyptian, above referred to, is enough to show that the messianic demonstration on the Mount of Olives, as described in the synoptics, is not in itself improbable. But the story they give us is derived from Old Testament texts.[46] The same is true of the expulsion of the traders from the temple, a story much less easy to accept as recording a real event.[47] Tradition has constructed for Jesus a Jerusalem ministry analogous to the Galilean; but the long invective against the Pharisees seems no more authentic in its substance, as the real teaching of Jesus at Jerusalem, than the discourse on the end of the world.[48] It is, moreover, improbable that Jesus would have been allowed to teach publicly in the temple for many days without suffering interference. Our choice lies practically between two hypotheses: a riot created by the followers of Jesus, if we may suppose them numerous enough to make it, immediately on their arrival in Jerusalem,[49] and the prompt arrest of their leader by the Roman authority; or a popular movement excited by the preaching of

Jesus in the temple, which would very quickly have brought on the intervention of the priests, followed at once by recourse to the procurator. In either case the affair would have borne, or would seem to bear, the character of a politico-religious demonstration which the procurator would suppress severely and without a moment's delay, as happened to the movements led by Theudas and the Egyptian. But the affair of Jesus, at the time when it occurred, seemed of less importance than theirs. He did not march on Jerusalem, as they did, with thousands of followers behind him, and his presence in the city would do no more than provoke a tumult to be suppressed at once.

All the evangelists have to record of the final evening is connected with the mystical meanings attached to the Last Supper, the Christian Passover in which the death of the Christ was commemorated. The treachery of Judas is accessory and it is by no means easy to say what, in reality, can have corresponded to this incident; it may have been invented as a mythical amplification of the punishment inflicted on Jesus.[50] The previsions attributed to the Christ on the same occasion are intended to throw a stronger light on his person; they come from the realms of drama and apologetic. One may be a fiction built up on a real fact; thus, the passing consternation of the disciples at the arrest and punishment of their Master is the basis for his prediction of their flight (Mark xiv, 27).[51] Another may be a fiction co-ordinated to another fiction or to a supposed fact; thus, the announcement of the coming betrayal[52] may be co-ordinated with Peter's denial—if, as is probable, the denial is an invention of Paul's party directed against the chief of the Galilean apostles.[53] In the same manner, but more surely, the announcement of the coming resurrection, interpolated into that of the flight (Mark xiv, 28) paves the way for the fictitious story of the discovery of the empty tomb. The words of the Eucharistic institution correspond to the interpretation of the Supper given by the First Epistle to the Corinthians:[54] they signify not only the presence of the Christ among his own at the common meal, but also the mystical relation of bread and wine to the commemoration of his saving death, of which the Supper is, in a manner, the mystical reiteration. And this interpretation, which can hardly go back to the apostolic age, is superimposed upon an older one in which the Supper is understood as a symbolic foretaste of the happiness of the elect in the Kingdom of God after the Great Event.[55] But even this earlier interpretation is the work of tradition which attached it typically to the last meal taken by Jesus who may very well have himself suggested it in the course of his ministry at the daily meals with his disciples. Finally the scene at Gethsemane[56] brings together and endows with material form the speculations of primitive Christianity concerning the great ordeal undergone by the Christ. Incidentally, the editors of Mark, followed by Matthew, have given that story a turn unfavourable to the Galilean apostles.

Of the circumstances of the arrest in the Garden of Olives not one, perhaps not even those of place and time, can be retained as historical.[57] The economy of the Gospel narratives is related to the ritual commemoration of the Passion; taking them literally we run the risk of transposing into history what are really the successive incidents of a religious drama. True it is that behind this drama lie the brutal facts, the condemnation to death and the crucifixion. But the real physiognomy of the facts has been transfigured in the drama which was conceived, not for reproducing the history reflected in it, but for its own purpose, that of bringing out its mystic significance, as well as in the interests of apologetic. Strictly speaking, it is possible, though there is nothing to make it probable, that Jesus was arrested at night, outside Jerusalem, by a sudden surprise organized by the temple police or by the Roman. If we suppose that Jesus was violently seized during an affray occasioned by him, and not without resistance by his partisans, we may be sure that tradition would have been careful to preserve no record of it. For not only has it not preserved the real circumstances of his burial, which it had perhaps an interest in falsifying, but it has no clear story to tell of his trial and condemnation.

For a long time past discussion of the Trial of Jesus has proceeded on the assumption that our texts contain an authentic account of its successive stages. What they do contain, let it once more be repeated, is the liturgical dramatization of the trial together with an apologetic commentary. Mark and Matthew report two trials and two condemnations: first, the Sanhedrim tries Jesus and condemns him;[58] then the procurator Pilate takes up the affair for confirmation, examines the case, finds Jesus innocent, tries vainly to save him and, finally, disclaiming all responsibility, ratifies the sentence of death.[59] According to Luke, the Sanhedrim prepares the accusation, then submits the affair to the Jews, passes the case on to Antipas; Antipas finding no ground for condemnation, Pilate then concedes the execution of the accused to the clamour of the Jews, after another vain attempt to pardon Jesus as in Mark and Matthew. In the fourth Gospel Jesus is first examined about his teaching by the High Priest, Annas (Hanan), who was not High Priest at that time.[60] Annas then sends Jesus to Caiaphas and the Jews carry to Pilate an accusation which they are not able to formulate (John xviii, 28–32); Jesus then explains to Pilate that his Kingdom is not of this world: Pilate pronounces him innocent and has recourse to the expedient of pardon; but the Jews persist in their demand and Pilate makes another attempt to deprive them of their victim, going so far as to present Jesus in kingly state and saying he will not crucify their King; the Jews reply they have no King but Caesar, and Pilate yields them Jesus for crucifixion. Let those who can find their way through this judicial phantasmagoria.

The one stable fact is the crucifixion, a Roman punishment reserved for rebels and inflicted on Jesus on one of the days preceding the Jewish Passover. It follows that the sentence was pronounced by Roman authority after a trial in which that authority acted in its own right,[61] and not as ratifying a sentence passed by the Sanhedrim.[62] It is easy to understand how the agitation fomented by Jesus would be construed as subversive of the sovereignty of the Emperor, even though it would not be regarded as a serious menace to the security of the Empire. Pilate would pronounce the sentence of death without a moment's hesitation; nor is it easy to see, in view of the historic circumstances and the probabilities, how he could have avoided doing so. Jesus was not condemned because he had been misunderstood. He had exposed himself to suspicion by the attitude he had openly adopted and by the tenor of his message. Only by his death did he triumph over his accusers. Had Pilate, *per impossible*, decided to keep him in prison, the Christian religion would not have owed its birth to him.

Was there an accusation by the Sanhedrim? We cannot

answer in the affirmative with certainty nor even with much probability. Our texts, repeatedly cut about and surcharged, are not an historic record of the death of Christ. More than that, they are not even founded on any historic record discoverable by literary analysis. It would seem indeed that the fundamental document of Mark agreed with the fundamental document of John in the date of the Passion, that is to say in fixing the death of Jesus at the day and hour when the Jews sacrificed the paschal lamb. But the date is not historical; it proclaims itself symbolic and liturgical. It reflects the primitive Easter observance of the Christian communities retained to the end of the second century by the communities of Asia from which the others had long been divided by their custom of celebrating Easter on Sunday, as the day of the resurrection.[63] The Christian religion had its birth in history, but only began to write its history with Eusebius of Caesarea, when it was too late. Let us then recognize the simple fact that the oldest tradition now perceptible about the death of Jesus, like that about his ministry, has already become a liturgical legend, the evolution of which in the gospel literature preserves throughout the same ritual character, complicated by apologetic interests.

While the chronology of the Passion was retouched in a way which distinguishes and clearly separates the Christian Passover from the Jewish, as the two were distinguished and separated in object, in like manner the story of the trial has been given a turn for the purpose of throwing back upon the Jews the initiative and the responsibility for the sentence of death. Hence the doubling of the procedure and, in the Synoptics, the improbable nocturnal sitting of the Sanhedrim during the holy night of the Passover. At this sitting Jesus is condemned for professing a Christology which was that of the second generation of Christians.[64] But the evangelists get embarrassed by the saying in which Jesus is made to avow an intention to destroy the temple. Taking the words literally, they would, if authentic, place Jesus on the same level as Theudas and the Egyptian mentioned above. The saying may, indeed, have been brought up in evidence at the trial before Pilate, to the ruin of him who had pronounced it, but has no natural context in any of the Gospel stories. The nocturnal arrest of Jesus by servants of the

High Priest is all of a piece with the trial before the Sanhedrim. But the story in the Fourth Gospel about Judas at the head of a band of soldiers and temple rabble who fall to the ground on their backs before Jesus in the garden is in no better keeping with historical tradition.

The incident of Barabbas is a fiction of which the origin is obscure, but the purpose evident.[66] The best device its authors could find for shifting responsibility for the sentence from Pilate to the Jews was to make the procurator offer pardon to Jesus and the Jews prefer its bestowal on a brigand. In like manner the intervention of Herod is to procure an unexpected witness to the innocence of Jesus in the person of the tetrarch. Originally this fiction must have been a parallel to that of Barabbas, but bolder, in that Herod was substituted for Pilate as condemning Jesus and taking the initiative in his execution, as he is said to have done in the Gospel of Peter.[67] It is obvious that the lofty declarations of Jesus before Annas and before Pilate have interest only for the history of Christology. Generally speaking it may be said that the statements and attitudes attributed to Jesus by the Gospels on this occasion are clearly devoid of meaning except in relation to Christology and to the liturgical drama of the Passion. To the historical reality of the arrest, condemnation and crucifixion they have no relation.[68]

In regard to the place of execution the traditional indication can be retained, although there is ground to suspect that tradition in placing the tomb has taken over an ancient grotto of Adonis, as it took over the cave at Bethlehem.[69] The whole setting of the scene of the crucifixion suggests dramatization, theological and ritual, even to the incident of Simon of Cyrene who saves Jesus from the humiliation of carrying the cross.[70] Other incidents[71] are introduced for the fulfilment of prophecy: the two robbers (Isaiah liii, 12);[72] the wine mixed with spices or gall (Psalm lxix, 19); the division of the garments;[73] the insults of the passers-by (Psalm xxii, 7-9); the words of Jesus on the cross (Psalm xxii, 1).[74] In other cases these incidents have symbolic value: the darkness;[75] the rending of the temple veil;[76] the earthquake; the dead rising from their graves. Symbolism is most pronounced in the fourth Gospel which, careless of probability, brings the mother of Jesus and the beloved disciple to the foot of the cross, shows Jesus issuing instructions till his last breath and discovers the mystic economy of the Christian sacraments in the effect that followed the thrust of the lance.77 The reality of it all was on a level less exalted than this drama, but more poignant and more cruel. Jesus was promptly condemned and promptly executed; he died in torment and, save for his executioners, there can hardly have been any to witness his agony.

Chapter III

BIRTH OF THE BELIEF IN JESUS AS THE CHRIST

WE have seen that the circumstances of Jesus' death are far from being defined in their details, even in those which would be of considerable importance to the historian, such as the date, now impossible to determine not only as to the day, but equally so, and primarily, as to the year. A still deeper obscurity reigns over the question now to come before us. Under what conditions did the disciples of Jesus acquire their faith in the victory over death which they quickly came to believe had been won by the Master they had lost: under what conditions did they acquire the eager desire, the strong will, the firm resolution, to spread this faith abroad as the sole means of admission to the Kingdom of God which Jesus, now glorified as the risen Christ, would soon bring down to earth?

We may assume that Jesus was crucified in one of the years between 26 and 29 and that the event occurred a little before the feast of the Passover. How then shall we explain the reaction of the disciples to a blow which might well have shattered their faith, but which actually ended by exalting it to new heights? In what conditions did they set about the propagation of the faith thus newly enhanced? How came it to pass that the propagation of it was so promptly carried beyond the borders of Palestine? These are questions which legend and myth have answered with much assurance and equal simplicity, but to which probable answers based on certain significant traces, debris of a deposit left by a true tradition and not entirely overlaid by legend and myth, are the best answers the historian is able to offer.

1. COLLAPSE AND RECOVERY OF THE DISCIPLES' FAITH

On the evening of the day when Jesus breathed his last, no man living could have foreseen the incomparable future awaiting the unfortunate prophet whose hopes of a renovated world had received from the course of events a refutation so complete and so cruel. The executioners who took down his body from the cross doubtless flung it, perhaps after giving a finishing blow to the half-dead sufferer, into some trench reserved for those deemed unworthy of honourable burial, in conformity with the Jewish law which forbad the bodies of executed criminals to be exposed after sunset. Perhaps the place of burial was "the field of blood," Aceldama,[1] to which Christian tradition has clumsily tacked on the legend of Judas, making Judas into a substitute for him who was not to be thought of as buried for ever in such a place. However that may be, the legend of the laying-out and burial of the body by Joseph of Arimathea, conceived as the fulfilment of prophecy (probably Isaiah liii, 9) and of one piece with the apologetic fiction of the empty tomb, is also a fiction.

The usual practice was to cast the body of an executed criminal into the common grave, unless the family obtained permission to bury it in their own way. At the time when the tradition was born it was known that in the case of Jesus nobody intervened. But later on, when the need was felt to give the Christ an honourable burial, which the family was thought unable to do, tradition imagined for the part a person of consideration alike for his social standing and character. But the invention of Joseph of Arimathea to play the part of intervener is a perceptible artifice, so, too, is the invention of women, in default of the disciples then in flight, as the most likely witnesses of the burial and afterwards of the resurrection. Even in the Fourth Gospel we get glimpses of an older story in the background which represented the executioners as putting the body into a grave that chanced to be at hand near the place of execution.[2] The stories in Mark about the burial and the tomb found empty are fictions which the other evangelists have elaborated so as to give them a better consistency. The object aimed at was to furnish the resurrection with a proof hitherto unthought of. The part played by women in funeral rites suggested the Galilean women, who, having ministered to Jesus in his native province, might be supposed to have followed him to Jerusalem, been present at his passion on Calvary, then at his burial and finally to have found his tomb unoccupied. Joseph of Arimathea was the male figure indispensable for decency of burial and boldly selected as a member of the Sanhedrim. Pilate, before granting the authority demanded for the removal, is informed by the centurion that Jesus is quite dead—a point intended to meet the theory, brought forward in a controversy between Jews and Christians, that the body had been carried away before death, neither party knowing more than the other how the matter had really gone.

Mark makes Joseph buy a new winding sheet: according to the other evangelists the tomb is also a new one;³ the Synoptics describe it as hewn out of the rock—doubtless in fulfilment of prophecies such as Isaiah xxii, 16, xxxiii, 16. The great stone blocking the entrance is intended to enhance the miracle of the resurrection.⁴ John adds to Joseph a second male figure in the person of Nicodemus, a figure peculiar to this evangelist; to give the burial a higher dignity and to complete the symbolism he has Jesus embalmed, contradicting the Synoptics. All this is supposed to take place on the evening of Friday so as to keep Jesus in the tomb for the whole of the Sabbath and a few hours of the following night; this has the secondary purpose of excluding the theory that the body had been carried off. With the same purpose, but more directly, Matthew has the fantastic fiction of a guard of soldiers stationed at the tomb. But the main object of the whole arrangement is to make the resurrection take place on the day of the Sun, which thus becomes the day of the Risen Lord. Apologetic and symbolism are thus equally satisfied.⁵

The discovery of the empty tomb by women is arranged in Mark with surprising artlessness. Never has fiction more childish found so many to believe it true. The concluding statement "they said nothing to any man, because they were afraid," which suppresses the testimony invented for them, by leaving it with no guarantee but the word of the evangelist, has the simple and very evident object of explaining how the discovery of the empty tomb was unknown to anybody until the moment when here recorded by him. As this plainly will not do, the other evangelists have taken pains to improve upon it, and first of all by omitting Mark's unfortunate explanation. Matthew, Luke and John⁶ all release the tied tongues of the women. But in spite of all they can do to improve on Mark it is clear enough that the whole story came into the tradition long after the accounts of visions and apparitions on which the earliest faith was nourished; and equally clear that the connexion is artificial throughout between the story of the empty tomb, with its secondary purpose of authorizing the Roman custom of celebrating Easter on Sunday, and the oldest recollections, whether concerned with visions of the Risen Christ or with the beginnings of Christian preaching. A like artificiality may be discerned in the way the burial by Joseph of Arimathea is bound together with the discovery of the empty tomb. But, though of earlier date than the story of the empty tomb, that of the burial by Joseph is no better founded on reality.[7]

The dead Jesus was left to his fate. But what became of the memory of him? What became of the faith he inspired in his disciples? It is certain that his arrest and execution put a stop for the time being to the proclamation of his message, and equally certain that the preaching of it by apostles did not begin in Jerusalem till some time had elapsed after the tragic end. How long the interval was cannot be exactly discerned, for the chronology in Acts is artificial and bound up with an imaginary and tendentious account of the facts. The perspective unrolled in the first two chapters of Acts, which are continuous with the end of Luke, omits entirely what may be called the interregnum of the faith or, more strictly, its period of crisis. It reveals nothing of the confusion into which the disciples were plunged by the arrest and death of Jesus, nor of their flight into Galilee nor of the real conditions under which their faith was re-established by the conviction that Jesus, risen from the dead, was about to return in glory as the Christ. Suppressing all this, Luke and Acts keep the disciples in Jerusalem, limiting the period of their anguish almost to the time while the Christ was in his tomb, and making them the recipients of a new and higher initiation, which begins on the very evening of the resurrection, is then continued for forty days by instructions from the Risen Christ in person, and consummated by the descent of the Holy Ghost and the foundation of the Catholic and Apostolic Church on the day of Pentecost. All of which is gnosis[8] and fiction, disguising a highly complex reality, the fiction serving only to baffle our conjectures as to the real course of events.

As Jesus cannot have been allowed to teach in Jerusalem for any length of time, if indeed he was able to teach there at all, it is improbable that he recruited many followers in that city. Thus the whole future of the Gospel came to depend on the believers from Galilee, the most ardent and faithful of whom, or at least those who were his regular followers, had doubtless accompanied him to Jerusalem. The third Gospel and Acts, as we have seen, keep them in Jerusalem, under the express order of Jesus, to the hour of Pentecost when their preaching is supposed to have begun. In this way the ministry of Jesus is prolonged after his death up to the time of his ascension into heaven; some days are then passed in prayer during which a twelfth apostle is chosen by lot to fill the place of Judas until finally, on the day of Pentecost, regarded as the anniversary of the promulgation of the Law, the Spirit descends from heaven upon the apostles and opens its victorious activity in the Church by the public preaching of Peter. All this is artificial and of late origin. The institution of the Twelve is not likely to have preceded the organization of the earliest community, while the idea of the Church as the Kingdom of the Spirit and a kind of substitute for the Reign of God, whose coming it still awaits, is relatively recent and certainly later than the foundation of the first groups of hellenizing Christians. We may add that the object the apostolic preaching is said to have aimed at—that of proving the Gospel by the fulfilment of prophecies (Luke xxiv, 43–47)—is not that with which it really began, but presupposes the evangelical tradition already grown to the form represented by the common source of the Synoptics.9

The sum of the matter comes then to this: the perspective of Luke and Acts, in itself symbolic throughout, is radically false from the historian's point of view. It deliberately contradicts an older and more probable tradition according to which the followers of Jesus returned at once into Galilee. It is true that this tradition, in the form in which it has come down to us, has already taken up a legendary element in the texts which inform us that Jesus, before his death, appointed a rendezvous with his disciples in Galilee, and that the order to repair to Galilee was repeated by the angel whom the women found in the empty tomb. All that is pure fiction, conceived for the purpose of disguising the collapse of the disciples, and their flight into Galilee in presence of the catastrophe which fell on their leader, and, at the same time, of buttressing the myth of the resurrection. Had the disciples really remained in Jerusalem and there found confirmation of their faith, the tradition would not have started by localizing the apparitions of the Risen Christ in Galilee. But the fiction of the rendezvous in Galilee proved somewhat embarrassing; for, if the disciples were actually in Jerusalem on the morning of the resurrection, why were they sent to distant Galilee to get the evidence of it in apparitions of the Christ risen from the dead? Luke (xxiv, 6) gets out of the difficulty by substituting for the rendezvous in Galilee the reminder of a prediction made by Jesus in Galilee to the effect that he would suffer and rise again; after which Luke localizes all the apparitions in Jerusalem. The perspective is still further distorted in the fourth Gospel,[10] where we find it completely upset by the addition of the last chapter, an overload impossible to fit in with the setting of chapter xx. All this elaborate staging, constructed for the purpose of providing an entrance into evangelical history for the resurrection-myth, and of adjusting thereto the origin of Christian preaching, comes to one result—that of obscuring, if not rendering quite undiscoverable, the real sequence of events between the execution of Jesus and the dawn of apostolic activity in Jerusalem. The scripture version of the tradition has thus created, but without perceiving it, an irreducible gap in its own evidence, thanks to which the mythologues of our time have been able to produce their theory that Jesus never existed.

We can well believe that Jerusalem was a dangerous place for the disciples after the arrest of their Master. The circumstances of the arrest seem to have been such that none of them was caught; doubtless the affair had gone too swiftly to give the authorities time to pick them out at the prophet's side. The instant his doom was pronounced they made off in all haste to their own country, overwhelmed by the blow which had struck down their leader and having no thought for the moment but that of their own safety. To call them disillusioned by the terrible outcome would not be strictly accurate; disillusion would imply a fuller participation in the tragedy than had actually been theirs, were it only to the extent of seeing with their own eyes the ignominy of their leader's execution and burial, which they did not see. But they were in utter consternation and amazement and needed a little time and freedom from danger to pull themselves together. The shock was violent; but their faith had a deep root and was bound in course of time to assert itself against the violence of the shock. And this reaction would come the more easily inasmuch as they knew only by rumour of the horror of the crucifixion and the infamy of the burial.

According to the tradition their faith was awakened, or rather created anew, by sensible apparitions of Jesus come back to life. It is easy to see that these apparitions, fitted with time and place and given material form in the traditional stories, are based upon *visions* in which faith was able to find nourishment and confirmation, and for the good reason that faith had created them. Taken as they stand, the Gospel stories do not show us the growth of the disciples' emotions into the belief that Jesus was risen from the dead. It cannot be repeated too often that the object these stories are aimed at is to transform what was essentially an inward conviction, insight or vision of faith, into external fact attested by the witness of the senses, and so make the conviction a part of factual history. To give substance to the apparitions as external facts, pains were taken to mark the day, with all the circumstances of their occurrence co-ordinated to those of the death, and with these again adapted to the day and circumstances of the burial. In this way the inward visions were objectified into outward occurrences, into material phenomena at once verifiable and verified. This done, the facts were arranged in serial order so as to form a posthumous life of Jesus. The faith was thus defended against objectors by fictions which faith produced for its own justification, but which were not the source from which it sprang. Belief in the immortality of Jesus risen from the dead existed long before anybody imagined or professed to know the day on which he rose, or that his tomb had been found empty, or that he had afterwards given the disciples their capital instructions, conversing and eating with them as he had been accustomed to do before his death. There is, however, good reason for adding that the authors of our texts are to be credited with relative sobriety in the shaping of their work. The tradition they have handed down has deliberately avoided the worst extravagances, such as those displayed by the story of the resurrection in the Gospel of Peter.

In those who first believed in Jesus the working of faith was deep and masterful. Their belief that he had risen from the dead was the fruit of that inner process. Needless to say the process was never analysed by those in whom it worked. History knows it directly only by its results. We have seen that the violent death of John the Baptist did not prevent the survival of his sect and that his followers did not believe that he had perished in the grave. But fortunes more resounding than John's were in store for Jesus. Let us not forget how, in the last days, Jesus and his company were convinced that the Great Event was *at hand* and that to-morrow might see them enter, alive and glorified, into the felicity of the Kingdom. There is little risk in assuming that in these solemn hours the disciples believed that Jesus was about to become the Messiah promised to Israel and that Jesus himself, in one way or another, accepted the idea. Nothing is impossible to the ardours of faith. On a faith which knows not how to criticize itself, and would not if it could, disillusion has no hold. Then, too, we must remember that, to minds habituated to the belief in resurrection or in immortality, death is an accident of no significance. Jesus and his followers were in that condition: they believed that the resurrection of the just in the Kingdom of God was *at hand*. One of two things, then, was inevitable, either the faith of the disciples would founder, which it neither could nor would; or it would gather up its forces for a bolder affirmation, continuing to proclaim as before, that the Kingdom was on the point of coming, but with the addition that Jesus, now raised to glory at God's right hand, would personally bring it in.

In fact there was nothing to prevent the disciples from continuing to expect what they had expected all along. He whom they mourned was not, in their eyes, a mere teacher who had converted a few simple souls. They had lost their Master, and their Master was none other than the King of Glory into whom Jesus was now transfigured and about to reveal himself to the world in the swiftly coming Kingdom of God. The Kingdom would descend from the high heavens, whence many besides themselves had begun to look for the coming of the Messiah, whence they had always thought he would come, but now expected him with confidence raised to the highest pitch of certitude. If all the righteous would be raised from the dead at the coming of the Kingdom, was it not fitting that Jesus, its prophet and founder, should be raised in advance of the resurrection of his followers, so soon to come? Since God must needs send him with the Kingdom would He not at once take him up to His right hand instead of leaving him in the abodes of the dead? Even if we suppose that Jesus himself had predicted his death in their presence, he could not have pictured his future otherwise either to himself or to them. God would not forsake him. The Kingdom was coming and Jesus, immortal and glorious, would come with the Kingdom.

What is religious faith? Essentially nothing else than the whole mind, reason, imagination and will, putting forth their combined energy in an effort to break a way through the natural framework of existence and escape from the mechanism which seems so inexorably to govern the destiny of all things. Thanks to the force of that effort, the difficulties aroused in our modern minds by the idea of resurrection, difficulties familiar also to the mind of Greece, had no existence for these Jewish believers, accustomed as they were to thinking in plain terms of survival after death, and incapable of conceiving it otherwise. Many apologists in our time have been wont to argue as though the resurrection of Jesus had to be demonstrated to the disciples by tangible and indisputable proofs such as would satisfy impartial investigators in a scientific age. In reality the first believers accepted the resurrection precisely because they were men for whom proofs of that kind had no interest. The power of their antecedent faith made it impossible for them to think of Jesus as one to whom death had put an end; they believed that he had been raised from death because otherwise they could not think of him as living. The "how" of the raising troubled them not the least: that was God's affair. It was only at a later stage, when the Gospel was being proclaimed among people of non-Jewish mentality that objections began to arise. Then it was that the effort was made to prove the resurrection by arguments convincing to critical minds: then it was that material form was given to the fugitive visions which had been nourishment enough for the earliest faith: then it was that the story of the tomb found empty was invented in order to prove that Jesus had not remained in his grave; then it was that he was represented, in apparitions clearly characterized, as conversing with his followers, eating with them and offering to Thomas the wound in his side and the holes in his nail-pierced hands. This array of proofs, so far-fetched and yet naïve, was not imagined till long after the birth of the belief that they were intended to support. The earliest faith had not sought them; one might almost say it would have found them meaningless. It never paused to speculate on the where and when of it all; cared not to know what had happened to the dead body of Jesus; raised no questions about the re-animation of the corpse and never asked how it had been done. Had the first believers been men with a turn for scientific inquiry into these matters they would have had no belief. Those who first came forward as witnesses that Jesus was risen were indeed persuaded that they had seen him alive in their visions, but they told no stories of his resurrection as a fact materially attested.

Thus did belief in the resurrection of Jesus come to its birth, and the manner of it may be called spontaneous. The faith of the disciples in his Messianic future was too strong to admit of self-contradiction, too strong to give way under the refutation thrown upon it by the ignominy of the Cross. Faith raised Jesus into the glory he expected; faith declared him living for ever because faith itself was determined never to die. Quickened by the ordeal, faith produced out of itself visions that brought balm to its anguish and strength to its affirmations. With the fragments of a shattered hope, and building on the death of Jesus, which might well have killed their faith outright, the disciples founded the religion of Jesus the Christ. Astonishment that faith can work such a miracle will be felt only by those who know not what religious faith really is and have no experience of the realities it can summon into being when once the power of it gets hold on a group of ardent souls. Unconsciously faith procures for herself all the illusions she needs for the conservation of her present possessions and for her advance to further conquests. But, humanly speaking, the work she accomplishes in availing herself of illusion is not always illusory.

Attempts at greater precision, if only by conjecture, in defining the process by which the faith of the disciples took form, are apt to end in fantasy. Renan, working on the theme of the resurrection, made out of it a little romance. J. Weiss, pressing hard on the meaning of Mark xiv, 28 ("after my rising I will go before you into Galilee"), concludes that Jesus had promised to lead his disciples after his resurrection into Galilee where the Kingdom of God would then appear. R. Schütz, improving on this idea, describes the disciples returning to Galilee with as much enthusiasm as if Jesus were really with them; Nazareth is saturated with Hellenism; Jesus himself and his Galilean disciples are full of it; the order of the day is rejection of the Law (*Los von Gesetz*); a Hellenist-Christian community is formed with which a Jewish-Christian community enters into competition. Thus everything is explained. But the whole construction rests upon air.[11]

2. THE CONTRIBUTION OF SIMON PETER

A name which we shall find in the forefront of the apostolic propaganda must here be introduced as that of the man who, in all probability, was the first to give out that Jesus was risen. Simon called Peter is, according to the tradition, one of the earliest disciples recruited by Jesus and the head of the apostolic college established by the Christ as the foundation and guide of the Church. Round him there has grown up an imposing legend to which his admirers are not the only contributors. None the less his share in the birth of the Christian movement was assuredly of the highest importance.

Legend has made great capital out of the surname Peter which Jesus himself is said to have conferred on Simon. But legend would not be legend if it developed consistently. According to Mark (i, 14–20) Jesus, at the very beginning of his ministry, peremptorily summons to his side two brothers, Simon and Andrew, as they were fishing in the sea of Galilee, near to Capernaum, and immediately afterwards, in the same sovereign manner and under the same conditions, two more brothers, James and John, the sons of Zebedee; this done, he expressly reveals his intention to make the four fishers of fish into fishers of men. To endow the event with greater significance Luke enlarges the story with that of the miraculous draught of fishes, which the appendix to John connects with an apparition of the risen

Christ. There can be no doubt that the story of the Miraculous Draught was originally comprised in the myth which related the foundation of the Christian apostolate: in the arrangement presented by John, which is probably the earlier version of the story, the apostolate is a creation of the immortal Christ. Mark as well as Luke has antedated its institution. John, in his account of the Vocation (i, 35–42), gives precedence before Peter to Andrew and to an unnamed but doubtless the "beloved" disciple; notwithstanding this, the change of name, intended to mark Peter as the foundation apostle, is made at his first encounter with Jesus—"thou art Simon son of John; thou shalt be called Cephas"—the evangelist being at pains to explain that Cephas means Peter. From all of which the historical fact to be retained is that the Simon in question was among the first adherents of Jesus, that he lived at Capernaum and was a fisherman by trade.

In reporting the choice of the Twelve, Mark (iii, 13–19) puts Peter at the head of the list and adds, as though the surname had been given on that occasion, "and he gave him the name Peter." But the importance of this mystical title is somewhat diminished by the prominence which the evangelist immediately gives to the resounding surname Boanerges conferred on the sons of Zebedee in the same circumstances. Luke (vi, 12–16) follows Mark. Matthew (x, 1–4) in reproducing the apostolic list says simply "first Simon called Peter" without intimation that the surname was bestowed at the time. He leaves us to suspect that the surname was not chosen by Jesus. And possibly not by the Christ. It may have been a mystical development of tradition, and this is the more likely inasmuch as the incident to which Mark connects it has no historical consistency.

In the incident of the Confession at Caesarea Philippi ("thou art the Christ") Mark brings Peter to the front, the idea being that Simon Peter must be the first to proclaim that Jesus is the Messiah on occasion requiring it. The original intention in recording the confession was, no doubt, to make it a merit on Peter's part. But the evangelist, as though he would destroy this favourable impression, forthwith makes Jesus address him as "Satan" for having tried to prevent the Christ from predicting his death. "Get thee behind, Satan, thou hast no feeling for the things of God." Peter does not understand the necessity and

BIRTH OF THE BELIEF IN JESUS AS THE CHRIST

mystical power of the Passion. Needless to say that if the Messianic confession has been antedated by the evangelist, this lightning reproach is still more so. It is a product of the Pauline tradition in its hostility to the older apostles. Luke omits it—an omission that tells its own tale. Matthew has retained it, but follows up the Messianic confession by intercalating a eulogistic response of Jesus in which the confession itself is presented as a revelation of the Spirit and Simon Peter as the man who would hold the Keys of the Kingdom of Heaven, regulate the discipline of the new community (more or less identified with the Kingdom of Heaven) and would become the foundation of the Church—the only passage in the Gospels when Jesus speaks of his Church, and assuredly not the most authentic.[12]

In all probability this development of the Confession was originally Jewish-Christian and anti-Pauline, for it was not without purpose that Peter is said to have been favoured with a revelation from on high in which flesh and blood had no part. We can almost see in it a discreet response to certain ambitious claims put out by Paul in Galatians (i, 11–12, 15–16). At all events there is enough in it to neutralize what is said, a few lines lower down, about Peter's lack of feeling for things divine. We may add that the bishops of Rome, who apply the eulogy to their order, have abstained up to now from claiming the reproach. John is content to idealize the Messianic confession, turning the profession of faith into a profession of fidelity, and avoiding the need to add either approbation or corrective (vi, 68–69).

The transfiguration of Jesus (Mark ix, 2–8) seems to have been conceived originally as the story of an apparition of the Risen Christ, afterwards antedated to his earthly life and lodged immediately after the Confession, with the insertion of a blunder made by Peter, who is judged to have no understanding of the manifestation, Mark and Luke excusing him as not knowing what he said. We have already seen that the Apocalypse of Peter connects the blunder with the rebuff administered by Jesus, which Mark has placed after the Confession and the first announcement of the passion. It is the same Peter who figures at Gethsemane in an attitude little to his glory, sleeping, spite of his Master's warning, while Jesus is at prayer in the Agony. All the evangelists, moreover, describe, with a kind of complacency,

Peter's triple denial in the High Priest's house during the trial of Jesus, and all are careful to make Jesus predict the denial before the event: in this way the offence is, as it were, palliated and then corrected by the repentance of the culprit. It is to be noted that Mark (xiv, 50) begins by saying that all the disciples took to flight, after which one hardly expects to find Peter following Jesus even "afar off" (54) as the armed band led him away. The same incoherence in Matthew. Luke omits the flight but records the denial. In John xviii, 15–18, 25–27, the denial, cut in two, seems to have begun in the house of Annas and ended in the house of Caiaphas, without Peter changing his place. On this anomaly see *Le quatrième Evangile*, 458–460; 463–464.

Exegetes have made it a merit in Peter that he himself revealed his weakness, which the world would never have known if he had held his tongue. There are better grounds for believing that the incident is in line with the other fictions invented to belittle an apostle who became the grand authority of Jewish Christianity.

Amends of a kind are made to Peter in the stories of the resurrection. The angel names him to the women for a special injunction to return to Galilee, where, it would seem, the coming manifestation of the Risen Christ is to concern him more than the other disciples (Mark xvi, 7). In Matthew there is no mention of Peter.[13] Luke changes the whole character of the angel's discourse to the women, but represents Jesus as predicting to Peter, during the Last Supper, that his faith would be unshakable in the coming torment and that his part would be to strengthen the shaken faith of his brethren. This prediction seems to have been conceived at an independent source which, if not ignorant of the story of the denial, left it aside. As Luke knew of Peter's vision (xxiv, 34) but abstains from giving an account of it, he must have known also that it was this vision that enabled Peter to revive the faith of the other disciples; and of that, too, he says nothing. In the Fourth Gospel the coming martyrdom of Peter is announced twice over (xiii, 36 and xxi, 18–19) and the Risen Christ, after the apparition on the Lake, where Peter is the leading figure, solemnly confides to him the guardianship of his flock.[14] From all of which it is clear enough that the Gospel and the Acts of the Apostles have done their best to reconcile two divergent tendencies: one, Jewish-Christian, in which the rôle of Peter was magnified; the other characteristic of certain Pauline circles, in which it was belittled: the reconciliation being effected, more or less happily, by upholding Peter as the head of the apostolate not only to the Jews, to which the Epistle to the Galatians (ii, 7–9) would limit him, but also to the world at large. The editor of Acts exhibits him in this universal character even at the risk of making him profess the doctrine of salvation by faith alone before the elders of Jerusalem after the affair of Cornelius, which symbolizes the opening of salvation to the whole world, with Peter as the opener of the door. The reality of Peter's contribution was of dimensions much more modest than this, but it led to results no less important.

Putting all these indications together we may conclude that Simon Peter was a fisherman, perhaps a master-fisherman of Capernaum, that he was an early adherent of Jesus, whom he accompanied in his wanderings and then followed to Jerusalem. If Jesus in his lifetime was not hailed by him as the Christ at Caesarea Philippi, Peter certainly entered with his whole being into the Great Expectation, and came to Jerusalem to share in the coming of God and the revelation of Messiah in that city. His faith survived the catastrophe. Returning to Galilee, to the surroundings and atmosphere whence the Great Expectation had its birth, coming back also to himself, his thought leapt to the conviction that Jesus could not have perished in death and that God had taken him to Himself that He might reveal him to the world in the day of his coming, straightway believing that he could see the Master thus, immortal with God. Such is the meaning of the firm tradition that the first vision of Jesus had come, in Galilee, to Simon Peter. No account of that first vision is to be found in any of the documents. Mark gives an advance hint of it (xvi, 7; cf. 1 Cor. xv, 5). Luke is content to mention the bare fact (xxiv, 34). The appendix to John (xxi) attaches it to a miraculous draught of fishes, where it is difficult to recognize, except in the symbolic meaning of the prodigy. But it may be said with confidence that the primacy of Peter's vision is implied by the whole tradition relating to apparitions of the Christ.

It may well be that Peter himself never described his vision, just as Paul never described the vision which converted him, for the triple story of the vision in Acts cannot be considered as coming directly or indirectly from Paul himself. Whatever the content of the vision may have been, its occurrence was a sudden explosion produced by the intense and inward workings of faith; out of which there leaped forth the answer to the riddle of the crucifixion. The answer was this—death has not held Jesus captive: he is alive with God, on the point of returning as the Christ with the Kingdom. What Peter was able to see in his vision escapes us and would seem to us insignificant if we knew it; what matters far more are the deductions that were made from it. The idea of a blessed survival was certainly not strange to Peter. His mind kept turning it over, and turning it over with Jesus as the focus of his thought. Then came the shining day when he thought that Jesus was visibly, and perhaps audibly, before him. His faith filled the vision with all he longed to believe and gave him the assurance that what he saw was a reality. Neither historian nor psychologist need inquire further. Even if we had before us a detailed account from Peter himself of what he believed to be a vision of Jesus clothed with immortality we should hardly know more, nor better understand the certitude of his faith.

We may be equally sure that Peter's faith immediately became contagious among those about him, the former disciples of Jesus, who, like Peter, were already prepared for it, one might even say were being carried along by it. He "strengthened the brethren"; that is, he regathered the now scattered group who had staked their hope on Jesus the Nazorean, and imparted to them his own confidence. Removed to the invisible world, the object of their faith was beyond the reach of the accidents which might otherwise have shaken belief. True, the Kingdom of God was in no haste to come; true, the Messiah delayed his appearance among the clouds. But what of that? One can always wait a little longer. They waited.

What length of time was needed to bring about this rekindling of their faith? We can only conjecture. But since a faith which hesitates or remains dormant for long is unlikely ever to revive, we are entitled to think that the interval was fairly short and the tempo rapid. We may assume that Peter had his vision in the days immediately following his return to Capernaum, days filled with the thought of his lost Master. Arrived at a clear conviction, he at once imparted it to his companions, and immediately these humble folk were back on the summit of the idealism to which Jesus had led them. More than that, they were persuaded that the Master was still alive and beyond a doubt was about to "come" again, but this time with the "Kingdom" and in "the glory of the Father." Back, then, to Jerusalem, appointed scene of the Great Event, there to wait for his coming! Only a naïve and superficial psychology would interpret this bright dawning of the faith as the product of material proof, such as the empty tomb, or of a parcel of gross illusions, and spend effort in searching for these proofs while knowing them to be false when found. Not through preoccupation with such proofs were the disciples possessed with their ardent belief that Jesus was alive with the Father. They believed it ardently because they desired it ardently and felt him near to them in the ardour of their desire, while fugitive and dreamlike visions, perhaps pure dreams, sufficed for the time to nourish and confirm their faith. Then came the discovery of confirmation in the Scriptures. Only at a still later period, when discussion had arisen, did the search begin for more palpable arguments; but it was not until the second, or possibly the third, Christian generation that the need for such arguments became urgent. This was the stage at which the story of the empty tomb was invented, but too reflectively for our liking; and then it was that the fugitive visions of the Risen One, the memory of which had sustained the faith of the first age, were transformed into apparitions and presented as tangible realities.

We have endeavoured to reconstitute the faith of Peter on lines which follow as closely as possible the faith which Jesus had, the faith which had led him to Jerusalem. In this we have been on fairly safe ground. The prompt return of these first believers to the capital of Judaism and their continued residence there have to be explained, and what other explanation can be given? The members of the pious band had no intention to make Jerusalem the centre of an apostolic mission to distant lands; it may be doubted if they had any conception of apostleship in the strict sense of the term. They came back to Jerusalem to await the Christ, and remained there for that purpose as long as they could. The last believers of this type quitted the Holy City when Roman armies were about to invest it, having doubtless come to the conclusion that Jerusalem, deaf to their warning, must be destroyed and trodden down of the Gentiles before the new and eternal Jerusalem, the true City of God, could be established in its place.

It was the march of events that first brought the apostolic office into existence and then gave direction to its work. But before we reconstitute the evolution of that office, at least hypothetically, it behoves us to weigh the importance of the forward step the disciples had now taken in raising their dead master, Jesus, to the dignity of Christ alive in heaven. Without a suspicion on their part of what was involved, their belief was already an essential transformation of the Gospel announced by Jesus; but nothing could be less intended by it than to form the followers of the Christ they were proclaiming into a particular sect either at the centre or the circumference of Judaism. Right up to the moment of Golgotha inclusive, Jesus and his companions seemed in their own eyes to be standing on the ground of a hope common to all the Jews. As to the complicity of the Jewish leaders in the sentence of death pronounced by Pilate, if complicity there were, it could be passed over as a human error and an injustice to God's Ambassador. The preaching of Jesus may well have prepared the way for a split in Judaism, but had not yet created it. But the split was bound to occur if the partisans of the crucified prophet took the line of openly proclaiming that he, their Master, now raised to life at the right hand of God, was the Christ, and that his coming was at hand. Such a profession of faith could not be a matter of indifference to the religious authorities of Judaism nor to the Jewish mass which obeyed them. The vast majority of the Jews would have refused at once to recognize the Christ in the man crucified on Calvary; he would seem to them in nowise qualified for such an honour, and the hope that, after such a prelude, he would presently descend on the clouds of heaven to judge the earth, would be counted a chimerical absurdity. True, a Christ in heaven was less of a political danger than a messianic agitator on earth but, apart from that, many would regard the partisans of the Christ as merely troublesome fanatics, while the majority, from the religious leaders downwards, would proclaim them heretics, and as such drive out of the fold whoever would persevere in such a faith. Thus condemned and driven out these obstinate believers would, without any will of their own, become a sect more or less under suspicion or even shameful and despised. That point reached, the road which led from the new Gospel to a Christian religion separate from Judaism would be opened to traffic.

3. Proceedings of the First Believers

So Peter and his companions, brimful of their hopes, went back to Jerusalem. Whether the Feast of Pentecost had anything to do with their return to the city they had recently quitted in their extremity cannot be stated with confidence. Certainly it was not only as a pilgrimage that the return journey was undertaken. They went back with the intention of remaining in the Holy City and, so to say, of making a home there. Formed plan of active propaganda they clearly had not; perhaps it was not within their means; moreover the indications are that they were somewhat cautious at the beginning in communicating their faith. We may suppose they found lodgings with friendly people, perhaps with those who had entertained them when they came up with Jesus for the Passover. Living on little, they kept up assiduous attendance in the Temple at the hours of prayer. Without any attempt at public preaching in that neighbourhood they found opportunities to impart their hope to a few of the pious Jews whom they met in the outer court. The grand scenes of preaching described in Acts (ii, iii, iv, v) have no more reality than the sittings of the Sanhedrim convened to put a stop to the apostolic propaganda (iv, v). The conviction that had kindled the ardour of John the Baptist and of Jesus in their ministries was at work to the same effect in them, and long continued to work as the driving power of the Christian apostolate. The Kingdom being at hand, nothing could be more urgent than to warn men of goodwill, wherever they could be met, to make ready for the Great Event. And, like John in his day, and Jesus in his, they met from time to time with simple souls who believed their message and joined their little company.

It is also probable that Baptism was administered to their

proselytes in association with their profession of faith in Jesus the Messiah. For the Christian religion made its entry into the world as a baptist movement, and must have so begun since Jesus himself had turned it in that direction. It would be hard to understand why Peter and his companions decided to baptize the newcomers unless the rite had seemed a matter of course as conforming to the practice of Jesus. In like manner it was customary for the new initiates to share in the simple meals of the brethren, when the bread was broken in memory of Jesus and in lively expectation of his coming.[15]

If we are to believe the book of Acts, which at this point seems to reflect an authentic tradition of the earliest community, it was a miraculous incident which first drew the attention of the temple priests to the followers of the new faith. This was the cure of a paralytic operated by Peter in the name of Jesus the Nazorean.[16] After making whatever reserves may be needed in regard to the supernatural character of this adventure, only a paltry rationalism would deny the probability that Peter made the attempt and even succeeded, or that Jesus ever risked it and with like success. We may be sure that the Christian missionaries would not hesitate to practice exorcisms for the cure of maladies by invoking the name of Jesus. Somebody must have made a beginning: it was Peter who made it on the day in question. On seeing the paralytic walk, a crowd formed, a great uproar rose round Peter and the miraculous walker; the temple police naturally came on the scene and the priests, informed of what had happened, asked Peter "by what power or in what name" he had done that. To their utter amazement they learnt that the potent name was "Jesus-Messiah the Nazorean" and that the men before them were followers of the Galilean recently crucified at the Passover. Whereupon "they strictly commanded them not to speak at all nor teach in the name of Jesus." And "when they had further threatened them, they let them go, finding nothing that they might punish them, because of the people; for all men glorified God for that which was done. For the man was over forty years old on whom this miracle was shewed" (Acts iv, 21–22).[17]

Prodigies of this kind increase the vogue of a nascent religion. One was enough to raise the credit of our pious band in the eyes of the common people. If the editor of Acts has not multiplied the number of them—as when he makes the shadow of Peter heal the sick brought in from neighbouring towns to attend his walk (v, 15–16)—we may be sure that public rumour did. As people watched the band at prayer or conversing with adherents under the Porch of Solomon, the most part would keep at a distance knowing that the priests now regarded their doings with no friendly eye. That, however, did not prevent increasing recruitment by private propaganda (v, 52). But the anger of the authorities would certainly be roused by any rash attempt at public preaching; nothing more was needed to bring down the arm of the law.

There is evidence that cohesion was rapidly acquired by this ardent group. Tradition has it that their meals were taken in common and that each contributed of his substance for the support of the fraternity. That this was the practice of these latter day saints may well be true. The Christ might come at any hour, and what else remained to do but help one another in the brief interval before his coming, the better-off ministering to the wants of the poor and bringing provisions to the common table. "There was not among them one person in want," remarks the editor of Acts, no doubt with a touch of exaggeration. It is true, nevertheless, that the Jerusalem community was always poor. But this was not, as many have thought, the result of a communistic system established at the outset; such a system certainly never existed in the rigorous form suggested by a literal reading of Acts. The poverty of the group was due to the fact that the nucleus of Galilean believers found themselves in Jerusalem almost without resources; that the new members seldom came from the richer classes of the city's population; that the generosity of the few better-off was insufficient to overcome the general indigence; that indigence was not unwelcome, since the Kingdom was for the poor; that, in their preoccupation with the coming parousia, they had little concern for the business of this world, fell into poverty and remained poor as the inevitable consequences of neglecting it. It does not follow that any of them died of hunger. The condition in which they were is supportable enough when religious faith is intense and the needs of the body restricted to the bare minimum.[18]

Precarious and rudimentary as the organization was, it was

yet organization. This society of friends had leaders, and we know who they were. They were the Twelve, whom tradition has made into apostles, and even into apostles *par excellence*, though some of them were not very active as missionaries of the new faith. Strictly speaking, the Twelve were the administrators of the first community; this is implied in Acts iv, 34 and v, 11, whatever doubts may be felt about the passage as a whole and the adventure of Ananias and Sapphira. But the Twelve certainly had no existence as a separate group prior to the formation of the community from which they were chosen. The committee of the Twelve—if that were the real number, as it probably was—was created in order to give the little society the elementary organization that would be needful in the early stages of its growth. The number of these committee-men, assuming it to have been twelve, seems to betray a symbolic intention; it corresponded to the arrangement imagined for the Kingdom of God in which the hopes of Israel were to be fulfilled. The saying about the twelve thrones, to be occupied by the twelve apostles judging the twelve tribes bears witness to the ruling idea (Matthew xix, 28). But the function there assigned to the Twelve is one of government rather than of preaching. Quite naturally our twelve overseers would be chosen from among the original disciples of Jesus in Galilee, with Peter as some sort of President. But it cannot be said that "apostle" was their title from the very first.

Certain ecclesiastical writers long since pointed out[19] that the name "apostle" belonged to the emissaries maintained after the fall of Jerusalem by the Jewish patriarchate to carry the letters of the central authority and to collect the subscriptions paid by the Jews of the Dispersion. On the strength of this it was supposed by Harnack and many others that the function must have existed before Jerusalem fell, and that the name passed to the Christian preachers who also organized collections in the communities, as appears from the testimony and example of Paul. But, if these envoys existed before the year 70, which is possible, it is difficult to understand how their name could have been applied to the messengers of the Gospel who were not sent out to visit already established communities, nor were chiefly collectors of offerings; while, as we have just seen, the Twelve, who seem to have been the first to hold the apostolic office, were not sent out anywhere and were neither professional preachers nor collectors of alms in the strict meaning of the term. Moreover the evidence of the New Testament on the matter is confused enough to make the problem difficult of solution, apart from any question that may be raised about a connexion between the Christian apostolate and the office of the Jewish collectors.

A close examination of the Book of Acts shows clearly that it knows of no apostles save the Twelve, understanding their title of apostle as meaning that they were missionaries of the Word and qualified for the work, inasmuch as they had been witnesses of the resurrection and followers of Jesus from the beginning of his ministry to the final hour of his ascent into heaven. Though the definition is systematic, and as such not without interest, we are not entitled to transport it into history. But Paul's Epistles reveal a much wider application of the term which bestowed it on Christian missionaries in general, and first of all on Paul who, while seeming to give express recognition to the apostleship of the Twelve, claimed the title for himself also, a claim which the Twelve and their party appear to have contested. The Epistles mention "the Twelve" only once (1 Cor. xv, 5). Luke affirms that Jesus himself named the disciples "apostles" (vi, 18), and throughout his Gospel, as in Acts, the Twelve and the apostles are the same persons, while Mark, who makes Jesus not only choose them but "send them out" as well, only once calls them "apostles" (vi, 30) and speaks constantly of "the Twelve." Matthew in like manner has "the twelve apostles" once only (x, 2), but often "the twelve disciples" or "the twelve." In the fourth Gospel "the twelve" are mentioned twice, but not called apostles (vi, 67, 71; xx, 24).

From all this confusion the certainty seems to emerge that the Twelve were not called apostles at the time they were formed into a group, nor did they become apostles merely by their membership. They were elected from among "the disciples," that is, the existing body of believers, not to preach, but to order the affairs of the first community, so far as this was necessary. Their importance grew as the Gospel spread. Viewing the matter from a standpoint in the present and giving full confidence to the Pauline literature, we might be tempted to conclude, as

Edouard Meyer has done, that the attribution of the title to the Twelve only was a reaction against the claim of Paul to be an independent apostle and missionary to the Gentiles, appointed thereto directly by the Lord—a reaction which went so far as to exclude Paul from any right to the title. This would explain why, in Mark, instructions intended for all the Christian missionaries are addressed to the Twelve in particular,[20] a transference the more easily made since Peter himself turned missionary after the year 44, together with his colleagues in Jerusalem and the brothers of the Lord (1 Cor. ix, 5).

It may well be that the transference of the title to the Twelve was not made quite so simply, promptly and mechanically. When indications furnished by our sources, themselves of later origin, are interpreted as reflecting the first beginnings of the Christian movement, we run the risk of immensely shortening a development which took a much longer time to mature. It is obvious that no *missionaries* (apostles) can have been appointed until *missions* had begun, and we can see both how and why the Twelve were not instituted as apostles; for not only is it true that not all of them were missionaries at any time, but those who were missionaries, that is employed in the propagation of the Gospel, were not *missioned* (if the word may be used) from any source outside or above; properly speaking, no mission had been given them as apostles in the service, to which they were devoting themselves, of propagating the Gospel. The apostolate in the sense indicated by our texts, does not begin until the business of propaganda has an organized basis, at least of a rudimentary kind; and this, it seems, did not happen until after the dispersion of the group of hellenizing believers which we are about to consider in the next chapter. When that has happened then, to judge by what we shall see taking place at Antioch, the apostles are definitely *missioned*, delegated and approved by a group which supported them. In this way, as we shall see, Paul and Barnabas were at first appointed to the propaganda in Syria and Cilicia.

At that time Paul had not put forth his claim to a unique and special mission conferred upon him by the Christ alone. In the epistles he would seem to have first made this claim when he decided to go his own way. As one no longer *missioned* by a group, he would despise henceforth the attribution of a human commission, and proclaims himself *missioned* by the Christ. Meanwhile the number of missionaries was rapidly increasing both in Palestine and beyond, but always it would seem in the same conditions under which Paul and Barnabas had been *missioned* at Antioch, Paul remaining alone in the singularity of his claim. It must be added, however, that this claim, clothed in the absolute form given it by various passages in the epistles, does not correspond with the reality of the situation and must have been conceived after the event. It belongs to the development of the literature called apostolic. The same is true of the systematic limitation of the apostolic title to the Twelve said by the evangelists to have been *missioned* by Jesus in the course of his ministry. This last point, which reveals the opposition to the Pauline tradition, was reached only when the conditions of Christian propaganda had completely changed and the primitive apostolate had become hardly more than a memory preserved in legend and surrounded by a halo. But let us now turn to the event immediately followed by the apostolic propaganda, of which it seems to have released the spring.

4. Stephen and the Hellenists

From a story in Acts (vi, 1–6) superficially clear, but intentionally confused, the fact emerges that the group of Jerusalem believers, whose recruits, after its first formation, had not been all of one type, was quickly divided into two parties. It soon counted among its members a certain number of hellenizing Jews, that is, Jews whose ordinary language was Greek, and whose ways of thinking, perhaps also their manner of life, were not quite the same as those of the believers speaking Aramaic and called "Hebrews," who had been gained over in the beginning by the disciples from Galilee. The hellenizing believers presently began to hold separate meetings with an organization of their own. What Acts tells us about the choice of the seven deacons is a fiction which too thinly disguises the distinct organization set up by these messianist Jews whom we must suppose to have been better acquainted with the pagan world than were the believers from Palestine. The greater part of them had probably lived more or less in Greek or in hellenized countries and had come to Jerusalem either on temporary business or with the intention of establishing a permanent abode. It must not be forgotten that the regular relations established between Jerusalem and the communities of the Jewish Dispersion, which facilitated travel from place to place, helped greatly at the outset in spreading the Christian propaganda.

Even on the strength of the fiction arranged by the editor of Acts, one is driven to suppose that the community of Jerusalem believers found itself, after no long time, composed of two elements which were not slow to separate more or less completely. In addition to that, since it was the hellenizing group only which, compromised by the action of one of its members, was driven out and dispersed, we may take it as certain that these hellenizers already constituted a distinct body having its own directors, the seven so-called deacons, and that the propagation of the Christian religion beyond Judea was begun by the scattered members of that group. The great outburst of evangelical preaching outside Palestine, to say nothing of that already inside, did not come from the Twelve and their group of Hebraizers. This fact the editor of Acts takes pains to hide, but without succeeding; and here is the point of departure to which he co-ordinates many other fictions in the course of the book. (Later on a bolder step was taken by representing the twelve apostles as having left Jerusalem after dividing between them the world to be converted.) In order to preserve the union of the Hebrew and Hellenizing groups in a single community, as his perspective required, the editor makes out that the Twelve constituted a kind of priestly body which administered the spiritual affairs of the community, and changes the seven heads of the hellenizing party to the lower status of deacons or helpers to the Twelve, appointed for the service of tables and the distribution of alms, in other words, for the administration of the temporalities—a type of organization which was in fact adopted in the Christian community, but only at a later stage.

The list of the seven deacons is neither better nor worse guaranteed than that of the twelve apostles. But the Seven were not helpers subordinate to the Twelve. They were formed as the governing body of the hellenizing group as soon as it acquired a separate existence. The existence of the group is certain. How exactly it was formed escapes us. Some difference of opinion analogous to that mentioned in Acts may have given occasion for the split; but the cause was other and profound. And we cannot invert the chronological relation of the two groups, as if faith in Jesus had begun with the hellenizing party. All the names on the list of deacons are Greek. Only one of the seven is a pagan by origin, but circumcised; he comes from Antioch; the others are Jews by birth but not "Hebrews" by language. It should be noted that the number seven, like the number twelve, has a symbolic meaning, being the cypher for the gentile or universal world, as twelve is for Israel. For that reason a strict interpretation of the names on the list would be out of place.

One individual alone stands out before us detached from the hellenistic group as having taken the initiative in the public propagation of the Gospel message in Jerusalem, and with results of considerable importance. Stephen, whom Acts describes as "full of grace and power"—animated, that is, by a zeal outstandingly effective in preaching—seems to have been the first to carry the Gospel into the arena of public discussion, not in the Temple, but in certain synagogues of the Greek-speaking Jews in Jerusalem. According to the statement in Acts, which seems to have been tampered with, "there arose certain of the synagogue which is called the synagogue of the Libertines, and Cyrenians and Alexandrians, and of them of Cilicia and Asia, who disputed with Stephen, and they were not able to resist the wisdom and the Spirit by which he spake" (vi, 9). The text insists on the opposition to Stephen's discourse, but tells us nothing of what the preacher said to provoke it. The source-document on which the editor was working no doubt indicated this in place of the miracles attributed to Stephen in v, 8. But having just placed Stephen among the *deacons*, he would naturally be unwilling to exhibit him too plainly in the preaching function of an *apostle*. The reference to synagogues is probably to several where Stephen found opportunity for delivering his message to the congregations gathered there. It is in keeping with the sense of the above passage to assume that the disputes in question were not confined to private conversations, and that Stephen took his turn to address the congregations, as any private person, even one not recognized to be a qualified preacher, could do. That his teaching raised objections should cause no surprise; and it is not impossible that the ardour of his convictions reduced his adversaries to silence. The certain fact is that instant animosity was aroused against Stephen by these actions.

Let us recall at this point how the cautious propaganda of the Galilean disciples came into being and was allowed to continue, even for several years after the affair of Stephen, without serious interference from the authorities. If Stephen's efforts to win converts were quickly followed by forcible official reaction the reason must be sought in its publicity, and, very probably, in the character of his teaching. This, at certain points, differed from the teaching of the original disciples. They announced that Jesus was risen from the dead as the Christ and about to return with the reign of God; but they did not speculate on the economy of the coming kingdom, nor on the changes it might involve in matters concerning the established cult of Judaism. Stephen, it seems, was less reserved. The witnesses who appeared against him at his trial before the Sanhedrim are reported to have said: "This man is for ever speaking against the holy place and the Law: for we have heard him say that this Jesus the Nazorean will destroy this place and change the customs which Moses delivered to us."[21] Although the deponents are described as "false witnesses" the charge is not said to have been denied, but was rather confirmed by Stephen who, in an ecstatic outburst and with transfigured countenance, answered the question of the high priest by simply exclaiming: "I see the heavens opened and the Son of Man standing at the right hand of God." Without taking these indications for an official report of a judicial inquiry, which they are not, we are entitled to infer from them that this hellenizing Jew went to the length of saying that the temple, the bloody sacrifices, the legal observances and whatever was specifically Jewish in the established cult would pass away at the coming of the Christ. Such, we are given to suppose, was Stephen's comment on the saying attributed to Jesus concerning the temple which he would destroy and rebuild.[22]

As already pointed out, closely analogous doctrines or opinions are to be met with in certain of the baptist sects and to some extent among the Essenes. Their converts from paganism were dispensed from an array of prescriptions which, said they, were

BIRTH OF THE BELIEF IN JESUS AS THE CHRIST

due to be abrogated under the coming Reign of God and the imposition of which was found a serious obstacle to the propagation of the faith. In the sequel, the destruction of the Temple in the year 70 was soon to give these practices and doctrines a measure of justification. Was it not clear that God, by that event, had condemned the outward and material economy of the Jewish cult?

In that lies the starting point for explaining the conduct of the missionaries who went out from Antioch, the work of Paul, and even the foundation of hellenistic Christianity. The long and curious indictment of the Jews attributed to Stephen (vii, 2–33) is conceived in the same anti-Jewish spirit. It is a digression, serving the dominant purpose of the editor of Acts, which is to prove that notwithstanding the recriminations and fury of those who are Jews by race and name, it is not these always hardened and rebellious Jews but the Christians who represent the religion which claims the authority of Abraham, Moses and the prophets. The author had an ampler experience than Stephen could have had towards the year 30 of our era.

The exact date of his martyrdom, just indicated approximately, is uncertain. Unless we abandon all the indications of time in Acts and Galatians, we are led to place the martyrdom of the sons of Zebedee in the year 44; a little earlier than that, the meeting in Jerusalem at which the question of legal observances was discussed; and the conversion of Paul about the year 30. With these data as our baseline we must place the crucifixion of Jesus in 26 or 27 and the martyrdom of Stephen in 28 or 29. This leaves the sequence of events somewhat compressed, for it is obvious that the Christian propaganda had reached Damascus and made some progress there before the conversion of Paul. It is true that the faith was rapidly contagious; nevertheless a minimum of time was needed for its formation and diffusion.

Here then is Stephen, the first martyr of the Christ and in some sense his first apostle, condemned to death, apparently after regular trial in the courts for blasphemy against the Law. He died by stoning in pursuance of the sentence pronounced by a Jewish tribunal. Until quite recent years it has been taken for granted that the Sanhedrim had no power to pronounce a capital sentence and least of all to carry it into execution without ratification by the Roman procurator, and, since there is no mention of Pontius Pilate or of his successor, it is supposed that Stephen's execution was an affair of mob-law and carried out in a riot, as the conclusion of the story gives us to understand. To this it is often added that the execution probably took place in 36 during the interval between the departure of Pilate and the arrival of his successor, as if, on anything of the kind happening, there was no representative of Roman authority in the city to give ratification. It seems certain on the contrary that the Sanhedrim retained complete jurisdiction in all religious matters and that its competence was limited on the political side only. The false perspective in which the Evangelists have set the trial of Jesus has contributed more than anything else to lead criticism astray at this point. It was only after the destruction of Jerusalem that the religious authorities of Judaism were deprived of the right to pass sentence of death, by losing the National Council which possessed the right.

Repression of the new movement was not limited to the execution of Stephen. Menaced and hunted down, the whole group to which he belonged scattered and lost no time in clearing out of Jerusalem. Whatever the editor of Acts, who contradicts himself, may say, it was not the entire community, Hebrew and Greek believers alike "except the apostles" (viii, 1), that was persecuted and driven into flight. (If they were bent on exterminating the Hebrew group why did they spare its chiefs?) It was the hellenistic group only. The Hebrew group was not disturbed, no doubt because it was less disturbing.

The story in Acts of repressive proceedings against *both* groups hangs together with the equally fictitious particulars about Saul-Paul taking part in the affair. The elements of the latter fiction are adjusted to the course of the story. By way of introducing him it opens by saying that the witnesses, who had to cast the first stones, "laid down their garments at the feet of a youth named Saul" who was "consenting to the execution."[23] A few lines further on the youth finds himself promoted, somewhat rapidly in view of his age, to the office of Grand Persecutor of Christianity in Jerusalem: it would seem, moreover, that he went about it by himself, proceeding on his own authority to search all the houses of the city in his hunt for Christians, and to take men and women to prison; while next day a commission from the High Priest charges him to continue the business at Damascus; though it is not easy to see how the Gospel could have so soon found its way into that city.

Later we shall discuss the legend of Paul's conversion. The preliminaries found in the story of Stephen's martyrdom are totally unworthy of credence. The "youth," even if we suppose him to have aged ten years as he went home after the execution of Stephen, could not have organized and carried on all alone the persecution of the Christians here ascribed to him. According to Galatians (i, 22–24) the Christian communities in Judea, prior to the Jerusalem conference, knew Paul only by reputation. Paul was not in Jerusalem when Stephen was executed. As general persecutor of the nascent Christian religion he is a creation of legend. The motive of the editor of Acts in calling him "a youth" is to present him as having been brought up at Jerusalem and a pupil of the famous Gamaliel (xxii, 3; v, 34). The editor has also made Gamaliel his victim by putting a discourse in his mouth, which the good doctor never made, on the occasion of a trial of the Twelve, which never took place. What we are told of the relations of Paul with Gamaliel has every likelihood of being no less fictitious than the rest.

From the time of the persecution onwards we find the entire community of Judaizing believers established in Jerusalem, just as it was before. There Peter and his companions remained, without any one of them being molested, till towards the end of the reign of Agrippa I. But never again was a Hellenizing group, such as Stephen's had been, formed in that city. Obviously Jerusalem was unpromising ground for the open propaganda of their Messiah—Jesus, especially if it was thought to offer any kind of threat to Jewish nationalism and the superstitious regard for the Law. But those who had driven the group of Stephen into flight turned out to have assured, by that very act, the future of the Christian religion.

Chapter IV

THE BIRTH OF
APOSTOLIC PROPAGANDA

AN ardent, regulated and almost methodical propaganda was now to be launched which, in less than thirty years, would carry the Christian religion to all the countries of the Eastern Mediterranean and as far as Rome, but under conditions which only permit us to catch glimpses of the chief stages in a mighty movement and to follow a few of its protagonists. As far as we can judge, this was not achieved by the proper and direct initiative of the Aramaic-speaking group of believers gathered in Jerusalem. The propulsive force that carried the new religion into the Mediterranean world was the force of the blow that had struck Stephen. Up to that moment the effort to make converts, in the conditions we have just studied, had been confined to Jerusalem. It is not certain, as some would have it, that small groups of believers existed in Galilee at that time, to which we might attribute the spread of the Gospel to Damascus. The invective against the Galilean towns (Matthew xi, 20–24; Luke x, 12–15) and the symbolic check to the preaching of Jesus at Nazareth (Mark vi, 1–6; Matthew xiii, 53–58; Luke iv, 15–30) would rather invite the conclusion that there were no groups of believers in Galilee in apostolic times. It may well be that the Jewish-Christian propaganda was roused into activity only by the Hellenistic-Christian, and did not become effective in North Palestine, Transjordania and Syria until after the migration thitherward of the Jerusalem community at the beginning of the Jewish war.

If the Christian religion which spoke in Aramaic was not without a future, if it was even destined to exert indirectly a profound influence on Christianity as a universal religion, that religion could not exist, and had in fact no existence, so long as the pagan world was unreached by its message. And the pagan world was not even touched so long as propagandist activity was confined to Jewish circles in Jerusalem, or even in Palestine. By the action of the Sanhedrim, the most active among the new believers, the most open minded, or if it be preferred, the least imprisoned within Judaism were driven abroad into various provinces of the Roman Empire where, in a very short time, they did a work remarkable in its results and astonishing in its success.

On evidence derived from the Epistles preserved under his name, the foundation of hellenistic Christianity, that is of the Christian Church, of the historic Christian religion, is still generally attributed to Paul. But, if his rôle was of such capital importance, how comes it that ancient Christian documents, the *Didache* and the so-called Epistle of Barnabas, seem to ignore him, and that the Apocalypse of John, though more judaizing in style than in spirit, makes his school, if not his memory, the object of attack? It is the Paul of the Epistles who is aimed at in the letters to the Asiatic Churches in Revelation ii, 2, 9, 14–15, 20–24; iii, 9. Notwithstanding that he was a contributor to founding the churches of Asia, they did not claim him, in the second century, as their founder, while the silence of the apologist Justin in regard to him is outstandingly significant. In the course of the second century, circumstances furnished him with an important collection of epistles, now gathered into the New Testament, and these, together with the combinations worked up in Acts, which give a considerable place to his missions, have made it possible to construct a scheme of Christian Origins partly false and too simple in relation to the complicated reality. Paul, for us, is the best known of the first Christian missionaries to the pagan world; but he was not the one and only missionary, nor even quite the first; he was simply the most active. The influence which his epistles came, ultimately, to acquire ought not to be credited entirely to his apostolic career; for the problem which now presents itself is just that of finding out whether the elaborate gnosis developed in the Epistles really belonged to their presumed author, to Paul. Even if that problem be set aside, it seems beyond doubt that the diffusion of the Christian religion in the pagan world had begun before Paul became a partner in the work, and that, notwithstanding his large contribution, it went on its course to a great extent independently of him.[1]

In order that our departure may be taken from a point of utmost certainty, let us fix attention on the following incomplete but trustworthy account in the Book of Acts (xi, 19–21): "They that were scattered abroad by the persecution in the time of

Stephen travelled as far as Phoenicia"—that is, to the hellenized towns of the Phoenician coast, including Caesarea, which, though the residence of the procurator of Judea, was not a Jewish town—"and to Cyprus and to Antioch, speaking the word to none save only to Jews. But there were some of them, men of Cyprus and Cyrene who, when they were come to Antioch, spake to the Greeks also, preaching the Lord Jesus. And the hand of the Lord was with them and a great number"—of uncircumcised as well as Jews—"believed and turned unto the Lord. And it was at Antioch that the disciples"—the believers in Jesus—"were first called Christians." In the pagan world the name of the sect is the name here indicated by Acts, and the foundation of the first hellenist-Christian community was the occasion of its adoption. In the Jewish, aramaic-speaking world, on the other hand, the adherents of the new faith, according to the same book of Acts, were called Nazoreans, following the title given to Jesus himself. "For we have found this man (Paul) a pestilent fellow ... and a ringleader of the sect of the Nazoreans" (xxiv, 5).[2]

The text previously cited (xi, 19–21) comes from the same source as the account of the hellenistic group at Jerusalem and of the martyrdom of Stephen, to which it forms the natural sequel, but is here converted into a brief introduction to what the author is intent on telling about the foundation of the first community to be recruited, at least in part, from among the uncircumcised pagans. Phoenicia and Cyprus are quickly passed over, but the author's meaning is, clearly, that in these two countries, as in the first place at Antioch, the word was carried to the Jews, but "to Jews only." If the source has nothing to say about the results of this preaching, it is because its author was in haste to get on to the mission at Antioch and the exploits of Paul. The editor of Acts, for his part, presupposes, in what he has to tell of Phoenicia, the existence there of groups of Christian recruits from the Jewish population, and contents himself with a few legends about the ministry of Philip, one of the Seven, in Samaria, before his settlement at Caesarea. It is probable that some of the fugitives found their way also to Alexandria, whence Apollos was later to come, but Acts knew nothing of them, or preferred to say nothing. Believers in Jesus also came early to Rome, but we are left equally in the dark as to the conditions. Let us not overlook the fact that the missionaries who "spoke to the Greeks" were strangers to the country, this one from Cyprus, the other from Cyrene. (We shall learn their names a little later.) From this it would seem that the hellenistic believers who fled from Jerusalem after the death of Stephen did not seek refuge in the countries of their birth, and were not merely bent on saving their lives, but concerned also to carry on elsewhere a propaganda to which Jerusalem gave no support. Beyond that we cannot say what considerations and what circumstances suggested to these propagandists the choice of their destination. But it seems clear that the desire to proclaim their message held priority over personal interest. Without this ardour of apostleship it is indeed impossible to explain the prompt diffusion of the sect. To make known to the Jews of the Dispersion that Jesus was about to return as the Christ was to them a mission of extreme urgency. Nevertheless, however urgent they deemed their message to be, they believed they had time to deliver it, and that belief brought some enlargement of perspective to the hope which had caused the Galilean disciples to return to Jerusalem.

What these passages tell us about the foundation of the Antioch community contradicts the traditional legend presented elsewhere in Acts, which gives Peter the initiative in the conversion of the Gentiles; and it contradicts the legend, also traditional, but scientifically exaggerated in recent times, which makes out that Paul was the first apostle, and the universal apostle, of the Gentile world and indeed the veritable founder of the hellenistic-Christian Church.

According to the first legend, Peter, during the interval between the death of Stephen and the foundation of the mixed community at Antioch, and after the propagators of the Gospel had made some converts in Samaria and the coast towns of Phoenicia, undertook a sort of pastoral visit to the new groups there recruited by evangelists who were not apostles. In Samaria, accompanied by John, who remains a dumb figure, we find him bestowing the Holy Spirit on Philip's converts, which Philip had been unable to bestow upon them, and confounding one of the converts, the famous magician, Simon, who had offered for cash down to buy the power to confer the Spirit, so that he, Simon, might bestow the gift himself.[3] After which, we are given to understand that Peter, making a similar tour of the coast towns, where he at once performed some miracles,4 travelling this time alone, was guided to carry the Gospel to the centurion, Cornelius, a man of substance friendly to the Jews—the guidance being furnished by a paraphernalia of revelations constructed on the same model as those by which the Book of Acts prepared the baptism of Saul-Paul by Ananias, and also to be met with in the mysteries of Isis.5 The interview of Peter and Cornelius, their reciprocal explanations and the subsequent discourse of Peter are somewhat lacking in interest. The object of the discourse is to exhibit Peter as the very first to proclaim before a pagan audience the principle of universal salvation by faith in the Christ, the principle which this legend of conversion is designed throughout to illustrate and figuratively to set forth.

The third act of the pious drama is the baptism of Cornelius and his household under a kind of mandate from the Holy Spirit, who descends on the catechumens before the sacrament is administered. This legend, somewhat abbreviated, is repeated in the account of his conduct which Peter is represented as rendering to the community at Jerusalem. As the conversion of Cornelius symbolizes the conversion of the Gentiles, so the misgivings of the Jerusalem community symbolize the opposition of the Judaizing party, while Peter's answer to their complaint is designed to show that the little Pentecost of Caesarea puts the pagans on the same footing as the believers of Israel baptized in the Spirit at the great Pentecost in Jerusalem. Thus the question of the salvation of the uncircumcised, by faith alone and baptism, is answered, always symbolically, before it arose in reality. But there is matter for a smile when, after hearing Peter, under reprimand for eating with Gentiles, prove so solidly that he has done well, one goes on to read in the Epistle to the Galatians (ii, 11–14) how Paul fell foul of this same Peter for refusing to sit at the same table with the uncircumcised.

Simon Peter may well have been the leading spirit in the genesis of the faith, but his rôle in reality was always little more than that of an apostle to the circumcision. No doubt it was impossible for him to be anything else, although, when the time for it came, he did not oppose the admission of pagans into the community by baptism without circumcision—so much may be retained from Galatians ii, 9, 12. There is no evidence of his going far away from Jerusalem before the year 44. Peter, James and John, the sons of Zebedee, and "James, the brother of the Lord"[6] were the chief figures of the Jewish-Christian community in Jerusalem during the first twelve or fifteen years of its existence. The legend of Cornelius is the creation of a time considerably later when an effort was made to give Peter prominence in relation to Paul, to exhibit him as representing the authentic and primitive apostolic tradition, the founder and first appointed leader of the universal church embracing both Jewish and pagan elements.[7]

The legend of Paul has undergone a parallel amplification to that of Peter, but on two different lines: first, by his own statements or by the tradition of his Epistles designed to make him the possessor of the true Gospel and of a strictly personal mission for the conversion of the Gentile world; and then by the common tradition for the purpose of subordinating his rôle and activity to the work of the Twelve, and especially of Peter regarded as the chief instrument of the apostolate instituted by Jesus.

Relying on the Epistles and disregarding their apologetic and tendentious character, even in much that concerns the person of Paul, though this perhaps is secondary, criticism is apt to conclude that Paul from his conversion onwards had full consciousness of an exceptional calling as apostle to the pagans, and that he set to work, resolutely and alone, to conquer the world, drawing in his wake the leaders of Judaic Christianity, whether willing or not. And this, indeed, is how things happened if we take the indications of the Galatian Epistle at their face value. There we encounter an apostle who holds his commission from God only, who has a gospel peculiar to himself given him by immediate revelation, and has already begun the conquest of the whole Gentile world. No small claim! (Galatians i, 11–12, 15–17, 21–24; ii, 7–8).

But things did not really happen in that way, and could not have so happened. Paul did not arrive in Syria and Antioch in order to preside at the foundation of the first community of hellenizing Christians and to place himself at the head of missionaries who had come there before him, as Galatians ii, 1–10 might very naturally lead us to infer. Not only does the quite trustworthy account in Acts xi, 20-21 make it clear that the first conversions of the non-circumcised were made by believers from Cyprus and Cyrene, while a supplement, otherwise needing caution (xi, 22-26), sends Barnabas to seek out Paul at Tarsus[8] not till after their conversion had taken place—not only this, but another notice entirely consistent (xiii, 1-3) which enumerates the prophets and teachers in Antioch at the moment when it was determined to carry the missions abroad, heads the list with the name of Barnabas.[9] Him we may identify without hesitation as the Cypriote who had a preponderant part in the evangelization of Antioch; while the fifth and last name on the list is Saul-Paul, whom nobody would suspect of choosing the last place for himself, but who filled it quite naturally after the others who belonged to the group of founders. Barnabas, moreover, takes precedence of Paul in the mission entrusted to them jointly by the community (xiii, 3).

Interpret how we may the over-statements in the Epistle to the Galatians,[10] it is certain that Saul-Paul did not make his entry on the Christian stage as the absolute innovator, the autonomous and independent missionary exhibited by this Epistle. The believers in Damascus to whom Paul joined himself were zealous propagandists imbued with the spirit of Stephen, and there is nothing whatever to suggest that he was out of his element among them. Equally, he was quite unaware at that time of possessing a peculiar Gospel or a vocation on a different level from that of all the other Christian missionaries. That idea he certainly did not bring with him to Antioch, where he found a community which others had built up and which recruited non-Jews without imposing circumcision. For long years[11] he remained there as the helper of Barnabas rather than his chief. When the Jerusalem community took offence at what was going on at Antioch, it was Barnabas and Paul, with Barnabas in front, who went to plead the cause of liberty before the elders. Paul's only initiation into the apostolate to the Gentiles was the initiation he received at Antioch by the side of Barnabas. That apostolate was established before Paul appeared on the scene and continued to be exercised by others at the same time as by him. Paul was simply one of the greatest missionaries of the earliest period. In the conventional histories of primitive

Christianity he has eclipsed the true founders of the hellenizing movement, as well as eclipsing Barnabas, who has almost been turned into a modest companion of his missionary labours, like Timothy and Titus at a later stage. But he owes this eminence far more to the exploitation of his memory by one part of the Christian tradition, and to the writings that were assigned to his name, than to any first-hand evidence of his apostolic activity and its successes.

The legend in Acts on the other hand, while magnifying him in its own way, has unduly subordinated him, along with Barnabas, to the founders of the first Christian community. Although edited Acts tell the story of his conversion in detail[12] and has it twice told by Paul himself in speeches put in his mouth, all that we can retain from this as certain is that Paul came from Tarsus in Galicia and that suddenly, in consequence of a vision, he was converted at Damascus to faith in the Christ whom he had previously opposed. Paul's native country is not mentioned in the Epistles, but Tarsus is no invention of the editor of Acts; it is even the most certain piece of information he has left us concerning the antecedents of the great apostle. We may believe in like manner that the apostle's Semitic name was Saul and that the name Paul, always used in the Epistles, is a surname; as it is probable that Paul was a Roman citizen the surname may be a *cognomen*. Nothing is known of his family. Perhaps the trade of tentmaker, which we shall find him following at Corinth in the house of Aquila, was learnt from his father. There were flourishing schools at Tarsus, but there is nothing to prove that Paul frequented them in his youth. By education he was a Pharisee, but the editor of Acts is responsible for making him a disciple of Gamaliel, which he never was; his culture was Jewish; he read the Scriptures in the Septuagint and may have known Aramaic as the traditional speech of his family as well as from his later travels. Needless to say our assessment of the influences to be recognized as having moulded his thought depends on the credit we attach to the Epistles. The gnostic ways of salvation to be met with in the great Epistles and in Colossians and Philippians—not to speak of Ephesians—suggest many and varied contacts with the mystical thought of the period. Retaining only what is most probable, it seems that Paul was of Jewish culture and a Jew of strict observance, but, with experience of life in a pagan environment, rendered capable by that experience of embracing without repugnance the programme of evangelization adopted by the missionaries of Antioch.

The Book of Acts gives us the romance, not the psychology, of his conversion. There is every reason to believe that Paul himself never examined the process that led up to it and never analysed its motives; nor has he described the vision which seems to have suddenly changed the orientation of his being.[13] The event took place at Damascus, but we have no knowledge of what brought him to that city, nor do we know whether he had previously been a zealous opponent of Christian groups elsewhere. He was never the general commissioner in charge of an official persecution. He must have been a Messianist, bewildered at first but afterwards gained over by what the followers of Jesus had to tell of their Christ. The inner process which issued in his conversion is not to be discerned either in the Epistles or in Acts. The Epistles say nothing about it, although commentators have pretended, and often still pretend, to discover it there. The editor of Acts has run the story of his conversion into the conventional mould of miracle and interpreted it according to the notion he is bent on giving of the providential mission to be assigned to Paul.[14] That he stirred up the Jews in Damascus by preaching immediately after his conversion, the Christ he had come to oppose is contradicted by Galatians (cf. Acts ix, 20–22; Galatians i, 15–17);[15] which equally contradicts the story of his setting out at once to Jerusalem to join the old disciples and of his preaching there in the synagogues only to provoke a plot from which he escapes again by flight.[16] As to the story of Barnabas, departing under orders from the apostolic community, to meet Paul at Tarsus and to bring him to Antioch, this is only another effort to exhibit Paul as an auxiliary of considerable importance recruited and patronized by the Jerusalem apostles. All these fictions must be set aside if the movement of primitive evangelization is to recover its true physiognomy.

1. FIRST IMPACTS OF THE GOSPEL ON THE PAGAN WORLD

The author of Acts in its original form seems to have had before him fairly precise information concerning the Jerusalem community, the foundation of the Antioch community and the missions of Paul. The editor of our canonical book has not enlarged the framework of the story; he has merely modified the contents, drowning them in his legends about Peter and Paul, and arranging them to suit the needs of his apologetic or to edify the Church. But missionary activity and the expansion of the Christian religion vastly exceeded in reality the scope assigned to it in Acts. In this respect the wholly fictitious scene of Pentecost, in its catalogue of the Mediterranean peoples, may give us a truer idea of the work accomplished during the first forty years of evangelization than can be gathered from the subsequent narratives in the book.

It is true that Acts gives summary information that the Phoenician towns and Cyprus were evangelized before Antioch (xi, 19), but tells us nothing whatever of how the preaching of the Christ came to Damascus so early in the day. The most probable conjecture is that some of Stephen's companions were able to reach that city; there is, however, the possibility that, when the Hebrew group also finally embarked on propaganda outside Jerusalem, Jewish Christianity may at once have thrown outcasts in Palestine and found its way into the neighbouring countries of Transjordania and Syria. Both Egypt and "the regions of Libya round about Cyrene" are mentioned in the story of Pentecost (ii, 10). Ought we not also to recall that a Cyrenian is said to have carried the cross of Jesus to Golgotha? It is at least significant that Jews of Cyrene figure at the side of Barnabas among the founders and teachers of the Antioch community—Lucius of Cyrene and probably "Simeon called the Black" (xiii, 1).

It is a reasonable conjecture that some believer in Cyrene evangelized his own country. But the probability is very high that the faith of Jesus, having once left Jerusalem and crossed the frontiers of Palestine, quickly penetrated Egypt and found its way to Alexandria. Christian propaganda does not seem to be aimed at in express terms in a letter addressed by Claudius to the Alexandrians shortly after his accession, although many have thought the letter condemns it;[17] but it is virtually impossible that Christian propaganda was not active at that time, or soon afterwards, in Alexandrian Jewry, and the more so in view of the contact of Stephen and his group with Jews of Alexandria.[18]

It is not until near the end of the second century, at the time of the pascal controversy, that the Christian community of Alexandria makes its appearance in history. But by then it had become of considerable importance and fully formed; it had a great teacher, Clement, a profound and learned mystic; it had behind it a long and, for us, extremely obscure past, of which our chief knowledge is that it supplied the Christianity of that time with many notable heretics. Although its origin must date back to the dawn of the Christian religion, we are completely ignorant of how, when or by whom the Gospel was carried into Egypt,[19] and of the conditions under which it lived and spread in that country. We have already indicated all that is known about *the Gospel of the Egyptians*. In the highly syncretist atmosphere of Alexandria Christianity seems to have taken a strong turn towards gnosticism. It is a misfortune, doubtless attributable to that atmosphere, that the writings of the Alexandrian gnostics of the second century have not come down to us, any more than *the Gospel of the Egyptians*. The consequence is that Alexandrian Christianity eludes the grasp of the historian until the time when it was caught up in the general current of the catholic movement, into which the gnostic crisis was later canalized and compressed.

Similar observations apply to the Roman community. When Paul wrote to it about the year 56 this community was not a thing of yesterday; yet a quarter of a century earlier the Gospel propaganda had hardly begun and must therefore have been carried to Rome in the earliest period of its activity. An edict of Claudius against the Jews, issued under conditions obscure to the historian, may have been occasioned by agitation provoked in Roman Jewry by the preachers of the Christ. It seems that the edict came out in the early years of his reign and was caused by the Christian propaganda; this it chiefly aimed at repressing, but without restricting the liberty of the Jewish cult.[20] Perhaps we may consider as probable the hypothesis that the Christian propaganda was not of the inoffensive political character it affects in the writings of the New Testament, and that it led to serious messianic agitation in the great Jewries, like that of Rome and especially that of Alexandria.

Who were the first and real founders of the Roman community? Certainly no important person from the first community in Jerusalem; certainly not Peter; otherwise Paul in his letter to the Romans would have had to pay regard to such notables and would not have been able to claim the field as freely open to him. They must have been Christian Jews from Palestine, hellenistic rather than Hebrew, who had not come to Rome for the sole purpose of propaganda, but had none the less exercised it there both among the Roman Jews and among the pagan frequenters of their synagogues; and with rapid success, since the community —or, more exactly, the Christian groups in Rome—had attained considerable importance, though as yet unable to claim that importance under any apostolic name.

The time is long past when critics ought to have recognized, or at least more deeply understood, that Christian propaganda was not at first, and was not to become until more than one generation had passed, a methodically conducted enterprise for the foundation of communities planned on a model predetermined by the first missionaries, or even determined after the lapse of several years. It was the kind of agitation that arises from personal communication, one might call it a contagion, and remained so from the time when Jesus began to preach till that of the Apocalypse. The promptitude with which the propaganda was begun and its almost staggering success would be inexplicable, though without being more miraculous than a world-epidemic, unless we took into consideration the free outburst of enthusiasm which started the first migration of the Gospel on its way, together with the whole assemblage of conditions under which the preaching of the Gospel was born. As the fever of extravagant hope cooled down, system and rule came in to the same measure.

Let us never forget that the message which fired this hope was at once urgent and easy to deliver; *God and His Christ were on the point of coming*. Every Jew had an interest in knowing that. Is it likely that any Jew would not be eager to hear of it? And those who carried the message, with a simple-minded conviction of its truth, never doubted for a moment that multitudes would be ready to believe them. Their faith gave them assurance of success. Moreover the utmost alacrity was imperative for the sake of every man whom the message might reach; the Great Event was bound to come suddenly and without warning: let every man then be ready. It must be admitted, however, that some groups of Hebrew believers refused to treat the message as an article for export, and represented Jesus as commanding his missionaries not to go to the Samaritans nor to the pagans, because the Son of Man would come before they had time to make the round of the cities of Israel (Matt. x, 5, 23). Superfluous orders for propaganda already on the wing and which nothing thereafter could stop!

There is, however, no need to exaggerate the meaning of the texts just quoted. They reflect the programme of the Judaizing party. They are easily explained by saying that their authors were resolved to keep their propaganda within the regions to which Jesus had confined his own activity. But, from the fact that this programme is here turned into a precept of the Christ, it does not follow that it was intended to make the example of Jesus into a binding rule for all. We must first consider how the Great Event was understood. Certain it is that the Judaizers were not bent on excluding all the Jews of the Dispersion from the coming Kingdom of God; they believed that the accession of the Dispersed to the Kingdom would be effectively brought about after, and as a consequence of, the Event, which the original believers feverishly awaited from day to day. On the other hand, the hellenistic believers, who proclaimed Jesus as "Lord" had begun to preach the *religion* of the Christ also, and not merely his imminent advent, and were early convinced that the message of this religion ought to be carried at once to the Gentiles, and to all nations, since faith in the Christ was, for all, an indispensable condition of entry into the Kingdom. "This Gospel of the Kingdom shall be preached in all the world as a witness to all nations; and then shall the end come" (Matt. xxiv, 14). As the Second Coming did not take place the delay was explained by the necessity of completing the world-wide proclamation of the Gospel. In any case, what was now more and more aimed at was the gathering, in hope of his coming, of recruits to the faith of the Christ who was acclaimed "as a god." Thus understood, the Kingdom of God was something very different from the enthronement of the Messiah-King at Jerusalem, and came more and more to be felt as already realized in the Christian community.

In this way the evangelical message was continually passed on from one locality to the next in the Jewish colonies of all countries, where it naturally gained a hearing and then came under discussion. It was not accepted by all who heard it—how could it be?—but a certain number received it as a hope imparted by contagion. To all appearance the Jewish authorities were not as prompt in discrediting the propaganda as the Christian missionaries were in spreading it. These authorities could not measure in advance the harm which the propaganda was about to inflict upon Judaism. At first they must have thought that the execution of Jesus would suffice to break down the agitation which the Galilean preacher had started. The formation of the Jewish-Christian community took them, so to speak, off their guard; they scented no great peril in that. Disquieted, later, by the formation of the hellenistic group and the preaching of Stephen, they reassured themselves by executing the new preacher and by dispersing his associates. But this dispersion of the hellenistic believers had also the effect of spreading their belief, and when information came to the authorities of the growing success which the propagation of it everywhere was achieving, they found themselves powerless to stop it. It was doubtless at their instigation that King Agrippa I resolved to strike down the leaders of the community holding on at Jerusalem. But Peter escaped. To set the law in motion against the whole group of Hebrew believers would have been too risky, while the hellenistic preaching was beyond the reach of violent repression. Before the fall of Jerusalem in the year 70 it seems improbable that the faith of Jesus was considered in any of the Jewries as altogether incompatible with the profession of Judaism.

Considered in itself the Gospel message appealed in the main to simple souls, who awaited the day of the Lord in good faith, and to the poor, who had need of its coming. Although the Christian movement was not, strictly speaking, socialism coloured by religion, it had from the very beginning and long continued to have, indeed has never altogether lost, the character of a popular association which offered a promising asylum to the disinherited classes of contemporary society, to the Jewish plebs, to the pagan plebs and to the pagan slaves. The participation of the more fortunate classes was for a long time on a small scale, but this favoured rather than hindered the organization of the new religion as a vast mutual aid society, in which the unfortunate of all classes found moral support and material help. In short, Christianity brought to its adepts something more than an unrealizable hope continually frustrated. It brought solace to great miseries, and led on to the founding of an equalitarian society less crushing for the oppressed victims of the old civilizations.

The expansion of the constituency of the new cult was effected from the side where the synagogues themselves recruited proselytes more or less complete but fairly numerous, that is, from the pagans. That Christianity was able to make such remarkable progress in so short a time is due to the fact that Judaism had previously spread itself over the entire Mediterranean world, and that the synagogues had everywhere throughout the Roman Empire, and even beyond, become centres of active propaganda. The missionaries of Jesus made all haste to carry their message to the synagogues. Gaining them, they came, almost without premeditation, into contact with the pagan proselytes, and when the missionaries, after drawing away a large part of these, were driven out of the synagogues, they addressed themselves directly to the pagans. This first happened at Antioch and it must have repeated itself everywhere.

Although Acts (xi, 19–21) give a highly summarized version of the doings at Antioch, it leaves us with the certainty that the believers in Jesus began by addressing themselves to Jews in the synagogues; that thereby they made an impression on a few pagans friendly to Judaism, and were thus led to recruit uncircumcised persons who were willing to hear their message. But, in all this, there was no question of a rupture with the synagogue, doubtless because the preachers had done nothing to provoke it, and also because the spirit of the Antioch Jewry was not bigoted. (The protest against preaching the Gospel to the Gentiles without requiring circumcision did not come from the Jews of Antioch but from Judaizing believers sent there by Jerusalem.) No official repudiation of the Christian propaganda was issued by the Jewish authorities till long after the year 44;

for we find that Paul, to all appearances, had been everywhere able to present himself in the synagogues of Asia Minor, Macedonia and Achaia without any ban being imposed from the outset on the reception of his message, which was obstructed only by local reactions. When he was taken prisoner in Jerusalem, his person was the object of attack. The Judaizing Christians of the earliest community continued to be tolerated and to frequent the temple, perhaps also the synagogues, without constituting a group separate from traditional Judaism, as the hellenistic-Christians organized by Paul in Asia Minor had by this time become.

It may therefore be taken as certain that the Gospel would have found no easy way out of Palestine if Judaism had not established colonies in almost every part of the Roman Empire, and beyond it. Christian propaganda would have taken no hold on the pagan world had not Judaism begun the conquest of it in advance and initiated the pagans, to some extent, in the hope of the Jews. But, Judaism being there, Christianity—a Jewish heresy—was enabled to make its appearance at every centre of the ancient world where Judaism was firmly rooted. In the environment where Judaism had won victories Christianity won them also, and more easily. For the Gospel seemed to bring, and did bring, the same hope, even a better hope, for it was on the way to fulfilment; at the same time it dispensed adherents from Jewish observances repugnant to the habits of the Greco-Roman world. With the way into pagan territory thus opened, Christianity found there an immense clientele of the disinherited, to whom it offered substantial help in their present misery, moral in the first instance but material also, with the expectation of felicity in the coming age.

2. The Headquarters at Antioch

The texts before us make it possible to see how, when once the Antioch community had been constituted, the propagation of the Gospel was organized for the countries of Syria and Cilicia. Although the members, at least the Jewish-Christian part of them, still frequented the synagogue, the community had nevertheless a life of its own, but without breaking away from

Judaism. Private meetings of believing groups for instruction and for the Eucharist had, in Antioch, a greater importance than in Jerusalem, because in the former there was no temple to serve as a common meeting place for the pious Jews and followers of Jesus.

Paul, in the Epistle to the Galatians, speaks of having preached in Syria and Cilicia for at least ten years.[21] The following notice in Acts (xiii, 1–2) concerning the initiative, taken by the Antioch community for the preaching work in question, refers to the beginning of this period.

> Now there were at Antioch,
>   in the community of that place,
>   prophets and preachers:
> (Joseph called) Barnabas (of Cyprus)[22]
>   Simeon called the Black
>   and Lucius of Cyrene
> Manaen, friend of Herod the tetrarch,
>   and Saul (called Paul, of Tarsus). . . .
> And as they worshipped the Lord and fasted,
>   The Holy Spirit said:
> "Separate me Barnabas and Saul
>   to the work whereto I have called them."

In the edited or canonical book of Acts this preamble introduces a common and prolonged mission of Barnabas and Paul to Cyprus and Asia Minor (xiii, 4–xiv) which is represented as taking place before the meeting at Jerusalem which settled the question of the legal observances. But this arrangement is contradicted both by the Epistle to the Galatians (cf. Gal. i, 21–ii, 1), which puts the Jerusalem meeting immediately after the mission into Syria-Cilicia, and by Acts themselves (xv, 23) to which, in their account of the meeting, the only hellenistic-Christian communities known are those of Syria-Cilicia. Moreover, it seems impossible to place this mission, with E. Meyer (iii, 421) and others, between the Jerusalem meeting and the subsequent conflict between Peter and Paul at Antioch, after which Paul, now separated from Barnabas, followed his personal inspirations only. Far more probably the Cyprus mission was undertaken by Barnabas alone after this separation, and the mission to Lycaonia and Galatia by Paul alone on the same occasion; the editor of Acts having thought well to combine these two missions into one, and to anticipate certain events in each of the two in the common mission he proceeds to imagine.[23]

The text just cited, then, concerns a mission of which the story is not told in canonical Acts. It can only be that of which the whole credit seems to be attributed to Paul in the Epistle to the Galatians. In fact our text supposes the mission to have been carried out under conditions very different from those implied by the Epistle. Following the latter, one might think that Paul set forth entirely alone in order to carry out a programme laid down by himself at the time of his conversion. We here see that he did nothing of the kind. At a meeting of the congregation, assembled, we must suppose, in the name of the Holy Spirit, the Spirit, doubtless with one of the prophets for spokesman, commands the congregation to make provision for the support of two missionaries, whose whole time is to be devoted to making converts, both in Antioch itself and especially in the neighbouring regions of Syria and Cilicia. The two missionaries selected were evidently the two judged to be most gifted for this kind of service, the first being Barnabas who heads the list of prophet-teachers as chief founders of the Antioch congregation, the second being Paul, the last on the list as having been admitted to the congregation when it was already founded, but whose zeal and gifts as a maker of converts had speedily won recognition.

It is not very difficult to see how the decision to undertake the mission came about. When the community had grown, through the adhesion of new recruits, to fairly large proportions, though the apostolic office had as yet no definite form, it became obvious that the time was ripe to organize teaching, for the furtherance of propaganda, by delegating it to those best fitted for that employment. Now the Antioch congregation was well furnished in this respect, having five "prophets and teachers." To support the home propaganda, in the conditions under which this had been carried on hitherto, half of the total force would be enough, while the most active, enterprising and—may we guess?—the youngest could then be more usefully employed on outside work. For various reasons Barnabas and Paul were the likely candidates for a travelling mission. Both of them, moreover, and Paul especially, were acquainted with the region

THE BIRTH OF APOSTOLIC PROPAGANDA

in which their zeal was to be exercised; the purpose being to radiate outwards from Antioch and as far as Cilicia—Paul's country of origin.

We can only conjecture how the Antioch community attained the degree of development at which we find it when the apostolic expedition of Barnabas and Paul was set on foot. To begin with, a few Jews would be won over by the fugitives from Jerusalem; then the Cypriots and the Cyrenians—Barnabas, Simeon the Black and Lucius—would recruit a certain number of uncircumcised proselytes to Judaism, whom they found attached to the synagogues. Since the synagogues had accepted them without demanding circumcision our new preachers would do the same, and would have little scruple in doing so if they thought, as Stephen did, that in the Reign of the Christ the non-moral observances of the Law would be swept away. So they confined themselves to baptizing their uncircumcised converts before admitting them to fellowship, just as they also baptized the circumcised Jews. For the rest, we may conjecture that at Antioch, as at Jerusalem, the new believers, while perhaps continuing to frequent the synagogues, would in addition have meetings of their own, especially in the form of meals for the solemn breaking of bread in memory of Jesus, and in celebration of his approaching advent. Assuming that complete separation from the synagogue was not soon effected—and it is probable that the bond was not broken for a considerable time—the final result is that the new community would have a life of its own and, we may add, its own meetings for worship, as we are in effect told it had.

In these meetings at Antioch strange phenomena were produced which can hardly have been forthcoming at Jerusalem in the same degree or in the same form. For the scene at Pentecost described in Acts is entirely fictitious; so too is what the same book has to tell us elsewhere about "speaking with tongues" (ii, 1–13; x, 46; xix, 6). Moreover there is no evidence of prophets or inspired teachers appearing in Jerusalem, except casually in stories of secondary origin and poor credibility (xi, 27–30).[24] At Antioch instructors in doctrine were regarded as endowed by the Spirit with the gift of Knowledge, and as able, on occasion, to deliver true oracles under the Spirit's dictation, as happened in the case of the mission entrusted to Barnabas and Paul. There seems to be no ground for dividing the list of the five "prophets and teachers" into two parts, as if the first two or three had been "prophets" and the others "teachers." A prophet does not prophesy without intermission. The same individual who at exceptional times seemed to be speaking to the direct dictation of the Spirit would, in ordinary times, deliver his teaching with its help and presence, that is, under the simple inspiration of his faith, but without emotional transports. Conversely, there were few teachers at this time who had not, at certain conjunctions, their moments of trance and prophetic revelation. In the case before us the suggestion which pointed to Barnabas and Paul was obviously the outcome of circumstances, and it matters little to know by the mouth of which prophet it was uttered, though we may be sure it did not come from either of the two persons interested.

It would no doubt be somewhat risky to assume that the spiritual gifts, which play so large a part in the history of primitive Christianity, were not first manifested at Jerusalem but had their beginning at Antioch. Mystical and visionary exaltation infectiously communicated is contemporary with faith in Christ risen from the dead, and helped to fortify it, the disposition to yield to it being strengthened by anxious expectation of the parousia. But Antioch may well have marked a stage onwards in the evolution of this mysticism, the stage of prophetical teaching, which is not said to have accompanied the delirious "speaking with tongues." Incomplete as our documentary evidence may be, it is an important fact that the Antioch community was organized under the direction of teaching prophecy.

Not less important to note at this point is the way in which the apostolate was instituted under the form of a *delegation*. Barnabas and Paul are teaching prophets at Antioch whom the community, at the suggestion of the Spirit—the Christ-Spirit—delegates for a mission abroad. This delegation clearly makes them "apostles," that is to say envoys of the community which had given them the mission at the bidding of the Spirit of Christ. "The work" referred to is a real or genuine apostolic mission, its significance as such being underlined for the sole reason that it was, at least in the writer's thought, the first of its kind;

an enterprise declared to be necessary in the name of Christ at a meeting of believers, and entrusted to delegates whom the community, while accompanying them with its prayers, provides with letters of recommendation, with money, and all else needful for the journey. Otherwise such expeditions would not have been possible. The passage before us, then (xiii, 1–2), is an account of the first institution of the travelling apostolate, the narrator being fully aware of it as such, as well as of the close collaboration of Barnabas and Paul for several years, a collaboration which the Epistle to the Galatians tends to disguise. A commission from the community to which the traveller belonged, with a contribution to the expenses of his journey, leaving the rest of his entertainment to his prospective converts, was a normal feature in the constitution of the primitive apostolate.

We lack the details of the preaching tours made by Barnabas and Paul in the regions of Syria and Cilicia.[25] All we know of it are the results. Several Christian groups were formed in these countries under the same conditions as those at Antioch. They were partly recruited from the pagans, so that now there were many communities, using the name of Jesus and sharing the Jewish hope, in which adherents were to be found who had not submitted to the obligations of the Jewish cult.

One may well ask whether the Antioch missionaries had weighed the consequences of what may perhaps be called their liberalism. No doubt the two envoys conformed to the broader tendencies of Judaism as observed in the Dispersion, putting the essentials of religion in a belief in the One God and in the salvation promised by him to Israel subject to observance of the Jewish moral law. These tendencies would be in agreement with the opinion attributed to Stephen regarding the abrogation, in the final economy of the Kingdom, of the material observances required by the Mosaic ritual. We may believe further that they had some sense, perhaps confused, of the great opportunities which the abandonment of these practices could not fail to bring for their propaganda. But neither could they disguise from themselves that these easy-going ways would give rise to opposition, and they would need to have their answer ready. What they probably did not suspect nor aim to bring about was that, in reality, they were laying the foundation of a new religion and that soon, in consequence of their exertions, the faith of Christ, the religion of Jesus would be separated for ever, and immediately, from Judaism.

3. Paul Breaks With Antioch

Between the new community at Antioch, with its offshoots, and the community at Jerusalem, the first and chief centre of the faith, there existed relations, just as there were relations between the Judaism of the Dispersion and the metropolis of all the Jews. It was not very long before the saints in Jerusalem began to be alarmed by the news that groups were being formed in Syria and Cilicia of persons more or less strangers to Judaism inasmuch as they were outside its ritual economy. The problem which the liberalism of the Antioch missionaries had found so easy of solution did not seem so simple to the Hebrew believers of the original community. How, they asked, could the promises be inherited by those who bore not the mark of the chosen people, by those who were not partners in the holy covenant with its ritual conditions fixed by revelation direct from God? Perhaps the chiefs of the community hesitated to pronounce judgment in the matter, the teaching of Jesus, so far as there was any to refer to, having never touched this problem, nor furnished a principle for its solution. At an early hour in the development of primitive Christianity, Jesus was represented as having predicted the accession of the Gentiles to the Kingdom, and even as having realized it symbolically by miracles performed at the request of the Canaanite woman and of the centurion at Capernaum. But he was not made to declare that circumcision and the other observances were of no value for salvation. The Judaizers made him say the flat contrary and openly declare that he had not come to abrogate the Law (Matthew v, 17-19).

There were, however, some zealous individuals, more or less imbued with the pharisaic spirit, who pronounced against the practice of the Antioch missionaries and took upon themselves the duty of travelling to that city and catechizing the proselytes, explaining to them that salvation was impossible unless the Law of Moses was observed.[26] Perhaps the Jewish believers in Antioch were easily shaken; but the hellenistic believers resisted, and their chiefs refused to yield to the injunctions of Judaizing extremists. By way of putting an end to the trouble the community resolved to send a delegation which would go into the matter with the elders in Jerusalem. Paul in the Epistle to the Galatians gives us to understand that this step was taken under orders from the Spirit (ii, 2),[27] the text describing it, however, as a private revelation in consequence of which Paul decided to betake himself to Jerusalem. But the thing happened quite differently. There was no question either of the affairs or of the doctrines peculiar to this apostle. Either Paul, after the event, immensely exaggerated his own importance in it, making the whole negotiation centre on himself, and claiming as his personal inspiration the step taken by the community, under injunction of the Spirit, in delegating, not Paul alone, but Barnabas first and Paul second—either this, or the text, written in eulogy of Paul, is apocryphal. The Epistle also mentions a certain Titus, an uncircumcised believer, as having been chosen by Paul himself as his companion. If Titus really accompanied the delegates, he too may have been appointed by the community. The journey probably took place towards the end of the year 43. Agrippa I died in the course of 44; Peter fled from Jerusalem in the spring of that year; the apostolic meeting took place some time previously.

The problem was not settled without a clash of argument. Reading the Epistle to the Galatians one might think that Paul and his doctrines were the sole matters in the debate. In fact the whole work of the Antioch missionaries, which had not been started by Paul himself, was in question. At the general meetings of the community little was spoken of beyond the results obtained by the missionaries. But Barnabas and Paul had long private audiences with the chiefs, of whom the Epistle mentions Peter, John and James—according to the context not the brother of John, but James the brother of the Lord.[28] To them the Antioch apostles gave their reasons and defended their practice. The elders of Jerusalem were at last convinced. If we could believe what the Epistle to the Galatians has to say of the matter (ii, 7–9) it would seem that the "pillars" recognized in Paul a unique and universal vocation as apostle to the Gentiles and a parallel vocation for Peter as apostle to the circumcision.

Nothing could be less probable than such a convention. The book of Acts has no suspicion of its having ever existed. Either, then, Paul immensely overstates his own importance in describing his providential mission, or the text is not authentic. The elders of Jerusalem were hardly more capable of claiming for themselves alone the evangelization of all the Jews in the world than they were of confiding to Paul alone the evangelization of all the Gentiles. Such a division would have been an outrage upon common sense. To render it more acceptable Edouard Meyer arbitrarily supposes that the Jerusalem believers, not knowing Greek, confined themselves to the evangelization of the Jews in Palestine and left all the other countries in the world to the hellenists. This in fact is what happened, but is not what the text of the Epistle means.[29] The debate was not aimed at the theoretical object of determining the vocation of the chief apostles and their respective spheres of influence, a problem both abstract and retrospective. From beginning to end the one question at issue was whether or no salvation could be assured to the uncircumcised by virtue alone of faith in God and His Christ Jesus, along with a change of heart and observance of the Jewish moral law, but without circumcision and the ritual practices obligatory for Jews by birth. This was the only question examined and it was so important in itself that to seek another theme for the debate in the personalities that were parties to it is a gratuitous expenditure of effort. On this, the only point at issue, the Jerusalem elders finally came to terms with the Antioch missionaries. This, doubtless, was done the more easily because Jewish opinion on the necessity of circumcision for the salvation of proselytes had not been at that time determined. The Galilean believers, moreover, cannot have been very deeply versed in the problems of theology. At this period they seem to have had no thought of leaving Palestine, nor even Jerusalem, and to have willingly given consent that others should carry the Gospel to the outside world, whether Jewish or Gentile, and under the conditions which the Antioch missionaries had adopted. Their sole request was the preachers to the countries of the Dispersion should not forget "the poor"—that is, the Jerusalem community, where material poverty was common enough. The help thus to be given was doubtless understood as a sign of communion, not to say as a kind of allegiance. Notwithstanding the story in Acts (xv, 13–20)[30] it may be doubted whether the arrangement carried other conditions, such as the interdiction of blood and of "things strangled." But it is morally certain that the general picture in Acts reflects the real practice, that of a compromise adopted in mixed congregations to allay the scruples of Jewish believers, and sanctioned from the outset by apostolic authority. What the chiefs had decided the Jerusalem community accepted, and letters were written disavowing the disturbers of the peace at Antioch; they were carried by two notables of Jerusalem, Judas Barsabbas and Silas who accompanied the Antioch delegation on the return journey. Thus the danger of division at the moment when the Christian religion was in process of being born was averted, and the continuation of the propaganda on pagan soil assured. But the external peace enjoyed by the Jerusalem congregation was about to pass through a time of trouble; while the agreement reached by the missionaries was soon, by the action of Paul, to be shattered also.

In the years when these things were happening the old Kingdom of Herod the Great was provisionally reconstituted for the benefit of Herod Agrippa the First, a dependant of the Emperor Claudius, and previously the friend of Caligula. This prince, after a life of many adventures and of mediocre edification, thought to win the favour of his subjects by putting on grand airs of piety.[31] Like the procurators, he resided by preference at Caesarea, but coming to Jerusalem for the Passover in the year 44 he made it his duty to persecute the heads of the Christian congregation. It is possible that the decision to do this was not entirely his own, but was made in response to solicitation from the Jewish ecclesiastical authorities. Since his reign began in 41 it may, however, be asked why had not the priests and the Sanhedrim made an earlier appeal to him? Perhaps the success of the Christian propaganda outside Palestine was beginning at last to alarm them, and it may even be that the Antioch affair, and the solution in which it resulted, had come to their knowledge and caused them particular irritation.[32] There is also the further possibility that the attitude of Agrippa may have been determined by that of Claudius towards Jewish agitation. For the rest, it is to be noted that action was not taken against the congregation as a whole, nor against James the brother of Jesus, who enjoyed a great reputation for fidelity to the Law. To begin with, the two sons of Zebedee, James and John, were arrested and put to death, probably after trial by the Sanhedrim.33

Peter was the next to be seized and, the time of the Passover having come, was thrown into prison to await his trial at the conclusion of the solemnities; but he made his escape under conditions which the book of Acts represents as wholly miraculous, and of which the least to be said is that the romancer and the dramatist have been hard at work (xii, 3-19). The alternatives seem to be that either he took to flight under the menace of arrest and that pains have been taken to cover up his inglorious retreat, or else some influential person found means to get him out of prison, and the incident became dramatized as a miracle. In either event he left Jerusalem in haste and in all probability never returned. But whither did he go? The editor of Acts is deliberately silent about the locality to which he betook himself, and for a twofold reason; first, because his purpose was to ignore the conflict between Peter and Paul; and, second, because by postponing the discussion about legal observances till after the events just related, he made it impossible to bring Peter, whom he supposes to have reached the solution of the problems at the conversion of Cornelius, on to the ground where the discussion had its birth. It may be that Peter left the city accompanied by John-Mark34 and by Silas.35 Palestine, now almost entirely under the rule of Herod Agrippa, being no safe place for him, he betook himself to Antioch.

Then arose the conflict which was to lead Paul on a road all his own and to wholly new fields for the proclamation of his Gospel. If we are to believe the Epistle to the Galatians (ii, 11-13) Peter found the Antioch community at peace under the recent decision of Jerusalem, and lived in the city for some time, participating without scruple, among the uncircumcised believers, in the meals where bread was broken in memory of the Lord Jesus. But soon there arrived certain emissaries from James who were scandalized by this promiscuous association of the circumcised and the uncircumcised. Save for indications in the Epistle to the Galatians, which are open to suspicion, there is no evidence that these emissaries attempted to cancel the Jerusalem decision and force circumcision on pagan converts. Their intention was to make it clear that the Jewish believers ought not to evade the obligations of the Jewish Law as interpreted in Pharisaic tradition. As they had on their side a little logic and a good deal of hereditary fanaticism, Peter gave way to their reproaches; so did the other circumcised believers; so, too, even Barnabas seems to have done, thinking no doubt that separation of circumcised and uncircumcised at meal times was preferable to schism between Antioch and Jerusalem on a matter of secondary importance.

Paul judged otherwise, and, if we may believe the Epistle to the Galatians,[36] lost his temper, denouncing Peter and the other Jewish believers as hypocrites, Barnabas included. He accused them roundly of being false to the Gospel, charging Peter in particular with attempting, in contravention of the Jerusalem agreement, to force circumcision on the Gentiles. The accusation, if it was ever made, seems to have had no foundation in fact. Barnabas, who had no thought of betraying the principle he had followed in evangelizing the pagans, did not change. Christian propaganda went on as before without imposition of the legal observances. It was largely owing to the absence of any such condition that it continued to succeed on the one hand and, on the other, that official Judaism was finally brought to the point of condemning it. We do not know whether Peter and Barnabas submitted indefinitely to the pressure of the Judaizers in governing their relations with the pagan converts. It is improbable. We may suppose that a compromise was soon effected—the very compromise in fact which the editor of Acts puts into the discourse of James and the apostolic decree for allaying the scruples of the Judaizers (xv, 20, 28–29).

The Epistle to the Galatians does not inform us what the sequel was to the controversy raised by Paul.[37] But it may be conjectured from the situation of which the Epistles, that to the Galatians to begin with, give us a glimpse. In that Epistle we see Paul isolated, proud of his isolation, and glorying in the consciousness of a unique vocation for which his isolation is, as it were, the natural price he has to pay. He sees himself, and describes himself, as pursued by unrelenting hostility, which he takes pains to discredit by attributing it to a difference of opinion about the essential principles of salvation and to certain unworthy intentions, but which we may suspect was mainly personal, caused by the way in which Paul had created solely for himself a schism from the other missionaries. But the question still remains for us of how far the view of the matter thus disclosed corresponds to the reality. If account be taken of the Epistle only, Paul is never again to be found in the relations of fraternal communion, existing up to the time of the Antioch quarrel, with Barnabas, with Peter or with other leading figures of the Christian propaganda, whoever they may have been. But, though Paul's independent turn of mind made him seek a field for his apostleship where he would have no competitors, there is no evidence that the communities founded by him formed a dissenting group, or even that there was a final breach between him and the authentic representatives of Judaizing Christianity. Just as he went to Jerusalem with Barnabas to obtain guarantees for the communities in Syria and Cilicia on the principle of freedom from circumcision, so later on we find him a second time in presence of the mother-community—this time with a collection taken up from his converts, as though with object of obtaining recognition from the Jerusalem leaders of the work he had accomplished all alone. But it may well be that confidence was not complete on either side, though matters were not yet at the pitch of anathema and excommunication.

Our canonical book of Acts is deliberately circumspect about the whole of this affair and firmly resolved to say nothing of the difficulties Paul had to encounter later in consequence of his separation from the other Christian missionaries. It confines itself to falsifying the true motive which prevented Barnabas and Paul, returned to Antioch after their journey to Jerusalem, from continuing to preach together as hitherto they had been doing. Barnabas is made to express a wish that Paul and he should be accompanied by John-Mark on a projected mission to the South of Asia Minor. Paul not wanting this companion, a lively contention then arises between the two which comes to such a pass that Barnabas goes off to Cyprus with John-Mark, and Paul to Asia Minor with Silas. The two departures, which we must suppose to have been almost simultaneous, belong, no doubt, to history. But the circumstances which led to them were not those indicated by the book of Acts.[38]

THE BIRTH OF APOSTOLIC PROPAGANDA

For different reasons the two missionaries judged it best to abandon the Antioch community which for many years had been the centre of their apostolic activity. Barnabas, certainly, might have stayed there. But perhaps, after the quarrel that had just arisen, he preferred to deliver the Gospel message in Cyprus, his native country, whither he had probably fled after the dispersion of Stephen's followers, but where he did not remain very long (xi, 19–20). If one may believe the Epistle to the Colossians, John-Mark was his nephew (Col. iv, 10); while according to Acts the house of Mary, John-Mark's mother, was a place of rendezvous for the Jerusalem believers.[39] It was to this house that Peter came, after his escape from prison, to bid them farewell on departing for Antioch. Of what Barnabas accomplished in Cyprus we know nothing, and can only presume that this true apostle, whose action was so decisive in carrying the Gospel to the pagan world, continued to labour fruitfully in the work he had been the first to set on foot. Tradition has pitched upon him as author of the Epistle to the Hebrews and of the so-called Epistle of Barnabas. But his real work was of greater value than Epistles or any treatise in theology. As to John-Mark, he was an evangelical worker of the second rank whose relations with Peter[40] made his name useful as a commendatory title for the oldest of the canonical Gospels.

Chapter V

THE APOSTLE PAUL

In Christian tradition Saul-Paul has become a massive influence embodied in a personality ever dear to Protestants as that of a father, but not easily grasped nor understood by the critical historian. The perplexity of the critic in presence of this more or less authentic patron saint of religious individualism is due to the fact that the human figure of him whom we conventionally name "the Apostle," which seems clear-cut so long as our faith is unshaken in most of the writings that bear his name, progressively loses its outlines in proportion as we become aware of the artificial elements in the documents concerning him. The present author does not claim to reconstitute his figure but only to fix its main features by means of probable hypotheses based on the glimpses we can get of his real activities.

1. From Antioch to Corinth

We have seen how, when Barnabas went off to preach the Gospel in his own country of Cyprus, probably at the end of the year 44, Paul took the road into Asia Minor accompanied by Silas. That his expedition received the unqualified blessing of the Antioch community, as the Book of Acts affirms (xv, 40), we take leave to doubt. For never again did Paul return to that neighbourhood,[1] and never did he speak of the Antioch community as his base of operations; even in the Epistle to the Galatians he recalls no memory of his ministry in the city at the side of Barnabas. The link between him and that centre of the apostolate was finally severed; for it was there that he had broken with all his brother apostles.

His little schism, however, did not deprive him of all his friends. Silas, as we have seen, had been the bearer of the letter from Jerusalem and time had been given him to become acquainted with Paul and Barnabas. Returned now to Antioch, we find Silas, if not taking the side of Paul—for his conduct proves that he was of neither party exclusively—at least associating himself with the new work Paul was about to set on foot. This work no doubt attracted Silas, Paul himself having personally gained his goodwill. Paul, though at variance with the other missionaries, did not regard himself as excommunicated, nor was he so in fact, nor did Silas think of him as being in that condition. So, without reserve, he joined himself to this pioneer of the Gospel withhis grand projects for the cause of the Christ and his capacity for giving them effect. In the sequel Silas did not remain permanently at the side of Paul and we shall have to ask why he left it, just as we have asked why he came to be there in the first instance. It is worthy of note that Silas was a Jew by origin and that Titus, a converted pagan who had followed Paul to Jerusalem did not follow him in the mission he undertook with Silas; only after some years, and then transitorily, shall we find him at Paul's side, in Corinth. Perhaps there were certain aspects or peculiarities in Paul's character which exhausted the patience of collaborators otherwise loyal and of goodwill. After all, we have no ground whatever for interpreting his rupture with Barnabas in a sense unfavourable to that apostle. It is probable that another companion, Luke (Lucas), a convert of Antioch, and pagan by origin, joined Paul and Silas in their apostolic expedition.[2]

It was quite natural, but is also highly significant, that Paul, who was a native of Tarsus, began his work as an independent apostle in regions bordering on his native country, regions which could not have been altogether unknown to him, instead of at once proceeding to some important centre of the empire, Ephesus, Corinth, Alexandria, Rome. It suggests that he had no thought, at the beginning of his ministry, of the unique and universal mission to the human race usually attributed to him; certainly he can have had in his head no map of the Mediterranean world, with the stages marked in advance, province by province and city by city, as far as Rome and thence into Spain. His first attack was on the place nearest at hand and, keeping continually on the move, he would pass from one to the next as opportunity offered and the course of events made possible. His first thought accordingly was to make for Pamphilia and Pisidia, where he knew of Jewish communities which perhaps would give the Gospel a favourable hearing.

The first halt of our wandering preachers was at Derbe where they had some success, for a Derbe man, Gaius, is found soon afterwards in the company of believers that went on with Paul (Acts xx, 4); but Acts gives no detail about the mission there.3 From Derbe Paul made for Lystra where there was further success, this being the place where he recruited Timothy, most faithful of all his disciples and the one who followed him to the end (xvi, 1–3). If Acts are to be believed, Timothy was the son of a Jewish mother and of a pagan father, and was circumcised by Paul "because of the Jews which were in those quarters." This indication, implicitly contradicted by the Epistle to the Colossians,4 is probably a tendentious counterbalance to what is said in Galatians about the uncircumcised Titus (Gal. ii, 3).

From Lystra the apostolic company passed on to Iconium where it had to make a rather long stay, Paul preaching in the synagogue and recruiting both Jews and proselytes. But the majority of the Jews proved refractory and soon became hostile, even stirring up the pagans against the new preacher, with the result that a riot broke out and Paul was stoned.5 Quitting the scene he now conveyed himself to Antioch of Pisidia where he preached under the same conditions and had a like experience. The next project of the missionaries was to evangelize the coast towns of Asia Minor, but they were "forbidden by the Holy Spirit" (xvi, 6), by which we may understand that the obstructions they had met with suggested a dream or mystic vision which turned the steps of the apostolic group towards Phrygia and Galatia proper. If the Epistle to the Galatians can be trusted Paul fell sick and remained for some time in these regions.6 But he continued to preach and not without success, founding several communities recruited mainly from among the pagans.7

"After they were come to Mysia," the Gospel heralds, who now seem to have been steering a rather haphazard course, "assayed to go into Bithynia but"—circumstances not favouring the plan—"the Spirit of Jesus suffered them not; and passing by Mysia"—without any attempt to preach there—"they came to Troas." Painful experiences, of which no detail is given, here lie concealed. We can hardly fail to see that after his rupture with Barnabas Paul had plunged into Asia Minor somewhat at a venture, without formed plan and without great resources, and that he went on his way guided by opportunities, or turned back by difficulties, to which the revelations of the Spirit adapted themselves, as best they could. He had not come to Troas to preach, for it was only at a later date that he was to find there "an open door" and was able to form a group of Christians. His object was to get clear of regions where an ugly reception awaited the good news, and so he took ship at Troas without yet knowing where he would disembark. A vision, which we may suppose to have been occasioned by some useful information picked up on board about the Jewries of Macedonia, settled the matter. "A vision appeared to Paul in the night: a man of Macedonia appeared before him who appealed to him and said 'Come to Macedonia and help us.' And when he had seen the vision we at once endeavoured to enter Macedonia, persuaded that God so called us to preach the Gospel unto them."[8]

The travellers disembarked at Neapolis (Cavalla) whence they took the road to Philippi. Knowing nobody in the town they went on the following Sabbath to the place of prayer beside a watercourse and sitting down waited for the chance of encountering some Jews. That day the only people to come were women, among them one who was well-off, a seller of purple and a native of Thyatira "whose heart the Lord opened, so that she was interested in what Paul told her" (xvi, 11–14). Soon afterwards this Lydia, now baptized, takes the missionaries into her house and so puts them into a more favourable condition for launching their propaganda in the town, with the result that Paul gets together a considerable group of converts consisting mainly if not exclusively of pagans. But the success of their propaganda got them into difficulties. There came a day when Paul and Silas were violently laid hold of by people who dragged them before the magistrates of Philippi and charged them as follows: "these men are a serious nuisance to our town: the fellows are Jews and teach customs which it is unlawful for us Romans to have anything to do with." The two missionaries are then whipped and put in prison, but soon afterwards released on the intervention of some friendly people who go bail for them, on condition, however, that they clear out of the town forthwith.[9] The statements about the beginning of the Philippi mission (xvi, 11–15) are plain and precise, probably coming from the source of Acts:

but the sequel is cut about, the editor introducing at the start of it the incident of the pythoness, which, had it occurred, would at once have compelled Paul to quit Phillipi, where he must have remained long enough to form a numerous and very faithful group of believers. The story of the pythoness exorcised by Paul, whose cure is said to have caused his arrest (xvi, 16–19) if not invented entire by the editor, can only be his romantic version of something that really happened. The only offence charged against Paul was his propaganda and the charge must have been sustained by the evidence of that alone. The editor had his reasons for trying to put readers off the scent. For the significant point here to be remarked is that a popular rising was caused by Jewish propaganda which directly and openly ran counter to the religious foundation of the Roman empire. That was the objection brought against the Christian religion up to the moment of its final victory. That the objection was brought against it at the very beginning is entirely natural.

At Thessalonica, where Paul made his next halt, "there was a synagogue of the Jews," the Jewish colony there being much more important than at Philippi. For three sabbaths in succession the apostle was able to discourse "on the Scriptures explaining and proving that the Christ must needs suffer and rise from the dead, and that Jesus is the Christ." A few Jews were convinced by these arguments and "a much greater number of Greeks and among them several persons of quality" (xvii, 1–4).[10] But the mass of the Jews showed an ugly temper and Paul was compelled to continue his teaching outside the synagogue. By this outside preaching he had time to recruit a considerable band of believers; the difficulties which followed seem to have come chiefly from the Jews. Under similar conditions he was able to found a community at Berea.[11]

Leaving Silas in the latter town he now comes with Timothy to Athens.[12] Here he spends himself to no purpose. The editor of Acts has attempted to conceal his failure by the fiction of his speech to the Areopagus (xvii, 22–31). He would here give us a specimen of the teaching which Paul, according to him, was wont to address to audiences of highly educated pagans;[13] it is a philosophical apology in the style of those published by Aristides, Athenagoras and Justin in the second century—a trait which would suffice to date the editing of Acts. A verse from the poet Aratus is somewhat playfully quoted,[14] as though by way of replacing the quotations from the prophets with which the editor adorns Paul's other discourses, all the rest of the story being contrived to furnish this fine oration with a framework and stage-setting. The failure encountered at Athens might easily have been foreseen; nowhere else could audiences have been found less ready to be impressed by an apocalyptic message.[15] Before quitting the place Paul had received news from Thessalonica which decided him to send Timothy to that city,[16] giving him a rendezvous at Corinth and charging him to bring Silas along with him (1 Thess. iii, 2, 6; Acts xviii, 5). It will be noticed that Paul's auxiliaries move from place to place as freely as he does, and that the new Christian groups keep him informed of what is going on in their midst by messengers and correspondence. Without these frequent contacts the improvised communities might easily have dissolved.

To Corinth accordingly the apostle, travelling alone, now betakes himself, probably in course of the year 50. He seems to have arrived there without resources and in low spirits after the check he had received in Athens. Meeting Aquila, a Jew of Pontus already won over to faith in the Christ, together with his wife Prisca or Priscilla, he installed himself in their house, these people being tent-makers, which was his own trade. There he remained, working for his living, until the arrival of Silas and Timothy[17] who brought him money furnished by the communities in Macedonia—in particular, doubtless, by the group at Philippi and the good Lydia (2 Cor. xi, 9).[18] Thanks to this he was now at leisure to devote himself again to his preaching and took lodgings near to the synagogue in the house of a Judaizing pagan named Titius Justus.[19] Thus for a time he was able to teach in the synagogue and to make a fair number of conversions, including Crispus the chief ruler. As in other places, the majority of the Jews were not slow to declare themselves against the Gospel, so that Paul had to continue his teaching outside the synagogue and henceforth to make his converts for the most part among the well-disposed pagans. Here his harvest was outstandingly plentiful, insomuch that the Corinth community may well have been, at least in point of numbers, the most considerable of all his personal foundations. For eighteen months[20] his Corinth mission went on (xviii, 11). The Epistles show that, by his own activity and that of his auxiliaries, Christian groups were founded at Cenchrea, the Port of Corinth, and in some of the towns of Achaia (Rom. xvi, 1; 2 Cor. i, 1).

It is hard to say what elements of authentic reminiscence are contained in the story of the Jewish riot which is said to have resulted in Paul being haled before the pro-consul Gallio. As arranged by the editor of Acts the story comes in as a surcharge and outside that of the mission at Corinth. Gallio's proconsulate there must have covered the second half of the year 51, and the first of 52.[21] This date would be priceless for fixing the Pauline chronology, and could always be used provisionally, were it not, unfortunately, that the editor of Acts may have got his information about the Corinthian magistracy of Gallio from other sources than Luke's original document, and exploited the name for his own ends, just as he exploited the name of Sergius Paulus in his story about the mission to Cyprus which in all probability Paul never made (xiii, 4–12).[22] Taking the Gallio incident as it stands, all that is clear in it is the apologetic purpose of the editor. He had risked the conversion of Sergius Paulus, but to make Gallio turn Christian was beyond his editorial courage; so he contented himself with ascribing to him the attitude which in his, the editor's, view the Roman authorities ought to take in regard to the conflict which separated Christianity from Judaism, the attitude, namely, of refusing to be mixed up in a Jewish theological quarrel, of not confirming the excommunication of the Christians by the Jews and of leaving the former to go their own way under the official protection guaranteed to the latter. A doubt is permissible as to whether Gallio understood the matter quite in that sense.

2. From Corinth to Jerusalem

His work in Corinth nearly done, Paul, in company with Aquila and Priscilla, embarked for Ephesus, probably in the fall of the year 52, but immediately left his two companions in that city, being anxious to revisit the communities he had founded in Galatia.[23] Perhaps he had been warned that a great effort was in preparation to detach them from his Gospel. While he was absent on this business there arrived at Ephesus a disciple named Apollos, native of Alexandria, a learned and eloquent man well versed in the Scriptures, who got a hearing in the synagogue.[24] The editor of Acts seems much concerned to prevent Apollos from being regarded as the original founder of Ephesian Christianity which, in point of fact, he seems to have been. For the anecdote about the twelve disciples, found by Paul at Ephesus on his return,[25] who were unacquainted with the baptism of the Spirit must refer—if it has any historical reality—to converts made by Apollos, here fictitiously presented, along with Apollos himself, as Christians insufficiently taught and in need of further instruction—Apollos by Aquila and Priscilla and the twelve disciples by Paul himself. This distinction has probably no greater weight than the similar story by the same editor about the converts made by Philip in Samaria who, though baptized, had not received the Holy Spirit, of which we are invited to think the Jerusalem apostles were the depositaries.[26] To transform Apollos and the twelve disciples into disciples of John converted at Ephesus into disciples of the Christ, as most critics and some mythologues are eager to do, is a somewhat risky procedure. The facts are simply that Apollos, having set the evangelization of Ephesus well on foot, decided to go on to Corinth, and that "the brethren," among whom doubtless were chiefly Aquila and Priscilla, furnished him with a letter of recommendation to the community (xviii, 27).[27] At Corinth his success was as brilliant as at Ephesus and his reputation soon began to outshine that of Paul.

There may be significance in the fact that Apollos, who has had such good success at Ephesus in the absence of Paul, disappears before Paul's arrival there; and the same will happen at Corinth, whence Apollos will again depart before Paul comes back. We may suspect, but without committing ourselves to risky conclusions, that the two teachers thought it wiser not to meet on the field of their missionary activity, and that their friends encouraged them, or at least encouraged Apollos, in that precaution. On returning to Ephesus as soon as Paul was ready to quit that city for Corinth, Apollos appears to have been extremely reserved (1 Cor. xvi, 12). He cannot be represented as holding entirely with the Judaizers, but neither was he exactly on the line of Paul from the hellenic-Christian point of view. We should regard him as a teacher less jealous for his own doctrines and apostolic privilege than Paul was, and ready, like Paul and the others, to go wherever he could find an open door. His position may have been similar to that of Barnabas, inclining to hellenism, but in good relations with the old believers in Palestine; in Corinth we shall find his partisans associating with Peter's on lines somewhat opposed to Paul. He was probably urged to go to Corinth by friends he had made in Ephesus, perhaps even by Aquila and Priscilla, who knew the many advantages of the Corinthian field. Moreover, notwithstanding their relations with Paul, Aquila and Priscilla were of the same way of thinking as Apollos in regard to the common Christianity.

In this connexion it should be noted that Silas (Sylvanus), who was still with Paul at Corinth, having borne him company all the way from Antioch, is now no longer at his side. As a companion of Paul he makes no further appearance and tradition puts him later at the side of Peter (1 Peter v, 12). It was at Corinth that the two apostolic labourers took their separate ways, perhaps in consequence of some personal coolness. The source of Acts can hardly have failed to leave a record of their separation, which the editor would be very careful to omit. To remain for long the companion of Paul a docile temper was necessary, like that of the good Timothy. Luke was not always at his side; however deeply he may have been attached to his person he does not seem to have been as closely associated with his ministry.

Meanwhile Paul returned to Ephesus and preached in the synagogue for three months on end. But a lively opposition declaring itself and the Jews scoffing openly at the faith he was offering them, he carried his teaching elsewhere, and continued it for two years[28] in a room he had hired from a certain Tyrranus, where he taught daily, thus exchanging, so to say, the pulpit of the preacher for the platform of the public lecturer. From all of which we may infer that a wide currency attended this teaching, to us so extraordinary in its contents and yet indisputably successful to a degree which baffles our reason. The angry opposition it awakened, of which the detailed manifestations escape us,[29] was commensurate with the success. But, as happened in the case of Corinth, the Ephesus mission was fraught with consequence not only for the development of the Ephesian community, which owed its beginnings to Apollos, but for the evangelization of other towns in that region.

Having taught at Ephesus for two years under these conditions, Paul formed a project which, with his past achievements in view, should not strike us as too ambitious, that of carrying the Gospel to Rome, but not until he had gone to Jerusalem with the collection he would first take up from the groups of believers in Macedonia and Achaia, as well as from those he was now forming in Asia.[30] These collections were to some extent imitated from those regularly made among the Jews for the support of the temple worship; and that no doubt is the reason why the editor of Acts is perseveringly silent on the subject.[31]

The true motive which led Paul to go to Jerusalem before making for Rome is not clearly indicated in the Epistles and we can only guess what it was. During his stay at Ephesus Paul had received the news that divisions, not entirely due to the activities of Apollos, were growing apace at Corinth. It seems that believers, or wandering preachers coming from Palestine or Syria to Corinth, as also to Galatia, had given it out to the communities founded by Paul that their apostle was not a genuine apostle and was not recognized as such by the authorized custodians of the Gospel. It is impossible to say what authority these people had to denounce him in this manner, but at least there can be no doubt that they expressed the general uneasiness of the earliest formed communities as to the doings of an apostle whose independence was too pronounced for their liking.[32] It must have been for the purpose of allaying their alarm that Paul found it opportune to fulfil the promise he had made twelve years previously to the elders of Jerusalem (Gal. ii, 10).[33] But it seems likely that the state of affairs at Corinth determined him to keep this promise with the least possible delay and in a manner most likely to defeat the manœuvres of the enemy.

Reading the Epistle to the Galatians one might think that the extreme Judaizers were trying to compel the uncircumcised believers in Galatia to submit to the Jewish observances. But this conclusion falls to the ground on closer scrutiny of the facts. For the credit of Paul was being undermined in the same way at Corinth as in Galatia without the apostle saying a word to the Corinthians about the legal observances. The Epistle to the Galatians falsely accuses Peter and Barnabas of trying to impose Judaism on the uncircumcised converts at Antioch, and consequently exaggerates the danger of Judaization by which the Galatians were threatened, but about which Paul says nothing to frighten the Corinthians; moreover, while explaining to the Romans the economy of salvation by the sole means of faith in the Christ, his arguments are not in the form of a defence against high authorities who would deny the principle of that faith, but against those who have accused him of failing in respect for the Law of Moses and for the people of the Promise. (Cf. Romans ix–xi.)

His experience at Corinth could not fail to induce in him some degree of moderation. Before quitting Ephesus he had sent out two of his auxiliaries, Timothy and Erastus, to hasten the collections in Macedonia and Achaia.[34] But Timothy had promptly returned to Asia with bad news: the conflict in Corinth between Paul's party and his enemies was going from bad to worse. As he had written to the Corinthians, before sending them Timothy, and had told them that he would come to Corinth himself after visiting Macedonia, he now judged it expedient to go there immediately. He did so, and came off badly.[35] His presence in Corinth, far from causing appeasement, gave rise to a grievous dispute in which he seems to have been humiliated before an unscrupulous opponent (2 Cor. ii, 5–11).[36] Returned to Asia he wrote, in a kind of despair,[37] a severe letter which he described later on as having afflicted the Corinthians for the health of their souls.[38] What proved more useful than the letter was the mediation of Titus who happened to be at Corinth at the very moment when his help was most needed to pacify the Corinthians.[39] There are grounds for thinking that this man, a member of the Antioch community who had formerly taken part in the Jerusalem meeting (Gal. ii, 1), had come to Corinth with the original intention of pacifying Paul himself, and that, fortified by his first success, he then consented to intervene in making peace between the Corinthians and Paul who was now disposed to be more agreeable to the old missionaries and to the Jerusalem community.

Paul meanwhile was at Troas where he founded a new Christian group while he waited for Titus who was returning by way of Macedonia. Becoming impatient he went back to Macedonia himself and met Titus who had made peace with the Corinthians. The immediate result was a new letter, full of joy and consolation, and incompletely reproduced in 2 Cor. i–ii, 13; vii, 6–16. Paul pardons the wrong done him (2 Cor. ii, 5–11). Titus wishes to go a second time to Corinth to complete the collection (2 Cor. viii). The good Titus then disappears from Paul's company, having no doubt more important business on hand elsewhere. We should think of him as an effective and conscientious worker for the peace of Christianity in the time of its birth when it was threatened with schism by the doings of Paul and by his pretensions. Let us remember that Titus did not follow Paul when he went his own way after the conflict at Antioch; we must suppose him to have been on good terms with Peter, Barnabas and the Antioch headquarters.

Returning to Corinth for the last time[40] at the end of the year 55 or 56,[41] Paul spent three months in the city. Then it was that he wrote the Epistle to the Romans,[42] that is to say the authentic parts of it, the document on which the canonical Epistle is based. The letter was addressed to a community mainly recruited from uncircumcised pagans with no inclination to Judaism, not at least to the point of themselves accepting circumcision and the Jewish observances. Thus we read (i, 13–15): "I would not have you ignorant, brethren, that often I purposed to come unto you —and hitherto I have been prevented—that I might have some fruit among you, as among the other Gentiles. I owe a duty to Greeks and to barbarians, to the wise and to the ignorant. So, to the utmost of my power, I am ready to preach the Gospel to you also." On looking closely into the matter we perceive that Paul, in developing his idea that the Gentiles must share the faith of Abraham in order to share the promise made to that patriarch, was less concerned in confuting the advocates of circumcision than in establishing the authority of his own mission. And he explains why the business of the collection obliges him to go to Jerusalem before coming to Rome: "But now I go to Jerusalem to do a service to the saints. For it has pleased them of Macedonia and Achaia to make a charitable offering to the poor among the saints at Jerusalem" (xv, 25-26).

From this we gather that Paul regarded his friendly action towards the mother-community in Jerusalem as likely to raise his credit when he arrived in Rome and to ensure the support of the Roman believers for his intended mission to Spain. For to Spain he certainly meant to go. But why to Spain? Because, in his view of the world, Spain represented its uttermost limit, and that the Gospel would have been preached everywhere when he had completed the "circle" of the Mediterranean (xv, 19, 22-23)—a somewhat imaginary framework for his ever overflowing activity. Strange as these particulars are to our minds, account of them must be taken by those who would understand the man and his work.

The projects of Paul were not realized according to plan. In the spring of the year 56 (or 57) he embarked at Cenchrea with Macedonia as his first destination. The Jewish plot mentioned in Acts (xx, 3) must be an arbitrary explanation of this detour, the true reason being that the bearers of the collection from the Macedonian communities had not arrived in Corinth, as soon as Paul desired, to set out with him on his pilgrimage to Jerusalem; he would go himself, then, and gather them together. We have already seen how the editor of Acts is deliberately silent about this collection as likely to upset his apologetic aim by showing, as it would, that from the very first Christianity tended to organize itself outside Judaism. It was not Paul's intention to be himself alone the bearer of the money collected among his Gentile converts for the saints at Jerusalem, partly because he would not have it suspected that he was actuated only by his personal interest, but also because he was eager to bring the representatives of the communities he had founded in person before the elders at Jerusalem. The list of Paul's travelling companions (xx, 4) is made up, for the most part, of the gift-bearers: Sopater of Berea, Aristarchus and Secundus of Thessalonica certainly carried the subscriptions raised in their respective communities. It is surprising that no mention is made of a representative from Philippi; but it may well be that the list is not complete. The two Asiatics, Tychicus and Trophimus, would take the collection from Ephesus; they were not due to come to Corinth and Paul would pick them up at Miletus. Timothy and perhaps Gaius[43] figure as Paul's assistant missionaries, not as representatives of the Galatian communities whose collections were not to be passed through Corinth, but sent directly to Jerusalem—as mentioned incidentally in 1 Cor. xvi, 1. None the less the apostle and his associates constituted a small embassy to Jerusalem from the converted Gentile world.

As a pilgrim under a vow, to be accomplished in Jerusalem at the feast of Pentecost,[44] Paul, on departing, shaved his head. This vow has perplexed certain critics who regard Paul as no more capable of such a thing than a good Protestant would be of taking a vow to Our Lady. And it is true enough that to find the author of the Law-sin-death theory acting like a fervent *nazir* is not what we expect. But Paul did not necessarily conform to all the theories his writings impute to him. It is certain that the information comes from the source of Acts, for the editor, either not understanding it, or thinking he might cut it into two, has made it unintelligible. While the real Paul did not impose the Law on his Gentile converts he seems himself to have meticulously observed it, at least in regard to cult practice.

The delegates from Corinth went with him, bearing the contribution from Achaia. But Paul lingered by himself among the groups in Macedonia, gathering the delegates from those regions, and, having stayed at Philippi for the week of Unleavened Bread, only after reaching Troas rejoined a part of the company which had embarked with him at Corinth;[45] there was now a Christian group at Troas to receive the travellers.[46] Thence he went on to Assos by land, his companions going by sea; after which they all kept to the sea route, sailing by short stages along the coast. "Paul," we read, "had decided to pass Ephesus by, so as to avoid losing time in Asia; for he hasted in the hope of reaching Jerusalem in time for the Day of Pentecost" (Acts xx, 16). This motive does not, by itself, explain why Ephesus was avoided, seeing that the company was making a stop at Miletus. The community at Ephesus might have put pressure on Paul to remain among them at a time when a stay there had become dangerous for him. The rendezvous for the delegates from Asia was therefore fixed at Miletus.[47] At

Patara a ship was found on the point of sailing for Phoenicia; this carried them to Tyre,[48] thence to Ptolemais, whence Paul proceeded on foot to Caesarea.

Here the whole apostolic company was entertained by Philip. This former companion of Stephen and one of the Seven had established himself at Caesarea immediately after the dispersion of Stephen's group and had gathered round him a small band of believers. A special point is made of informing us that he had four virgin daughters endowed with the gift of prophecy (xxi, 19). The purpose of the original author of Acts in mentioning them was certainly to make them utter a prophecy analogous to that which the later editor thought would be more decently placed in the mouth of a male prophet. All that concerns Agabus is fiction of the editor who has already made use of the same person for another fiction (xi, 27–28). The prophecy was that Paul would fall into enemy hands at Jerusalem.[49] Everybody, his companions no less than the local believers, now implored him to go no further. But Paul replied that he would not renounce his project, even though it meant that he would perish in the Holy City: whereupon they all abandoned themselves to the will of God. Perhaps the scene has been to some extent arranged by the original author, Luke. But the attitude ascribed to Paul is intelligible. At all costs the task to which he had committed himself in preparing his journey to Jerusalem must be carried out to the end. A few of the Caesarea believers added themselves to Paul's company and went on with him to Jerusalem where they had procured the hospitality of Mnason, an "old disciple." Evidently this Mnason, who came from Cyprus, was, like Philip, a "hellenist" and well disposed to Paul.[50] It remained to make contact with the Hebrew believers, on whose account the expedition has been undertaken.

3. From Jerusalem to Rome

Next day Paul and his retinue were received by James and the collection from the communities was presented to the Jerusalem elders.—Omitting all mention of the collection, which was the principal object of the expedition, the editor of Acts confines himself to saying that Paul, after saluting the company, proceeded at once "to set forth in detail all that God had done among the Gentiles by his ministry" (xxi, 15–16).—The offering was accepted; Paul's account of his mission was then heard and due satisfaction expressed. But the elders did not disguise from Paul the danger he was running from the Jews who regarded him as no better than the preacher of an apostasy. They then proceeded to advise him, by way of making himself less conspicuous, to join up with four *naẓirs* of their community, who were on the look out for some charitable person to pay their expenses,[51] and to fulfil his vow as one of their company. Such at least seems to be the meaning of the elders' discourse as it was given by Luke in the original document. But the editor of canonical Acts would have it understood[52] that the "believing" Jews who were seeking Paul were Jewish-Christian believers, and that it was to them, Jewish Christians, that Paul must prove, by becoming a *naẓir*, that he was not an apostate to the Law, as he was accused of being. All this, in the given circumstances, is wholly unintelligible and irrelevant. These Jewish Christians were not to be counted by "thousands," as the edited text declares, but were chiefly to be found in the very audience to which Paul had just recounted his triumphs. The members of that audience knew perfectly well why Paul was accused of being an apostate to the Law, but they also knew that in strictness the charge was unfounded, since Paul dispensed with the Law only in the case of Gentile converts. Apart from that, the advice to take on the character of a *naẓir*, as the elders are made by the editor to recommend, would, if adopted, prove nothing by itself; in point of fact Paul's adoption of it was not proclaimed, and his recognition came about by chance. Now, since the normal observance of the vow was for thirty days,[53] the nature of the case makes it morally certain, and our texts confirm the certitude, that Paul took his vow as a *naẓir* on leaving Corinth and timed it to be completed in Jerusalem; he was still under the vow on his arrival and could not do otherwise than join up with persons in the same condition,[54] not for the purpose of showing himself more openly but for the opposite purpose of being less conspicuous, as appears plainly in the course of the narrative. Perhaps the editor was unwilling to represent Paul as one who would hide himself; but his chief concern was to maintain his thesis—that Paul and the Christians were the best Jews in the world, Christianity when rightly understood being the true Judaism.55

Paul accepts the elders' advice, repairs to the temple with the four *nazirs* of the Jerusalem community and the day is fixed for the discharge of the vow (xxi, 26). But on that day, the seventh or eighth after Paul's arrival, some Jews from Asia, who have met him on the street with Trophimus of Ephesus, catching sight of him in the holy place, cry out on the profanation, believing or pretending that he has introduced an uncircumcised person into the sacred precincts. The crowd rushes in; Paul is dragged out of the temple and the priests close the gates. Paul would have been killed had not the tribune of the cohort in barracks at the Tower of Antonia received timely notice that a mob was gathering and violence afoot; he hurries to the spot with his soldiers, gets possession of Paul, puts him in chains and asks the cause of the trouble. Getting no clear answer in the tumult he carries Paul off to the fortress and orders him to be put to the question. Whereupon Paul declares himself a Roman citizen and his chains are at once taken off. Meanwhile the Jewish authorities, informed of what has happened, at once put in a claim to the prisoner demanding that, as guilty of an offence against religion, he must be given up to them.56 Fortified by a vision,57 and perceiving that his sole chance of safety lies in his status as a Roman citizen, Paul insists on his right to be judged by Roman Law. Without further delay the tribune then despatches him to Caesarea and tells his accusers to state their case before the procurator Felix.58

This simple and well co-ordinated story has been dismembered by the editorial fictions of canonical Acts. In the story of Paul's arrest by the Roman soldiery, and before they carry him to the Tower of Antonia, a gross interpolation, easily recognizable as such,59 has been introduced. It represents him, when half beaten to death by the blows he had received, as capable of delivering on the spot a long speech for the benefit of the tribune and the mob, in which he expounds his merits as a faithful Jew and tells the whole story of his conversion and calling to the Gentiles (xxi, 37–xxii, 22) —a fine opportunity to represent the Jews, on hearing the latter proposition, as lifting up their voices in protest against the conversion of the pagans (xxii, 22)! From what follows our interpolator would lead us to infer that Paul disclosed his status as a Roman citizen[60] only in order to escape the torture; in fact the legal conditions of the affair are thrown into confusion by any device that occurs to him, and always for the purpose of closing our eyes to the fact that Paul's manœuvres were consciously aimed from the first at escaping from the jurisdiction of the Sanhedrim, which was bringing the charge against him. He forgets to say that the Sanhedrim claimed to judge Paul, and that Paul rejected its right to judge him, not for having profaned the Temple, but as a cause of trouble in the synagogues outside Palestine. In contrast to this the editor has imagined a sitting of the Sanhedrim convoked by the tribune to get information about Paul, which ends in nothing because the Pharisees and Sadducees fall to quarrelling about the resurrection;[61] in all of which he is aiming to show that orthodox Judaism and Christianity agree in principle about the survival of the dead. But that was not the question at issue. Finally we are given to understand that Paul was transferred to Caesarea merely to put him out of range of Jewish plots on his life. At this point the editor gives the rein to his imagination and creates for Paul an unexpected nephew whose revelations induce the Tribune to despatch Paul to Caesarea.[62] The editor even goes the length of inventing an official report from the tribune Lysias to the procurator Felix containing cautious testimony to Paul's innocence.[63] To avow the simple reality of the facts would not have served the editorial purpose. He would say nothing about the Sanhedrim claiming the right to judge Paul, because, by doing so, he would have been led to admitting that Paul had denied the right of a Jewish tribunal to judge him, and that this was the reason why the tribune had referred the case to the procurator and sent Paul to Caesarea, admissions he was not willing to make. The plain fact is that Paul escaped from the clutches of the Jewish authorities only by establishing his Roman citizenship; but, for all that, he was not yet saved.

Arrived before the procurator Felix, Paul undergoes a simple interrogation as to his identity and is then remanded under guard to Herod's pretorium pending the presentation of the Sanhedrim's petition.[64] When this has been done, Felix, who was well informed about the Christian sect, adjourns the final solution of the affair and keeps Paul in custody, leaving him free to see his friends and receive their ministrations.⁶⁵

As a political measure the adjournment had the double advantage of keeping the accused agitator quiet for the time being and of not handing over to the Sanhedrim a Roman citizen whom the procurator had no right to abandon to its jurisdiction. It is conceivable, moreover, that the question of the legitimacy of the Christian propaganda from the Jewish point of view was not clear to the first Roman magistrate called to adjudicate in the matter, even though he understood his duty no more rigorously than Felix is said to have understood his. And there was yet another question of equal if not greater import, of which Paul himself does not seem to have thought, but demanding urgent consideration. Was not this propaganda, which the Jews declared to be an infraction of the traditional law of their religion, equally condemned by the laws and fundamental principles of the Roman Empire?

It is a common practice with the editor of Acts to amplify his story by repeating an incident twice over. When, therefore, we find the judicial action taken by the Sanhedrim before Felix repeated before Festus who succeeded him as procurator, we might suspect, in view of the editor's habits that we have here another instance of his duplications. But, in the present case, the duplication seems to be only partial, the change of procurator⁶⁶ coming from the source document and the editor merely antedating to the time of Felix the fuller debate under Festus. The question at issue, which Felix had decided to adjourn, was a question of jurisdiction; this, when referred to him, Festus considered his duty required him to decide in favour of the Sanhedrim. Paul's appeal to the tribunal of the Emperor was determined by that decision, with the result that the root question, that of Paul's culpability, though touched upon during the debate on competence, was not directly examined and adjudicated till the accused arrived in Rome. Thus we may conclude that the adjournment by Felix, the change of procurator at the end of two years and the measures taken for the cusody of the prisoner in the interval come from the source. But the *mise-en-scène* of the judicial enquiry before Felix, the discourse of the accuser's advocate and Paul's defence are all in the editor's manner, though a few of the details he may very well have picked out from the source document.

Felix became procurator of Judea in the year 52. The exact date of his recall in uncertain, but not earlier than 55 and, probably, not later than 58. Festus remained procurator till his death in 61. It is not surprising that Felix, who had been some years in office, was tolerably well informed about the Christian movement, at least as the Jews understood it,[67] in contrast to Festus who found the case of Paul brought before him in court at the very beginning of his magistracy. But this explanation of the adjournment does not, in the source document, imply the personal interest in the case which our canonical text attributes to Felix. Luke's object was rather to indicate the political motive of the delay, which lay in the difficulty of the case and the danger of a hasty solution. The private interviews with Paul of Felix and his wife Drusilla, daughter of Agrippa I, are editorial fiction, doubling the grand scene which the editor will construct later on, in which great persons, Agrippa II and his Queen Berenice, brother and sister of Drusilla, make their appearance on the stage. From what we know of the private characters of Felix and Drusilla, their qualifications as Paul's catechumens were of mediocre promise.[68]

Paul had been kept prisoner at Caesarea for two years (probably 56–58) when Felix was replaced by Porcius Festus. Hardly was Festus installed when the Sanhedrim, judging the occasion opportune for taking up the case again, renewed its plea in his court. Festus, no doubt, was unwilling to begin his tenure of office by disobliging the subjects of his administration; he yielded to the demand and soon afterwards received the delegates of Jewish authority in his official residence at Caesarea. Having heard a statement of the case, he declared himself incompetent to deal with it, on the ground that the matter in dispute was distinctly of a religious nature and of interest only to Jews; he would therefore remit the case to the judgment of the Sanhedrim. But Paul, as a Roman citizen, was not without means of escape from a decision which would deliver him to judges from whom he knew what to expect. Using his right of appeal, he invoked the jurisdiction of the emperor and demanded trial by Caesar. The appeal, legally formulated, was granted. Festus, after conferring with his

Council, gave his verdict: "thou hast appealed to Caesar; to Caesar thou shalt go" (xxv, 1–12).

It may be that the Sanhedrim had calculated that Paul would not dare formally to repudiate its jurisdiction, since, in so doing, he would place himself outside Judaism. Paul, on his side, having staked his hopes on Roman justice, had probably flattered himself that the procurator would pronounce the petition of the Sanhedrim unfounded, and order his discharge; he was a Roman citizen and his conduct was in keeping with Roman law. But the previous attitude of Felix must have caused him to reflect, and perhaps suggested to him the idea of having recourse, if the need should arise, to the higher jurisdiction that every citizen could claim. It is even possible that Festus, on deciding to send the case back to the Sanhedrim, as one with which he was incompetent to deal, himself reminded the prisoner of his right of appeal to Caesar. In any case, Paul, when the decisive moment came, seems to have had no hesitation. The choice before him being only between the sentence of death which the Sanhedrim had in store for him and the chance of a discharge offered by appealing to Caesar, he chose the Emperor's tribunal. Such was the door, so to speak, to which the Christian, escaping from Judaism, ran for safety. Did Paul indulge in illusions as to what the attitude of the imperial tribunal would be? We cannot say. Did he think that Caesar in Rome would be less accessible to Jewish influence and less inclined to consider the interests of Judaism than his procurator in Palestine? Did he even hope that Caesar, by giving him his liberty, would recognize the legality, or rather the permissibility of the Christian propaganda? Perhaps. But the contrary was to happen, insomuch that one might almost accuse the apostle of some imprudence in bringing the cause of Christianity in his own person before Caesar. But it may well be that it was but the faintest glimmer of hope that decided him to do what he did. His appeal would take him to Rome, and, if Caesar were pleased to declare him innocent, the years of his captivity would not have been wasted time.

The essential features of the proceedings are preserved in canonical Acts. But there are a few retouches and interested additions. The preliminary petition of the Sanhedrim is falsely presented as a request for a favour, and the editor has added, on his own responsibility, a plot of the Jews to kill Paul before the judgment asked for had been delivered (xxv, 3). The judicial inquiry is sketched from the source, but probably shortened, the arguments having been partly anticipated, as we have seen, in xxiv, 1–21. The decision of Festus to refer the case to the Sanhedrim which resulted in Paul appealing to Caesar is turned into a benevolent proposition, designed to oblige the Jews by the procurator, who asks Paul if he is "willing" to be judged by him at Jerusalem[69]—a false perspective of the case in which it is implied that the procurator would hold the proceedings in the presence of the Sanhedrim, whose sentence of death would be ratified by him before execution. Paul's appeal to Caesar is intelligible only on the assumption that Festus recognized the competence of the Sanhedrim to deal with the main issue; this it was that left Paul with no alternative but an appeal to Caesar. The terms of the appeal and the final sentence of Festus cannot be otherwise explained. But the editor has left his mark in what he makes Paul say about Festus being persuaded of his innocence and wanting to make his person a "present" to the Jews.[70]

The meeting of Festus with Agrippa II and the pomp and ceremony of the conference arranged for the satisfaction of this Jewish kinglet are mere editorial padding intended to provide a setting for a new speech by Paul in his own defence and a new testimony to his innocence in which the Herodian prince backs up the Roman procurator. Superficially at least this concoction is better balanced than many of the others and shows that the editor spared no pains in its composition; Paul's speech for example being constructed in the amphigoric style deemed proper in addressing royal personages. None the less the fiction taken as a whole is founded on a ludicrous improbability, the supposition, namely, that Festus had nothing to put into the report which he was bound to send to Rome along with the prisoner and hoped to get matter for the report after Paul's examination before Agrippa (xxv, 25–27).[71] It is clear that the procurator, on deciding to send Paul back to the Sanhedrim, judged that there was a real case for the Jewish tribunal and that, on the appeal intervening, it was no longer for him to furnish an account of the matter at issue, this being sufficiently furnished by the complaint of the Sanhedrim annexed to his report. But, in making Agrippa declare (xxvi, 31) that Paul would have been set at liberty if he had not appealed to Caesar,[72] the editor gives us a clear hint that Caesar in the upshot did not set him at liberty, and that he was the victim of judicial error, if not of gross injustice.

4. IMPRISONMENT AND DEATH

A few days after the session of the court into which Paul had flung his appeal to Caesar, he was remitted with other prisoners to a centurion named Julius, of the cohort Augusta, for conduct into Italy. They embarked at Caesarea in a ship of Adramyttium which made sail for the coast of Asia; Luke was with Paul;[73] Aristarchus of Thessalonica being also of the company. The Adramyttium ship not being a government vessel the companions of Paul[74] would be entered as passengers, unless they had been granted permission to go with him as his servants. Next day the ship made Sidon where Julius allowed Paul to visit the brethren in the town. Thence, after a trying voyage, they arrived at Myra in Lycia where the centurion transhipped his charges to an Alexandrian vessel about to sail for Italy. But navigation became more and more difficult, and the ship, in manœuvring to winter in Crete, at the port of Phoenix, was caught by a tempest and buffeted about the Mediterranean for fourteen days, till finally it struck a rock near the island of Malta, whence the shipwrecked company saved themselves by swimming, or on rafts hastily put together.[75]

The inhabitants of the island treated them with great humanity, and the head man of the island, Publius by name, sheltered them for three days. In Malta they were forced to remain for three months, until the return of weather favourable for navigation. The shipwreck took place towards the end of November and the departure from Malta the following March. The story of Paul bitten by a viper and receiving no hurt, and the cures operated by him on the sick of the island are within the range of possibility, but not beyond the editor's power of invention.[76]

Julius and his prisoners left Malta in another ship of Alexandria bearing the sign of the Dioscuri; three days were spent at Syracuse, one at Rhegium; after another day's sailing, anchor was dropped at Puteoli and the perilous voyage was ended. Soon they were in Rome.

The procession of Christians from Rome coming out to meet the prisoner at Appii Forum is obviously an insertion by the editor; the Forum was a day's journey from Rome in the Appian Way, and to give the captive apostle a triumphal reception at that place would have been neither easy nor well timed. So far as our information goes, the believers in Rome do not seem to have rallied round Paul during his captivity, which explains why the editor shows them so eager to meet him. The stay among the brethren at Puteoli (xxviii, 14) which ends the story of the journey, prepares the way for a display of devotion by the Christians of Rome.

The reality was more sombre. Arrived in Rome the prisoner was remitted by the centurion to the prefect of the pretorium. This person, Burrus, who held the post till the year 62, it must have been who authorized Paul, as Acts relate,[77] to take a lodging in the city, where he was to remain, with a soldier charged to guard him, until the arrival of delegates from the Sanhedrim to lay the charge against him. These conditions, we are told, continued for two years, Paul enjoying a relative liberty and unhindered in preaching his Gospel to those who came to visit him.

It is of set purpose that the editor of Acts allows no word to pass of what followed. Had the trial of Paul ended in acquittal, 'most assuredly he would have put it on record. The doubled scene of interviews between Paul and the Jews (xxviii, 17–28), enhanced by the final gloss[78] on the liberty given to Paul for private preaching, fictitious if anything is, constitutes the conclusion of the Book of Acts as our editor would have it. In that conclusion he gives a symbolic summary of the apologetic thesis which dominates his editing of the book: Christianity is the true Judaism, now represented by the Gentiles, because it has been rejected by the blinded Jews, and is entitled to that liberty of preaching which was not refused even to Paul in his captivity. An ideal and a theory!

One fails to see by what means or by what authority Paul, just arrived as a prisoner in Rome, was able to gather around him the leading persons of the Jewish community; and the motive of their eagerness to satisfy him is equally obscure. The speech attributed to Paul (xxviii, 17-20) is intended to show that his appeal to Caesar must not be construed as a repudiation of Judaism. The assertion which concludes it, "for the hope of Israel I am bound with this chain," in which the apostle of the Gentiles poses as the authentic representative of the Jewish faith, is the very thesis of the editor, but a thesis which Paul himself would have had some difficulty in upholding as an account of the true meaning of his apostleship. The conclusion of the second interview (xxviii, 23-28)[79] gets lost in allegorical symbolism. The editor, employing the same methods as for the fictitious session of the Sanhedrim before Lysias, represents the Jews as divided on the value of the Christian thesis, without the better disposed adhering to it more closely than the most determined of its adversaries: whereupon Paul, for the edification of posterity, hurls a text of Isaiah[80] at the wrangling group, the classical text employed in the New Testament for this purpose, in which the Eternal passes judgment on his hardened people. Israel having defaulted, the turn of the Gentiles has now come! The artifice of these stage-effects is apparent from the way in which Paul is given the air of announcing, for the first time, the rejection of the Jews for their hardness of heart; but it was important to repeat once more, as the last word, how the conversion of the pagans had directly resulted from Jewish incredulity (xxviii, 28). Thus the reader could not possibly mistake the moral of everything the canonical Book of Acts has told him. In default of believing Jews the bearers of the Gospel must needs carry it to pagans: *but the believing pagans, in virtue of their religious profession, have won the right to be counted the heirs of the promise and the only real Jews.*

The interests of history would be better served by the smallest authentic information about the issue of Paul's trial. It is certain that some time elapsed before a decision was reached, and probable that the verdict when it came was a sentence of death for the apostle and that his execution followed. To know the grounds on which the judgment was based, which we can only guess, would be knowledge of immense value to the historian. As to the delay of the trial, we may suppose that the Jewish authorities were in no hurry to get on with the prosecution and imperial justice no more hurried in terminating an affair of which, at first, it did not grasp the significance, taking it merely for a quarrel among the Jews. But this only makes us the more curious to know why, at some given moment, the case was reopened and settled. This new and final phase occurred, no doubt, at the end of the two years mentioned in Acts. If that brings us to the year 64, it follows that the occasion for suddenly taking up the trial of Paul would be that which set on foot the persecution of the Christians in Rome after the burning of the city.

But this plausible view does not seem the most probable. The somewhat abrupt conclusion of Acts has a didactic purpose: the book ends where it ought to end to serve the intentions of the editor who has foreshadowed a tragic close to the trial, but is unwilling to disclose the precise nature of the end because, by so doing, he would ruin his apologetics, while his object would be better attained by insinuating that Paul was innocent of the charge on which he was condemned, whatever that charge might be. It has been maintained by some critics, whose procedure would certainly be somewhat naïve were it not for the interested motives that often prompt it, that Paul was freed from the first accusation before the imperial tribunal, that he resumed his apostolic labours for some time afterwards, even went to Spain as he intended,[81] or, if not, returned to the East—although Acts gives us clearly to understand that he never returned—and finally came back to Rome and was put to death with Peter in 64. All of which is legend and conjecture. The two apostles were not destined to die together, but a later tradition brought them together in death, after they were dead, by way of honouring them as founders of a church which neither of them had founded, but whose prestige was enhanced by the legend of such founders. It is more probable that Paul died first, say in the year 62, and that Peter, if he died in Rome, according to an obscure tradition, not contradicted by any ancient evidence, was swept away in what is called the Neronic persecution.

The so-called Epistles of the Captivity, if written from Rome, as they probably were, contain little precise information about the two years which were beyond a doubt the last of Paul's life. Almost nothing is to be derived from the Epistles to the Colossians and to Philemon, except that Paul during the first part of his detention in Rome was full of confidence in the future: he tells Philemon to prepare a lodging for him because he is hoping soon to return to his friends. Timothy is with him acting as his scribe; Philippians (i, 1) assign him the same position. Aristarchus and Luke ("the dear physician") are there also. Tychicus who had probably been with him since his journey to Jerusalem with the collection, will carry his letter to the Colossians and visit them on his behalf. Mark, who figures in tradition as the interpreter of Peter, here turns up in the retinue of Paul: a preaching tour may soon bring him to Colossi and the brethren there are bidden to give warm welcome to this "cousin of Barnabas." The information is scanty and perhaps fragile.

In Philippians the outlook to the future is more sombre. While, on the one hand, he can say that his case has attracted much attention "throughout the pretorium"—that is, the imperial tribunal—and outside it, and that the Gospel has had some profit thereby; while, at the end of the Epistle, he seems proud to send to the faithful at Philippi salutations from "the brethren who are of Caesar's household"; while he affirms that his imprisonment "has given many of the brethren confidence in Christ," encouraging them by his presence, though a prisoner, to speak the Word without fear—yet, after all this, he has to add that other propagandists are equally zealous to stir up ill will and to increase his afflictions. Resignation touched with melancholy. Here we find him still hoping for his liberty but facing the possibility of his death. In praising Timothy, whom he will send to Philippi as soon as he can, he writes as one who feels himself all alone (ii, 19–23). Of the Roman community he says nothing. If his trial ends well he will himself come to Philippi. So he thinks no more of going to Spain; nor will he stay in this Rome, so long the object of his dreams; to the East he will return though, if we may trust the Epistle to the Romans,[82] there was no place left there to which he could carry his message (Rom. xv, 19, 23–24).

That the presence of Paul in Rome gave rise to propagandist effort in the two directions he indicates, and that the effort was crowned with success, should cause no astonishment: it explains why the number of victims in the Neronic persecution was so large. Whether Peter was among those whom he discreetly accuses of adding to his afflictions we can only conjecture. The Christian world was then a small one, but the whole of it had an interest in Paul's case. Nothing is more natural than that agents of the Gospel, considerable in number and weighty in influence, should be found active in promoting it at the time, and in the place where the least clairvoyant could see that its fortunes would be determined. That these gospellers were not all eager to come into close relations with Paul is also, given the quarrels of the past and the distress of the present, what we might expect. Needless to say the groups of believers recruited under the two types of apostleship did not constitute a single, homogeneous and centralized community. They were distinct fraternities, carrying the same label and sharing approximately the same hope. We cannot say whether the persecution, which made no distinction between the two, had the effect of uniting what remained of them or whether unity came little by little, until completely achieved at the end of the first century or the beginning of the second.

Had Paul's case been examined in Palestine its Jewish interest would have been apparent and, had the Sanhedrim been judge, what was at stake quickly understood. Paul would have been condemned as an adversary of the Law, as a debaucher of faithful Jews, as a maker of false proselytes, as the founder of a pretended Jewish sect whose root principle, the abrogation of Law, at least in all that concerned the admission of the uncircumcised and the insignificance of Law for salvation, was the very negation of Judaism. It was in these terms that the charge was brought to Rome. That it remained in this form to the end is not certain, nor even probable. The condemnation may have been obtained by a Jewish intrigue which brought into play some powerful influence at the imperial court. But it is also possible, in view of the probable date of the verdict, that the case was examined under all the rules of procedure and that the attention of the judge had been called to the true character of Christianity. In that case the question to be decided by the court would be the legality of the Christian propaganda, as the Epistle to the Philippians seems to say (i, 16), a question brought into the law courts for the first time in the trial of Paul; and it would be upon that propaganda, represented in the person of its great apostle, that sentence of death was pronounced by a Roman judge. Continuing the hypothesis, the court would understand, or at least glimpse the fact, that the new sect was not to be confounded with Judaism, since it claimed to have its place outside Jewish nationality and tradition, and that it embodied only the intolerance of the Jews, now converted into universal propaganda against the established cults and so against the Roman empire which recognized them all as more or less its own. Thus the Roman government, here acting with full knowledge of what it was about, would have declared the Christian propaganda illegal in the highest degree, and Paul by appealing to Caesar in Rome, would have brought about the official denunciation of the Christian religion in that city.

But the main interest of his career is to be sought elsewhere. Thanks to the meagre information preserved for us in the Book of Acts and completed by authentic elements in the Epistles, we are able to form some idea of the way Christianity spread itself between the years 30 and 60, from the East to the West; we see it rejected at its birth by Judaism, and yet making headway everywhere by the help of Judaism, in spite of Judaism and at the expense of Judaism. We may think of it as a train of powder winding into every part of the Roman empire where Judaism had found a footing. Most assuredly the career of Paul is a remarkable sample of this astonishing propaganda. But no more than a sample, and very far from epitomizing or representing the whole movement. Official Judaism, which supported the Sadducees side by side with the Pharisees, and tolerated the Essenes, repudiated Christianity, with violence and from the very first, as treason, as apostasy. It did so because the Christians in claiming Jesus as the Lord Christ and making him an object of worship, with salvation depending on faith in Jesus alone, insulted the Law and destroyed it. Of this new religion Paul was one of the initiators but by no means the only one, nor the first. The Christian propaganda had other agents, some known to us and many more unknown, who laboured in the pagan world under the same conditions as Paul, undeterred by the minor differences among them, all of them more than suspect in the eyes of Judaism, all destined to speedy condemnation by the imperial authority of Rome.

Chapter VI

PERSECUTION BEGINS

THE personal activities of Jesus brought him into collision with constituted Judaism as organized in Palestine under the Roman government. A like collision awaited the propaganda of Stephen in Jerusalem and the later propaganda of Peter and the two sons of Zebedee at the time of Agrippa I in the year 44. Paul in his turn had almost everywhere to undergo hostility from the rulers of the synagogues and, in many towns, an account to settle with the civil magistrates, until finally, caught between the Jewish Sanhedrim and the Roman procurator, he made his appeal to Caesar, an action on his part which brought the question of Christianity for the first time under the jurisdiction of the imperial law court. We have seen in what sense the first decision in the matter was given by that tribunal. That decision was the opening stage of a conflict, hardly foreseen at the time, which was to continue for two centuries and a half and to end in the triumph of the Christian religion. But the jurisprudence applied by the imperial tribunals to the Christian affair was not created by the trial of Paul; the fact to be noted here is that the era of what Christians are wont to style "the persecutions" properly began in the year 64. Our next task will be to define more precisely the position of Christianity under Roman law or, more strictly, under the empire as a political institution, and to ascertain the reasons which caused the empire to "persecute" the Christians. And since the empire not only "persecuted" Christianity, but attempted its suppression and extermination, it behoves us to find out why it did not succeed in either attempt.

1. WHY WERE THE CHRISTIANS PERSECUTED?

A superficial reading of the passage from Tacitus quoted on a former page (*Annals*, xv, 44) might lead us to believe that the persecution under Nero had its origin in a personal caprice of the emperor. But Tacitus is at pains to inform us that the crime alleged against the persons arrested, so far as the mass of them was concerned, was far less that of setting Rome on fire than that of "hating the human race"—an accusation hardly in legal style and vague enough to the modern mind, but charged with precise meaning to the Roman historian and involving the highest political interests of the empire. For Tacitus, "the human race" meant the population of the Mediterranean world then in subjection to Rome.

It was a world organized by the conquering power of Rome; in her drive for domination a single city, the City, had taken possession of it piece by piece. Both City and world now owed obedience to the emperor in whom the power of the City over the world was incarnate. In the sphere of religion, the City not only had gods of its own who had shared with it in the conquest of the world and to whom it paid honour, but itself was also a divine personification and, mystically speaking, a divine personality. Here, then, were two divinities. In one sense the Genius of Rome was the supreme divinity of the empire; beside that divinity was the emperor, the Genius of the living emperor, his imperial personality; he, in practice, was the high god, holding the world in balance. The ancient empires of the East, to which Rome had succeeded, were founded on a like conception. All the gods of the conquered peoples, like the many other gods of Rome itself, continued to function under the shadow of the two protecting deities aforesaid, attending them as helpers, so to speak, but always helping them by a dutiful obedience.

Now there was one god who managed to escape from that duty, at least in principle. This was the god of a despised people, the god of the Jews. He claimed to be the only God. This god, we know, had never been the ruler of a great kingdom, but only of a petty province, and had moreover been conquered at almost regular intervals by all the great monarchs who held successive sway in the East until the arrival of conquerors from the West, who in turn overthrew them, and that with no great effort. But, notwithstanding these humiliations, this god of the lowest of the peoples put forth a claim to be the only god in existence and his worshippers, the Jews, believed him so to be. For them there was no other god but God. Not without some impatience did Rome and her emperor tolerate this insolent caprice of a god and a people so conspicuously remarkable for their own intolerance.

PERSECUTION BEGINS

No symbol of the imperial cult found its way to Jerusalem; Caligula alone, who was mad, set about the introduction of his divine image into the Jewish temple, and would have provoked the bloodiest of all the Jewish revolts had not a timely death put an end to his antics. Things went no further than the offering in the temple of a sacrifice for the emperor on whom the Jewish god was supposed to bestow a blessing, but without the slightest recognition of him as a protector. The empire, reciprocally, was willing enough to recognize this outrageous deity of the Jews, but not for a moment would it accept his claim to the exclusive homage of all the world. In the eyes of the empire at large and the emperor in person, the public proclamation by open propaganda of this deity's intention to impose himself on both of them, to the detriment of all the other existing gods, Rome and Caesar included, would be highly offensive.

Thus it came to pass that when the attempt was made to set up the Jewish god as an effectively independent deity, and when the authority of Nero was challenged by the Jews, under the leadership of men who refused to recognize on earth any master but their God, both god and people at once became the objects of pitiless repression. This was repeated under Hadrian. Rome would not leave to God even the space occupied by his temple in Jerusalem, and did not. This notwithstanding, the Jews preserved the right to worship their god in private and after their own fashion, provided they abstained from propaganda against the gods of the empire and from recruiting proselytes turned into Jews by circumcision. On these terms the Jews were able to keep their religious rule of life, and their god was tolerated as a national deity, but always watched by the police for possible offences to the imperial religion. Rome would tolerate any god who was not intolerant to Rome.

In these conditions Christianity found itself in a position delicately balanced between opposing considerations, of which the mind of that age could neither grasp the meaning nor feel the weight. Although Christians claimed to have the same god as Jews, they were not Jews and had no wish to be, while the Jews on their part repudiated them for the good reason that Christians put themselves outside the Law and its observances. Whatever might be claimed for the god, the religion was not the same. And more, as Christians were not Jews, neither were they another particular nation, side by side with the Jewish. They were only the worshippers of a highly jealous god, no less absolute in his sovereignty than the Jewish deity, having indeed only pretentions to that sovereignty, but unprovided with a nation of hereditary devotees, as were the Jews. This Christian god laid claim to the rule of the whole world, refused to be written down in the catalogue of national divinities and announced his intention to dispossess them all, without delay and without mercy. He was no abstract and remote divinity, with theoretical rights of which the time for enforcement was indeterminate; he was a present god, demanding the prompt submission of all men and the denial, equally prompt, as false and wicked of all the gods to whom the imperial power extended its recognition. In the studied and cautious language put into the mouth of Paul for his discourse before the Areopagus the editor of Acts frames the matter thus: "Passing by the times of ignorance, God now gives warning, to all men everywhere, to repent, because he has fixed the day on which he will judge the world in righteousness by the man he has appointed to be judge, whereof he has given assurance to all men by raising him from the dead."

If the invitation to repent was declined by philosophers with ironical politeness, or greeted with laughter considered permissible in the circumstances, the politicians were quite unable to see the humour of the situation, and that mainly for two reasons: first, because Christian preaching was not carried on in the calm tones affected by the Areopagus discourse; second, because popular fanaticism allowed no leisure to constituted authority for pondering the philosophical bearings of propaganda subversive of all received ideas, at enmity with all the imperial divinities and intervening, with provocative condemnation, in all the forms of worship and superstition current in the pagan world. When the missionaries of Jesus set out on their errand, their purpose was not precisely that of announcing the end of the Mosaic Law and calling for obedience to a law purely moral (they annulled the Law *de facto* without rejecting it *de jure* and were not simply pleading for moral reform); what they announced was the speedy coming of Christ on the clouds of heaven, the overthrow of Satan and his kingdom, which meant nothing less than the complete collapse of idolatry and final end of the idolatrous empire, and the Christ in place of the emperor. So they understood their errand and so their errand was understood by those to whom it was addressed. We can see at a glance why authority was disturbed, why Nero's judges put the same construction on the case of Paul as Pilate had put on the case of Jesus, and why public opinion in the pagan world long regarded the Christians as atheists and horrible examples of impiety and sacrilege. They were judged to be capable of the most abominable crimes, and not only capable, but guilty. And the public would have believed it even if the Jews had not made a contribution of their own to the libel, as the apologists of the second century accuse them of doing. But it was not upon Jewish information that Tacitus, speaking of Jesus and the Christians, based his epithets "disastrous superstition," "plague," "atrocity and shame."[1]

The first collective persecution of the Christians took place at Rome under Nero, towards the close of the year 64, very soon after sentence had been passed on Paul. The occasion was the fire which destroyed a great part of the imperial city. Beginning on July 19th it continued for six days and despite the efforts made to check it broke out again, when thought to be under control, and lasted for three days more—an event of ample scope to give free play to the imagination. When at last the calamity came to an end and the first and most urgent remedies had been applied, and the gods placated, as was fitting, by solemn propitiations, the hunt for the guilty was taken up in earnest. Pure chance may well have been the chief criminal, some common accident occurring under conditions favourable to the spread of fire. But in all such cases it is the way of the populace to seek for causes proportioned to the magnitude of the disaster; to account for a conflagration so monstrous incendiaries must have been at work whose criminal capacities were out of the ordinary. If Tacitus is to be believed, public rumour fixed on no less a person than Nero, who thereupon sought to clear himself by accusing the Christians: "ergo abolendo rumori Nero subdidit reos et quaesitissimis poenis afficit *quos per flagitia invisos vulgus christianos appellabat.*" Perhaps Nero had no need to invent this calumny, his friends merely taking advantage of a tale already in circulation, by way of deflecting from his person a charge which, it is permissible to think, he had not deserved.

According to Tacitus the first victims seized were some persons "who confessed." But what did they confess and under what conditions? The question will long be discussed whether they confessed to incendiary acts or merely to being Christians.[2] It may well be that the last offence was held to involve the first, the Christians being judged in advance as the worst of criminals. Remembering, moreover, the expectations and hopes by which every Christian was animated, is it not likely that many of them, as they watched the flaming city, must have thought that the end of Satan's reign was at last coming and the punishment of the wicked actually begun? To explain the accusation against them we have no need to suppose that a few were mad enough to lend a helping hand to the judgment of God.[3] But not for them was the horror, the panic, the desolation of the Roman populace; some perhaps were caught in the act of expressing their joy. Such being their general attitude, there is no need to go further in seeking the origin of a calumny which must have seemed a probable truth to those who first gave it utterance and found ready belief among the masses. It is not true, however, as Duchesne asserts (i, 64) that Tacitus allows us "to see that nobody attributed the fire to the Christians." Preferring, for his own part, the hypothesis of Nero's guilt, and insinuating it as the true explanation, Tacitus confines himself to saying that the motive of the condemnation, as it fell on the mass of the condemned, was not their supposed incendiarism but "hatred of the human race." The people, he remarks, at length took compassion on the victims "although they had deserved the extremity of punishment," the ingenuity displayed in varying the modes of execution having made it apparent that they were rather designed to satisfy the cruel instincts of him who ordered them than to meet the lawful demands of public anger: "Unde, quanquam *adversus sontes et novissima exempla meritos*, miseratio oriebatur, tanquam non utilitate publica, sed in saevitiam unius absumerenter." Thus it would appear that common opinion, fully shared by Tacitus, approved prosecution and the death penalty as justly due to the Christians, although the majority of them were not chargeable with the burning of Rome and do not seem to have been charged.

The last of the accused, like the first, were condemned as criminals under the common law without the need arising to create *ad hoc* legislation against the new religion. Tertullian himself asserts that the precedent of Nero determined the judicial position for his successors without further difficulty (*Ad Nationes*, i, 7). The correspondence of Pliny and Trajan in the year 111 does not presuppose the existence of a law directed against Christians in particular; it merely implies the point of view, a natural and spontaneous product of established institutions and customs, that the profession of Christianity was, by itself, a crime to be punished by death. No edict proscribing the Christians was issued under Nero; but on the occasion of the fire there took place at Rome a hunt for Christians which led to a great number of them being done to death. There are no grounds for thinking that a general persecution was then set on foot, but we can well believe that both then and later popular ill will in various places caused many a Christian to perish, however little the Roman magistrates, from good nature or policy, were inclined to take part in their destruction. The principle *non licet Christianos esse*, though never formally inscribed on the statute book, was in the air and governed the practice of the court whenever a Christian was put on his trial.

The multitude of martyrs who perished at Rome in the year 64 left no names behind them; for us they are anonymous. Taken by surprise, and doubtless thrown into utter confusion, the Christian community was in no shape to draw up a prompt balance sheet of its losses. Moreover, at this early date it were better to speak of Christian groups than of a single organized community. The victims, at the mercy of chance denunciation, increased in number from day to day, but there was no governing body to register their names and construct a martyrology. The Epistle of Clement to the Corinthians (5–6) speaks of these victims, but only by allusion and in terms more vague in substance, if not more general, than those used by Tacitus. In this document we find the leading place among the martyrs of 64 already assigned, it would seem, to Peter and Paul, presented as the two great founders of the Roman church, Peter, as the presumed founder of the Roman episcopate, being given precedence to Paul. If the letter of Clement was composed at Rome only some thirty years after their martyrdom it is surely matter for astonishment that the references it makes to the two apostles contain not a single informative detail as to the circumstances under which they met their death. We are inclined to think that the author knew hardly more about Peter and Paul, except the bare fact of their martyrdom, than anyone may read for himself in Acts and Second Corinthians. Although legendary tradition seems to place the death of Paul at the end of the persecution of 64, and liturgical tradition leaves us to suppose that both apostles died on the same day,[4] the probability, as we have pointed out above, is that Paul perished some time before the persecution.

The fate of Peter is far more obscure than that of Paul. Of Paul we know fairly well both the time and the circumstances of his coming to Rome. Of Peter's coming to the city we know nothing. The chief argument in support of the Roman tradition that Peter came to Rome and perished there is that no other tradition and no evidence of any kind in Christian antiquity can be found to contradict it. This argument, though not absolutely decisive, is not without weight. True it is that Ephesus, during the pascal controversy, could make claim to the apostle John without meeting a protest, and Rome might well have made an equally unfounded claim to Peter without encountering opposition; but there is a difference; ancient Christian documents give the critic ground for contesting the pretension of Ephesus to John, but contain nothing to authorize an off-hand denial of the pretention of Rome to Peter. On the other hand, direct evidence as to Peter's fate is neither very old nor very precise. From the Epistle to the Romans (especially xv, 17–23) we may deduce, at least with some probability, that Peter was not then in Rome and could not have been there up to the time when the Epistle was written. We learn from the Epistle to the Galatians (ii, 11) that Peter arrived in Antioch in the year 44 or a little later;[5] but the Book of Acts which records his departure from Jerusalem at that date says not a word of what happened to him afterwards. But the editor of this book, who may well have had a motive for saying nothing about Peter going to Antioch, had seemingly no motive for keeping silence about his being in Rome when Paul was there, and would presumably have mentioned it if precise information had been in his hands about a ministry carried on by Peter in Rome before the conclusion of Paul's trial.[6] We have just seen the contribution made to the subject by the letter of Clement; it amounts to a probability in favour of Peter's martyrdom in Rome. The letter of Ignatius to the Romans seems to regard Peter and Paul together as Apostles of Rome;[7] but this letter, if later than 150, adds nothing to Clement's testimony or to the more recent Dionysius of Corinth.[8] The name "Babylon" in First Peter is probably intended for Rome as the place from which the Epistle was written:[9] but the Epistle is not authentic and this trait, while proving the relative antiquity of the Roman tradition, brings us little nearer to the time in question than Clement does. The same holds true of the allusion to Peter's martyrdom in the last chapter of the fourth Gospel and in the Apocalypse of Peter.[10] The Epistle to the Hebrews (xiii, 7), if we may take it as addressed to the Roman Christians, vaguely attests the same tradition as Clement, but at an earlier date. We conclude, then, that the Roman tradition has an old, firm but rather narrow and bare foundation in traditional reminiscence. Peter had been in Rome for some time, beginning perhaps at a date just before the death of Paul, when he became engulfed in the *multitudo ingens* which Nero so cruelly put to death. The survivors of the slaughter may well have known but little of the circumstances of his death. Whether the tradition concerning the place of his burial is exact or conjectural is a question of very little import to the history of the Christian religion.[11]

2. Roman Law versus the Christian Religion

Roman Christianity was not entirely destroyed in the year 64 and even if it had been would not have been slow to form again, as it was formed before, by the influx of believers coming in from outside regions to carry on their propaganda and increase the number of adherents in the city, as it had done from the first. But there seems to have been no solution of continuity. The action of Nero did no more than create a temporary arrest and great disturbance in the process of its growth. Soon enough, under the Flavian Emperors, it was destined to win back its first importance. By the destruction of Jerusalem and of the temple in the year 70, Christianity lost its original centre and, we may add, its point of attachment to Judaism. The community of old believers in Jerusalem had been scattered abroad before the date of the siege and continued to exist only in a few small groups in the North of Palestine and beyond the Jordan.[12] The time was not far distant when the capital of the Roman Empire would become in fact, and then proclaim itself by right, the metropolis of the Christian world. But that great development had its own dangers.

Though fanatical Judaism had been suppressed in the year 70, but not completely extinguished—for the fire smouldered under the ashes till the time of Trajan and Hadrian—and though moderate Judaism, represented at Rome by persons in credit with the Emperors, retained its legal status, the position of Christianity in presence of Roman law was not thereby made any clearer. Speaking more exactly, it cleared up to the detriment of Christianity in proportion as the new religion became completely independent of Judaism and was recognized as independent by the Roman authorities. The Jews were not likely to countenance any confusion of the two religions, and the efforts of the Christians to acquire parity of treatment by the law were all in vain. They profited only by the favour shown to Jewish monotheism in certain circles of Roman society, and these not the least considerable.

The "foreign superstition" of which Pomponia Graecina, a Roman lady, was accused in the time of Nero (Tacitus, *Annals*, xiii, 32) and for which she was pardoned by her husband who, as head of the family, claimed the right to judge her, was probably the Christian religion. There were clearer cases under Domitian. Acilius Glabrio, consul in 91, is a probable case; that of Flavius Clemens, consul in 95, is certain.[13] According to Dio Cassius, Clemens and his wife Flavia Domitilla "were accused of atheism, an accusation which in those days made victims of many among the followers of Jewish morals." Domitian's financial policy may well have led him, not quite without intention, to confuse the Christians with the Jews, and so make the most of the *fiscus judaicus* by treating as adherents of Judaism all who adopted Jewish morals, even though uncircumcised. It should be noted, however, that what we have now to do with are the legal trials, few or many, of individuals accused of Christianity and ending in the death penalty or confiscation of goods. Clemens was executed; but this did not prevent Domitian keeping the two sons of Clemens near his person and having them educated, as his presumptive heirs, by Quintilian the rhetorician. No doubt political considerations had their part in the affair of Clemens whose uncommon "incapacity," *contemptissimae inertiae*, attested by Suetonius, may have been partly the result of his preoccupation with a mystical religion. Before that, Flavius Sabinus, father of Clemens, brother of Vespasian, and prefect of Rome under Nero, was reputed a man of very gentle disposition whom some, in his old age, had accused of weakness, though the worst to be said of him was "a man of moderation and sparing of the blood of his fellow citizens" (Tacitus, *History*, iii, 65–75). There is an affinity between the temper of this family and the spirit of the Christian religion.

An idea of the legal position of Christianity at the beginning of the second century can be derived from the correspondence between Pliny the Younger, who was legate in Bithynia in 111–112 (or 112–113), and the emperor Trajan about the procedure to be followed when Christians were on trial for the offence of their religion. We learn in the first place that this Roman magistrate, up to the time of his assuming office, had never taken part in the trials of Christians. "Cognitionibus de Christianis interfui nunquam; ideo nescio, quid et quatenus aut puniri soleat aut quaeri." All Pliny knows is that the profession of Christianity is punishable by death, but he is ignorant how the charge should be defined in judicial practice, which he had been obliged to define for himself, as best he could, according to his sense of justice, in the numerous cases when denounced Christians had been brought into his court. Neither he nor the clerks of the court knew of anything in the statute book to guide them in the course to follow in such affairs. In his answer Trajan shows that he knew no more than they did and gives no positive instructions, contenting himself with an approval of the procedure discreetly recommended by Pliny in his own letter.

This letter reveals that, to begin with, certain denunciations had been brought before the court which Pliny had dealt with as follows: a threefold interrogation of the denounced persons under threat of the death penalty if the Christianity of which they were accused were not denied; execution of those who admitted the charge and persisted, unless they had the status of Roman citizens; remand to the imperial tribunal of those who had that status. It seems clear that renegades were pardoned and set free without further formality. The ground assigned by Pliny for the condemnation of the others is their obstinacy, a seemingly insufficient offence, since mere stubbornness is not itself a capital crime. All the same it was the best reason Pliny could assign for passing sentence on the Christian "Name"—setting aside the crimes attributed to the Christians by popular rumour, of which crimes he, for his part, was inclined to think them innocent. It must not be overlooked, however, that he considered himself to be legally empowered to require the accused to offer sacrifice to the gods and to the image of Caesar, and regarded an obstinate refusal as a kind of rebellion. On the other hand, he judged the religion, on which the refusal was based, to be an extraordinary superstition, but harmless enough in itself. In all of which we discern the mind of an experienced politician.

The first trials led on to others, and a multitude of denunciations came out in an unsigned document containing a long list of names. Though the charges were not in regular form, Pliny, at this further development, proceeded with greater severity than before, probably because his Council had found him too lenient in the earlier trials. Some of the persons named in the list declared they were not Christians and never had been; if these made no difficulty about invoking the gods and doing homage to their images and to the emperor's, by libation of wines and burning of incense, and finally by cursing the Christ (all flatly refused, we are told, by true Christians), their cases were dismissed. Others confessed to being Christians, but were induced to repudiate Christianity under threat of the death penalty for persisting; there were also some who said they had been Christians, but were so no longer, having given up the religion three years ago, or even twenty years ago: all these consented to perform the same acts as those who declared they had never been Christians. This notwithstanding, Pliny would not let them go scot free, but kept them prisoners pending the arrival of the emperor's instructions, doubtless because his counsellors had again advised him to hesitate before taking the apostasy of these people as proof of their innocence. Meanwhile he continued the inquisition, of which the results up to date are here passed on to Trajan.

All these renegades or apostates from Christianity emphatically affirmed that they had committed no offence or misdemeanour beyond meeting habitually on a fixed day before the dawn (*ante lucem*) for the purpose of singing together a hymn to the Christ, as to a god, and that the oath[14] they had taken as Christians, far from pledging them to commit crime of any kind, pledged them not to commit theft, brigandage, adultery, betrayal of trust or appropriation of trust-money. They alleged further that after singing their hymn, they gathered together for an innocent meal in common, and that they had discontinued even this since the legate had promulgated Trajan's decree against associations.[15] Clearly these people were regarded by Pliny as harmless enough. From the reports submitted to him he had formed an idea of their Christ identical with that of Tacitus; it was that the Christians in their meetings celebrated as a god the man who had founded their sect, and this founder he knew, as Tacitus did, under his surname of Christ.

It is to be noted from the above that one effect of the imperial edicts in Bithynia had been to change the custom of the Supper, which was no longer kept in the evening as an ordinary evening meal, but in the early morning. That it was completely suppressed is hardly probable.

A last feature to be noted in the correspondence concerns the interior economy of the congregations. To obtain fuller information on all these points Pliny caused two women employed in serving at the meetings, and having the title of "deaconess" proper to that employment, to be questioned under torture. It is clear that these women did not abjure the Christ; but the legate was able to learn nothing more from them than the renegades had already told him, unless it were the perversity and extravagance of their superstition, "*superstitiam pravam, immodicam*"—which we may understand as referring to the fanatical stubbornness of the women in their intolerant and absurd belief. The legate says nothing to indicate the existence of any priestly organization, though doubtless the Christian groups in Bithynia had their elders and deacons. We need hardly ask how Pliny finished with the obstinate deaconesses: he had them put to death in common with all the other persons denounced in the list who confessed to being Christians and did not apostatize.

He had no desire, however, to multiply these executions and his writing to the emperor was an attempt to induce him to lay down a policy of moderation. The fact plainly is that the number of people denounced was too great for prosecution to be desirable, especially if punishment had to be inflicted on the renegades who had apostatized under threat as well as on those who had abandoned Christianity of their own accord after practising it for some time; they included persons of both sexes, of all ages, of every condition, and were found in the country districts as well as in the towns. A moderated system of repression, says Pliny, had already produced good results: the congregations which had abandoned the temples of the gods, are now beginning to come back; there is better attendance at the festivals and a better sale for the sacrificial meats. Clearly the contagion has been checked, and there will be no great difficulty in recovering the deluded masses if pardon be granted them on repenting of their folly. "Visa est enim mihi res digna consultatione, maxime propter periclitantium numerum. Multi enim omnis aetatis, omnis ordinis, utriusque sexus etiam vocantur in periculum et vocabuntur. Neque civitates tantum, sed vicos etiam atque agros superstitionis istius contagio pervagata est: quae videtur sisti et corrigi posse. Certe satis constat prope jam desolata templa cœpisse celebrari, et sacra sollemnia diu intermissa repeti pastumque venire victimarum, cujus adhuc rarissimus emptor inveniebatur. Ex quo facile est opinari, quae turba hominum emendari possit, si sit pœnitentiae locus."

In all this Pliny may well have been under some illusion as to the efficacy of his tactics. But he was a philosophical magistrate, sincere and goodhearted, whose pity for the Christians was greater than his hatred of Christianity, a man who regarded persecution to the last extremity as hardly less absurd than the extremes of Christian fanaticism. So, with a pretty clear notion of what answer he would get, he decided to bring the following questions in plain terms before Trajan:

(1) Whether in the trial of Christians, account should be taken of the tender age of children who might be denounced.
(2) Whether a person who has been a Christian, but is so no longer, is not entitled to pardon.
(3) Whether the mere profession of the Christian name is a punishable offence without other proof of criminality or with only such proof as was given by common opinion of the crimes attributed to the name.[16]

These questions Pliny places at the head of his letter, the whole of which is framed in a manner likely to suggest the answers he considered suitable.

Trajan approves what Pliny has done. The problem is complicated and the particular differences make it impossible to apply a uniform rule. There must be no hunting down of Christians, as though the intention of the government were to make an end of them at a blow. When denounced and convicted they are to be punished, and about that there are to be no half measures; the punishment will be death. Christians who recant must be pardoned subject to the conditions observed by Pliny in the judgments given first. And that is all. Trajan evades the distinction Pliny had proposed between the crime of adopting the Name and the crimes connected with the Name in the opinion of the public. Pliny inclines to pardon those accused of the Name but not of the crimes: Trajan answers as though, like Tacitus, he regarded the Name and the crimes as really inseparable. But he fails to see that in letting renegades go scot free he is either pardoning criminals or contradicting himself. Of the two correspondents Pliny was the more humane and the more sagacious; Trajan was the more astute politician, his treatment of the affair revealing a mentality of mediocre good sense conformed to the popular opinion of his time. Obstinacy, in his view, is a real crime. If he understood Pliny's meaning he may have said to himself that popular opinion, after all, was not very far wrong in regarding the Christians as criminals and that these people, even if innocent of the ritual and other abominations charged against them, lived, thought and laboured in ways opposed to Roman law and order. Some political reason it must have been that induced Trajan to pass over without notice Pliny's distinction between the Name and criminality, or that referring to the age of the accused in which Pliny had shown himself inclined to confine conviction to responsible adults. (In fact women were often condemned and adolescents occasionally.) Had he not said, moreover, that a few examples would be enough to bring back the mass of Christians into the common road of fidelity to the gods? On the other hand might we not say that Trajan shows himself a man of greater moderation than Pliny by forbidding him to receive anonymous denunciations? "*Sine auctore vero propositi libelli in nullo crimine locum habere debent. Nam et pessimi exempli nec nostri saeculi est.*"

We cannot but believe that both Pliny and Trajan did their best in their respective positions, but that the problem was one of those which go beyond the ordinary reach, always relative, of the human mind. How is it possible, without provoking violence and revolution, to reconcile an established social order, which seems to satisfy the demands of reason, with the consummate folly of a movement which aims at setting up a new and better order for mankind? In cases of this kind the road into the future has its course marked out not by men, but by events; and it is a road that has no ending.

The rescript of Hadrian to Minutius Fundamus (*Eusebius*, iv, 9) is on the same lines as Trajan's letter to Pliny. The emperor's instructions are that punishment is not to be inflicted on Christians in response to popular clamour; their trials are to be conducted in legal form on the strength of accusations drawn up according to the rules, the exact observance of which the judge will see to. If the accusation is unfounded, the informer is to be punished. But if the accusation is proved, if the accused confesses and declares his intention to remain a Christian, he is none the less to be sentenced and put to death.

With the measures prescribed by Trajan, Hadrian and Antoninus,[17] goodwill towards Christians had nothing to do; the real motive was regard for public order, for moderation, for sound policy. Not for a moment did the idea of protecting Christianity enter their minds; their aim was to keep it in check and repress it with the minimum of violence. So far was this from providing Christians with security, that the right to be Christians was always denied them. They were continually at the mercy of denunciation, of popular passion, of the hostility by which a magistrate, municipal or imperial, might chance to be animated.

Was there any sign of response from the Christian side to this relative appeasement? Was no effort made to mute the strings of that "hatred of the human race" which Tacitus pretends to have been proved against the martyrs of 64? It now behoves us to attempt an answer to these questions.

We search the Book of Revelation in vain for the faintest sign of mitigated hatred. This book reflects the mentality of the Christians in Asia, at least of their notables, of those whose part it was to animate and sustain the faith of the others. Not only did the author live in hourly expectation of the Second Coming; he lived also in the atmosphere of martyrdom, and dreams only of persecution and death. At the time of his writing few were being made martyrs on the earth, but a considerable number had already arrived in heaven and the immediate future was to be a time of trial for every believer still alive. The prophet comes little short of counting all the saints as martyrs and seems to believe that every true Christian will come to a violent end. He beholds in heaven a multitude of souls supplicating the Eternal to take vengeance on their persecutors. "And a white robe"—their glorified body—"was given to every one of them, and they were bidden to hold their peace a little longer until their fellow servants and their brethren had all been slain, as themselves had been" (Rev. vi, 11). In his vision of triumph, those who have been marked on earth with the seal of the living God, and now stand before God's throne and before the Lamb, are all in one class: they are "those who have come through the great tribulation and washed their robes and made them white in the blood of the Lamb" (Rev. vii, 14; xx, 4). But we have only to read attentively the letters to the seven congregations which introduce the great revelation (ii–iii) to satisfy ourselves that all the believers of that time were not quite in harmony with the grand diapason of the author's words; he bemoans and chides the lukewarm, puts it on record that fervour is declining in many quarters and foresees a time of positive defection. It would seem that Pliny's repressive action in Bithynia had produced as many renegades as martyrs, if not more. But the spirit of the Church was not in the renegades. It was incarnate in those of whom Pliny says that nothing could stir them from their outrageous superstition. These were the martyrs and their prophet was John.

John and his martyrs are not among Rome's well-wishers. They are preoccupied with the prospect of her coming overthrow. From end to end the Apocalypse is filled with the recital of calamities about to overwhelm the pagan world, persecutor of the children of God. Rome is the abominable Beast whom the Dragon has raised up against God, Christ and his faithful ones. It is Satan who makes men worship the Beast and his image, and compels all the Beast's worshippers to bear his mark. Inasmuch as the Beast is Rome he is also the Emperor of Rome; his image, which all must worship, is the image of Caesar (xiii, 16–17)—and let us not forget how Pliny compelled the renegades to burn incense in its honour. But here are the angels to proclaim the end of the empire and vengeance on idolators. One cries out: "She is fallen, she is fallen, Babylon the great, who made all nations drunk with the wine of fury and of her shamelessness" (xiv, 8). Another makes proclamation: "If anyone worships the Beast and his image and bear the Beast's mark on his forehead, or even on his hand, he too shall drink wine of fury, the fury of God, which is poured out without mixture in the cup of his wrath: he shall be tormented with fire and brimstone in the presence of the angels and of the Lamb, and the smoke of his torment shall go up for ever and ever" (xiv, 9–11). And then a word of warning to the renegades; for them, as for the idolators, eternal death is in store. Finally (xvii–xviii) our author describes with relish the punishment of the Great Harlot, before passing on to the triumph of the Christ and his saints.

We look in vain for documents of the same period inspired by a less fiery zeal for the annihilation of Rome and her empire. Unfortunately the New Testament books which evince some degree of respect for established order and constituted authority are of uncertain date. If the Epistle to the Romans were the authentic work of Paul in all its parts he could be cited as having taught the faithful in Rome to reverence the temporal powers and render them sincere obedience as instituted by God, as all authority is, for the protection of the good and the punishment of the wicked.[18] But this wise instruction is a late addition which can hardly be as early as the first century. The same must be said of the First Epistle of Peter where the same lesson is given in analogous terms (ii, 13–17) with a commentary which suggests a date near the time of Pliny. In effect the author insists not only that Christians are under strict obligation to be irreproachable in their conduct, but also that the calumnies now pursuing them make such conduct both necessary and expedient. From his own point of view he draws the same distinction as Pliny does between the "name" Christian and the crimes attached to it by common opinion. "If ye are insulted for the name of Christ, happy are ye! That any one of you should suffer as a murderer, a thief, a rogue or as guilty of sedition, must not be. But if he suffers for being a Christian, let him not be ashamed of that, but let him thank God for it. For this is the time when judgment begins in the household of God; and if it begins with us what will be the fate of those who reject his Gospel" (ii, 14–17). A day is coming, then, when punishment, as foretold by the author of Revelation, will fall on the unbelievers. Meanwhile, let the Christian govern his conduct in loyalty to the powers that be, even though they persecute him.

The First to Timothy goes further: "Before all else I lay it upon you to make supplications, prayers, intercessions, thanksgivings for all men, for kings"—meaning emperors—"and for all in authority, that we may lead a quiet and peaceful life in piety and honour, which is a good and acceptable thing in the eyes of God our Saviour, who will have all men to be saved and come to the knowledge of the truth" (ii, 1–4). Here was a believer with a mind wholly set on peace, whose hopes were centred on the conversion rather than the destruction of the Roman empire. In like manner, Clement, concluding the long prayer inserted at the end of his Epistle, calls down all the blessings of heaven on the bearers of the imperial mandate, to the end that their power may be used according to the will of God (*Corinthians* 61). We may conclude that by the age of the

Antonines the Christian mind had turned definitely towards appeasement.

Need it be added that the Gospels and Acts are in a current of feeling less embittered and more deferential to Roman authority? Pilate, when confronted by Jesus, is represented by the Gospels in an attitude identical with that of Pliny toward the Christians in his province. His goodwill for the Christ, suggested in the drawing of the scene, is intended not only to remove all suspicion of rebellion against the empire from the presumed founder of Christianity; it is introduced for the further reason that some Roman magistrates were by the time the story was told adopting a policy of moderation in dealing with the Christians, in spite of the fact that official jurisprudence, supported by popular fanaticism, required their condemnation to death. The belief, thus indicated, that moderation was on the increase, cannot have risen in the Christian mind at the time when it was under the impression of the frightful experience of the year 64, nor while Christians were suffering the hardships imposed by Domitian. It belongs to a period later than the reign of Domitian (81–96) when Roman policy had consciously and of set purpose adopted the rule of go-slow in its persecution of the Christians. The saying attributed to Jesus about tribute owed to Caesar was intended, by whoever conceived it, to put Christians on a higher plane than Jewish zealots; it may have been invented at an early date among the Jewish Christians of Palestine who had not joined the Zealots in their great revolt. But the birth of the fiction cannot be confidently dated and may be no earlier than the period when the Jerusalem ministry of Jesus was systematically arranged in the common tradition of the Synoptics.

The apologetic of Acts is constructed in the same spirit as the passages from the Epistles cited above: constituted authority—with the exception of the Jewish—is always shown as either indifferent or benevolent to the cause of Christianity, nor does the editor despair of a coming time when Christian propaganda, represented by him as ever respectful to the Roman government, will be tolerated, as Judaism actually is; while the discourse to the Areopagus goes so far as to hint that pagans, without their knowing it, may be worshipping the same God as the Christians. The apologists of the second century adopt the same conciliatory attitude, though the regime of persecution has not been abandoned either in theory or practice, and they themselves are under its threat.

3. Philosophers Intervene

The popular dislike, in some respects profoundly unjust, which had fallen on the Christian religion and the strange jurisprudence which condemned Christians to death by approving suspicions which made them guilty of crimes of which they knew they were innocent, was bound to raise up apologists as soon as Christianity could produce men of sufficient capacity to put the case before the reading public and explain the extraordinary position in which Christians were placed by the joint action of common opinion and public authority. On the other side the reading public in general and the philosophers in particular began to take an interest in Christianity, but without the least sign of goodwill. Justin, the apologist of whom we shall soon have to speak, had at his elbow a Cynic philosopher named Crescens who was out for Justin's head and eventually got it; Fronto, the tutor of Marcus Aurelius, accused the Christians, in a published writing, of practising the rites of Thyestes; and Celsus was soon to come forward between 170 and 180, with an almost scientific refutation of the new religion, ending, however, by proposals for a sort of compromise with Christianity.

Of the apology presented to the emperor Hadrian by a certain Quadratus we know next to nothing. The moderate policy of the emperors evidently encouraged the Christians in efforts to gain acceptance for their claims. Quadratus, who lived in Asia, seems to have been a Christian prophet. The most remarkable feature of his apology, retained by Eusebius (iv, 3),[19] is the mention of persons raised from the dead by Jesus, of whom some were said to be still alive in the time of the apologist. As the evangelical tradition has no knowledge of these numerous resurrections, we must conclude that Quadratus was either exaggerating or that his only knowledge of the raised persons came to him in a vision. The proceeding of Quadratus had been prompted by vexations inflicted on the Christians in his part of the world.

The apology of Aristides, an Athenian philosopher, was

addressed to the emperor Antoninus[20] in the early years of his reign (before 147). The author, after presenting the neoplatonic idea of God as the Christian idea—which reminds us of the discourse to the Areopagus—gives summary refutation to the chief forms of polytheism, and then discusses Judaism, true in theology and ethics but a cult of angels;[21] finally he expounds the Christian faith and way of life. Christians, he says, acknowledge one God and one only, creator of the world, and they obey his commandments while waiting for the age to come in which they will see the Christ and receive the fulfilment of his promises. The description of Christian morals has a close affinity with the moral part of the *Didache* and with what Pliny's letter tells of the declarations made by the Christians; evidently the basis of it all is some catechism widely used in those times. But of Christology there is virtually nothing, unless we count as Christology the statement that the precepts of God are the precepts of the Christ, that Christians are willing to suffer all things for his name and their supreme hope is that of seeing him. The dominant purpose of the author is to present Christianity as a lofty religious philosophy, imposing irreproachable conduct on its adepts; this last point receiving particular attention in view of the current calumnies. The attenuated eschatology may betoken deliberate avoidance of a dangerous subject; but it may equally result from the fact that by this time expectation of the Second Coming had considerably cooled down and the attention of believers become more concentrated on the needs and duties of the present life.

It was to Antoninus also that Justin, about the year 152, addressed his *Apology*. He, too, professed to be a philosopher, "going about," as Duchesne describes him, "from city to city, dressed in his short cloak, and bearing the message of an independent thinker."[22] He was born at Neapolis in the country of the Samaritans. Never a great philosopher, he knew the different schools, notably that of the Platonists, but he was a troubled soul on whom the constancy of the Christian martyrs, of which he has been sometimes a witness, had made a deep impression. Becoming instructed in Christianity he adopted it about the year 133, probably at Ephesus, where about 135 he had a debate with the Jewish doctor Trypho. Thence he came to Rome and seems to have remained there a considerable time. He continued to wear the garb peculiar to the philosophers and to practise their manner of walking, discoursing in public on Christian doctrine and presenting it as a philosophy, or speculation of wise men, on the meaning and purpose of life, as were the other philosophies of that time, some more or less coloured by mysticism. Many writings came from his pen, not only in defence of Christians' faith against pagans, but also against gnostic heresies then swarming within the fold, and notably against Marcion. At Rome he had a public debate with Crescens, a Cynic philosopher who, like most of the philosophers of the time, was hot against the Christians. Crescens, however, knew very little about them and having the worst of it in the debate, he tried to get his adversary judicially condemned; whereupon, Justin quitted Rome, to return a little later under Marcus Aurelius. He resumed his teaching, was arrested with other Christians, tried and put to death.

With the freedom proper to the philosopher, Justin, in his *Apology*, presents his plea to Antoninus, the "pious" emperor; to his adopted sons, Marcus Aurelius, the "philosopher," and Lucius Verus, to the Senate and the entire Roman people. It is a plea "on behalf of men of every race who are hated and persecuted, himself, Justin, being one of them" (1 *Apology*, 1). Men such as those for whom he is appealing, "truly pious men and philosophers," ought not to be judged by preconceived opinion but by reality. Christians should not be condemned, except for proved crimes (if they have committed them) and not for a mere name which, by itself, proves nothing for or against those who bear it (2–4). Justin admits that some sects claiming to be Christian may not be quite irreproachable: all the more reason to make inquisition only for crimes and not to condemn a name honourably borne by the majority[23] of its bearers (5). Certainly the allegation is true that Christians worship God only and no idols, and look upon sacrifices as futile; they know very well that idolatry was the work of "evil spirits who had appeared in olden time."[24] Socrates denounced it, and the demons had him put to death as an atheist and a man of impiety; and now they are treating Christians in the same way, because the Logos, who spoke by the mouth of Socrates, "become man and named Jesus-

Christ," has revealed the truth to the barbarians. So far as these false gods are concerned the Christians are atheists; but they worship and reverence the true God, His Son Jesus-Christ, whom He has sent, and "the host of other good angels who resemble him and follow in his train."25 "When you hear it said that we await a kingdom, rightly you suppose that we mean a human kingdom; but it is of God's Kingdom that we speak, a kingdom in the life that is eternal, persuaded that God will render to every man according to his works; moreover it is the Christians' belief in this coming judgment that makes them, "of all men, the greatest lovers of peace." If all the world were penetrated by a belief so salutary, not a single wicked man would remain in existence. "In truth you seem to fear that all men will become virtuous and that nobody will be left for you to punish" (i, 11–12).

We are almost led to think that Justin takes no interest in the common eschatology, in spite of the fact that he knows the Apocalypse of John and professes millenarianism in his *Dialogue with Trypho* (81). The reason is that the *Dialogue* was intended for the edification of Christians while the *Apology* was written for pagans. Moreover, even in the Apology, the attenuation of apocalyptic eschatology is more apparent than real: in Justin's outlook the days of the Roman empire are numbered, and the best the emperors themselves can do is to make ready for the Day of Judgment (i, 68).

Justin expatiates widely on Christian ethics, citing the Gospels with a copiousness unknown in all the earlier Christian literature, and not overlooking the story of the tribute. In his commentary on that saying there is a note of pride. "Since it is our duty to render to Caesar what is Caesar's and to God what is God's, our adoration is wholly given to Him; in all other things we willingly obey you, recognizing you as kings and leaders of men and praying that in you the wisdom of reason may be one with the power of kingship" (17). For emperors must die like other men and they will be judged like other men. Dilating on that, Justin proves that men do not wholly die, appealing to necromancy, possession by spirits, oracles, the descent of Ulysses into Hades, and then caps his argument by adducing the probabilities in favour of the resurrection of the dead. As to the final destruction of the world by fire, do not the Stoics teach almost the same?

All is grist that comes to the mill of this brave apologist. What Christians tell about Jesus, he remarks, is precisely what pagans tell of the sons of Zeus, Hermes, Dionysus, Hercules, the Dioscuri and others. But all these stories are the work of demons and offer no example for human conduct. By contrast, everything is pure in Jesus; he is the veritable word and messenger of God, like Hermes; born of God, since, like Perseus, he was conceived by a virgin; resembling Dionysus in being put to death; and let us not forget his miracles, which allow of comparison with Asclepius. But in reality, the Christ alone has the special gifts which befit his name—the Son of God. The stories told of the false gods are wicked caricatures concocted in advance by bad demons, or fictions put by them into the minds of poets. Since then and until quite recently the invention of false gods has been going on: it was the demons who helped Simon Magus to get himself accepted as a god in Samaria, and has he not a statue even in Rome?[26] After him his disciple Menander fooled plenty of people at Antioch; and at this present moment there is a fellow named Marcion, of Pontus, going about everywhere proclaiming that he has a better god than the Creator of the universe.[27] The followers of these gentry are not to be confounded with true Christians. Them he goes on to defend, contrasting their well-ordered life with the debauches of the pagans, and not hesitating to mention the scandalous affair of Antinous, the favourite of Hadrian, drowned in the Nile and afterwards deified by the emperor.

Man has ever been an inventor of gods and invents them still; such at least is the opinion of Justin. But the fact emerging from this development of apology, which the modern reader will find most instructive, is that, all things considered, the mentality of a second century Christian, even an enlightened one, was not so far removed as one might think from the mentality of his pagan contemporaries; and this should help us to a better understanding of the atmosphere in which the Christian mystery, to be discussed in the next chapter, was gradually formed and of the influences contributing to its formation. The difference between Christianity and paganism is much less in theology—

than it is in mythology—and much less in metaphysics than in moral idealism.

Then comes a long dissertation on the fulfilment of Jewish prophecy in the person and history of Jesus. By the boldest of anachronisms Justin recalls how King Ptolemy had demanded the Hebrew books from Herod for the purpose of having them translated into Greek (31). From this part of the *Apology*, continued and completed in the *Dialogue with Trypho*, the most important fact to be learned is that the evangelical tradition had by this time been put into definite shape, so that the apologist could confidently and triumphantly point out the correspondence of the legend with the ancient texts, and celebrate the correspondence as a work of divine providence, ignoring the fact that the legend had, for the most part, been ingeniously drawn from those very texts by the faith of earlier Christian generations. This was not an argument to carry weight with educated pagans and has never been convincing, except for believers. Nevertheless we must take it into account if we are to understand the mystical element in the thought of second century Christianity. The extreme *naïveté* of our philosopher is seen in his daring to refer the emperors, for evidence about the birth of Jesus, to the registers of the enrolment made by Quirinius, whom he makes the first procurator in Judea (35); and for evidence about his miracles and death to official records made in the time of Pontius Pilate[28]—as though these registers and records were preserved in the archives of the empire.

To avoid the air of omitting something, the omission of which from his picture might rouse suspicion, Justin next describes the rites of Christian initiation and worship. As this part of the *Apology* deals with the new Christian mystery we shall return to it in the next chapter. Suffice it for the present to note that, according to our author, the demons, having discovered an announcement of baptism in the prophecies, at once proceeded to make rules about washings and such like purifications; the same with the eucharist which these wicked beings had imitated by setting up a similar rite in the mysteries of Mithra—the presentation of a loaf and a cup of water accompanied with certain well-known formulas. Justin seems to imply that these formulas also are not without their counterparts in the mystical language used by him in explaining the Christian rite. It does not seem to have occurred to him that some of his pagan readers might be inclined to think that it was not the pagan mysteries for which the intervention of devils was responsible, and thus derive from his analogies an idea not altogether favourable to the Christian religion.

None the less the concluding words of the *Apology* are the utterance of a sincere and courageous soul: "If that which we have submitted to your judgment seems reasonable and true, act accordingly; if you think it folly, treat it as folly, but do not condemn to death, as enemies, people who do no evil. For we forewarn you that you will not escape the judgment of God if you persist in injustice. As for ourselves, our cry will ever be 'let God's will be done.' " By way of postcript he adds the Latin copy of Hadrian's rescript to Minutius Fundanus forbidding the punishment of Christians for the profession of their faith unless they were proved guilty of offence against the law.

The so-called "Second Apology" is a sort of complementary writing published by Justin some time afterwards in which he deals with three sentences of death passed upon Christians by Urbicus, prefect of Rome. In this he addresses himself directly to public opinion and speaking to the people as brothers urges them in the name of humanity to protest against these acts of injustice, now being committed by the magistrates, under cover of the law, at Rome and throughout the Empire. He discusses three cases which have occurred in Rome. A Christian woman, tired of an intolerable husband, had finally given him notice of the *repudium*, on which the husband had denounced her as a Christian; the woman having obtained judicial delay for the preparation of her defence, the husband, by means of a centurion friend of his, caused the arrest of a certain Ptolemy who had converted the wife to Christianity; summoned by Urbicus to abjure the Christ, Ptolemy refuses and Urbicus has him put to death; a person present at the trial, named Lucius, protests against the sentence; Urbicus asks him if he is a Christian and on his answering "Yes" orders him to be led off immediately to execution; another man protests and meets the same fate (ii, 2). From all of which it is clear enough that under Antoninus the Pious, and at the seat of the imperial government, the hand of Roman justice was not asleep when Christians had to be dealt with.

Having discussed these cases, Justin, with remarkable temerity, proceeds to ridicule the "philosopher and swaggerer," whom he knows to be on the warpath against him, with the determination to bring him, Justin, to a like end (ii, 3–4). He responds with dignity to the bad jesters who ask why Christians don't kill themselves and go quickly to their God without bothering the magistrates to send them thither: God, he says, has put us in the world to do good and we confess ourselves Christians that truth may be spoken. But why, it is asked, does God let you be persecuted? The answer is—because the world has been corrupted by the doings of wicked angels and of their offspring, the demons, and because God, on account of the Christians, delays the universal catastrophe which is to sweep away for ever the wicked angels and the sinners.[29] But some will say: "Is that certain?" Justin answers: "If there were no chastisements, either there would be no God or only a God who had no interest in men; and so there would be neither good nor evil; the Logos is truth and virtue; him, and not falsehod and vice, it behoves us to follow even at the cost of our lives. As to the evil rumours current about Christians, the demons have invented them that the disciples of the divine Logos might be done to death. Oh that men will understand at last where truth is to be found!"

For the time being it was all wasted labour and the law continued its unjust chastisement of the Christians. Feeble, in many respects, as the apology we have studied may appear in our eyes, it was inspired by deep human feeling and spoke the language of reason in all sincerity. The judge—it was still Urbicus—who sentenced Justin about 165 sent an upright man, who was no fanatic, to his death. In the reign of Marcus Aurelius, other apologists, Melito of Sardis, Apollinarus of Hieropolis, Miltiades, Athenagoras, produced writings in the same sense and equally barren of immediate results. But these books were the means which turned the attention of the public to Christian literature. If the apologies cannot precisely be said to have established and propagated the faith, they began to compel adversaries to take it seriously, and some of these adversaries responded otherwise than by denunciation and sentence of death.

Celsus

The True Discourse which Celsus published against the Christians towards the end of the reign of Marcus Aurelius, perhaps in 178, contained no violent denunciation and had no resemblance to a pogrom. The attitude of Celsus is still that of one who considers Christianity a ridiculous superstition, but he knew enough about Christians to prefer their conversion to their annihilation. Here is no new edition of popular calumny, but rather appreciation of the Gospel morality. He expresses satisfaction at finding the doctrine of the Logos among the Christians; is acquainted with the sacred books which Jews and Christians have in common as well as with the books specifically Christian, the Gospels in the first place, and with other writings both of orthodox Christianity and of the gnostic sects; makes correct distinctions between these sects and the Great Church, although, from his point of view, all the forms of Christianity fall under a common reprobation.

It may be said that in this book Celsus takes a direction contrary to that of the order of proof planned by Justin, with its point of departure in Jewish prophecy. He starts off with what is, virtually, a refutation of Christianity by a Jew; that is to say, he gathers together all the objections which Jews bring against the foundation of Christian faith, namely, the Messiahship of Jesus; then, having thus deprived Christianity of its historic-theological base, he lumps the two religions together and refutes them as one, arguing, against the apologists of Judaism and Christianity alike, that the ideas of Greek religious philosophy are of superior value and greater antiquity compared with those either of Jews or Christians—a thesis not less disputable, in certain respects, than that of the Christian apologists.

Celsus applies severe criticism to the Gospel legend, especially to all that concerns the resurrection of the Christ, proving that the whole legend has been repeatedly worked over, in one Gospel after the other, in order to guard against objections which it could not overthrow. Finally, he appeals to Christians to abandon their uncompromising attitude, to accept the common religion and not to create schism in the State nor weaken it by division.[30] In the main Celsus is willing to let Christianity live, on condition of subordinating itself, in common with the ancient Eastern cults, to the imperial religion of Rome and Augustus, and of tolerating the other cults as legitimate forms of worship. Philosophically and politically, nothing seemed to him more natural, logical and necessary. But the real force of Christianity, which aimed at a goal beyond the Roman Empire, lay in its refusal to compromise. That refusal it could not abandon without being false to itself and compromising its future.

There are no signs that the writing of Celsus made any deeper impression on the Christian leaders than the apologies of Justin and the others made on the leaders either of imperial policy or of Greek thought. Christian writers contemporary with Celsus make no mention of him. By a chance encounter in the year 246 Origen came into possession of *The True Discourse* whose existence had hitherto been unknown to him; nor did he even know who Celsus was. Only through Origen's conscientious refutation of the book has it come to the knowledge of the Christian world and been preserved there. Thus did the apologists vainly attempt the instruction of the persecutors; thus did Celsus vainly attempt the enlightenment of the persecuted.

4. Later Persecution

Persecution continued. What admirers of Marcus Aurelius can help deploring that, during his reign, in the year 177, the city of Lyons was the scene of martyrdoms comparable in horror to those witnessed by Rome in 64 under Nero?[31] At the time of the Lyons martyrdoms there was a Christian congregation there and another at Vienne, both still small in number and of recent formation; their founders and a part of their converts perished in the persecution we are about to describe. Some members of the Lyons group were of Asiatic or Phrygian origin, but many were natives of the country. An old man of ninety, Pothinus, ruled the church as bishop and was assisted by the priest Irenaeus, who came from Asia.[32]

As often happened at this time it was popular passion that forced the Roman authorities to take action. The Christians were regarded with no friendly eyes by the pagan populace whose imaginations had been excited by the strange tales in circulation about what went on at the Christian meetings. In the absence of the provincial legate a large number of believers were laid hold of by a mob and, after brief interrogation by the tribune of the cohort and the town magistrates, were remanded to prison to await trial. On the return of the legate the trial began. At the outset a notable of the place, Vettius Epagathus, having announced his intention to defend the accused, was himself at once arrested as a Christian on his own confession. Various incidents marked the course of the trial and there were ten apostasies.33 New arrests took place both at Lyons and Vienne. Some pagan slaves of Christian masters were seized and these slaves, in their terror and under prompting by the soldiers, "lyingly imputed to the Christians banquets of Thyestes, incest of Oedipus and all the things which are not to be spoken of, nor thought of, nor believed to be ever possible among human beings." This evidence created a bad impression even on people who, being related to the accused, had shown themselves less hot against them.

This made the legate and the soldiers all the more determined to get confessions under torture. Sanctus "the deacon" of Vienne, Maturus, a neophyte, Attalus of Pergamus and the young slave, Blandina, showed unshakable courage. Blandina especially astonished and exhausted the torturers, who, all day long, took their turns at her. They were amazed at the obstinate hold that life kept in that broken body. Still less could they understand the mysterious relief the sufferer found in the words she would repeat whenever they urged her to confess—"I am a Christian girl and we do nothing bad." Sanctus also was put to repeated and atrocious torture but never a word could they get out of him, save these two in latin: *"Christianus sum."* Condemned to be thrown to the beasts, the four confessors were despatched to the amphitheatre. The first to succumb were Maturus and Sanctus, after they had been scourged, dragged along by the beasts and forced on to an iron chair made red-hot. Blandina, chained to a post and offering prayers, seemed to the brethren "as one clothed with the Christ"; the beasts would not touch her. Yells from the frenzied crowd demanded the punishment of Attalus, and he had already been dragged round the amphitheatre when the legate learned that he was a Roman citizen. Thereupon Blandina and Attalus were sent back to prison. The legate, for his part, thought it best to consult the emperor. Perhaps he was disturbed by the turn the affair had taken; perhaps the evidence of the slaves against the Christians made him unwilling to take responsibility for releasing the apostates, whom he was keeping in prison. The case was identical with that which Pliny had referred to Trajan.

By the time Maturus and Sanctus came to suffer Pothinus was dead. Weakened by age and hardly breathing the old man had been carried into court amid the shouts of the infuriated mob. In presence of the judge he showed a bold front. Asked by the legate what kind of being the god of the Christians was, he answered: "If you are worthy of him you will know him." He was taken back to prison, insulted and beaten by the mob and, after lingering two days longer in the jail, breathed his last. Other confessors, younger than he, were chained in a filthy dungeon and died before receiving the final punishment in store for them. But, during the days in which the local authorities were waiting for the emperor's answer, the conscience of those who had apostasized began to trouble them. These unhappy wretches who, notwithstanding their recantation, had been kept in prison under suspicion of having previously committed the foul homicide and impurity commonly attributed to Christians, perceived that they had become objects of contempt to the pagans and of pity to their more courageous brethren. Touched by the sincere compassion of these latter, many of the apostates felt ashamed of themselves and made up their minds to withdraw their recantations.

Such was the posture of affairs when at last the answer came from the man whom modern historians are fond of calling the saint-emperor. Moved either by political considerations, or by the knowledge of the little truth there was in the tales about the crimes of the Christians, in whom he finds little to reproach beyond their obstinacy, Marcus Aurelius repeats the order formerly given by Trajan to Pliny; the renegades are to be set free; those who persist in the faith are to be put to death.

It was the time of year when deputations from the cities of Gaul were pouring into Lyons for the yearly fêtes held at the altar of Rome and Augustus; the time also of the games in the amphitheatre, and here was a supply of Christians ready for the wild beasts. The legate accordingly lost no time in rounding off the judicial business that remained to be done: all the confessors who were Roman citizens were sentenced to decapitation. There remained the apostates, whose case was not tried with that of the confessors, no doubt because sentences of release would not be pronounced in public. Those who had recovered the courage of their faith were immediately added to the group awaiting execution. None was released, says the letter which tells this dramatic story, save "the sons of perdition."[34]

During the public interrogation of the Christians there was among the audience in the court room a certain physician named Alexander, Phrygian by origin, but some years resident in Gaul, who kept encouraging the accused to be firm by making signs to that effect. The crowd, seeing what he was after, called out that it was he who was making the renegades renew their confession of the Christ, as some of them were doing. Questioned by the legate, Alexander declared himself a Christian and was sentenced to death on the spot. The very next day he made his appearance before the public in the amphitheatre along with Attalus, whose status as a Roman citizen the legate, anxious to conciliate the mob, had chosen to forget. A variety of tortures were inflicted on the two: Alexander, his mind concentrated on God, died without saying a word: Attalus, roasting on the red-hot chair, called out to the crowd as it yelled with delight on sniffing the odour of the grilling flesh, "Here is a man being cooked for the table; you seem to be fond of that diet. But we people are not cannibals, we leave that to you, nor do we harm to any man." Blandina was kept back for the last day of the show, and with her a boy of fifteen named Ponticus. The crowd present that day was debased enough below the human level to take a furious delight in the sufferings of these two children. They were heroic; Blandina, like an elder sister, speaking words of encouragement to Ponticus in the midst of their common torment. Ponticus was the first to expire. As to Blandina, the talk was that nothing could kill her. But at last, after the scourge, the wild beasts, the fiery chair had been tried in vain, they tied her up in a mat and flung her before a bull which tossed her about from side to side until, after a long time, she was dead.

As though the fury of man were more insatiate than the hunger of wild beasts, the mangled remains they left undevoured were denied to the survivors who would have buried them. The bodies of those who had died in prison were thrown, under supervision, to the dogs; watch was also kept over the debris of those who had perished in the amphitheatre; after six days' exposure to the public it was all raked together and burnt, that nothing might be left save the ashes. Then the ashes were thrown, amid laughter, into the Rhone, which was near-by, so that nothing at all might remain. "Now let them rise from the dead" was the comment of those who arranged this beautiful programme, and the merry jest of those who carried it out.

Here is a unique page, not, alas, in the history of the first persecutions, but in the history books, in the documentation which has preserved for us the record of them. Raise Marcus Aurelius to what height of greatness you will, there is a page in Eusebius' history that cries shame on the memory of him, illustrious as his name may otherwise be. For reasons of State Marcus Aurelius gave his sanction to the jurisprudence announced in the rescript of Trajan, sanctioned by him for the same reason.

This philosopher-king, accounted the wisest of the wise and the most humane of his time, could he not see the facts as Pliny had seen them sixty years earlier; could he not suspect that in Christianity also there was "something human" and forbid these odious and futile massacres? A girl and a boy triumphantly accuse him before the bar of posterity; their names are Blandina and Ponticus. Faced by the accusation of these innocent victims of his brutal legislation the lofty reason of the philosopher-king is overthrown and put to silence. That lofty reason of his was shortsighted; it was narrow in outlook; the prisoner of a fixed idea called common sense by the "enlightened" of those days.

Like Trajan, Hadrian and Antoninus, the mind of Marcus Aurelius was fettered to the notion of Christianity as a pestilence and a scourge, a sect of absurd but dangerous rebels, while yet he was well aware that Christians were generally innocent of the infamies charged against them by the ignorant multitude. These emperors were men of high intelligence and moderation; but they never paused to question the prejudice and bigotry on which the current notion of Christianity was founded. All they could see, and they thought it clear enough, was the contradiction offered by the new religion to the principles on which the Roman empire was, or seemed to be, established. But were these principles incapable of improvement and expansion? Had not Christianity now become a very different thing from what it was in the time of Nero, before the explosion of the Jewish war more than a hundred years before? Had not the attitude of Christians towards imperial authority changed, since the end of the first century, to an attitude of respect? Whence came the ever increasing success of the new religion? Came it not largely from the insufficiency of the others for human need? And if Christianity could draw to itself such a multitude of the disinherited, so many troubled souls, was it not because the disinherited were far too numerous in Roman society, and because the current doctrines of philosophy and official religion were too unconvincing or too hard-hearted, or too impoverished on the moral side?

It is true that the Antonines did not display towards the Christians a wanton cruelty like that of Nero, nor were they deliberate and systematic persecutors like Decius and Diocletian, though system of a kind they certainly had, with room in it for some outstanding atrocities. But this abatement was not due to any feeling for justice or to half-hearted goodwill towards Christianity. As Duchesne remarks: "it followed naturally from the contemptuous indifference of the authorities to these conflicts of sect and doctrine, their contempt arising perhaps from excessive confidence in the resisting power of philosophy and in the tendency of sects to spend their power for mischief one on another." These emperors, indeed, had good reason to count on the force of the many cults, old and new, which existed in self-ordained subordination to the imperial religion; they counted also, and knew they could count, on the force of good sense, that indefinable divinity of which philosophers are prone to consider themselves the high priests. They never asked themselves whether the no-compromise attitude in which the Christians differed from the other sects might not itself be a force—the force of a deep-seated consciousness of higher truth and a more excellent morality. In reality it was precisely that consciousness to which the tireless and charitable labours of the Christian apostolate owed their life and vigour, and which made the

Christian religion so rapidly contagious that it burst the dikes built against it by the "good-sense" of philosophers.

But a new "good-sense" more attractive than learned and lordly reason had been brought into being—the common sense of Christian equality; and with it came a type of virtue less harsh than the Stoic—the practical brotherhood of the Gospel. The wrangling of sects did not prevent the Christian communities inside the pale of the Church from forming compact bodies held together in close solidarity. The fact of that consciousness was apparent whenever the Christians confronted their judges in court; it was seen on every eager face among the brethren as they pressed round the prisoners at the risk of their own lives. When all was over the Christians were still there to beg for the ashes of the martyrs and give them honourable burial. Their beneficence was generous, and it was organized. Already the great congregations, like that of Rome, had their treasure chests, regularly and abundantly replenished, for ministering to the needs of the poor. After Justin has described the eucharistic service, the mystical banquet of the brethren, centre of their religious life and hearth-fire of their mutual love, he goes on to say: "Those who have the means and are men of goodwill give freely, each giving as he pleased, and the collection is then laid before the president"—the bishop who presided at meetings—"who distributes it among orphans and widows, the sick and the poor from any cause, the prisoners, and travellers on their journeys"—the Christians of other congregations always received as brethren—"in short, he is the helper of every one who is in need" (1 *Apology*, 67). Under these conditions the rapid growth of the bishop's person to great consideration is easily understood. Nor need we wonder that the Friendly Society over which he presided recruited new members every day.

It remains to add that the Christianity of Justin, of Melito, or of Irenaeus, even when judged by intellect and reason, made no mean showing. In what was it inferior to the philosophy of a Plutarch, of a Celsus—nay, of Marcus Aurelius himself? Was it indeed so very different in the matter of reasonable ideas and reasoned ideology? Supreme Being, Ruling Providence, subordinate spirits, justice at the summit and sure of final vindication, and the primacy of the moral consciousness over all forms of knowledge—were not all these analogously conceived by both sides, but with more precision in Christianity and with a measure of practical achievement in daily conduct, in family life and social relationships, peculiar to itself? The good Justin was not in error when he presented Christianity as a great philosophy—a philosophy whose speech in Justin's time was the lisp of an infant, but an infant full of life and vigour and with the future in its grasp.

At the death of Marcus Aurelius the triumph of Christianity, though not due to burst upon the world till a century and a half later, was already assured, but unforeseen by the pagan world. The Christians foresaw it in faith, and were quick to note the signs of its coming as events took their course in the contemporary world. As the third century unfolded Roman paganism more and more came to resemble a vast hoarding behind which the Christian religion was gradually being built up. And so in our day it may be that Christianity in turn has become a façade behind which men are building the religion of humanity. The tree which Constantine and his Christian successors let fall, or cut down, was no longer a living thing. Thus it came to pass that Christianity, with persecution at an end, soon became master of the house. Would that it had never forgotten the lesson, taught by its own first experience, of the fundamental iniquity and ultimate futility of persecuting men for the offence of religious belief.

Chapter VII

BIRTH OF THE CHRISTIAN MYSTERY AND OF ITS RITES

In the preceding chapters we have seen with what rapidity the Gospel was propagated and have followed the course of a persecution that was powerless to stifle it. Behind all that, we have caught glimpses, but glimpses only, of a group life, an intense life, that gathered power in the silence and, as it were, underground, until it shook the foundations of the empire. We have already seen enough to make it clear that this life was a profound religion, and we know that the essence of it was the worship of the Lord Jesus Christ, of him who died and rose again, prince of the age to come. Our next task must be to study this worship, this cult, from the inner side and to see how it expressed its character in practice. In this chapter we shall have before us a Mystery of Salvation, figuratively presented in worship, and to some extent foreshadowed in the mystery of the Church, that strange Society of Friends which proved itself stronger than Rome and outlasted her empire. Then, in the chapter following this, we shall watch the Mystery taking form and crystallizing in a system of doctrines.

1. THE MYSTERY IN EMBRYO

The Book of Acts, in an idealized picture which has become conventional, shows us the first believers in Jesus gravitating towards the temple and publicly frequenting it every day, like other Jews, but privately breaking bread together in their own houses (ii, 42, 46). They spoke of Jesus risen from the dead and about to come again; they healed the sick in his name; they even baptized, already perhaps in the name of their Christ, those who rallied to the hope of his coming (iv, 33; v, 42). Thus, at the very beginning of the Christian religion there existed a mystical faith in Christ Jesus, a mystical bond uniting the faithful, with a ritual of membership and communion in which their unity was expressed and fortified. Before it overflowed into the pagan world, before it was officially and relentlessly repudiated by Judaism, the Jesus-sect had within it the seed of a faith and worship which soon would open the way for its growth into an independent religion.

From the very first, then, it had a faith all its own: the Master, Jesus the Nazorean, active no more on earth, was risen from the dead; he had become the Christ now at the right hand of God and ready to return with the Kingdom which he had declared would come immediately. The ardour of this faith, first kindled by Jesus himself, grew hotter in proportion as he himself became its object and its warrant, as his exaltation to heaven and glory seemed to make his coming in power to establish the Kingdom, if one may dare to say it, a thing easy to accomplish. In the atmosphere thus created by faith were born the uncriticized visions and hopes which fanned the enthusiasm of the preachers into a fire that nothing could put out.

Thus it came to pass that Jewish hopes for a new and better world, hitherto varied in form and wavering in outline, were crystallized, centralized and systematized round a personal figure, but henceforth a transcendent figure above the danger of the shipwrecks which had inevitably overtaken the wild ventures of violent Messianism. Judas the Galilean, Theudas and the Egyptian mentioned by Josephus and the Book of Acts, the fanatics of the great revolt and Barkochba left no religious sects behind them to continue their work after they had met their end. But John the Baptist, Simon Magus and Jesus were all the founders of sects which lasted on, perpetuating and exalting the founder's memory after each had suffered a violent death, which, however, in no way disconcerted his followers, but served rather to quicken their faith. A success all its own awaited Christianity. It sprang, at bottom, from the faith and vigour of the human element in the heart of that religion. Viewed from the outside, success came to it from the concatenation of causes which, to all appearance, had brought it into being: first, the tragic death of Jesus and his sudden removal from the scene had repercussions on the fortunes of his main idea which could not have happened if he had died a natural death after a long captivity; then the forcible dispersion of the hellenist believers had the effect of flinging the Gospel message into the

Mediterranean world; finally came persecution which gave the new sect a wide publicity and glorified it by the sufferings of its martyrs.

But the growth of faith in Jesus was not dependent on favourable external circumstances. Eager to magnify its Object with new dignity it soared to great heights by the sole force of its inner life. Once raised to the heavens, Jesus became immediately the Son of Man presently to come on the clouds. Up to that time it would have been a hard task for the historian to identify the Son of Man with a definable personality. But faith settled the matter: Jesus in heaven was the Son of Man making ready to come again. That the term could be applied to Jesus is proved by the fact that the application was realized; and it is not without analogies. The notion of "the Man" was easy to assimilate; a passage of the Book of Enoch applies it to Enoch himself (lxxi, 14). The application to Jesus was made early and is found fully developed in the Jewish-Christian tradition of the apocryphal Clementines. It exalted Jesus in two ways: on the one hand it made him transcendent and pre-existent; on the other it gave to his death an intelligible place in his appearance as a man on earth, of which the chief object was to prepare the way for his Great Coming as the Christ. In the Synoptic Gospels, however, the idea of the Great Coming dominates the whole presentation. There Jesus is not so much the Heavenly Man incarnate for the salvation of mortals as the Christ who is to die that he may come again in his glory. Such was the Christ of the first believers. He it was who had announced the coming Kingdom to the poor, promised pardon to repentant sinners and given his bond that the powers of God would soon be displayed on the side of the righteous. Conqueror of death, and already ruling in the heavenly places, he was about to come in his glory; "He who is Coming and we look for no other" (Matthew xi, 3) was their byword and formula in greeting the brethren. The oldest symbol of the Christian faith seems to be enshrined in the Aramean *Maranatha*—"The Lord cometh," or "Come, Lord."[1]

They spoke of him as "the Lord"[2] as an alternative to "the Son of Man." The long continued employment of the *Maranatha* formula, even in the liturgies of the Greek-speaking Christians,[3] proves the Jewish-Christian origin of "Lord" as a title applied to the Christ. In its religious and ritual sense the use of the title was evidently applied to Jesus only as risen from the dead; but it was given him immediately when the belief arose that, after dying on earth as Jesus, he had risen to heaven as the Christ. The application of the term to Jesus was unpremeditated and entirely natural but it was big with consequences as no other title could have been. The title of "Lord" had a meaning for worship, a cult meaning, not carried, at least with the same force, by the theological title "Son of Man." To Christians speaking Greek, "Lord" would unquestionably be a divine name or, more strictly, it was a name that tended to deify the figure to whom it was applied; on the one hand it placed Jesus among the divinities worshipped in the mystery cults who were familiar to pagans as mediators of salvation, subordinate to the Supreme Being; on the other hand the hellenic Christians who read the Old Testament in the Greek version found there a multitude of texts when the word "Lord" is the substitute for Jahveh,[4] the unspeakable name of God Himself and, applying these to Jesus, inevitably raised him to the level of Deity.

The first of these results—the coupling of Jesus with the mystery gods—is clearly brought out as the following passage (1 Corinthians viii, 5–6):

> For if there be many named gods,
>   be they in heaven, be they on earth,
> And as there is many a god
>   so there is many a lord,
> For us there is no God but one, the Father,
>   of whom are all things, and we for him.
> For us there is no Lord but one, Jesus Christ,
>   by whom are all things and we by him.

The paganism of that time was familiar with many lords and divine heroes and had placed Caesar among them in the first rank, even with the added attribute of Saviour. In the text cited above Jesus is not God absolutely, nor even one among many gods: he is a divine *lord*.[5] As "Lord" he is at once below the Supreme Deity and above all other created beings, possessing the maximum of godhead compatible with his nature as created, the fullness of the godhead belonging only to the uncreated Supreme.

BIRTH OF THE CHRISTIAN MYSTERY AND OF ITS RITES

Meditation on biblical texts led Christian thought towards the same result. Many a speculation of that early age sprang from meditation on a verse in the hundred-and-tenth Psalm:

> The Lord (Jahveh) said to my Lord (master)
> "Sit thou on my right
> While I make thine enemies
> a footstool under thy feet."

A picture, surely, of Jesus, risen from the dead and now seated by the side of God on his heavenly throne! Occasioned in the same way was the proclamation of Jesus as the Son of God, but in a sense quite other than that of the sonship which every believer could claim.

> The Lord said to me: Thou art my son;
> This day I have begotten thee.[6]

Faith went far in magnifying and exalting Jesus but, however far it might go, he remained very near to his own and in the midst of them. Stephen, as the story relates, saw him standing at the right hand of God, a vision born in the ecstacy of the first martyr; it was his answer to the high priest. But others had seen him before Stephen, or saw him afterwards. Of these visions tradition, as we said before, has retained only a few, and these typical rather than real, presented as proofs of the resurrection. What they really prove is the faith of those who had them, the faith of the first believers in the perpetual presence of their Christ. When they prayed together in their meetings, he was there; when the bread was broken at the fraternal meal which prefigured the Kingdom they waited for, he was invisibly with them at the table. Some said that they had seen him break the bread and bless it, and when others of the company, hoping to see him, saw him not, they still had the impression of his presence and felt that he was with them in spirit. According to Acts the spirit of Jesus never failed to come to the help of Paul and his companions in their difficulties, now leading them away from this plan, now guiding them to that. In very truth Jesus was a guiding genius, a guardian spirit to his own.

Quite early a particular day was consecrated to Jesus, "the Lord's Day." This was the first day of the week honoured among pagans as the day of the Sun. The day of the Sun was not consecrated to Jesus because the Christ rose on that day, but because it was the fitting day for his resurrection. In the beginning nobody knew either the day or the hour of the resurrection, for the sufficient reason that the resurrection was a matter of faith which nobody could witness as a sensible event and assign to a definite time and place. Long before the story was told of the tomb found empty on the Sunday, day but one after the passion, believers believed and preachers preached that Jesus, risen from the dead, was alive for ever with God. In a certain sense and measure the Gospel stories of the resurrection are the explanatory myth of the Christian Sunday. This at least is what the arrangement of the elements makes them: first, in all the Gospels, the discovery of the empty tomb on Sunday; then in the third and fourth, the report on Sunday of the apparitions. Sunday was also the usual day for the Christian Supper, which explains why some of the apparitions are both Sunday myths and Supper myths, jointly symbolizing the belief that the Christ was risen to heaven and yet present with his own at their common meal; for the myth of the risen Christ and the myth of the present Christ were, at bottom, one and the same. But why was the first day of the week chosen as the Lord's Day, birthday of the Christ in glory? This question remains to be answered.

We remark in the first place that the choice of a particular day could not be avoided. In the new communities, as in the first community at Jerusalem, the bond of union lay in the common meal of the brethren. It was of course impossible to maintain unbroken companionship at table; on the other hand the common meal would fail of its object unless it were held at fairly short intervals. The pattern of the week, established in Jewish custom and becoming generally adopted under the influence of the oriental cults, was bound to be followed as a matter of course needing no reflection. Once a week, then; but on which day of the week? Clearly the first day was indicated as the day most fitting for the Christians to come together, for the meal to be held in memory of Jesus and in celebration of his glory, and this, not because it followed the Jewish Sabbath or the least intention existed to link the two together, but quite simply because it was the first of the seven, the Chief Day, the day of the Sun, honoured as such, and not by pagans only. And was there not an analogy perceptible to all, and spontaneously accepted by all, between the risen Christ in his glory, and the sun in heaven and the solar gods abounding throughout the East? Need it be added that the Essenes worshipped the rising sun and that Sunday would be to them also the most honourable of the seven? Little wonder if this analogy instantly suggested itself to pagan converts as well as to Jewish converts living in pagan countries, even if they had never heard of it in Palestine.

The Christ in his glory was thought of as a Being of Light; light was the substance of his being. We need to search no further than the pages of the New Testament for proof that the object of the earliest Christian worship and prayer—the dying Stephen renders back his soul to Jesus—the Lord, the King on high invested by God with a part of his power, clothed in divine majesty and soon to come in his glory to found the Reign of God on earth—for proof that this luminous Being belonged from the first, his Jewish traits notwithstanding, to the family of the celestial gods, especially to that of the solar deities. What likeness do we see in the Christ of the Apocalypse, riding on his white horse, with his name of mystery, his eyes of flame, the sword coming out of his mouth, his flashing diadems and mantle red with blood?[7] We see the likeness of a solar deity, of Mithra as he is depicted on horseback in bas-reliefs. In that connexion a long story might be told of the Christ of the Apocalypse with his seven Churches, his seven attendant stars, his seven Spirits— he who is the Holy, he who is the True. It is the figure of an astral divinity, presiding over the heavenly spheres, like Mithra, like Attis and many another. These affinities are the natural consequence of faith's effort to see in Christ the Lord of the universe; they were felt in that effort and created by it. And so it came to pass that Jesus, prophet of the Kingdom, first becomes Messiah and rises from that to Lord of the Universe and Master of humanity. The communication to Jesus of attributes proper to the solar deities was all the easier inasmuch as they were gods of justice, gods of truth by the very fact that they were gods of light; all the easier because Jesus, identified with his own ideal of eternal justice and truth, was drawn into their company by the moral values represented as divine in their character. To Christians of the first age Jesus was the sun of justice and salvation newly risen on earth and now reigning in heaven: "the dayspring from on high which has visited us."

So the day of the Sun became the Day of the Lord, and Sunday the day of the risen Christ. How easy it was, after that, to make Sunday the day on which he rose. Once adopted as the Christian Holy Day, the justification of the usage would be complete when the Christian believed that on that day, and none other of the seven, his Lord rose from the dead. It was bound to come to that as soon as the Christians had to justify their observance of Sunday, and the more inevitably perhaps, when, under pressure of a later demand for proofs that Jesus really rose from death, the attempt was made to construct a co-ordinated story of the apparitions under a scheme of time and place. Thus, when the editor of the second Gospel would prove the resurrection by revealing the circumstances of the burial with the clinching evidence of the empty tomb, he inevitably places the discovery on the morning of the day of the sun, a little after its rising (xvi, 2). Having thus formed the picture in his imagination, belief that matters happened thus was bound to follow. The editor of the third Gospel, governed by a preconceived perspective, dates all the apparitions on the Sunday of the resurrection and places them all in Jerusalem (xxiv). The editor of the fourth carries system yet further: he notes two apparitions of the Christ to the disciples gathered in the room of the Supper with the closed doors customary at the ritual meal of the Christian communities; both apparitions take place on a Sunday, the first on the Sunday of the resurrection, the second on the Sunday following (xx, 19–29). These doubtless are intended to be reckoned the first two Sundays of the Church, made holy by visible manifestations of the Christ and indicating that all Sundays thereafter are consecrated by his invisible presence. Finally, the seer of the Apocalypse has his vision on a Sunday (i, 10).

Simultaneously with these developments, the great festival of Christian salvation, the festival of Easter, yielded to the attraction of Sunday as the day for its celebration. At the beginning this festival was held, as was natural enough, on the same day as the Jewish Passover which might fall on any day of the week, and with no difference except that it now commemorated the Christian's salvation, won for him by the death of Christ, the true pascal lamb, as the fourth Gospel teaches. The so-called quartodeciman usage, maintained by the congregations in Asia at the end of the second century and condemned by Pope Victor, was the primitive usage of all the Christian congregations and is indeed presupposed by the Gospel tradition. But the glory of the Sun's day proved irresistible, and this attraction, coupled with the growth of reaction against purely Jewish observances, soon shifted the Christian Passover to the Sunday following the Jewish celebration. Even the early Gospel of the Hebrews regards as canonical the observance of the Jewish Christians who celebrated Easter on Sunday morning after a fast lasting from the evening of Friday.[8] We are told of one great Sunday in the year when the final achievement of salvation was celebrated in the glory of the Christ rising from death to life. Thus the stories of the resurrection became simultaneously the myth of the institution of the Christian Easter and the myth of the Christian Sunday.

Let the apologist Justin bear witness. "On the day of the sun all our people come together for religious exercise, because that is the first of days, when God, having transformed darkness and matter, created the world,"—he means the spring equinox, the birthday of the world being that on which God made the light[9] —"and because, on that same day, Jesus Christ our Saviour rose from the dead. For they crucified him on the evening of Saturday, and on the morrow of Saturday, that is on the day of the Sun, he appeared to his apostles and to his disciples and gave them the teaching which we have just submitted to your judgment."[10] Here, then, is clear evidence that in Justin's time, and in the Christian circle for which he speaks, Sunday and, among them all, the great Sunday of the Passover,[11] was chosen for the joint commemoration of the resurrection of Christ, the creation of light and of the world, and the revelation of saving truth made by the Christ to his apostles. In all senses, it was the Festival of Light. In keeping with this, Christians adopted quite early, if not from the very beginning, the custom of turning to the East when engaged in prayer.[12] That this custom, explained as homage to the Christ as he rose to heaven, was borrowed from the Eastern solar cults admits of no doubt.

2. Baptism

In texts relatively old, baptism is presented as an "illumination" (φωτισμός) of which Jesus, needless to say, is the sun.[13] A baptismal hymn quoted in the Epistle to the Ephesians (v, 14), and more completely by Clement of Alexandria (*Protreptikos*, viii, 84), contained the following apostrophe:

> Awake, thou sleeper,
>   rise up from among the dead,
> And he who is Christ the Lord shall enlighten thee,
>   the sun of the resurrection
> Begotten before the dayspring
>   giving life by his beams.

Such were the hymns sung round candidates for initiation into the Christian mystery, but not in the earliest days of Christian religion. We have already seen how the little group of Galilean believers who, on returning to Jerusalem after the death of Jesus, announced that he was risen from the dead and coming with his kingdom—how this group baptized its recruits, as John the Baptist had done, and Jesus himself had probably done. This baptism was, before it became anything else, an act of purification, a cleansing of the whole body by immersion in water and, at the same time, a symbol of repentance, of a life changed in readiness for the Great Event expected from hour to hour. But, whether with or without first intention, it presently became the rite of admission to membership in the society of believers in Jesus and of union with Jesus himself, since it implied a profession of faith in him as the coming Messiah and as already glorified. In this way it created a kind of mystic bond between the believers and the Christ, although there was probably no thought as yet of assimilating the two, of identifying the one with the other, after the manner of the initiation rites of the pagan mystery religions which made the initiate one with his god. Its effect was that the believer belonged to Christ thenceforward and was in some way linked to him; he was baptized "in his name" and, as the name was being invoked, received the sign of Jesus-Messiah that he might be recognized as one of his own on the Day of Judgment (Acts ii, 38–41; x, 48).

Whether to disguise the fact that the rite was borrowed by the Christian sect from John's, or to emphasize the difference between the two, or because Christian baptism soon acquired a character all its own, the idea arose that it was essentially different from John's, his being only a symbol, while Christian baptism was a sacrament, a baptism of spirit charged with mystical power.[14] Strange to say, the Book of Acts gives us to understand that there were some Christians who had been baptized only in John's way (xviii, 25, 26; xix, 1–7). Apparently the intention of these texts is to represent the rite practised by the Judaizing Christians as no other than John's way of baptizing and inferior to the true baptism of the Christ. The same book, in its myth of Pentecost, has the first group of believers baptized in spirit and made, by the gift of the Spirit, into apostles of the new-born faith. By this the editor would intimate that Christian baptism carries with it a supernatural power, the infusion of a Spirit, that of God or that of Christ, who takes possession of the believer, endows him with the gift of tongues, makes him a prophet and, at times, imparts the power to work miracles.

Such a conception of baptism is what we might expect in the outburst of religious enthusiasm characteristic of the first generations and in keeping with the psycho-physiological disturbances which are frequent accompaniments of these outbursts. Johannite baptism, taken over by the earliest Christians, still closely akin to the legal washings of Judaism, was retained in its primative sobriety by certain groups of Christians inclining the Jewish way;[15] but to the hellenizing groups, which formed the majority, it seemed a feeble rite that effected nothing and as powerless as the legal purifications were supposed, however wrongly, to have been deemed. The water in the urns at Cana, said to have been turned into wine by Jesus, tells the same tale.

The last step was to provide Christian baptism with a suitable institution-myth. For this purpose the best that could be invented was to fix the institution of spiritual baptism on the occasion of the water-baptism conferred by John on Jesus. The opening of the heavens takes place at the very moment when Jesus, coming out of the water, leaves water behind him to receive the fullness of the Spirit and be consecrated Son of God.[16] This was intended to show that Jesus was there and then revealed as the firstborn of God, the direct offspring of the Spirit, and that, like him, the faithful underwent a mystical immersion in spirit which made them also the sons of God. Surely a naïve way of revealing the original identity of Christian baptism with John's by the very means taken to mark an essential difference between the two. Later on it was deemed advisable to attribute a command to confer baptism on all new believers to Jesus himself after he was risen from the dead (Matthew xxviii, 19; Mark xvi, 16).[17]

3. The Holy Supper

As baptism was not instituted by Jesus,[18] no more, in strictness of speech, was the Holy Supper. The daily meals of the first Christian groups in Jerusalem, necessarily taken in common under the conditions in which they found themselves, quickly took on a highly distinctive mystical character. The common daily meal was already established in Jewish custom as a religious function. If there is one thing certain in the history of the birth of the Christian rites it is that the point of departure for the development of the Eucharist, "the exercise of thanksgiving," the holy supper, characteristic of the Christian religion, is to be found in the prayers, recited in common, which accompanied the meals of the Jews, in the "grace said" to God for his bountiful gift of daily food, chiefly bread and wine: "blessed be He who caused the earth to bring forth bread" and "blessed be God who created the fruit of the vine." These are the prayers clearly referred to in the mystical stories of the multiplication of loaves (Mark vi, 41; viii, 6) and of the institution of the Supper. The former stories are in themselves myths of the institution of the Christian rite, but with this difference from the latter, that the stories of the multiplied loaves refer to a communion without wine, the "breaking of bread" of which Acts also speaks (ii, 42, 46), while the stories which relate the actual institution with bread and cup, with the attached symbolism of body and blood, refer to the mystical Supper commemorative of Jesus' death and the medium of communion with the Christ who died and rose again.

It is, moreover, clear that the Supper was not, in its first stage, a sacrament in which the death of the Christ, his crucified body and his blood, were mystically represented. "The breaking of bread," the name used in Acts to designate the Supper, shows clearly enough that no special significance was at first attached to the food of which the meal consisted. The cup of wine was not in any sense a necessary part of it, and all the indications are to the effect that it was often dispensed with (later on we shall produce evidence that it was often absent even after the Supper became figuratively the death of the Christ). It is therefore with this primitive form of the Supper, in which the breaking of bread for the common meal was the essential and characteristic feature, that we must connect the story of the multiplied loaves.[19] We have already seen how the chief apparition stories are also myths of the institution of the Supper, myths, we might say, of the Risen Christ's co-presence at table, his commensality, with his disciples and believers. The disciples at Emmaus recognize him "in the breaking of bread." In the supplement to John the Risen Christ offers bread and fish to the disciples, as in the multiplication of the loaves (xxi, 13). Here the fish is itself symbolic. The meaning lies in the symbol of eating together; the material of the meal is of secondary importance.

These myths reveal the original meaning of the Supper. In the first stage the only symbolism the meaning required was that implied by common participation in the same food eaten together under the belief that the Christ-to-come was invisibly present. We can see from the *Didache* (ix, 2) how thanksgiving for the spiritual gift of salvation, and for the hope of it, presently found its way into the thanks given for the food of the body, and how the former was substituted for the latter. Here is the "Eucharist," the formula of thanksgiving, to be pronounced before the holy meal began, and first of all over the wine cup:

> We give thee thanks, O our Father,
> for the holy vine of thy servant David,
>   which thou hast made known to us by thy servant Jesus.
> To thee be glory for ever and ever (*Didache*, ix, 2).

"The holy vine of David" is clearly the vine in Psalm lxxx, here taken mystically for the Spiritual Church, the vine of

Salvation. Follows the "Eucharist" over the broken bread (*Didache*, ix, 3, 4):

> We give thee thanks, O our Father,
>   for life and knowledge[20]
>   which thou hast made known to us by thy servant Jesus.
> To thee be glory for ever and ever.
> As this bread was scattered on the mountains,
>   then, gathered in, became one,
> Thus may thy Church be gathered in
>   from the ends of the earth in thy Kingdom.
> For thine are glory and power,
>   by Jesus Christ, for ever and ever (ix, 3–4).

The couplet on the vine and the first couplet on the bread are counterparts respectively to the two Jewish prayers quoted above. But the gift of knowledge (gnosis) and of eternal life replace the gifts of food for the body. Moreover the Supper has now become a meal restricted to initiates in which those only may take part who have been baptized "in the name of the Lord," and it is "the holy thing which the Lord commanded not to be given to dogs" (*Didache*, ix, 5). Here then we find not only a mystical meaning but a mystical power attached to the elements, the bread and wine, of the holy spirit.

Other prayers are indicated for use at the end of the meal, which, be it noted, still has the character of an ordinary meal regarded as now finished (*Didache*, x, 1–5):

> When you have eaten enough, this shall be your thanksgiving:
>   We thank thee, Holy Father,
>   for thy Holy name
>   which thou has caused to dwell in our hearts,
>   And for knowledge, faith and immortality
>   which thou hast made known to us by thy servant Jesus.
>   To thee be glory for ever and ever!
>   Thou, Master almighty,
>   Thou hast created all things to the honour of thy name.
>   Food and drink hast thou given for the making glad of man
>   for which they render thee thanks;
>   But thou hast also gladdened us with food and drink of the
>   spirit and of eternal life
>   by Jesus thy servant.
>   To thee glory for ever and ever!

> Remember thou thy Church
> to deliver it from all evil
> and make it perfect in thy love;
> Gather it from the four winds, make it holy
> in thy Kingdom which thou hast prepared,
> For thine are glory and power for ever and ever
> (*Didache*, x, 1–5).

In this chant it would seem that natural food and drink are recalled as a reminder that Christians have higher matters for thanksgiving than that for which the Jews offered theirs. Equal prominence is given to spiritual gifts and to the Church, but with the Great Event as the background of both. For there follows immediately a mystical dialogue of the highest interest between the president and the rest of the company:

> Come thou Gracious One and let the world pass away!
> Hosanna to the God of David
> Whoso is holy, let him come;
> Whoso is not, let him repent!
> Maranatha!
> Amen (*Didache*, x, 6).

In this the president announces and prays for the coming of the Gracious One, who is apparently Christ himself, announcement and prayer being uttered together in the mysterious "Maranatha"; at the same time he invites every man to search his conscience, the crowd answering with Hosanna and Amen to him who is to come, nay, who is come already. For the mystical presence of Christ in the midst of the company anticipates the parousia. At this stage the Eucharist is already a mystery; but it is the mystery of the Christian's hopes and of the unity of all believers in Christ the Spirit. Not yet has it become the mystery which continues and communicates his redeeming death; not yet have the bread and the wine become, in mystery, the body and blood of Jesus.

4. BAPTISM, BREAD AND WINE TAKEN UP INTO THE MYSTERY

In First Corinthians and in all the Gospels we find the bread and the wine charged with this mystical meaning and power as the body and blood of Jesus;[21] in the Epistle to the Romans baptism has undergone an analogous transformation (vi, 1–11). This we shall consider first.

In all it has to say about the ceremonial of baptism, the *Didache* shows a marked sobriety. The moral part of the book (i–vi) is a body of instruction to be given to catechumens in preparation for receiving the baptismal sacrament. This instruction, which consists of rules of conduct only, may be relatively old, although the collection of Gospel texts which accompany the precepts seems to be an addition later than the precepts themselves. As to the ritual, there is only this simple direction: "After expounding all that"—the moral precepts just mentioned which the candidate promises to follow—"baptize in the name of the Father, Son and Holy Spirit, in running water" (vii, 1). But running water is not indispensable: "if you have no running water, baptize in other water, and, if you cannot obtain cold water, use warm"—the word baptize here understood in its proper sense as total immersion. This is made clear by what follows: "If you have neither cold water nor warm, in quantity sufficient for total immersion—pour what you have three times on the candidate's head in the name of the Father, Son and Holy Spirit." Evidently this pouring out of a little water on the head as a substitute for the immersion of the whole body shows that the water is now symbolic. But a doubt may be permitted as to whether this Trinitarian formula goes back to the beginning of the second century.

Justin appears to be the oldest witness to the Trinitarian formula to whom a date can be assigned. "Those," says he (1 *Apology*, 61), "who are persuaded of what we teach and believe it true undertake"—reminding us of the oath mentioned by Pliny—"and are instructed to pray to God and ask him, after fasting, to pardon their past sins, we praying and fasting with them."—The *Didache* (vii, 4) also enjoins the candidate to fast for one or two days before baptism, the minister of the rite and fellow-believers fasting with him.—"Afterwards the candidates are taken by us to a place where there is water, and are regenerated by the mode of regeneration by which we ourselves were born again; to wit they are then immersed in water in the name of God the Father and Master of all things, and of our Lord Jesus Christ, and of the Holy Spirit." Justin

BIRTH OF THE CHRISTIAN MYSTERY AND OF ITS RITES

then proceeds to explain the spiritual nature of the new birth. He says that baptism is called "illumination" because the mind of the person baptized is illuminated by the doctrine he has learnt. His comment on the baptismal formula seems to turn it into a kind of symbol: The Son, he says, "is Jesus Christ who was crucified under Pontius Pilate" and the Holy Spirit he "who predicted by the prophets all that is told of Jesus."[22]

Although he never cites the fourth Gospel expressly, and is rarely inspired by it, he seems to have used it for his account of spiritual rebirth. In the discourse to Nicodemus he would read the theory of the sacrament stated thus:

> In truth, in truth, I say to thee
> Except a man be reborn of water and spirit
> he cannot enter the Kingdom of God.

In this theory of rebirth, water appears to be a principle or symbol of life rather than a purifying element. Elsewhere the fourth Gospel lays great stress on the virtue of running water as an element having eternal life and even represents the Christ as being, in his incarnation, the source of this running, life-giving water (iv, 14; vii, 37–39). It must not be forgotten that the fourth Gospel, like the others, was originally a catechism used in connexion with the rites of Christian initiation.

5. Baptism in the Epistle to the Romans

The Epistle to the Romans suggests a mystical symbolism somewhat different from the above, but one which had less influence on the subsequent course of Christian tradition (vi, 3–6):

> All we who were baptized to Christ Jesus
> to his death were we baptized.
> Thus were we buried with him
> by baptism in death
> To the end, that as Christ is raised from the dead by the
> glory of the Father
> we in like manner may walk in newness of life:
> For if we were associated to his death, by imitation,[23]
> we shall also be with him in his resurrection,

> Knowing this:
>> that our old man was crucified with him
>> that the body of sin might be destroyed.

What does this mean? Evidently that the baptismal immersion is a mystical burial in the water whereby the Christian is made one with Christ dead and buried, the effect being that our sinful flesh is also crucified, done to death and consigned to the grave. But, just as Christ rose glorious from death by the power of God, so the Christian emerges reborn from his baptismal immersion and comes forth from the water as one rising from his grave, mystically, inwardly and morally risen from the dead in readiness for the glory of his resurrection to immortal life. Once baptized he is a new man, dead to sin that he may live henceforth to God. We shall see later how this conception of baptism is connected with a general and balanced system of mystical gnosis in its bearing on the scheme of sin-and-redemption. In contrast to the Johannine theory in which water appears as a principle and symbol of life, it is here to be understood rather as a symbol of death, figuring the tomb of the carnal man from which the spiritual man is to emerge, but without water being the agent of the spirit's action. In this version the baptismal immersion is not a sacrament effecting the regeneration of the sinner but, if we may say so, a sacramental condition of its being effected. We get a somewhat different result, however, if we try to adjust what is said in First Corinthians (xv, 29) about baptism for the dead to the theory just summarized. So adjusted, the sacramental condition is no less indispensable and efficacious in its own way than the sacrament of baptism in the water of eternal life: baptism undergone by proxy on behalf of a person deceased is able to produce the same effect on him as it would if performed on the living man. To insist on so peculiar a feature would here, perhaps, be out of place, though it had importance in its own day. The tradition of the Church does not retain it.

Elsewhere (in 1 Corinthians x, 1–5) a parallel is set up between the Christian Sacraments and the sacraments of the Desert—the baptism of the Israelites by Moses under the cloud and in the sea, and a kind of Eucharist in the heavenly manna and the water struck from the rock. This apparently belongs to another gnosis, probably not less ancient than the former and with closer affinities to the gnosis of the fourth Gospel.

> For I would not have you ignorant,
> brethren.
> That our fathers were all under the wet mist,
> and that all went through the sea,
> That all were baptized to Moses
> in the wet mist and in the sea;
> That all ate the same spiritual food
> and all drank the same spiritual drink;
> —For they drank of the spiritual rock[24] that
> followed them;
> now the rock was the Christ,—
> But that most of them pleased not God,
> for they were destroyed in the desert.

Here is a warning that Christian sacraments will not preserve from reprobation those believers who sin as gravely as the Israelites sinned in the desert. But it would be a mistake to expect in this homiletical effort a system of sacramental theology neatly rounded off. What we here listen to are the lispings of Christian thought in its first attempts to understand the sacraments. But the movement of thought is not here towards the theory of baptism-burial as in Romans. The action of the spirit is introduced into all sacraments, even into those of the Desert, while care is taken to avoid too much magic by a warning that sacraments will not save those who offend against the Law of God. The chief interest of the passage lies in the way it links together the two sacraments of baptism and eucharist, and links them so closely that the two are carried back, in their connexion, to the Old Testament where, for our part, we should not expect to find them.

Justin gives explicit testimony that the two were thus linked together by his time (*Apology*, 65). Immediately after his bath of regeneration, the baptized person is conducted to the spot where the brethren are gathered. All then join in prayer, both for the individual baptized and for Christians in general, that their knowledge of truth may be joined to the practice of good and that eternal salvation may be theirs. "When the prayers are finished we kiss each other. Next in order, bread and a cup of water[25] are brought to him who presides among the brethren; and he, taking them, praises and glorifies the Father of all things, in the name of the Son and the Holy Spirit,[26] and delivers a long thanksgiving for all the benefits wherewith he has blessed us." Evidently the exercise of thanksgiving over the elements of the repast has become much longer since the time of the *Didache*,[27] and, equally evident, that this is not a meal that might satisfy hunger, except symbolically by the simple distribution and prompt consumption of the elements over which the prayers have been uttered. In other words we have now reached the stage when the meeting of the brethren has become wholly spiritual and nothing remains of their daily meal except the sacrament. "When the president has concluded his prayers and thanksgivings all the people answer by acclamation, saying: Amen." After which the "deacons" distribute the eucharistic elements among those present to be carried to the absent brethren (1 *Apology*, 65).

Admission to communion thus became an essential part of Christian initiation: but communion itself was no more than one part of the ritual of initiation and, for yet stronger reason, was not, even in its origin, part of the baptismal rite or an appendix to it. It was rather, in strictness of language, the rite of those who had been initiated; it was as already made Christian by his baptism that the baptized person was introduced to the sacrament. Justin himself tells us (i, 67) that the ordinary service of the Sunday Communion was performed in the same manner as that which he has just described as proper to baptism, except that it began with a more or less lengthy reading from "the Memoirs of the Apostles," that is, from the Gospels, or perhaps from the prophetical writings; the president then delivers exhortation based on the passage read; after which all rise up for prayer, eucharist (thanksgiving) and communion (*Apology*, 67). Originally the religious meal of the community, but a meal in the ordinary sense and for the ordinary purpose, the Christian Communion became a purely religious and somewhat complicated exercise, the chief liturgy of the congregations, in which the symbolic and sacramental rite of common participation in the same food remained essential and dominant.

Justin dwells at some length on the eucharist (i, 66), explaining why only those are admitted to it who have been baptized and are living conformably to the precepts of Christ, the reason being that this is no ordinary repast. "Even as Jesus Christ took flesh and blood by the Word of God, so the nutriment which sustains our flesh and our blood, blessed by the prayer of the Word, becomes flesh and blood of Jesus incarnate." By "prayer of the Word" our author understands the blessing pronounced by Jesus on the bread and the cup at the last meal he took with his disciples[28]—not the so-called formula of institution, "This is my body. This is my blood." Not till much later than Justin was the idea born which sees in these words what has been named the "form" of the eucharistic sacrament.

In his *Memoirs of the Apostles* Justin read the instructions given by the Christ with regard to the Supper. "Jesus, having taken bread, gave thanks and said 'Do this in remembrance of me. This is my body.' Having also taken the cup, he gave thanks and said 'This is my blood.' And to them alone he made distribution."—Note that Justin makes no reference to First Corinthians. Not once does he quote from the Epistles. He would seem to be unacquainted with the work of Paul, though he cannot have been wholly ignorant about him, for he knew Marcion well enough. The words which he quotes as evangelical are in approximate agreement, for the bread, to the text of canonical Luke (xxii, 19) and, for the cup, to that of Matthew (xxvi, 28).

In his *Dialogue with Trypho* (41) Justin refers to the offering of wheaten flour prescribed by the Law (in Leviticus xiv) to a purified leper, and writes as follows: "This prefigured the bread of the eucharist which Jesus Christ our Lord bade us consecrate, in memory of the passion undergone by him for the purification of men's souls from perversity, to the end that we might render thanks to God for having created for man the world and all that it contains, for having delivered us from the evil into which we had fallen and for having finally broken the principalities and powers[29] by him who came to suffer according to his will." In another place (70), commenting on Isaiah xxxiii, 16 ("bread shall be given him and his water[30] shall be sure"), Justin notes that the prophecy refers to "the bread which our Christ bade us consecrate in memory of his incarnation and of his sufferings for believers, and to the cup which he bade us consecrate in memory of his blood."

At this stage, then, the picture may be thus presented. The Christian Supper, in virtue of its institution as recorded in the Gospels, is a mystical commemoration of the death of Jesus, an exercise of thanksgiving for the redemption effected by his death, the thanks being added to those rendered to God for the gift of the created world, and a mystical participation and communion in the flesh and blood of the incarnate Word.

From a simple act of thanksgiving for an ordinary meal of bread and wine, when not of bread and water, Christian thought and practice has now arrived (*circa* 140) at a repast of which the meaning is purely religious. This has become a symbol, not very felicitous, of a unique sacrifice, an image of the Passion which saves the believer, a sacrament of communion with the dying Saviour, a communion which is the pledge of immortality. Such is the result at this stage, not arrived at all at once, but by long and complicated labour of Christian thought and as the outcome of a veritable evolution in Christian liturgy. The idea of the baptized person as made completely one with the dead Christ failed to take root in Christian tradition; but communion with the crucified Christ, by participating in the Lord's Supper, became the very centre of Christian worship. So Justin understood the matter, and this is what he found in existence, though the last step in the process cannot have been achieved long before his time.

6. The Johannite Eucharist

In its bearing on the tradition reputed to be apostolic the Fourth Gospel has a position all its own. The account of the last meal taken by Jesus is here the account of a developed eucharist lacking the essential words in the tradition we have just analysed (xiii, 1–17, 20, 31–xvii). With the sublimity fitting to his Person the Christ here holds the place of the presiding celebrant mentioned by Justin, but holds it as sovereign Master of the Mystery who, having himself accomplished the work of salvation, praises God that his work is done. He teaches, he prays, he offers thanks; he celebrates the banquet of divine love, of the union of the faithful in God and in the Christ who died for them; but says not a word of the bread and the wine, nor of any commemorative act. The canonical edition of the Gospel contains a double series of his instructions, xiii–xiv and xv–xvii. Both are conceived in an atmosphere purely eucharistic, and this is especially marked in the long prayer at the end of the collection (xvii), spoken by the Christ as author of salvation and first celebrant of the eucharistic mystery which shows forth his saving death:

> Holy Father, keep them in thy name,
>   those thou has given me,
>   that they may be one as we are . . .
> I ask thee not to take them out of the world,
>   but to guard them from the Evil One . . .
> For them I sanctify myself,
>   that they also may be sanctified in truth . . .
> And the glory thou gavest to me, yea to me,
>   I gave to them,
> That they may be one
>   as we are one,
> I in them
>   and thou in me
>   that they may be perfect in unity,
> That the world may know
>   that thou hast sent me
> And that thou hast loved them
>   as thou hast loved me.
> Father, those whom thou hast given me,
>   I would that where I am
>   They too may be with me,
> That they may see my glory,
>   which thou hast given me,
> For thou hast loved me
>   before the foundation of the world.
> Righteous Father, the world has known thee not,
>   but I, I knew thee;
> And they too have known
>   that thou hast sent me.
> And to them have I made known thy name,
>   and will make it known,
> That the love wherewith thou lovest me may be
>   in them and I in them.

This utterance of sublime mysticism which we would willingly have cited in full—whence came it? Is it a vain imagination to think that one Easter Day a Christian seer, speaking in the name of the Christ, chanted it for the first time to an assembly of the faithful in one of the churches of Asia where the Christian Easter, falling on the day of the Jewish Passover, celebrated the redeeming and triumphant death of him who was the Lamb of God?

It seems certain that, in the tradition of the fourth Gospel, the institution of the Supper goes back to the miracle of the multiplied loaves (vi, 1–14). Knowing, as we do, that this miracle is, in reality, one of the oldest of the Christian supper-myths, it is not surprising that the Ephesian Gospel presents it as the symbolic institution of the Eucharist. In the first part of the discourse on the bread of life (vi, 26–51a) the symbolic bread is, in reality, Jesus himself, but not as being present mystically in the bread considered as his body. As bread is the life of the body, as manna was the life of the Israelites in the desert so Jesus, for those who believe in him, is life itself, and eternal life.

> Verily, verily, I tell you,
>> Moses gave you not
>>> the bread of heaven.
> My father is he who gives you
>> the bread of heaven,
>>> the true bread.
> For the bread of God
>> is he who comes down from heaven
>>> and gives life to the world ...
> 'Tis I who am the bread of life,
>> who comes to me
>>> shall have no hunger;
> Who believes in me
>> shall never thirst ...
> 'Tis I who am the living bread
>> which came down from heaven.
> If any man eats of this bread
>> he shall live for ever.

Up to this point Jesus is supposed to be explaining in what sense he is the bread of life for those who believe in him. The bread is a figure, a figure of spiritual salvation as offered and guaranteed by Jesus. But far from being a mere figure of speech, the author of this commentary on the bread of life has in mind throughout the bread of the Supper, to which he gives the mystical meaning of the *Didache*. There is a real bread of life; thanks are given for it in the Christian Supper: it is the Christ with the life that he gives to the believer. By this insistence on the reality of the bread the discourse is none the less a eucharistic utterance; but in the spirit of the *Didache*.

Now comes a sequel to this discourse, apparently a later addition (vi, 51b–58) which connects with the tradition presented by Justin as that of the apostles:

> And the bread I will give
>   'tis my flesh
>   for the life of the world . . .
> Verily, verily, I tell you,
> If you eat not the flesh of the Son of Man
>   nor drink his blood,
>   you have no life in you.
> Who eats my flesh
>   and drinks my blood
>   has eternal life . . .[31]
> For my flesh is real nourishment
>   and my blood real beverage.
> Who eats my flesh
>   and drinks my blood
>   abides in me and I in him . . .
> 'Tis the spirit that makes alive,
>   the flesh serves for naught:
> The words I have spoken to you
>   are spirit, are life.

Here is a development presented as a commentary, or explanation given to the disciples, on the preceding passage, where the saying that bread is flesh is stated to have resulted in the amazement of the Jews (vi, 52; 59–62). It must, however, be the author of this assertion who speculates in the added passage on the mystic meaning of bread and wine as tantamount to flesh and blood.[32] According to this author flesh and blood is what they truly are, but only in a mystical or spiritual sense. What the believer eats, as he commemorates the death of Christ in the Supper, is not flesh, and what he drinks is not blood. The spirit of God and of Christ—that is the sustenance of which he partakes. A great lesson which the theologians of the age of iron no longer understand!

7. The Supper in First Corinthians

The same process of superimposing a religious rite on a common meal may be clearly seen in the accounts of the eucharist given in First Corinthians[33] and in the Synoptic Gospels,[34] with the difference that the lesson on the Supper in Corinthians seems to come from a single source while in the Gospels the introduction of the symbolic words of institution is added by a second hand. Moreover the lesson in the Epistle appears to be the older of the two, and is completed in the same Epistle by another passage (x, 1–22) in which the Supper is compared with the pagan sacrifices and given the character of a sacrificial banquet. In this passage the underlying idea is the same as that suggested by the Gospel account of the institution. This we shall consider later.

It would seem that the Corinthians, professing to carry out what their apostle had taught them, treated the Supper as an ordinary meal at which everybody ate and drank as he pleased without respecting the common bond which held them together (xi, 17–22). To make them ashamed of such abuse Paul will now recall the conditions in which the Supper was established by the Christ himself (xi, 23–25):

> I myself have from the Lord
>   that which I also passed on to you,
> That the Lord Jesus, on the night he was betrayed,
>   took bread and, having given thanks, broke it and said:
> "This is my body, which is for you;
>   do this in remembrance of me."
> Likewise also the cup, after the meal, saying:
> "This cup is the new covenant in my blood;
>   this do, as often as you drink it, in memory of me."

From this he draws the conclusion that the Supper is a solemn act commemorating the death of the Lord "till he come"; to partake of it in an unseemly manner is to eat and drink damnation; see to it, then, that everything is done in good order.

Some strange features confront us in this passage. It is strange that Paul, if he had really told all this to the Corinthians before, should here be obliged to recall it; strange that he should present it as a revelation received by him from the Lord;[35] strange that a doctrine implying the theory of redemption by the blood of the

Christ, and linked artificially to the benediction of bread and wine customary at Jewish meals, should see the light in the first generation, when Christians lived in expectation of an immediate parousia. On the other hand it is significant that regard is here paid to that expectation. Evidently the vision of the institution of the Supper which Paul professes to have had is conceived in the framework of a story relating the last meal of Jesus with his disciples in which preoccupation with the Great Event was the dominant feature. Mention of it accordingly is made as follows (xi, 26):

> For as often as this bread you eat
> and this cup you drink
> You proclaim the Lord's death
> till he come.[36]

In the economy of the Supper *as a mystic rite* this reference to the parousia, made at a time when it was no longer thought of as imminent, is out of place. The mention of it is due to an old and firmly established tradition. There is ground therefore for saying that mystic commemoration of the saving death, the mystic communion with the crucified Christ, is superposed on a form of the Supper as an anticipation of the banquet of the elect in the Kingdom of God, a form clearly indicated in a saying embedded in the oldest tradition of the synoptic Gospels:

> Verily, verily, I tell you
> that I will drink no more
> of the fruit of the vine,
> Until that day
> when I drink it new
> in the Kingdom of God.

The account of the mystic Supper, in First Corinthians, belongs to the evolution of the Christian Mystery at a stage in the development of that mystery earlier than Justin, earlier even than the canonical edition of the first three Gospels but notably later than Paul and the apostolic age. It must be dated in the period when the common meal was in process of transformation into a simple liturgical act. The passage in question is a conscious attempt to further the transformation by giving it the apostolical authority of Paul. In Justin's time the transformation was fully effected; in

Marcion's time it was a thing of the recent past; so, too, in Bithynia in Pliny's time, but only just effected, the imperial orders regulating the religious fraternities having contributed to bring it about. We conclude that this lesson on the good ordering of the Supper was drawn up towards 140 in some circle where the memory of Paul was held in honour.

The mystical sense of the Supper as here understood is explained in a long passage which warns the Corinthians against taking part in the sacrificial meals of the pagans (x, 1–22); in it there occurs the following (16–17, 20–21):

> The cup of blessing, which we bless
>   is it not communion in the blood of the Christ?
> The bread which we break
>   is it not communion in the body of the Christ?
> Being all one bread, all one body are we;
>   For of the one bread all we partake ...
> That which pagans sacrifice,
>   to demons and not to God they sacrifice it.
> Lo, I would not have you be
>   in communion with demons:
> You cannot drink the cup of the Lord
>   and the cup of demons;
> You cannot have place at the table of the Lord
>   and at the table of demons.

In this text, assimilation of the Supper to the sacrificial meal is as complete as it could be. The Christ, in his attitude to Christians who would associate with pagans in their sacrificial meals, is like a god roused to anger on seeing his altar abandoned or defiled. The eucharistic elements are assimilated to the sacrificial victims and offerings of both Israelite and pagan cults. The Christian Supper, endlessly renewed, is conceived as related to the unique sacrifice—the death of Jesus on the cross—in the same way as any sacrificial meal would be related to the immolation of the victims that furnished viands for the feast. Unnatural as this conception of the Supper was, it rested nevertheless on an analogy, mystically apprehended as a reality, between the elements of the commemorative Supper and the remains of the victims that were eaten after being offered in sacrifice to the gods. A strange position would seem to be assigned to the Christ; he is at once the divine president at the sacrificial banquet and the victim, served as meat and drink on the table. But the pagan gods, notably Dionysus and Osiris, were in the same position.

Our texts make much of the general idea of sacrificial communion which also implies the further notion of mystical communion between the victim slain and the god to whom it is offered; for, if the believer enters into communion with his god by eating the victim, the reason must be that there resides in the victim a certain mystic and divine power which acts as the medium in effecting communion between his god and him. In this respect the God of Israel, the gods of the pagans and the Christ stand on the same level: all three alike share a common table with their devotees and commune with them in the holy meal, united to them in partaking of the victim they all are eating. Although there is nothing divine in the sacrificial viands—at least so we are told (x, 19)—and nothing divine in the bread and wine of the Supper, a mystic union is nevertheless formed both in the sacrificial meals of the pagans and in the Christian Supper. But the union so formed is quite other than simple moral likemindedness between the divine beings, Jewish, pagan and Christian, on the one side, and on the other, their worshippers, be they Jews or pagans offering sacrifice, or Christians partaking of Eucharistic bread and wine. When the victim is eaten by the pagan, it is certainly not his god that he eats; neither is it the material body of the Christ that the Christian eats when he eats the bread, nor his blood that he drinks in the wine. (Let it be said in passing that this idea of communion with God by drinking the blood of a sacrificed victim was never born in the brain of a Jew.) No eating of the god's body is here, and no drinking of his blood; but a real communion of spirit is established between the god sacrificed, or sacrificed to, and those whose part in the sacrifice is to eat and drink the material of the oblation. This communion of spiritual power is in agreement with the common notion of the meaning of sacrifice, but not with the orthodox notion of Israelite sacrifice as a rendering of homage and mark of fidelity. In the texts before us it is intensely concrete and intensely alive. Not only is it a relation of reciprocal love but, more than that, a through-and-through penetration of the human by the divine in which the believer is completely possessed by the Christ-Spirit.

8. The Synoptic Account of the Last Supper

Many Protestant critics have maintained and many still maintain that the symbolic sayings "this is my body," "this is my blood"—at least the first of them—belong to the primitive tradition and are authentic words of Jesus, but spoken by him in a sense different from that given them by tradition and by Paul in the first instance. They contend that Jesus merely made a simple comparison between the bread broken, the wine poured out, and the fate that was awaiting him. An uncalled-for hypothesis and consequently a risky one. The sayings in question have a natural fitness to the mystical interpretation of the Supper, and to that only, and have to be teased before any meaning acceptable to reason can be got out of them—to the reason that is of those who insist on finding such a meaning.

These critics moreover overlook the hopeless incoherence in the account of the matter given in Mark (xiv, 22–25) on which Matthew and Luke are both dependent. This account is a kind of summary covering many implied meanings which the reader is supposed to understand without needing to have them mentioned. In the first rank of what is thus taken for granted and left unexpressed is the idea, which should be attributed to Paul, that the last meal taken by Jesus is the first Eucharist, the prototype on which the Christian rite is founded. In reality the Gospel account has Paul's teaching in view, and purports to be in accord with that teaching alone. But the elements of which the account is composed are not all in accordance with that. They are not homogeneous. The two types of the Supper which we have distinguished above are both represented—the ordinary meal and the mystical rite. The same occasion cannot have produced them both at a single birth, and we have therefore to look for their historical relationship. Here is the passage to be considered:

> And while they were eating,
>   he, taking bread, broke it after benediction;
> He gave it to them, and said:
>   "Take; this is my body."
> And taking the cup,
>   after giving thanks, he gave it to them,
>   and they all drank of it.

BIRTH OF THE CHRISTIAN MYSTERY AND OF ITS RITES

> And he said to them:
> "This is my blood of the covenant,
>   shed for many.
> Verily I say to you
>   I will drink no more," etc.

Let us examine this. We can see at once that the words "This is my body" would be utterly unintelligible for a reader unacquainted with the Christian Eucharist. Clearly then he is supposed to be acquainted with it. He knows—not indeed what Jesus, on the hypothesis of our Protestant critics, could not have failed to say in clearing up the enigma—but what was in the mind of the evangelist and what was thought about it all in the Christian group for which the second Gospel was written. The meaning of the mysterious saying "This is my body"[37] and of the mysterious saying "This is my blood" are co-ordinate to the same effect. They refer to the bruised and crucified body represented by the bread—not quite happily, the body of Jesus not having been broken in pieces—just as the wine (or water) of the cup represents the blood of Jesus (and not more happily, since the blood of Jesus was not poured out, as would have happened had he been, for example, executed by decapitation). All this would be intelligible enough to a Christian reader familiar with the developed eucharistic rite as practised in the group for which the Gospel was intended: but perfectly unintelligible on the occasion when the sayings are supposed to have been uttered. In short, it is hard to conceive or, rather, impossible to conceive why Jesus should resort to these dark sayings—for dark they then would be and there is no question of their being parable—instead of explaining in a few simple words why he was exposing himself to death. These mystic sayings have no natural sense except as referring to an established Christian sacrament, and as explaining it.

In the passage before us there is a difference in the manner of introducing the bread and the cup respectively, and it is important to note that the narrator hardly seems to have foreseen the mystic explanation of the latter. The mystic explanation of the bread is inserted at the appropriate moment when Jesus has given the broken loaf to the disciples. Coming to the cup the evangelist writes, "He gave it to them and they all drank of it" (Mark xiv, 23), whence it follows that the cup was empty when Jesus said "This is my blood"(24). There was no more *this*. Clumsy editing, one would say. Yes, and the clumsiness so flagrant that Matthew has corrected it, writing, when he comes to the cup, "Drink of it all of you, for this is my blood" (xxvi, 27, 28). But the blunder would not have been made if the words "this is my blood" had been present in the fundamental document of Mark on which the editor of canonical Mark was working. On the contrary, the formula "he gave it to them and they all drank of it" would lead on quite naturally to the sequel "I will drink no more of the fruit of the vine," etc., and this is the sequel it demands. In this sequence the implied meaning would be that Jesus himself drank of the wine-cup with the rest of the company, just as he is supposed to have shared with them in the eating of the bread. But the mystic words "this is my body," "this is my blood" are inconsistent with the supposition that Jesus himself partook of the bread and wine, which would be tantamount to saying that he was mystically nourished by his own flesh and his own blood. What could more clearly confirm the impossibility of attributing these words to Jesus in his life on earth? Mystical participation in the body and blood of the Christ becomes intelligible only when understood as referring to the spiritual Jesus, and not as referring to Jesus present in the flesh and conversing with his disciples. Moreover one need not be a master in critical science to see that the saying about the eucharistic body and blood of the Christ belongs to a wholly different current of ideas from that of the words, "I will drink no more wine," etc.

The overlaying of an earlier by a later version which is so apparent in Mark has an interest for the history of the Supper as well as for the criticism of the second Gospel. The first evangelical account of the Supper was one in which the meal was conceived as foreshadowing the banquet of the elect in the coming Kingdom, and not as a mystic and symbolical participation in the body and blood of the Christ taking place there and then. It is an old conjecture that the original story contained, in the place now occupied by "this is my body," words analogous to those spoken over the wine: "I will eat no more bread," etc., words which seem to have been preserved, with the substitution of "passover" for bread, in canonical Luke (xxii, 15–16).[38] In the original story of the Supper, Jesus was not represented as formally instituting a rite. The Supper was presented as a dutiful repetition of the last meal, in which was condensed, so to say, the memory of the many meals taken by Jesus with his disciples, together with a perpetual reminder of his death. This primitive Supper was no repetition of Jesus' death, but the recall of it in commemoration, and dominated throughout, as in the thought of Jesus himself, by an outlook towards the Great Event—in other words, an anticipation of the festival awaiting the elect in the Kingdom of heaven, accompanied by a lively sense of the invisible presence of Jesus who has died and was alive again. This type of the Supper was not confined to Jewish Christianity, but must have been the type common to both Hellenic and Jewish Christians for quite a long time. Needless to say this eschatological Supper did not suddenly give way to the mystical type outlined in First Corinthians. The approximate date would coincide with that of the modifications introduced into the Gospel books, or, let us say, the date when the Sunday Easter was substituted for the quartodeciman usage, and when the community meal ceased to be a meal and became a liturgy. This was not till after the year 70 and probably towards the end of the first century or the beginning of the second.

To sum up. We may take it as established that the eucharistic prayer in the earliest time was an outpouring of gratitude, on the occasion of a community meal, for the gift of salvation, which consisted in participation in the Kingdom of God, a gift added to the blessing of creation. Christ was thought to come in person, but invisibly, at the simple call of his faithful ones, and the meal was holy, the elements being consecrated by the prayer of thanksgiving. Then, under the general influence of the mystery cults, there was born spontaneously the idea of a mystic communion with the Christ in the elements of the Supper, a communion understood in terms of the Christ dying for the justification of men that he might rise for their glorification: the meal now becomes a wholly ritual and symbolic act around which there grows up a genuine liturgy. Finally, the idea of sacrificial communion thus introduced issues, towards the end of the second century, in causing the elements of the Supper to be regarded as an oblation which God is asked to fill with spiritual power in virtue of its assimilation to the body and blood of Jesus—as in the

Liturgy of Hippolytus. But, vastly as the Supper has grown in significance, the ritual of it still always and essentially remains an act of thanksgiving over the bread and the cup. Thus, notwithstanding the long evolution of mystic faith and theological doctrine, it still holds fast to its point of departure—the prayers of the Jew giving thanks for meat and drink.

Chapter VIII

EARLIEST THEORIES OF THE CHRISTIAN MYSTERY

It is obvious that the theory of the Christian mystery supported the system of its sacraments, the Christian faith which these reflect being widely different from the Jewish hope, conditioned, as it was, by the national restoration of Judaism. Much that is written in the New Testament books represents the efforts that were made, one after the other and from different angles, to equip the new religion with a balanced doctrine both in regard to the central object of the religion, the person and work of its founder, and to the form of its practice in the society of believers. To this process we now turn.

1. Theory in the Epistle to the Romans

The mystical gnosis developed in the Epistle to the Romans did not enter entire into the general current of Christian tradition, at least before Augustine, and even the influence of the Doctor of Hippo prevailed only within the Latin Church. This gnosis, however, with the additions and modifications given it in other Epistles attributed to Paul, constitutes the most complete, if not the oldest, known attempt made by Christian speculation to transform messianic faith into a theory of redemption, more or less analogous to the doctrine of pagan mysticism, but without abandoning the ground of Biblical revelation and of the Gospel message of the Kingdom of God.

In an apparently authentic part of the Epistle (iii, 27–iv, 24) Paul has proved that Gentiles were entitled to enter the Kingdom of God on condition of faith in Jesus, who became Christ by his resurrection. Abraham, he says, was justified solely by faith in the divine promise at a time when he was still uncircumcised; whence it follows that uncircumcised pagans can be saved in the same manner and on exactly the same terms as the Jews, the circumcised descendants of Abraham. Thus Gentile believers took their place, so to say, in the general scheme of Israel's hope, which was to come to fruition in the conversion of Israel itself after the Gospel has been preached to all the pagans.[1] Thus it stands in the passage before us. But the problem of salvation is resumed from quite a different point of view in the chapters which deal with the scheme of redemption. Here there is no longer question of the promises made to Abraham for his posterity, but of a plan of salvation intended by Divine Providence, from the beginning of the world, to embrace the whole of mankind, the revelation to the Jews being no more than an interlude connected with the fall of man, not the real basis of his restoration.

God, we are told, has proved his love for men in that Christ died for the redemption of the sinful human race. Here are the providential conditions under which this came about:

> As by one sole man sin entered the world,
>   and death by sin.
> And thus death passed to all men,
>   because all have sinned . . .
> As from one sole transgression
>   there followed condemnation for all,
> So from one sole deed of justice
>   there followed justification for life
> For, as by the disobedience of one sole man
>   the rest were all made sinners,
> So by the obedience of one sole man
>   the rest are made righteous.[2]

Nothing could less resemble an improvised letter than these studied declarations of which even the form is carefully balanced. But their importance lies in their matter. Two images, two men, two Adams dominate the whole of human history. The first Adam, "image of him who was to come," has by his sole transgression involved all humanity in sin and death. (A tragic interpretation of the old story of the first man being driven out of God's garden, where the Tree of Life was, for having disobeyed his Creator!)[3] The second Adam, Jesus Christ, by an act of justice, of perfect virtue, which was also an act of obedience, to wit his voluntary submission to death—the death due to all men as sinners like their father Adam, but not due to the Christ, a heavenly being by origin and nature and not descended from the first Adam—this second Adam has, by the aforesaid act of justice rendered men irreproachable before God. This, virtually, he has done for all mankind but, actually, for those who believe in him and who, through baptism, are mystically identified with him in his death and so participate in his resurrection.

The fifteenth chapter of First Corinthians is yet more explicit about the two Adams:

> Thus is it written:
> There was made the first man, Adam,
>   living soul
> The last Adam
>   lifegiving Spirit.
> But the spiritual is not first,
>   the first is the living,
>   then the spiritual.
> The first man, being of earth, is earthy,
>   the second man is of heaven.
> As is the one earthy
>   so are the many;
> As is the one heavenly
>   so are the many,
> And as we have borne the likeness of the earthy,
>   we shall bear the likeness of the heavenly ...
> Flesh and blood cannot inherit the Kingdom of God
>   and corruption will not inherit incorruption.

By an exigesis of extreme subtlety the two Adams are here deduced from Genesis, which is not to be wholly credited either with the Adam of perdition or with the Adam of salvation, very emphatically not with the latter. They are myth figures here adapted to Genesis and to the Gospel. The terrestrial Adam and his heavenly counterpart are the primordial Adam divided into two, the ideal prototype and its historical realization. This is the myth of Man, whence is derived the Son of Man of the Gospels, who is the pre-existing type of humanity and the destined agent in effecting his salvation. Philo[4] knew the two "men" in question, but gave priority to the celestial. Fundamentally our author has the same idea; but, taking his point of view at the historical manifestation, he puts the terrestrial man first, reducing primordial man to primacy in sin, misery and death and reserving the Celestial Man for the end of the ages.

Strange things are told us in Romans about the Law (v, 13, 20, 21):

> Until the Law
> > Sin was in the world;
> > But was not counted as sin,
> > > there being no law . . .
> > The Law came in
> > > that transgression might abound;
> > But where sin abounded
> > > grace abounded more,
> > To the end that, as sin reigned in death,
> > > so grace may reign by justice to eternal life,
> > > > by Jesus Christ our Lord.

The author's idea of the Mosaic Law, and indeed of law in general, could hardly have occured save to one born outside the Jewish fold, who, weighing the Law as an outsider, judged it impracticable. His view is, moreover, that man, being inclined to sin by the natural appetites of the flesh, the Law, by bringing to his notice the opportunities for sinning, would, so to say, incite him to commit the very sins it forbids. A strange mode, truly, of understanding social obligation and the reasons underlying legislation in general! Where, then, are we to look for a regulating principle and a criterion of good? Our prophet is embarrassed by no such trifles. According to him, sin, death and law are inseparably one and constitute, as it were, the Trilogy of damnation; grace, righteousness, eternal life are the Trilogy of salvation; immortality issues from righteousness, and righteousness from grace—grace granted to every man who, having faith in Jesus dead and risen from death, participates in his death and resurrection; such a believer dies to sin, lives to God, enters without effort into the way of righteousness, all under the impulse of a new spirit. All virtues are born of the spirit of grace. The logical consequence of the system would be that the believer is incapable of sin. But a formal admission of this is here avoided though it is hinted at in Romans vi, 14, and expressed in plain terms in 1 John iii, 6.

Dealing throughout with abstractions, our author believes he is dealing with realities. His conceptions are terribly ponderous, not to say mechanical, and yet not far removed from a primitive mentality. In the presence of death he is like a child seeking the key to a non-existent problem. Death, in reality, is the natural ending of every form of life on earth, and the miracle would be if man had escaped it. Death reigned before there was any sin to generate it. And what is our author's idea of sin? A fearful and monstrous abstraction, behind which, most assuredly, there is a fact only too real, but a simple fact quite otherwise explicable than by the innate corruption of the flesh and the pretended provocation of it by the law; a fact to be simply explained by human weakness in presence of the ideal born in social life, the weakness resulting from the limitations of reason, from the kind of constraint which our natural appetites impose on the reflecting will. The idea of grace is not less ponderous, nor that of redemption less artificial. Sin, the capital evil of humanity, innate in the flesh —though we are not told how—is suddenly annihilated because the Christ, having taken flesh, takes sin upon him also, but without being defiled by it, and then, by the destruction of his own flesh effects the destruction of sin in humanity at large. The idea at the back of this is not expiation, but elimination, as in most of the ancient sacrifices classed as expiatory, and notably in the scapegoat, mystically loaded with the sins of Israel, which he carries away with him into the desert. Thus the sin of the guilty human race is done away with in the body of the Man-Christ, who was himself untouched by it. Childish dreams worked up into a theological nightmare and adapted, by hook or crook, to a lofty moral conception!

To this strange system some corrections are applied by the Epistle itself (vii, 14–17):

> We know that the Law is spiritual;
> but, as for me, I am carnal,
> sold to sin.[5]
> For what I do, I understand it not:
> 'tis not what I would that I do,
> 'tis what I abhor that I do.
> Now, if what I would not is what I do
> I acknowledge that the Law is good;
> But it is no more I who do it,
> 'tis sin abiding in me.

Here are subtleties enough, but not without psychological meaning and moral insight. The Law, we are told, being spiritual, is so far good; but the flesh is turned towards evil, even when reason perceives the good and assents to the Law. Man now appears to be torn asunder between two tendencies, both permanent, in so much that, contrary to the system we have just examined, justification would not seem to be acquired once and for all, but to result only from a victory constantly renewed by the help of the spirit in a struggle that goes on till life ends (vii, 18–23). The conception is here more sober, more philosophic, being partly borrowed from the philosophers, and bearing marks of serious reasoning and genuine psychological experience. But we should completely deceive ourselves if we thought we could find in these theoretical views the profound and purely personal experience by which Paul was led to his faith in the Christ.

The chief author of this system had in his mind an idea of the whole world as subject, against its will, to corruption, and as sharing with believers in the Christ in the expectation of deliverance. Everything suffers violence in this lower sphere, still reigned over by evil spirits, "the princes of this world"; they it was who, according to First Corinthians (ii, 8),[6] without knowing him, "crucified the Lord of Glory." The final redemption of the suffering universe will be effected in the metamorphosis awaiting the elect. "The creation, impatiently waiting, longs for the manifestation of the Sons of God"—in their glory as they will appear in this new world; "for to vanity"—doubtless to the subordinate powers which govern it so ill—"has the whole creation been made subject, not of its own will"—having never desired such servitude—"but by the doing of Him who so subjected it"—doubtless God who appointed the evil powers to rule the visible world—"in hope that the creation also"—sharing the resurrection of humanity—"will be delivered from the bondage of corruption"—which the evil powers impose on the world chiefly through the pagan cults—"that it may attain the liberty of the glory of the children of God." And the author even speaks of the creation as "travailing" and "groaning" in company with mankind.[7]

Evidently the triumph of the elect is no longer conceived as the reign of the Christ on this earth in a Jerusalem made glorious; for the lower, material world will disappear to make room for the expansion and manifestation of the spiritual world. Nevertheless the spiritual world is not purely ideal; even the elect who will possess it are to have bodies, spiritual bodies of an ethereal substance, light, subtle and luminous (1 Corinthians xv, 35–44). As to the nature of this substance, the clearest information the writer can give us is that it will not be gross, like the matter of which the present world is composed.

So pessimistic a view of the material world might well suggest that foreign influence is here at work. It brings to mind the Persian doctrine of the world as created by the wicked Ahriman whom one day the good Ormuzd will destroy. But here the world is not the creation of a wicked god and, even if Persian influence can be detected in the idea of the world as badly governed from the beginning, that influence goes further back. The idea of "powers" which have abused the authority which God has given them over the world, and abused it both against the world and against God himself, is to be met with in Jewish apocalyptic literature of a period earlier than Christianity. But the idea appears in our texts under a stronger accent. Furthermore, the strangest of all the applications to which the idea has been put, that which presents the crucifixion of Jesus as due to the "princes of this world," is given support as sketched in the Old Testament (Zechariah xi–xiii, 8); to which the fourth Gospel gives precision by attributing the death of the Christ to one only of the princes, "the prince of this world," that is, to the grand master of the lower powers. The human agents who take part in the condemnation and execution are regarded as his tools, and as hardly responsible for what they do.

Here, then, is a profound and dauntless faith translated into the language of mythology. The author of the gnosis, of which we have just ventured an analysis, has experienced persecution, nor does he expect that persecution will soon come to an end. But, taking comfort from his belief that the elect will overcome all the difficulties and torments awaiting them, he now breaks forth into this fine outpouring of his mystical faith (Rom. viii, 28–30, 31, 35, 37–39):

> We know that, for those who love God,
>   everything converges to good,
>   ––for those called according to plan––
> Because, those whom he foresaw,
>   them he predestined to be conformed to the
>   pattern of his Son,
>   that he might be the first-born of many brothers.
> Now, whom he predestined,
>   them also he called;

> Whom he called;
>> them also he justified
> Whom he justified,
>> them also he glorified.
> If God is for us,
>> Who will be against us?
> Who will separate us from the love of the Christ?
>> Tribulation, distress, persecution,
>>> hunger, nakedness, peril, sword?...
> But over all that we triumph
>> by him who loved us.
> For I am persuaded that neither death nor life,
>> nor angels, nor principalities, nor powers,
>>> nor height, nor depth, nor any other creature
> Will avail to separate us from the love of God
>> in Christ Jesus our Lord.

This powerful summary of faith can hardly have been produced before the end of the first century, or elsewhere than in a circle faithful to the memory of Paul. We are tempted to say that the author of it takes his stand on the Scriptures only as on a platform from which to take his flight above them, for his Christ is placed under the Law only that he may deliver those in bondage to the Law (Gal. iv, 4-5). Was he also born of a woman and descended from David according to the flesh? (Rom. i, 3). The Epistles answer in the affirmative, and by the fact that he was woman-born in the lineage of David he would be identified with the Jewish Messiah. But the whole system is consistent only with a real epiphany conceived as historical and incarnate in a body of flesh which, wearing the semblance of sin, must have been real also. What is said on this subject gives no ground for understanding it in the sense of Docetism, the thought of our author being everywhere entirely matter-of-fact and of the kind that could never base the redemption of mankind on a phantom show. It remains to add that the Christ he presents was, by his origin, a "power" in the same category as those who crucified him in the flesh, but, unlike them, faithful to God from the beginning.

2. Theory in the Epistle to the Hebrews

The Epistle to the Hebrews, which there is reason to think was not originally attributed to Paul, contains another synthesis, probably of somewhat later date than the foregoing, which constructs the scheme of salvation after a widely different pattern. This gnosis is developed methodically and at considerable length, and elaborately fortified with biblical quotations,[8] though in reality the gnosis is not derived from the Scriptures, but rather attached to them by a subtle exegesis. The preamble announces the general theme of the Epistle (i, 1-4):

> Many times and in many ways
> > God, having formerly spoken
> > > to the fathers by the prophets,
>
> In these last of the days
> > has spoken to us by the Son,
>
> Whom he appointed heir to all things,
> > by whom also he made the worlds,[9]
>
> Who, being the reflection of his glory,
> > and expression of his substance,
>
> Upholding all things
> > by his word of power,
>
> Having effected purification from sins
> > sat down on the right of Majesty on high,
>
> Becoming so much superior to the angels
> > that he received for his share a name more excellent than they.

The intention of the author is to prove first that the Son, in virtue of his origin and nature as Son and reflected image of God who, by him, has built the universe, is superior to the angels—that is, to the "powers" made familiar to us in the Epistle of Paul, who are merely agents of the divine will but not mediators of salvation (i, 5-14). It is true that the Son, in his earthly manifestation, has been only for a time the Man spoken of in the eighth Psalm whose place is below that of the angels. (The Psalm is speaking of man in general and of his eminence in the creation as only a little lower than the divine condition.)[10] The Son's place is "below the angels," that is, below that of the heavenly race, in the sense that he took flesh and blood in order that, by dying in the flesh, he might break the power of the devil, who is the lord of death and imposes it on all men. Thus the Son became man that he might deliver men from their bondage to death and lead them forth into immortality (ii, 5-18).

Greater than the angels, the Son is next shown to be greater than Moses, who was merely a servant in God's house, while the

Son is builder and head of the house. This headship belongs to the Son—and here we come to the central point of the mystery as expounded in the theory before us—because he became, by means of his death, the unique High Priest of whom Melchisedec had been the prototype. A complete gnosis is now fitted on to the name Melchisedec, a more or less mythical figure which got attached at a late date to the legend of Abraham. The hundred-and-tenth Psalm shows that quite early, perhaps long before the birth of Christianity, speculation had been active about this Melchisedec. Our theologian has his own way of exploiting the statements in Genesis (xiv, 18–20), and draws conclusions from what they do not say no less than from what they say. Melchisedec is type of the Christ by his appearance as a unique figure in history: his name means King of Righteousness, and he is called "King of Salem," that is, "King of Peace";[11] neither father, nor mother, nor genealogy is assigned to him; neither beginning nor end of his days is indicated; as priest of the Most High he is shown to be priest for ever; which tallies with the eternity of the Son of God.[12] A deduction more remarkable for courage and ingenuity than for logic. The same must be said about our author's inference that Levi, as descended from Abraham, paid tithes to Melchisedec as Abraham had done, "for he was yet in the loins of his father when Melchisedec met him." But what we have especially to note is the idea which the strange comparison of the Christ with Melchisedec is intended to make good, namely, that whereas in the gnosis of the Epistle to the Romans the rôle of the dying Jesus is that of victim only, that rôle, while still retained, is here subordinated to that of the sacrificing priest, eternal priest of humanity for ever performing his office in the presence of God. "He rose up from Judah"[13] as a star might rise, but is not said to be descended from Judah's tribe, for the Christ appeared *in history* like Melchisedec without father or mother and without human ancestry. As applied to the eternal Son of God this would have no sense, for the Son in his eternity is not without father. The Christ, then, appeared historically in the flesh, but without being born of human parentage—an idea more natural for the earthly manifestation of a being conceived as pre-existent than would be his incarnation in an embryo subject to all the changing forms of human growth.

The expiations prescribed by the Law, he continues, were only a figure; incessantly repeated as symbols, they left sin uneffaced. But Jesus has, by his death, made expiation, at one stroke and for ever, for the totality of sin. By his death he entered at once into his glory, and laid his own blood on the altar of heaven, effecting by that unique oblation an eternal redemption for sinners, the new covenant, the real covenant, by which the covenant of Sinai was set aside (ix–x, 18). By the sacrifice of the Christ, accomplished once and for ever, the sacrifices prescribed by the Law are all rendered superfluous. Simultaneously, it is by his death that Jesus attains his priesthood and his inheritance in the glory of God. "In the days of his flesh," we are told, in the days, that is, of his appearance on the earth, he had "prayed, with great outcry and weeping to Him who was able to save him from death"—to save him, that is, not by dispensing him from death, but by raising him from it alive; then, his prayer now answered, he learnt "in his passion" what obedience is; finally "having been made perfect"—that is, fully initiated into his priestly office, and fully endowed with insight into the mystery on entering his celestial dwelling place—"he became, for all who believe in him, the author of eternal salvation and a true priest after the manner of Melchisedec" (v, 7–10). There, our author declares, is the great mystery.

It may be said in passing that the prayer, the suffering and the institution of Jesus as eternal High Priest are not, as commonly supposed, to be identified precisely with the prayer of Gethsemane, the passion and resurrection, as these are told in our Gospels. They are data borrowed from the Scriptures, in particular from Psalm xxii, all the descriptive imagery of which is transposed by our author into history, especially verses 2 and 3. On the other hand the Gospel stories of the passion are largely influenced, or rather supported, by the Psalms, in particular by the twenty-second from which our Epistle draws its inspiration. Thus our author stands, in regard to the Gospel tradition, on the same ground as the author of the salvation theory in the Pauline Epistles, who is almost indifferent to the real circumstances of the life and death of Jesus, and anterior at least in point of view, if not in reality, to the definite crystallization of the prophecies into an apparently historical tradition.

Our Epistle presents Jesus as a lofty example of human perfection both in his life and death. He patiently underwent all the trials possible to human nature without sinfully yielding to them—literally "tempted in all manner of ways, according to resemblance, sin excepted" (iv, 15).[14] His death was a token of obedience to God. Moreover his death is not conceived as a doing-away of sin, but as a satisfactory oblation for it, his blood being laid by him on the altar of heaven just as the blood of the victims was brought into the sanctuary by the levitical High Priest on the day of the great expiation. This is soteriology at once moral and liturgical from which conclusions are drawn less fantastic than the theory of a righteousness that cannot be lost. Without discussing the matter, the author admits the possibility of a relapse into sin after baptism, going no further than to point out the terrible consequences of such an event. The blood of Jesus opens the door for the sinner into the sanctuary of heaven, and with such a High Priest given to men, it behoves them to keep their faith in him alive and their hope firm, to incite each other to faithfulness and good works, and not to forsake the assemblies, as some wrongly do. For, if we sin voluntarily after receiving knowledge of the truth we have nothing to expect save punishment by devouring fire, since there now remains for us no other sacrifice to expiate our sin beyond that of the Christ, the benefit of which we have already had. A formidable inference which the Church has not upheld. It suggests a date for our Epistle earlier than the Shepherd of Hermas.

Our Epistle, equally with that to the Romans insists upon faith, but understands if differently. The faith here in question is no longer an absolute trust in the mediation of Christ and in the efficacy of his sacrifice. It is the certainty of what is hoped for, the conviction of the reality of what is not seen. Its essential object is summed up in the formula: "God exists and rewards those who seek him" (xi, 1, 6). It was by faith that all the righteous were saved and all the marvels performed of which the Old Testament, and the tradition founded on it, bear record.[15] Encouraged by this cloud of witnesses let Christians confidently run the course which is opened to them, their eyes fixed on Jesus who endured the cross before sitting down at the right

EARLIEST THEORIES OF THE CHRISTIAN MYSTERY

hand of God; let them bear with patience the trials God sends them for their good; let peace prevail between all and holiness be in every man. Jesus abides for ever, let no man be led astray by strange doctrines; the cult of the Law is out of date, our altar is in heaven, and there too is our abiding city; let us offer the sacrifice of prayer, by the Christ, to God. Let not the example of the great ones who died a glorious death be forgotten, and let obedience be paid to those who lead that they may have no cause for sorrow.

Here is morality, a morality strict and severe, but of peace and charity bound up with a gnosis of relative sobriety, and in such a way as to be a logical part of it. The gnosis, moreover, is profoundly spiritual. The author has no belief in the resurrection of the flesh; he even seems to know nothing of the imminent parousia and the reign of the elect on the earth. But, if he speaks of worship in spirit, he does not ignore baptism, the sacrament of "illumination" (vi, 1, 2), nor the Eucharist. For it is not for nothing that he exalts Melchisedec, whose only priestly action recorded in Genesis is the offering of bread and wine. There is little risk in supposing that, in the author's thought, the mystic offering of the Supper was already conceived as presented to God on the heavenly altar whereon was laid the blood of the Christ, in order that it might become, for those who took part in it, the body and blood of the Lord Jesus.[16] All that is worked out with an eye to Judaism, but from outside and afar off, and as if those whom it concerned were separated, and because in reality they had long been separated, from that religion, now regarded as a rival.

3. Theory in the Epistle to the Colossians

A gnosis analogous to the foregoing is worked out in the Epistle to the Colossians, not more in opposition to Judaism but directed, as it would seem, against a gnosis with Judaizing tendencies. Here is what we read of the Christ (i, 15–20):

> He is the image of the invisible God,
>   first-born of all creation,
> Because in him all things were made,
>   in heaven and on earth,
>   visible and invisible;

> Whether thrones, whether dominations,
>> whether principalities, whether powers,
>>> all was made by him and for him.
> Himself is before all
>> and all subsists in him
> And himself is the head of the body,
>> of the Church.
> He is the beginning,
>> first-born among the dead,
> That he may become in all things,
>> he, first.
> Because in him all the pleroma judged good to dwell,[17]
>> and by him to reconcile all things to Himself
> Reconciling (by the blood of his cross)
>> by him, whatever is on earth,
>>> whatever is in heaven.

Would that the author had himself commented on his text! Would that he had told us, in particular, what he understands by "pleroma," a gnostic term, taken by him as such in his adaptation of it to his monotheistic faith and to the saving rôle of Jesus Christ! Another passage in the Epistle (ii, 8–12), which presents the same doctrine in its contrast to a false mystery, throws some light on the last citation but not enough to resolve all our difficulties:

> Beware that no man capture you
>> by philosophy and vain sophistry,
> According to the tradition of men,
>> according to the Elements of the world,[18]
>>> and not according to Christ.
> Because in him there dwells
>> all the pleroma of Divinity as body,[19]
> And you are made pleroma in him,[20]
>> who is the head of all principality and power,
> In whom also you were circumcised
>> with circumcision not of hands,
> Putting off the body of flesh
>> in the circumcision of the Christ,
> Buried with him by baptism,
>> when you were also raised with him,
> By faith in the power of God
>> who raised him from the dead.

It is evident that the pleroma ("plenitude"), of which the former passage told us that it had chosen Christ for its dwelling place, is the pleroma of the Godhead. But what are we to think of it when we are now told that it dwells in Christ *after the manner of body*? First we are told that the body is the Church: here we are told that baptized believers are, in Christ, made integral to the pleroma-body or, as we might say, *pleromed*. That leads to a highly comprehensive notion of the Church, but throws no light on what the pleroma consists in. Fullness of what? The question is further complicated by what is said in the first passage about a reconciliation (which an apparent gloss turns into redemption by the blood of the cross), bringing order back into both the terrestrial and celestial worlds. On this matter some light is thrown by the following (ii, 13–15):

> And you who were dead in sins
>   and the foreskin of your flesh,
> You has he made alive with himself,
>   forgiving you all your sins,
> Cancelling the clauses of the account,
>   which was against us;
> And he caused it to disappear
>   nailing it to the cross.
> Having disarmed principalities and powers
>   he put them to shame
>   triumphing over them in that condition.

The Christ has here become "chief," or head, of the principalities and powers, because he is their conqueror, having overthrown them by dying on the cross. From this it is clear that an outbreak of rebellion is conceived as having taken place in the Pleroma, in the Whole, which the principalities and powers, as members subordinate to their head,[21] form with the Christ; that the death of the Christ has reconciled men to God by effacing their sins and annulling the act which declared them sinners, doubtless the Law of Moses; that, furthermore, it has established peace in the upper world, and reconciled the principalities and powers to God by bringing them under the dominion of the Christ. The ransomed believers are made integral parts of this sublime incorporation, which is the divine Pleroma and, at the same time, the Church.

A redemption poem analogous to the foregoing is sketched in chapter xv of First Corinthians, but is there founded on the myth of the Man and the distinction between the two Adams; the resurrection also is differently conceived.[22] This, in Colossians, does not appear as the change of the body into a finer substance. In principle, the resurrection of the believer becomes real in his baptism, although his immortality remains, for the time of his present life, "hidden with the Christ in God" (iii, 3).[23] From the following passage, moreover, the definition of this gnosis appears to be aimed in opposition to a mystery-cult, more closely related than itself to Judaism, at least in external form (ii, 16–23):

> Let no man judge you about meat and drink
>   about feasts, new moons, sabbaths,
> Which are shadows of things to come,
>   the reality[24] being of the Christ.
> Let no one condemn you
>   under pretext of humility and the right cult of angels,[25]
> Which he has seen in the initiation,[26]
>   vainly puffed up by his fleshly thought,
> Unattached to the head
>   by which the whole body,
> With joints and sinews provided and held up,
>   increases and grows by God.
> If you are dead with Christ to the Elements[27] of the world,
>   why, as though living in the world, suffer the orders
>   "Take not, taste not, touch not"
> All on things destined to corruption by usage,
>   a business of human laws and doctrines?
> That comes to you under the name of wisdom,
>   as "right form of worship," "humility,"[28]
>   "discipline of body"
> but has no value, save for fleshly satisfaction.

The terms of precision in the above passage are borrowed from the terminology of a determinate cult with its own forms of initiation and a great array of minute observances, clearly Jewish, and a worship of angels, but in which the Christ had no place. This Judaizing cult of external forms impresses our author as a materialistic religion devoted to the "Elements," στοιχεῖα, of the world. Pretending to be a philosophic gnosis it is, in fact, grossly unspiritual, and Paul is here made to oppose it with the spiritual gnosis of the Epistle. But the Paul who speaks in the Epistle (i, 23) of a Gospel entrusted to him alone and "preached to every creature under heaven (i, 23)"[29] can only have been some fervent follower of the long dead apostle, the whole Epistle being conceived, or rather adapted, some fifty years after his death, to fortify the Christians of Asia against the propaganda of a mystery-cult, possibly that of Zeus Sabazios,[30] then widely active in those regions.

4. Theory in the Epistle to the Philippians

In the Epistle to the Philippians a kind of theological enclosure within the text, unmistakably a hymn to the Christ, contains a gnosis of the same character (ii, 5–11):

> Being in the form of God
>   he judged it no lawful prize
>   to be equal with God;
> But stripped himself
>   taking slave-form
>   becoming human in figure;
> And, found a man in appearance,
>   he abased himself,
>   becoming obedient even to death
>   (the death of the cross)
> Wherefore God thus exalted him,
>   and gave him the name
>   above every name[31]
> So that at the name of Jesus
>   every knee should bow
>   of beings celestial, terrestrial, infernal,
> And every tongue confess
>   that Jesus is *Lord*,
>   to the glory of God the Father.

Pre-existing in form divine, the Christ restrains himself from usurping equality with God, as dared by the princes of this world, who cause the nations to worship them as gods. On the contrary, he threw off his celestial shape, took the form of a slave and accepted death in obedience. Here again the Christ forms part of the divine Pleroma which had been thrown into disorder by the attack certain "powers" had made on the prerogative of God, and restored to order by the Son's sacrifice of himself, all created beings, in their triple ranks of heaven, earth and hell, being subdued under him in consequence of that sacrifice. Jesus Christ is thereby proclaimed *Lord*, co-partner in the name, the power and the glory of God. All this however is but a rough outline which leaves us asking how the author would have filled in the detail of his conception. Notwithstanding the doctrinal affinity he can hardly have been the same person as the author who developed the gnosis of Colossians. The passage we have quoted is detached from its context and seems to have existed at first, independently of the Epistle into which it is incorporated, as the oracle of some Christian prophet. Colossians i, 15–20 may have a similar origin.

On the theme of the "descent" of the Christ, in which the oldest mythology finds an echo, the first Epistle of Peter has more knowledge and more to say than the Epistle to the Philippians (iii, 18–19; iv, 6):

> Christ also died once for sins,
> > that he might bring us to God,
> Put to death in the flesh
> > but made alive in spirit.
> In spirit also went he to preach
> > to the spirits who were in prison,
> Those who had been untaught in time past,
> > when the long-suffering of God waited,
> > > in Noah's day when the ark was built . . .
> For this cause was the Gospel preached to the dead:
> > that they may be judged humanly in flesh,
> > > but live according to God in spirit.

A persistent desire to extend salvation to the dead, especially to those drowned in the Deluge, or, one might say, to humanity at the first stage, is a curious feature of gnostic speculation. The author of First Peter seems to have formed a purely spiritual idea of the resurrection: it is as a spirit that Jesus goes to preach to the dead; he can hardly be supposed to have preached in vain; the converted dead will have risen up with him from their infernal abode, and it was doubtless in the course of his ascent to heaven that he enforced "submission on angels, powers and virtues" (iii, 22). In the Gospel of Peter, Christ on rising from the tomb is said to have already fulfilled his preaching-mission to the dead. The fourth Gospel seems to make an explicit allusion to it (v, 25, 28),[32] and perhaps it is implied in other parts of the New Testament.[33] Justin, in his reference to the matter, mentions an apocryphal text of Jeremiah which speaks of the Lord preaching to the dead.34 Marcion has his own account of the Christ's descent into hell, but here it is with the object of liberating all those who had been damned under the Old Testament.35

5. GNOSIS IN THE FOURTH GOSPEL

The gnosis of the fourth Gospel is distinguished above all the others by the sublimity, balance and harmonious development of its doctrine, announced in discourses which are really hymns, and figuratively presented by means of stories constructed in symbolic language. Here is mysticism at once profound and luminous; a scheme of salvation purely spiritual and yet throbbing with life; a transcendent Christology penetrated through and through by human tenderness and a unique mode of speech which one might think had been created for the lofty use here made of it. Many have thought that the hymn to the Logos which serves as introduction to the Gospel was inserted as an afterthought; but nothing could be less certain. If there is no further question of the Logos in the body of the book, the reason is that regard for tradition restrained the writer from putting the express formula of the logos-philosophy into the mouth of the Christ. Nonetheless the preamble fits in exactly with the book as a whole and with its general doctrine, to which indeed it furnishes the key:

> In the beginning was the Logos,
>   and the Logos was with God,
>   and the Logos was god.36

Reason and spoken Word of the Eternal, the Logos was before all things, and near to God, being of God and sharing His nature, but without being God himself.

> He, at the beginning, he, was with God:
>   everything was made by him,
>   and without him was nothing made.37

The Logos, and he *alone*—this, perhaps, pointed against some gnostic fancy about the process of the "aeons"—is said to be near to God at the very beginning, because he is the creative word of Genesis, without whose power and instrumentality no created thing has come into being:

> Whatever was made alive, in him is the life of it,[38]
> and the life was the light of men.
> And the light shone into the darkness,
> and the darkness quenched it not.[39]

Life and Light: that, precisely, is the Logos, and that, precisely, as the whole Gospel will tell, is the Christ, the Son of God. He was Life and Light in the world as it subsisted in him before his epiphany, that epiphany which was made real for the particular good of humanity, and of which the Gospel will now tell. But his influence met resistance and limitation from the darkness in which it worked. This "darkness"—be it said without play on words—is the dark point of the system. It would seem to be derived from Genesis, where the darkness is a negative element opposed to the organizing work of God.[40] Here the darkness is an influence permanently at work in the world; for the "prince of this world" is clearly also the prince of darkness, to wit, Satan.[41] At this point we encounter a dualism which the Gospel does not resolve; we are not told whence comes the devil, "the father of lies."[42] He seems to personify, so to say, the whole class of "powers," elsewhere described as mismanaging the world confided to their care. As the Gospel presents him, he is the greatest of the "powers," God's enemy, a moral personification of "the darkness," a kind of Ahriman-Antichrist, whose origin, like that of the darkness, is left unexplained. Possibly "darkness" is conceived as forming the stuff of the perishable world, though the statement is not expressly made.

> That was the true light
> that sheds light on every man
> who came into the world.
> In the world he was,
> —the world made by him—
> and the world knew him not.
> To his home came he,
> and his own welcomed him not;
> But all who welcomed him,
> to them gave he power to become God's children.[43]

These are general propositions concerning the activity of the Word-light which seemingly antedate the incarnation, unless they involve it by anticipation. It will be noted that the author of the hymn makes play with the words *light, darkness, world*, understanding them alternately in a material and in a spiritual sense. The "world" is the visible universe, but it stands also for humanity as reasonable and, again, for humanity as unteachable. The precise gift which the Word-light has to confer upon men is truth and life, the truth of the knowledge of God, and the life of immortality. By the gift of these they are made sons of God, as he is:

> Born of blood or of fleshly will he was not,
> nor of the will of man
> but of God was he born.[44]
> And the Logos became flesh,
> and he dwelt among us,
> full of grace and truth.[45]
> Of his plenitude[46] it is that all we received
> favour after favour,
> For the Law was given by Moses;
> grace and truth came by Jesus Christ.[47]

Following the above comes an explanation fully in the spirit of the text: "No man has seen God at any time," not even Moses any more than the self-styled prophets of the false divinities: "the only begotten Son, who is in the bosom of the Father" (i, 18), he it is who makes him known. The invisibility of God here asserted is a principle fundamental to the Johannine theology and to the mystical gnosis on which that theology depends.[48] The Law which Moses "gave" was taught him by intermediary angels. The Logos-Christ is the only Revealer, as he is the only Saviour; none but he imparts "grace and truth," because none but he knows God in himself and is able to tell of him and explain him to his faithful believers, to his initiates. He is the exegete of God, the Master of the mystery. The operating idea is that of the unknown God, inaccessible to common intelligence but revealed in mystical initiation by a divine mediator. And there is but one true mystery. It is the Christian.

How precisely the divine sonship of the Logos stands related to its incarnation is a question not easily answered. Nevertheless it is not without purpose that the divine sonship of the believer is presented as of the same type as the sonship of Jesus Christ, the incarnate Word. The author had no intention, and felt no need, to explain the origin of the human form in which the Logos was made visible on the earth. He presents it as a real form, just as he presents as real the miracle-signs which he makes the Christ perform, while giving them a wholly spiritual signification. Meanwhile, if men of flesh and blood are born anew in spirit by a spiritual generation which has nothing to do with the union of the sexes, the fertilization of woman and the natural growth of the embryo, that is because the Word itself, by taking flesh, became the prototype of the children of God, the only begotten Son.[49] As only begotten Son of the Father, the Christ Jesus has no mother in this world, any more than he has an earthly father: the Marriage at Cana makes that clear enough. The sublime mysticism of our author, which ignores, if it does not disdain, the virgin conception, is not any more in agreement either with the idea of the incarnation of the Logos as taking place in the womb of a woman naturally fertilized or with the pre-existence of the man Jesus before the Logos-incarnation. The Logos appears in the flesh when it becomes active as the Christ. To regard such a conception as more improbable than the traditional dogma of the virgin birth would be childish from the historical point of view.

Truth to say, the Gospel itself, both discourse and narration, is in a sense another incarnation of the Logos as light and life. For it is expressly under these images of Light and Life that narrative and discourses reveal the work of the Logos-Christ. The Johannine Christ is the spiritual light of the world, and he comes to bring life eternal to men. The miracle of the man born blind confirms him in the first as principle of light; the miracle of Lazarus in the second as principle of life. Before healing the blind man Jesus declares (ix, 4–5):

> Needs must I work
> > the works of Him who sent me
> > > while there is day.
> Comes the night
> > when none can work.
> While I am in the world
> > light am I of the world.

In like manner before raising Lazarus (xi, 24–26):

> I am the resurrection and the life;
> > whoso believes in me, though he die, shall live.
> And whoso lives and believes in me
> > shall never die.

To deny the symbolic character of these miracles reveals a strange preoccupation of mind in those who make the denial. The miracles symbolize in action what Jesus expressly says in the words which introduce them.

But the Light which the Christ brings to men is no promise of access to the Kingdom of God by repentance of sin; and the Life that he gives them is not immortality on the earth at the general resurrection of the dead. Whoso believes in the Son sent from God and in his life-giving power participates at once and from then onwards in the Son's eternal life. He who believes is thereby and already among the elect; he who believes not is thereby and already damned. No Day of Judgment is needed to judge them hereafter; and the resurrection of their bodies is uncalled for (iii, 16–18; v, 24).

> So God loved the world
> > that he gave his only begotten Son,
> That whoso believes in him should not perish
> > but have life eternal.
> For God sent not the Son to the world
> > to judge the world
> > > but that the world might be saved by him.
> Whoso believes in him is not judged;
> > whoso believes not is judged already . . .
> Verily, verily, I tell you
> > that whoso hears my word
> > > and believes in Him who sent me
> Has life eternal,
> > and to judgment is not exposed
> > > but has passed from death to life.[50]

As we have already seen, the visible and material sacraments of the faith have a wholly spiritual meaning, that of an inner rebirth with participation in the eternal life of the Christ. But the Christ died, as he had lived, in the real flesh of humanity and in a state of obedience even to the death of the cross, in order that believers might live in spirit. If he appeared in flesh without being born of flesh (i, 13; iii, 5–6), it was that he might accomplish his work in his own person, the work of preaching his mystery and making a gift to men of his mortal existence.

In the canonical edition of the Gospel this doctrine, in substance too fine for the faith of the multitude, is limited and made concrete by borrowing from the older Gospel tradition and from the sacramentalism of First Corinthians, which we have already found incorporated in the tradition of the synoptic Gospels. Certain additions to the original texts of the discourses join the resurrection of the dead with the parousia of the Lord (iii, 16–18; v, 24). The supplement added to the discourse on the bread of life introduces the symbol of flesh and blood into the eucharistic Supper, the symbol which betokens mystic participation in the life of the Christ by mystic commemoration of his death (vi, 51b–58). Without exaggeration it may be said that sacramental symbolism was developed to a point where it covered the whole career of the Christ as told in the Gospels. One incident of the passion betrays it very clearly—the issue of water and blood from the side of Jesus when pierced by the soldier's lance. On this there is a comment in the first Epistle of John (v, 6–8):

> This is he who came by water and blood,
>   Jesus Christ,
> Not in water only,
>   but in water and in blood.
> And it is the spirit that bears witness,
>   because the spirit is the truth;
> For three there are that bear witness,
>   spirit, water and blood,
>   and the three make one.

This is not the gibberish it might seem to be. On the contrary, it presents the quintessence of the Christian mystery conveyed in the language of gnosis. The Son of God was made manifest on earth by water, and in water, when he came to the baptism of John; he was made manifest by blood, and in blood, when he died on the cross.[51] In both cases the Spirit bore witness; at his baptism, by descending into the Christ (i, 29–34); at his death, when the Christ "gave up" the Spirit bestowed on him (xix, 30). For the breath yielded up, mystically understood, is the Holy

Spirit set free,[52] so to say, by the death of the Christ that it may be poured out at large on believers. The three make but one because, finally, it is the Spirit who bears witness to the Christ in water and in blood, in his baptism and in his passion.

But the meaning of our passage is not yet exhausted. It must not be overlooked that, according to the evangelist, water and blood issued, and issued together, from the side of the Crucified. By this the evangelist would signify the birth of the Church, in the manner of Eve's creation as issuing from the side of Adam; in this way he shows the fountain of eternal life flowing from the side of Jesus as the Christ had announced it would—"out of his body streams of living water will flow" (vii, 38). The stream is canalized, as it were, in the sacraments of Christian initiation; the water representing baptism, sacrament of spiritual regeneration; the blood representing the eucharist, sacrament of eternal life in union with the Christ who died for men and rose from the dead. It is by means of these two sacraments that the witness, three in one, still goes on as a present fact, the Christ continuing to come by water and by blood, the Spirit continuing to bear witness to him in water and in blood. The Holy Spirit which formerly bore witness to the Christ during his earthy mission, in his baptism, and in his death, now bears witness to him continually through the medium of baptismal immersion and the eucharistic meal. Thus the Christian mystery is evenly balanced by the attachment of its two sacraments to the two extremities of the saving Christ's career, baptism and death mystically interpreted by their spiritual effects. And thus the fourth Gospel, in the correlation of its two parts, takes the form of a sublime and balanced catechism, but always, like the synoptics, a catechism of initiation into the Christian mystery.

6. Birth-Stories and the Antedating of the Epiphany

Before entering upon our study of the mystery of the Church we must needs descend for a moment from the high regions we have been exploring to mark the upsurge of a lower mysticism, of a vulgar supernaturalism and mythology, which made its appearance in Christian tradition and became no less firmly anchored there, and no less amply developed, than the metaphysical mysticism whose first forms have just been described. Ancient speculation did not confine itself to the question of the heavenly Saviour's pre-existence in eternity; it became active also, and perhaps at an earlier date, about the conditions of his birth upon the earth.

The earliest Christian generation knew that Jesus had brothers and parents, nor have the mythologues who would suppress the historical Jesus been able to get rid of these by mere conjecturing. The first groups of Jewish Christians were not nourished on transcendental speculations. Quite early, however, the idea arose that since Jesus was the Messiah, he must be son of David, and indeed was his son, since it was so written in Scripture. Doubtless those who asserted this were in no great haste to find out how it was possible; but the unbelieving Jews would not be slow to ply the believing brethren with malicious questions about the matter. It occurred to the believing party that the difficulty might be met by producing a genealogy. Two were produced, Matthew's and Luke's, which contradict and reciprocally cancel each other. Both agree in naming Joseph as the father of Jesus; but they assign different fathers to Joseph and take us back on different lines of ascent to David, one (Matthew) following the series of Kings to Jeconiah, and the other (Luke) adopting Nathan son of David, of whom the Scriptures give only the name (2 Samuel v, 14). Of such fictions the historian need take no account, except in so far as they prove the absence at the beginning of any genealogical tradition about the Davidic origin of Jesus, and reveal the general belief, in the first times, that Jesus was born, without miracle, of Joseph and Mary. For both genealogies are based on the name of Joseph as father of Jesus, and it was through Joseph that Jesus was at first thought to be of Davidic blood.53 From this it is evident that the genealogies were invented in circles which as yet had no idea of the miraculous conception, and that the birth-legend inserted in the third Gospel was formed at first under the same conditions as the genealogies. It is true that Jesus, in this legend, is born amid miraculous circumstances, but as issue of the marriage of Joseph and Mary.

Where, when and how the idea arose of the virgin conception we can only guess. It was not in the first community of believers, nor in the very earliest time, and not without influence, at least indirect, from surrounding paganisms. Both of the birth legends represent, as they have come down to us, a somewhat complex elaboration, to which the Gospel editors have given the last touches. Matthew's legend, notwithstanding the mythological influences traceable in it, has the form of a Jewish *haggada* (anecdote) or of an haggadic collection, minutely and artificially built up on biblical texts, with formal emphasis on the connexion with scripture. From this we may conclude that this version of the legend was born in a circle of Judaizing Christianity, but of a Judaism somewhat unorthodox, in which the divine filiation of the Messiah was admitted without scruple, and pharisaic rabbinism held in suspicion. Northern Syria, between Antioch and the Euphrates, has been suggested for the birthplace not only of the legend but of the whole Gospel of Matthew.[54] In those regions Judaizing Christians known as "Nazareans" were still to be found as late as the fourth century. They used an Aramean Gospel containing the birth stories of our Matthew. In Luke the stories are dominated by the spirit of traditional Judaism and conceived in connexion with a legend of John the Baptist and in dependence on it; they would seem to have originated among Jewish Christians living in northern Palestine or in southern Syria.[55] The fulfilment of prophecy is hardly less implied than in Matthew's version, but is here clothed in a garment of romantic fiction.

On both sides the culminating point of the mythical legend is the miraculous conception by the operation of the Holy Spirit. Jesus is Son of God because, physiologically speaking, God is the operating cause of his generation. This is not offered in the grossly primitive sense of the old mythologies, the Greek for example, which describes the amours of Zeus and other gods, with metamorphoses appropriate to the different circumstances. Even among the pagans of that time a few pious and enlightened men were taking the matter more seriously, Plutarch holding the opinion of the Egyptians to be plausible that a woman might conceive by the approach of the Spirit of God. But this idea was not reached at a single bound from the starting point. In the ancient literature of Christianity we catch glimpses of the successive stages or, one might well say, the gropings by which the apotheosis of Jesus was realized in the faith of believers and in their catechisms.

We cannot remind ourselves too often that the point of departure for this apotheosis was the belief that Jesus had become Christ and made his entrance, so to say, into the sphere of divinity *by his resurrection*. This was the first apostolic Gospel, the Gospel of Paul and of Peter: the Son of God had been declared to be God's Son, and manifested as God's Son, *by his resurrection* (Romans i, 4). The Epiphany of the Christ, as first conceived, took place *in the resurrection itself*, and the evidence for it lay in apparitions or visions of him as risen from the dead. The earthly life of Jesus, in its relation to the postmortem manifestation of him as the Christ, had been an indispensable preliminary but of secondary importance. His great revelations, his essential instructions were not attached to the earthly preliminary. Criticism has for some time suspected, for example, that the scene of the Transfiguration of Jesus in the Synoptics had its origin in an apparition of the Risen One. We have it so presented in the Apocalypse of Peter where it is bound up with a revelation on the end of the age, the happiness of the elect and the punishment of reprobates. It will be noted that the same perspective, but more compressed, is maintained in the preamble to Acts (i, 3–11),[56] and that quite perceptible traces of it are retained in the closing passages of Matthew (xxviii, 16–20),[57] Luke (xxiv, 44–53),[58] John (xx, 21–26; xxi, 15–19)[59] and deutero-canonical Mark (xvi, 14–20).[60] In all these cases, essential teachings, and the command to preach the Gospel everywhere, are attached to manifestations of the Risen One.

This epiphany of the Christ in his divine character has been antedated by Mark and turned into a scene of transfiguration during his earthly life. The confession of Peter prepares the way for it. Six days after Peter has recognized Jesus as Christ, Jesus appears on the mountain in heavenly glory and the voice of the Father proclaims him Son of God. The result of this antedated apotheosis—and indeed the object of it—is to place the action of Jesus in going up to Jerusalem to die there, and to place the death itself, under the banner of the Son of God, so that the witness of the apostles may rest on a wider base, and an answer be given to those who decry their witness as a story made up after the event to overcome the scandal of the cross. Note also that the same evangelist has similarly antedated the revelations of Jesus concerning the end of the world (Mark xiii), representing them as given before his death. We are entitled to say that antedating, or anticipation, has here been systematically practised. The antedating of the Transfiguration in particular, its transposition from a revelation of the Christ after his resurrection to an event in the earthly life of Jesus, once admitted as a fact, has an importance for the history of the Gospel tradition not recognized by those critics who allowed it only as a hypothesis.

A new step towards apotheosis, the more easily to be recognized because the Gospel tradition so-called seems to have held back from it for a long time, was taken by antedating the epiphany of the Son of God to the very beginning of the Galilean ministry in the baptism of Jesus by John. The Gospel of Mark is written within this framework, which dominates the tradition of all the written Gospels known to us. As the scene of the Baptism is constructed, it includes, as simultaneous, the Messianic consecration of Jesus by the Spirit, the heavenly voice which acclaims him Son of God, the institution of Christian baptism and the witness to its superiority over the baptism of the sect called after John. At those points the framework of Christian catechesis remained for a long time fixed, while keeping an open door to all the teachings given in the name of Jesus and represented as having been spoken by him before his death. The Marcan framework is easily recognized in Matthew and Luke, to which the birth chapters seem to have been added at a later date, and we have just seen that the fourth Gospel keeps within the frame of set purpose. The connexion with John the Baptist shows us the circumstances under which our frame was elaborated. It had reference to the propaganda of the sect which claimed to be derived from John, proving that Christianity was born independently of it and was pre-eminent in regard to it. Whence we may infer that the elaboration took place in a region and at a time when Christian propaganda came into competition with that of the Baptist sect. This would again bring us to the countries of Transjordania and Syria and to a time when the rivalry of the two sects was still a matter of concern to the leaders of the Christian movement.

The opening chapters of Matthew and Luke are evidence that in course of time the Marcan frame came to appear inadequate and that the attempt was made to throw back the Epiphany of the Christ to the first moment of his human existence. Always the Son of God, he had been God's Son on his assumption of humanity; the fact has been made evident in the miracle of his birth and in its accompaniment of other marvels in keeping with an event so tremendous. Such was the new theory. In the Jewish-Christian circles for which Matthew was elaborated, it seems that care was taken to give prominence to the Davidic filiation of Jesus (while giving it at the same time a symbolic turn) with the special object of barring the way to certain conclusions which might be inferred from Mark. On the one hand it might be argued that Jesus became Son of God by adoption at his baptism (this adoptionist doctrine was not ill looked on in Rome); on the other hand it might be said, with Mark as authority, that a higher power had governed Jesus from birth to death and then departed from him; or again, forcing the meaning of the epiphany, the existence of Jesus before his baptism might be suppressed altogether, as the original author of the fourth Gospel and the author of the Epistle to the Hebrews seem to have suppressed it; or, again, various forms of Docetism might be fitted into the frame, as was done by some of the gnostics and, in his time, by Marcion.[61]

To give eminence to the new conception of the epiphany, the Gospel stories made use not only of Old Testament texts but of mythical themes then current, adapting them to the texts or choosing the texts to fit in with the myths. The theme drawn upon for exploitation in both versions was that of the divine child, born in a place of no repute, whose presence is miraculously announced to shepherds;[62] though the Lucan legend, working up the theme to make Bethlehem the birthplace, has not forgotten that David was a shepherd (ii, 8–20). Matthew's legend brings in its Magi and herald-star because it belongs to a region (Persia-Babylon) where the Magi and their astrology were well known; but the star is there to connect with the Star of which Balaam, the great soothsayer, had spoken long ago as destined to come out of Jacob (Numbers xxiv, 17). The time was not far distant when the same text was applied to the impostor Messiah Bar-

Cochba, "son of the Star."⁶³ The theme of the divine child, or child of destiny, menaced with death by hostile powers and miraculously escaping from a massacre, is similarly exploited in Matthew, but with an eye to Moses, as prototype, and to his flight from Egypt into Midian. The construction of a myth is of all things easiest to explain; it is also true that nothing is more arbitrary nor, at bottom, more incredible than the myth itself. But the Epiphany of the Son of God had to be magnified by one means or another. Even the fourth Gospel, with all its sublime symbolism, found no better way to give lustre to the Epiphany of the incarnate Logos than to bring Jesus to the marriage at Cana for the changing of water into wine, wherein the Christ "manifests his glory" by performing a miracle borrowed from the myth and ritual of Dionysus.⁶⁴

7. Theory concerning the Baptist: the Mandeans

In the last two stages of our advancing exposition we have seen, at each stage, how the Christ, on the way to apotheosis, was exalted at the expense of John the Baptist. At the stage before the last the movement came into contact with John and subordinated him to itself; and again, at the stage last reached in its mythical evolution, we have seen how this same subordination was repeated, with John's legend now expanded and apparently in a manner favourable to Jesus. The same effort to subordinate John and make capital out of him is to be met with in almost every one of the passages in which our Gospels, the fourth included, have thought well to mention the Baptist. To the impartial critic the meaning of this is evident enough. It can only mean that the Christian sect, born later than the sect of John, and in some way an offshoot from it, found it also a rival in the first period; and, further, that Christianity, striving for its own pre-eminence, took pains to disguise in part the extent of its debt to the Baptist's sect, and at the same time to interpret the Baptist's rôle as a function contributing to the rôle of Jesus, making John out to be a forerunner of the Christ and conscious of himself as such—an idea which never entered the mind of John nor that of his followers. And this notwithstanding that the founders of the two sects, Jesus and John, encountered a similar fate and had the same fortune of glorious survival in the faith of their adherents. Both movements must have shared a basic belief in the imminence of the Kingdom of God, and it was evident that one essential rite of Christianity, namely baptism, was borrowed by it from the sect of John.

Some recent writers have maintained that the question of the relation between the two sects has been put on a completely new footing by the publication of the religious literatures of the Mandeans,[65] said to be survivors of John's sect, and by certain commmentaries on this literature lately put out.[66] But, however interesting the greater part of the suggested comparisons may be, they do not seem to justify the conclusions the writers would draw from them, to the effect that early Christianity and the New Testament in general depend on Johannism to a much greater extent and more directly than careful criticism of New Testament books has hitherto been able to grant. It has not been proved that the religion of the Mandeans represents original Johannism more exactly than any Christian sect of our time, or all of them taken together, represent original Christianity. Mandean religion is certainly a great gnosis, but it is an historical growth which underwent diverse influence in the course of its development and was not a great gnosis at the beginning. And this beginning may well have been much later than the birth of Christianity. No proof has been given that any one of its writings is earlier than those of the New Testament. It is certain that the general compilation of the Mandean scriptures was made in Islamic times, not under the control of a homogeneous tradition, but by borrowing from different sects and with considerable incoherence in the total result. Nothing in it betrays the least knowledge of ancient Christianity, nor even, in regard to John the Baptist, the least souvenir which could be claimed as historical and independent of the Gospels. Mandean baptism, in its ritual economy, is, rather, dependent on the baptismal liturgy of the Nestorian Church. The gnosis was a belated growth whose original point of departure may, perhaps, be the same as that of the Christian gnoses, but it has no title to a place in the genealogy of traditional Christianity. Risky—to use no stronger term—as the pretention is which would explain the literature and evolution of Christianity before Irenaeus by reference to Marcion alone, it is more risky, certainly not less, to offer the religion of the Mandeans as the true key to ancient Christianity and to the New Testament.

A position much more in need to be made good would be the following.—Christianity did not make its entry into the world and into history as a great doctrine already defined in its essential parts, but as a Great Hope, flung at large over the Mediterranean world in the name of Jesus Christ and under the covering form of Jewish monotheism. Almost immediately and for more than a century, this Hope may be seen repeating itself in the diverse mentalities of those who now in this manner, now in that, gave it favourable reception, as light is broken up by a prism into a thousand colours. A boiling ferment of doctrines, a swarming of sects, a religious chaos was produced, which would soon have broken up into scattered fragments without future, had not certain steadying forces, due to its origin, been retained throughout. To these principles of stability, more and more resolutely affirmed in the last sixty years of the second century, the institution of the Catholic Church owes its existence. But the Church before becoming an institution was an idea. We make bold to say it was also a myth, for that reason a word must be said about the myth before we study the institution.

8. Birth of the Mystery of the Church

The mystic conception of the Church was born almost simultaneously with the birth of the Christian religion. There was no need to create it; no more was needed than to take it over from Judaism, detached completely from Jewish nationalism and enlarged by adaptation to the Christian mystery. Judaism, in spite of internal divisions, less felt among the Jews of the Dispersion, was a Church. It was made a Church by common faith and hope, by the bond of confraternity which united all the synagogues one with another and with their common centre at Jerusalem, a centre at once national and religious. Judaism in its own eyes was truly "the community of God" and was proud to be.

Of this mystic community, waiting for complete accomplishment in the Kingdom of God, Christianity professed at first to be only the realization hoped for, or its beginning, or the means, the instrument by which it would be made perfect. It was thus that the new religion proclaimed itself to the Jews everywhere and to all the pagan converts to Judaism: and when Judaism finally refused to recognize the Christ, it was thus that it maintained the claim to be the true "community of God," the true Church. Christianity then declared itself "the community of God," and from that time onwards denied the claim of the Jews to the very attribute it had borrowed from them.

And so all the mystic pride of the Jews in the consciousness they had of being God's chosen people, the authentic Society of True Believers, passed over entire to the Christians. Firmly entrenched in this conviction they saw with regret, but without dismay, that they were cast out of the Jews. Paul reveals his mind on the subject quite clearly in the Epistle to the Romans: surely it was his "great sorrow and unceasing pain" to see himself separated from his brethren in Israel—or, rather, to see their blindness in presence of the Gospel. But what could he do? They were blind to the fulfilment of prophecy in the Christ; the providential scheme of salvation by faith, open equally to Jews and Gentiles, interested them not. A sad affair! But it turns out that the teachableness of the Gentiles and the unbelief of the Jews were foretold by the prophets just as those qualities are now being shown (ix–x). Soon, under the indefinite delay of the Second Coming, the salvation of the Jews lost present interest and, the question becoming speculative, the idea occurred that the Jews had providentially fallen into temporary unbelief in order to give the pagans time to rally to the cause of the Christ; the turn of the Jews would come later (xi). Until that happened, and none the less for its postponement, the hellenist Christians were the true people of God.

Organization in the mystery had not proceeded far before hellenist Christianity began to conceive itself organized as the body of the Christ. In the characteristic prayers of the *Didache* we have already encountered the idea of the Church as assimilated to the bread of the Supper made out of grain at first scattered and now brought together; thus would the Church, at present dispersed over the earth—as the Synagogue was— soon be gathered up in the Kingdom of God, united in one body, as the bread was (*Didache*, ix, 4). First Corinthians shows further how, from this point, advance was quickly made to the conception of the existing Church, no longer as a scattered society, but as one living body, the mystic body of Jesus raised from the dead. In the words "there being one only bread, one only body are we" (x, 17), we encounter the same symbolism as in the *Didache* which likens the bodies of the faithful to the Eucharistic bread; but the words which follow: "for we are all partakers of that one only bread" go beyond the *Didache* by making the one bread of which every Christian partakes, no longer the bread he eats, but the very Christ who is figured in the bread, in such way that the mystic union of all the faithful in Christ is also figured in the bread of the Supper. The rules laid down for the eucharistic meal are founded on the principle that, in order to be "the Lord's Supper" the meal must be one at which the material consumed is shared *in common*, and not one in which each participant eats and drinks what he will, so that the same bread may be Christ in *all*, and *all* one body in the Christ and by the Christ (xi, 20–21).

The theory of the mystic body is expounded at length in the instructions about spiritual gifts (*charismata*), a part of the document (xii, xiv) later than Paul but earlier than Marcion.[67] It may be taken as almost contemporary with the *Didache*, since it knows of missionaries still travelling under the name of apostles and of prophets who prophesy in meetings of the community (1 Cor. xii, 28–29; xiv, 26–33). The instructions are intended to prevent the disorder which inevitably resulted when the spiritual gifts became competitive (xii, 4–6):

> Differences of gifts there are,
>   but the Spirit is the same;
> Differences of service there are,
>   but the Lord is the same,
> Differences of working there are,
>   but God is the same,
>   who works all in all.

If the principle is one, the effects are many. But the Church, the community, as well as the principle, must also be one. Like the human body, the Church, as the body of Christ, has many members, all necessary; these must not be jealous of each other but behave as mutually interdependent, which is what they really are. The mere enumeration of spiritual functions shows that the communities were suffering from an excess of riches, and it is clear enough that a lowering of their activities had become due—apostles, doctors, wonder-workers, healers, helpers, administrators, speakers with tongues. So let every gift-bearer do his best not to annoy the others. But all this upsurge of enthusiasm was conceived as going on within the body of the Christ, and wits were taxed to prevent it upsetting the organic equilibrium.

Other formulas were used to express the mystic conception of the Church. In Second Corinthians the Corinthian community is described as "a chaste virgin" whom its apostle has espoused to the Christ (2 Cor. xi, 2). Since each community was, with the others, the Church of God, what is here said of Corinthian Christianity might be repeated of the whole. It is the application to the Christ and to the Church of an image familiar to the Hebrew prophets—the marriage of Jehovah with Israel. The author of the Epistle to the Ephesians connects the mystic notion of the Church as the spouse of the Christ with the other mystic notion of it as the Christ's body (v, 23–24). "The husband," he says, "is head of the wife, as Christ is the head of the Church, he, the saviour of the body"—meaning the body which is the Church itself. He then goes on, in his bad style (v, 23–24):

> Husbands, love your wives
> > as Christ loved the Church
> And gave himself up for her to make her holy,
> > purifying her in the bath of water with speech,
> To offer the Church to himself in her glory,
> > having no spot, nor wrinkle, nor aught of that kind
> > but holy and spotless.

Finally he quotes the text from Genesis about the union of man and woman and notes that it contains "a great mystery"—a profound secret of mystic theology—"in regard to the Christ and to the Church" (v, 32). Here our author touches the fringe of certain pagan mysteries; not does he fall far short of making the Church a transcendant personification, an *aeon*, as it is in some of the gnostic systems.

The same reflection is forced upon us by the Pastor of Hermas.

Here, however, the Church is not the eternal Jerusalem described by the seer of the Apocalypse as ready to descend upon earth, but the visible institution ready to get organized here below.[68] The Church herself is the teacher who, in the form of an aged woman, instructs Hermas in the first part of his book. She is at first shown to him seated on a great white throne and holding in her hand a book of prophecy containing threats against the pagans and a consoling promise for the righteous. A year later the same woman comes back to Hermas and this time leaves him a little book to copy in which, among other things, there is a promise of pardon, but for one occasion only, to all Christian sinners, even to apostates, who repent before the great tribulation —that is, before the approaching persecution. Hermas then learns that this woman, whom he had believed to be the Sybil, is the Church. She is old because she was created before all things, and it was by her that the world was made.

This is not a solitary instance of fantastic speculation about the Church. The ancient homily, known as the second Epistle of Clement, has the teaching that he who does the will of the Father belongs to the primal Church, to the spiritual Church, created before the sun and the moon, which is the Church of Life.[69] Now the living Church is the body of the Christ. For Scripture declares that God made man male and female (Gen. i, 27); the male is the Christ; the female is the Church, spiritual as the Christ is. The Church was revealed for our salvation, at the end of the ages, in the flesh of the Christ, showing that whosoever keeps the Church unchanged in the flesh shall receive the Holy Spirit; for the flesh is the image of the spirit, and he who changes the copy shall have no part in the original, which is spirit, and spirit is the Christ. The flesh of such an one, when united to Christ, is made capable of receiving an incorruptible life from the Spirit, and no man can express or describe the good things which God keeps for his chosen ones.

This gnosis, nonsensical farrago as it may seem, is hardly more audacious in its mode of expression than that of the Epistle to the Romans, or to the Corinthians with the thesis of the two Adams, or than that of the Epistle to the Ephesians on the Christ and the Church as a transcendant husband and wife, to say nothing of the conception in the Apocalypse of the New

Jerusalem as "the bride of the Lamb."[70] Had this line of speculation been carried much further the homily would have joined company with gnosis in the most delirious of its expressions. But our author checked himself and reduces his gnosis to a moral lesson: the Church being in our flesh, as it is in the flesh of the Christ, and we, in our very selves, being thus the flesh of the Christ, it behoves us to guard our flesh in purity, lest we dishonour the Church and the Christ.

In his third vision Hermas still has the Church before him, but this time accompanied by six young men about to construct a building; the woman sits on a bench of ivory covered with a white veil, and makes Hermas sit down on her left hand, because the seats to the right are kept for the martyrs; and the young men set about building a tower on the water with stones brought to them by thousands of workers. The woman explains that the tower is the Church, that is, herself; it is built on water, because the life of the believer is saved by water—doubtless by baptism; the six young men are the first-created angels to whom the Lord has entrusted the government of all created beings; the countless workers are also angels, helpers to the six; the stones, squared and white, and fitting exactly, are the apostles, bishops, teachers and deacons with a record of good service; the other stones drawn up from the bottom of the water, are the martyrs—etc. etc. At this point it becomes clear that the building of the Church is leading up to a consideration of the end of the world. So, when Hermas asks the woman if the end is at hand, she answers that the tower is not yet finished, but soon will be, and that the end will then come; meanwhile the important thing is to spread abroad the warnings that have been received and to give heed to them. This said, the woman addresses a severe admonition to the faithful and especially to their leaders whom she reprimands for their divisions (*Vision*, iii, 8–9).

In his ninth parable Hermas takes up the theme of the tower in new detail. We now learn that the master builder, together with the rock which serves him for a foundation and the entrance door of the building, is the Head of the six angels, in other words he is the Son of God, the Christ himself, who thus comes first and not seventh in the group of higher beings; "the other six form his retinue, on his right hand and on his left." Hermas sees the Son of God in the fashion of "a man surrounded by glory and of colossal stature"—just as the Christ, rising from his tomb, is represented in the Gospel of Peter. Getting somewhat entangled in these speculations, the good Hermas informs us in the preamble to the parable that the Holy Spirit, who is the Son of God, and who formerly spoke to him under the figure of the Church, has since spoken to him by the Shepherd, angel of penitence (*Parable*, ix). But the Shepherd is not a simple figure. Neither is the Church which was created before all things. We may recall the feminine hypostasis of the Christ in the second Epistle of Clement, which the Church here resembles.

9. Birth of the Church-Consciousness

The letters attributed to Ignatius of Antioch seem to have been written when the flood of gnostic heresies was at its height, and may be described as a mystic canonization of the episcopate intended to secure the cohesion of the communities and to oppose the innovators by making the episcopate into the object of a veritable cult, in which the institution of bishops is no longer merely that of a corporate body, but is tending to become a sacred hierarchy. The author gives no place to the Church-myth of Hermas and must have written later than the date of his mythology. It is not enough that a man call himself a Christian, says the letter to the Magnesians, he must *be* a Christian, and he is no Christian when he holds to any kind of union in which the bishop has no part. "Let everything be done in the concord ordained by God, the bishop presiding in the place of God, the presbyters replacing the senate of the apostles, the deacons . . . charged with the service of Jesus Christ, who was at God's right hand before the ages and was revealed at the end of them . . . just as the Lord, united to the Father, did nothing without the Father, either by himself or by his apostles, so you, likewise, do nothing by yourselves without the bishop and the presbyters . . . One only prayer, one only supplication, one only spirit, one hope in charity and innocent joy—even that is Jesus Christ, above whom there is nothing." Obedience must be rendered to the bishop: "Be in submission to the bishop, and each to the others, as Jesus Christ, according to the flesh, was in submission to the Father, and the apostles to the Father, to the Christ and to the Spirit."[71]

There is other evidence that the object of these admonitions is to avert the danger of heresy. In the letter to the Trallians (6–7) we read as follows: "I beseech you nourish yourselves on Christian food only, and abstain from every foreign plant, that is from heresy"—the word has now acquired its traditional meaning. "Its professors, to make themselves respectable, mingle Jesus Christ with their doctrine, as if they were putting deadly poison into honeyed wine . . . Protect yourselves from such people. This you will do by not getting puffed up and by keeping yourselves inseparable from Jesus Christ, from the bishop and from the precepts of the apostles. No man has a clear conscience who undertakes anything in separation from the bishop, the presbytery, and the deacons." But the practical interest evinced by this advice detracts nothing from its essentially mystic character. It serves to show how, under the menacing pressure of heresy, a vague sense of unity among Christians is now rising into a clear consciousness of that unity in which, as we know from Justin, God and the Christ are seen as present in those who have become the effectual ministers of the mystery, the chief depositories and agents of the Spirit by whom the Church has been animated from the beginning. In reality these functionaries were become the guardians of tradition, and it was a tradition of which they themselves were about to fix the form. Our author, meanwhile, proclaims them representatives of God, substitutes for the Christ, successors of the apostles; and insists far less on their doctrinal function than on their strictly pastoral and mystical rôle. He would have Christianity range itself behind the ministers of the Christian mystery, and a deaf ear turned to teachers who are working to break Christian unity by proclaiming dangerous novelties.

It is important to bear in mind that our Ignatius, who himself claims to be a bishop, and has the surname "God-possessed," is an ardent mystic, a seeker after martyrdom, of which he tells the Romans they have taught him the lesson (*Romans*, 3, 1)—a probable allusion to the Pastor of Hermas. "I write to all the Churches and send word to all of you, that I shall willingly die for God, if you do nothing to hinder it . . . Food for wild-beasts let me be, that by them I may have access to God. God's wheat am I, and the teeth of wild beasts will grind me, that I may be formed purest bread of the Christ. Give the beasts your caresses for becoming my tomb and let no fragment of my body remain that any man should have the trouble of burying it. Then shall I be truly a disciple of Jesus Christ when the world sees nothing more of my body" (*Romans*, 4). Perhaps all this is a trifle overdone and a little finer than nature; perhaps our author himself, in a situation less imaginary, would have somewhat tempered his eloquence; but there can be no doubt that his enthusiasm is sincere and that his interpretation of the consciousness of the bishop-martyr, as a eucharistic oblation to God, is superbly done.

The thought of Ignatius is saturated in eucharistic mysticism: "I have no taste for corruptible food nor for the joys of this life: I would have the bread of God, which is the flesh of Jesus Christ, descended from David, and for drink I would have his blood, which is incorruptible love" (*Romans*, 7). This refers to the heavenly and wholly spiritual eucharist; but Ignatius speaks also of the Supper: "Deceive not yourselves . . . whoso follows a schismatic shall have no part in the Kingdom of God: whoso rules himself by strange doctrines, shall not share the benefits of the passion. Have a care then to use the one only eucharist, for there is only the one flesh of Our Lord Jesus Christ, and one cup for union in his blood, one only altar, as there is but one bishop, surrounded by the presbytery and the deacons. I go back to the Gospels as to the flesh of Jesus, and to the apostles as the presbytery of the Church. Love we also the prophets, for they announced the Gospel, they put their hope in it, they waited for it, they were saved by believing in it, being in the unity of Jesus Christ" (*Philadelphians*, 3–5).

Unity—all comes back to that: Old Testament is Gospel; Gospel is Jesus Christ; Jesus Christ is God of the Christian mystery, living Spirit of the Church. But what is the Christian mystery? It is that which the bishop with his helpers the priests and the deacons administers in every Church. Two Scriptures there are not; nor two Christs; nor two eucharists; nay, rightly speaking, there are not two Scriptures. All these are one in the Christ. In practice they are all one in the bishop, representative of the Christ in the Church. And outside of this mystery—what is there? Naught but the fantasies of professors without authority, naught but the error which is all they have to offer. And God, the Christ, the Church, the truth of the Old Testament and Gospel, the mystery of salvation—where are all these to be found? Nowhere else than in their one habitation—the Christian communities closely ranked round their several bishops.

In gaining this mystic consciousness of itself, as it stood firm against the gnostic flood, common Christianity became, in very fact, the Catholic Church. Come whence they may, these impassioned letters of church-mysticism contain something quite other than the first whisperings of theological formulas destined, when their voice has grown louder, to establish or defend an abstract and subtle dogma. They speak with the full voice of vehement faith, of Christianity established in that faith, and meeting the gnostic invasion with a bold front.

Chapter IX

THE GNOSTIC CRISIS

THE great work of mystic construction which we have been studying was not suddenly brought into being. It came forth from the Gospel, but without foresight in the Gospel that it was coming. The first missionaries had barely an inkling of what it would be; it was, so to say, the spontaneous issue of their labour, brought into being by an irresistible upsurge of faith achieving a result widely different from what the faithful had hoped for. They had hoped that the Kingdom of God would come; what came was the Church.

But the Church was not formed without internal conflicts no less dangerous to its growth than the conflict with outside forces and, in the end, no less fruitful. There were three main crises. The first, hardly perceptible to us, but pregnant with consequences, was that which led to the formation at Jerusalem of the Hellenist group of believers side by side with the Hebrew. The second was that in which Judaizing opposition arose to the work done by Hellenist preachers among the pagans. But hardly were communities of Hellenist Christians established on pagan territory, than their union was threatened by the intense religious fermentation which then broke out and was constantly changing its form under the influence of the varied elements drawn into the movement. This crisis of the growing age, the third to be encountered, begun almost in apostolic times, reached its height towards the middle, and was not finally overcome before the last quarter, of the second century.

During this period the Christian mystery, whose birth and development we have sketched, was threatened with disintegration. More exactly, as the movement increased in strength it had to disengage itself from a mass of strange excrescences and parasitic growths known under the general name of gnosis. This was an ebullition, sometimes superficial or near the surface, thrown up by that deep travail of faith of which traditional Christianity was also the outcome. Rightly understood Christianity itself is a disciplined gnosis born of the same movement which produced the gnoses called heretical, and brought to its own definition in the process of condemning them. The doctrine it proclaimed was a mystical knowledge of the divine secret and of the revealed programme of salvation. Thus Christianity, in its own way, was a gnosis, and so it has always remained. Nothing could be more *gnostic*, in the special sense of the word, than the declaration attributed to the Christ in Matthew xi, 27:

> None knows the Son, save the Father;
> None knows the Father, save the Son,
>   and he to whom the Son will reveal him.

But Christianity had to force a way for itself through a swarm of gnostic sects among which, had it been less sure of itself, it might easily have dissolved and perished. This process we have now to study.

1. SIMON MAGUS

The first point on which we have to remark is that Simon the Magician, a contemporary of Jesus and of the first missionaries, is presented in Christian tradition as the father of heretical gnosis. There is a sense, however, in which the gnostic crisis had its birth in Judaism long before the preaching of the Gospel, and had long been a factor in the religious syncretism which arose in the Eastern world as a result of the successive conquests of the Persians and the Greeks, and in which mysteries of salvation were flourishing elements. Writings such as the Book of Enoch and Book of Daniel may be truly described as monuments of Jewish gnosis influenced by science and mystic speculation of foreign parentage. The Jew Philo was a gnostic, if ever there was one; and the Gospel itself, born though it was from a popular current of Jewish hope, drew its first breath of life in an atmosphere of gnosis, and breathed that air more deeply as it grew up. The Christian mystery was, as it were, a rectified gnosis with the chaff and impurities sifted out, and equipped with a doctrine and sacramental mysticism all its own. The systems commonly known as gnostic are, in their relation to the Christian, parallel variations of the same movement, each with a tendency to absorb the Gospel; they are not, as they are often represented to be, the wilful and belated distortions of a Gospel to which gnosis of every kind was originally foreign. The Christian mystery, which assumed definite forms as Catholic Christianity, has never repudiated its Jewish base in the principle of absolute monotheism, where the First of Beings, the Creator of the world and the God of Israel are unconditionally identified as One. Nor has it ever cut its line of communication with the historical point from which the Gospel makes its departure in the historical manifestation of Jesus. Nor has it ever lost hold on the idea of universal salvation by the death, followed by the resurrection, of the Christ. Now this last idea, mystic through and through, and stamping Christianity as one of the mystery religions, is the creation of gnosis. Of this idea heretical gnosis took possession to sublimate it into various systems, just as it made the God of monotheism transcendent to the point where he becomes the absolute unknowable and, in the effort to spiritualize the Christ, dissolved his existence into vapour.

In representing Simon the Magician as baptized by Philip in Samaria and subsequently repudiated by Peter for attempting to buy the gift of conferring the Holy Spirit from the apostles, the legend in Acts aimed at disqualifying this founder of a rival sect, representing him as only a provisional and jealous adherent to the newly born Christianity, whom the chief of the apostles justly put to shame. This legend is not more consistent than those of a later date which show the same Simon engaged in a subsequent competition with Peter in the East, and even at Rome; but there is nothing in it to permit a distinction[1] between the leader of the sect, who figures in writers on heresy, from the magician who, according to Acts, led the Samaritans astray. The existence of Simon is not to be denied on the pretext that we know him only in legend. The fact is simply that Simon, notwithstanding that Christian tradition has made him the father of all the heresies, never was a heretic in regard to Christianity, for he never professed it. Although Justin incautiously lets himself be deceived about the worship paid to Simon in Rome it does not follow that we must reject as untrue what he says about Simon being born in such or such village of the Samaria to which he belonged, or about the doctrine held in his time by the Simonians, that is, by Samaritans. These worshipped Simon as "God above every principality, power or essence" (which should not be condemned as *a priori* improbable, seeing that Christians did as much for Jesus) with "his supreme thought" under the name Helena, made into an associated object of the cult (*Apology*, 1, 26, 56). The truth is that Celsus, twenty years later, knew of Simonians who called themselves Helenians[2] and took them for a Christian sect, the description meeting with a lively protest from Origen (*C. Celsum*, I, 57; vi, 15). Justin had already protested against it (*Apology*, 1, 26, 6–7) but without perceiving that he had supported it by representing Simon as the father of heresy in regard to the true faith. Some analogy between the two sects there must have been in doctrine, rites and propaganda, and some kind of affinity. Otherwise the pagan opinion echoed by Celsus and the attitude of Justin would be hard to explain.

The problem of Simon is complicated with the problem of Dositheus, another Samaritan sect-founder, sometimes represented as Simon's master and sometimes as his rival.[3] He might well have been both, but the documentary evidence is not decisive. Dositheus and Simon, both Samaritans, founded sects, each his own, which long survived them. They were two Samaritan Messiahs, both deified and worshipped after their death. Dositheus claimed to be the "prophet" announced by Moses for the last days (Deuteronomy xviii, 18). Though he denied the resurrection of the dead, as not taught in the Law, his disciples proclaimed him alive after death and carried up into heaven, like Moses and Elijah before him.[4] Simon's claim to be the Messiah was made under somewhat different conditions, and with more success. He seems to have been more independent of the Law and to have professed a kind of gnosis which his followers subsequently developed. The notice about him in Acts gives two indications, the second superimposed on the first. The first tells us that he made himself out to be "some great personage" (viii, 9)— a formula applied by Acts in analogous terms to Theudas (v, 36) and referring no doubt to their Messianic pretension: this was the account he gave of himself. His following, on the other hand, are said to have proclaimed him "that Power of God which is called the great Power" (viii, 10), meaning that Simon was an incarnation on earth of the sovereign power of God. The distinction here to be noted is that the latter definition represents in brief what Simonians were saying about Simon at the time (*c.* 130) when the editor of Acts was writing. First Corinthians says of the Christ in like manner that he was "Power and Wisdom of God" (i, 24). We may conclude that incarnation of these divine attributes was an idea familiar to the first forms of gnosis.

Among the Simonians the incarnation of Wisdom was alloted to Helena, Simon's female companion: she was the Supreme Thought, mother of all things; after issuing from the abode of divinity she brought forth the angels and the angels made the visible world, but they kept their mother a prisoner in order to conceal their origin and otherwise ignored God. After various metempsychoses—the most remarkable being that in which this feminine Logos became Helen of the siege of Troy—the Great Thought turns into a prostitute in a house of resort at Tyre; there the Great Power, incarnate in Simon, finds her, buys her freedom and attaches her to himself. In this gnostic poem (which the writers on heresy, to whom we owe the account of it, did not invent, though they may have put undue emphasis on some of its fearures) the Great Power is said to have been manifested in three forms; to the Jews, as Son, in Jesus who suffered death in appearance but not in reality; to the Samaritans, as Father, in Simon himself; to other people as the Holy Spirit. Salvation among the Simonians consists in the knowledge of this mystery; the knowledge carried with it freedom from the Law, which was a work of the creator-angels, and from laws of every kind, the distinction between good and evil being a human convention.[5]—In this outline we are following Irenaeus (*Heresies*, i, 28) and Hippolytus (*Philosophoumena*, vi, 19, 20).[6]

It was not Simon who elaborated the whole of this system, and the artifice by which the authors of it would make Christianity, not to speak of other religions, into a Simonism unaware of its own true character can only be an afterthought of a time when both Christian and Simonian propaganda had long been active. It does not follow from this that Simon and Helen never existed, nor that the essential features of the system do not go back to Simon, as de Faye would have it. Would it have been so easy to make him the father of gnosis if gnosis were something to which he was wholly a stranger? The points where the two systems meet are as striking as those where they part. From what has just been said it is clear that the Simonians were aware of the meeting points and made the most of them. Frail as is the testimony of the apocryphal Clementines in regard to Simon, it is nevertheless significant that they present Dositheus and Simon as disciples of John the Baptist. In historical strictness neither Simon nor Dositheus was a successor to John, any more than Jesus was, but affinity of origin and character there must have been between all these sects which arose in the same environment and almost at the same time. Both in reality and legend the case of Simon and Dositheus is not without analogy to the case of Jesus, their relative insuccess, compared with the fortune awaiting him, being due to the limits which their origin and circumstances imposed on their propaganda. But points of difference, as we have said, are equally striking. As regards Simon, his system lacked the prestige conferred on the Christian by its lofty ethic. What he said of the Law bears indeed a strong resemblance to statements in the Epistle to the Galatians (iii, 19) and in that to the Romans (v, 13, 20; vii, 1); but the rent these Epistles tear in the theoretical idea of duty is healed by the purity of the moral feeling which inspires what they have to say. Simon's gnosis, on the other hand, was largely compatible with superstitious magic and with some degree of moral licence, and continued to be compatible with both.

2. Menander

An analogous doctrine was preached at Antioch by Menander, said to have been a disciple of Simon. He too professed to be the heaven-sent Saviour of humanity. To his disciples he promised immortality—of what kind we do not know—and conferred a baptism which gave security for it.7 Justin names Menander between Simon and Marcion, as if these three were heads of the chief sects which the pagans were in the habit of confusing, under the name Christian, with the believers of the Great Church. Simon and Menander had taught, before Marcion, that the lower world was not created by the Invisible God whose intervention had brought about the salvation of mankind.

3. Cerinthus

Of Cerinthus as a human figure we know only the name, the

approximate time of his teaching and the place where he taught. He appeared in Asia Minor towards the end of the first century. Three-quarters of a century later the opponents of the Johannine writings attributed their paternity to Cerinthus, who had been a Judaizer and a millenarian in his eschatology, while professing a Christology more or less on the pattern of the fourth Gospel. If Iraeneus is to be believed (*Heresies*, i, 26) Cerinthus taught that the Supreme Being is too far removed above the world to take an interest in its affairs; a power ignorant of the supreme God had created it, another angel having created the Law and become the god of the Jews. A power ("virtue") from the supreme God had descended upon Jesus, son of Joseph and Mary, on the day of his baptism and dwelt in him up to the moment of his passion, when it forsook him; only the human Jesus suffered death and rose from the dead. It will be noted that the descent of the "virtue" is quite expressly indicated in the Synoptics and can be found also in the fourth Gospel as finally edited. The departure of the "power" is recorded in express terms by the Gospel of Peter in the words attributed to the dying Christ: "My power, my power, thou hast forsaken me." His dualism brings Cerinthus very near to Simon. He was also a precursor of Marcion. Justin seems to have had no knowledge of Cerinthus, but the Epistle of the Apostles, an apocryphal writing of mediocre importance,[8] which seems to have come out in Asia Minor in the second half of the second century, sets out to refute him by evidence derived, as so much other evidence had been, from imaginary conversations between the risen Christ and his disciples. The author was full of good intentions, but his work is sufficient proof that gnosticism had invaded the Church. Like Valentinus he represents the Logos as born from the Ogdoad, or combination of eight Principles; as receiving his "Wisdom" from the Father before descending into the world, and as bearing witness to himself under the figure of Gabriel. The opinion has often been advanced that Cerinthus is attacked in the Johannine Epistles (i, iv, 3, ii, 7); but the passages in question, like the apparition to Thomas in the fourth Gospel, aim rather at those who denied the reality of Christ's body, the Docetists, not at Cerinthus who did not deny, as they did, that Jesus suffered death as a real man.

4. The Satornilians

There existed in Justin's time a sect of Satornilians whose founder, Satornil, had taught at Antioch in the reign of Trajan (*Dialogue*, 35).9 Satornil was the offspring of Menander. According to Irenaeus he professed the existence of an unknowable God, creator of the angels and of other spiritual powers. Seven angels created man and the visible world. God, taking pity on a part of the human race, imparted to it the spark of a higher life. The creator-angels, to whom the god of the Jews belonged, are in revolt against God. To overcome them the Saviour Jesus descends from on high; he is not born on earth and is without a body of flesh; his office is to bring back to God the men who have received the spark of life. Satornil did not believe in the resurrection of the flesh; he condemned marriage and forbad the eating of anything that had life. In many respects, therefore, he was a forerunner of Marcion. Though much indebted to Simon and Menander, he, unlike them, does not set himself up as the Saviour sent from on high, but attributes that rôle to Jesus. Consequently, heretic though he be, we cannot deny him the qualification of Christian, while, from the Christian point of view, Simon and Menander qualify rather for Antichrists.

5. The Serpent-worshippers

Analogous conceptions are found in other systems insufficiently known or on which we have only conflicting information, sects not named, like the foregoing, after their founders, and of which we cannot determine the origin and the localization nor the transformations they underwent in the course of a history which mostly ended in decay and oblivion. Irenaeus describes a good many of them under the general name of gnostics (*Heresies*, i, 29–31). The name Serpent-worshippers (Ophites) fits only some of them in which the serpent was made the object of a cult and given a place in their doctrine which, whether deduced or not from the story in Genesis, was co-ordinated with it. Celsus was acquainted with the Ophites whom he took for Christians, which Origen denies (*C. Celsum*, vi, 24–38). As the Simonians are in the same case, it is not necessary to suppose (with de Faye) that the Church was still tolerating the Ophites in the time of Celsus. It is a fact, however, that the Naasenians, whose name alone proclaims them a serpent-sect, attributed the rôle of Saviour to Jesus; a Naasenian hymn cited by Hippolytus (*Philos.*, v, 1, 10) makes him intercede with the Father in terms which recall something of Marduk's intercession with Ea in certain Babylonian incantations. Unsatisfactory as Hippolytus' account of them is, few ancient texts give us a better idea than these Naasenian speculations of the intense fermentation of doctrine which broke out in Christianity and around it in the second century, or of the timeliness of the barrier hastily raised by the Church to restrain it.

Origen discusses a diagram made by the Ophites which Celsus, without naming the Ophites, alleges to have been an esoteric Christian document. It resembled, as we might expect, a map of salvation which Celsus compared, not without reason to the Mithraic cosmography. It showed ten concentric circles framed in a greater circle which was the soul of the universe and named Leviathan, whose name also figures at the centre of the whole apparatus; there are seven gates to be passed guarded by seven spirits in the form of animals (lion, bull, amphibian, eagle, bear, dog, ass) with their names indicated (Ialdabaioth, Iao, Sabaoth, Astaphaios, Eloaios, Horaios) with a password for each; a transverse black line represents hell; a square space guarded by a flaming sword has to do with the Tree of Knowledge and the Tree of Life. The seven angels, enemies of the angels of light, are called archons, their chief being the demiurge, the creator, and god of the Jews who gave man the knowledge of good and evil and is himself accursed for having cursed the serpent; a sacrament called "The Seal" as Christian baptism was often called (*Apoc.*, vii, 3-8) is conferred by a "father," the candidate being "son"; this sacrament involves an anointing, since the candidate has to pronounce the words "I am anointed with the anointing of the Tree of Life." On this, Origen exclaims that the Ophites who curse the Creator also curse Jesus and cause him to be cursed by all who enter their sect—though this is not in the diagram and not true of all the Ophite sects. A preposterous doctrine in which we catch some resemblance to Marcion's system, but not necessarily derived from it.

Among the sects of which we are speaking were some which placed a female aeon besides the Ineffable Being. This was "the Mother" with whom went the successive emanations of the aeons and the successive decay of one, the organization of the lower world under a demiurge without knowledge of the Supreme God, and finally the manifestation of the aeon "Christ" in Jesus, which was to gather up the sparks of Divinity scattered about the human world and re-establish the harmony of the pleroma.[10] It would be an error to make all this depend on Marcion even if these systems are later than his. The Syrian origin of many of their speculations is betrayed by the names given to the aeons.

It would be unwise to lay too much emphasis on the extravagance of these sects, which are often working with the same materials as the old Christian writers. The question is hardly more than one of degree. The gnosis of Colossians, that of 1 Corinthians xv, and that of Romans iv–vi are not conspicuous for rational sobriety, and the Woman of Revelation xii has some resemblance to the Mother who figures in the systems of certain gnostic sects.

6. Basilides

Basilides was of Alexandria where he taught in the reigns of Hadrian and Antoninus (117–161). He wrote a Gospel commentary in twenty-four books entitled τὰ ἐξεγητκά. In the system of Basilides as described by Origen, the unbegotten Father, or First Principle, gave issue to Nous; from Nous came forth Logos; from Logos, Phronesis; from Phronesis, Sophia and Dynamis; from these primal beings came the "virtues," powers and angels; together they formed the population of the first heaven. There were three hundred and sixty-five heavens of which we see only the last and lowest. This is inhabited by the angels who created our world, whose head is the god of the Jews; between this god, who aimed at enslaving all peoples to his own, and the angels of the peoples to be enslaved, there broke out a conflict, to which an end was put by the intervention of Nous who, sent by the Supreme Father, took on the semblance of humanity in Jesus. At the moment of crucifixion his form changed into that of Simon of Cyrene, who died in his place. There is no reason, therefore, for paying homage to the Crucified nor for undergoing martyrdom in his name. In order to be saved it suffices to know the truth of the system taught by Basilides.

Needless to say, the Old Testament, which was the work of the demiurges, had to be rejected. A kind of magic was practised against the lower powers, certain mysterious words being recommended for the purpose, especially the word *Abraxas*, the letters of which, turned into numbers and added, equalled the number of the heavens. The human passions were substantial appendages attached to the reasonable soul, which they led into sin; evil is the punishment of sin, the martyrs themselves, even if innocent of sin in this life, suffer for sins committed in a previous existence. Reincarnation was one of Basilides' doctrines. He and his son Isidore counselled celibacy, tolerating marriage as the lesser of two evils. Faith, in the system, is a kind of substance, or hypostasis, inherent in elect souls, who thus constitute a true aristocracy both as to number and quality. The ethics of Basilides as first announced were somewhat severe; but it seems that the sect was not slow to enter upon evil courses.

7. Carpocras

The sect of Carpocras, or Carpocrates, appears to be as old as that of Basilides, for there is no reason to distinguish the Carpocras who lived at Alexandria in the time of Hadrian from him whose doctrine was brought to Rome towards the year 160 by a woman named Marcellina. The case of the Carpocratians enables us to see how a certain form of gnosis could be made compatible with the most reckless immorality and furnish pretexts for the defamation of Christianity. There was, however, little enough Christianity about this sect. Epiphanus, the son of Carpocras, who died when he was seventeen, leaving behind him a book "on Righteousness," was revered as a god in the island of Cephallonia, from which his mother had come.[11] This youthful philosopher poured ridicule on the prohibition of adultery laid down in the Decalogue; the common and equal enjoyment of all things, said he, belonged to all men by divine appointment; human laws had invented the distinction between good and evil, with all kinds of private property, including the marriage bond; thus the law had created the robber and the adulterer; but community of goods and free love[12] is the law of nature. An unexpected use of Plato for achieving the downfall of Moses and the morality of the common man!

Carpocras acknowledged the unity of God, and a hierarchy of angels who had created the visible world. Human souls had also belonged to the spiritual world before they fell into matter, from which they can free themselves in all the states and actions implied in human existence by rising superior to the rules artificially established. Evidently Basilides, and Carpocras more distinctly, start off from a principle which might be called identical, save in respect of moral sense, with that which supports the theory of Justification in the Pauline Epistles, the principle, namely, that spirit and the spiritual have an eminent dignity above the Mosaic Law, and above law of any kind. But instead of making the renunciation of carnal pleasures the condition of a perfect life and a blessed eternity, the condition now lies in breaking free of the law which puts a social restraint on the lower appetites. Let sin be suppressed; but suppress it by suppressing the law which makes it sin. The satisfaction of the appetites is permitted to the wise man and even becomes, in the system of Carpocras, a positive means of his salvation, which is for that man only who has exhausted the lists of sensual pleasure in violation of every law which puts it under interdict.

As a single life would not ordinarily suffice for most men to achieve so complete a liberation, Carpocras introduced the doctrine of reincarnation to provide further opportunity for souls imperfectly liberated. Jesus, who was born and lived under ordinary human conditions, had been given as an example of the liberation which all men are called to achieve for themselves; he had triumphed over the creator-angels by breaking free from their rules and ascended to the Father from whom he came. Every man can succeed as well as he, or even better, in realizing a like liberty for himself; let him, by breaking the laws the creators have made, dissolve his partnership in their adventures. We are prepared to learn that magic had a great vogue with the Carpocratians especially as a means of combating the influence of the creators. They also offered worship to the images of the great philosophers, including an image of Jesus, of whom they professed to have a portrait made by orders of Pilate. Their morals were in keeping with their doctrine, Irenaeus declaring that he dared not believe what was told of them. Given their principles, it is permissible to suppose that their conventicles were not abodes of the purest innocence. Dregs of mysticism gone astray!

8. Valentinus

The influence of Plato is also to be seen in Valentinus, but his excesses were mainly of the metaphysical order and his vogue was greater than that of all the sect-leaders we have so far mentioned. Lower Egypt was his country of origin and he had studied at Alexandria, a city unique in those days for an intense fermentation of mind, of which it was a hotbed. There Valentinus had his first successes. Like other gnostics he was, in his own way, a Christian, but repressive action against heresy, so far as it existed when he began to teach his religious philosophy, had little severity, and less at Alexandria than elsewhere. He came to Rome, as Marcion did somewhat later, and there according to Irenaeus he made a long stay from the episcopate of Hyginus (139–142) to that of Anicetus (157–168). He lived there on the margin of the Christian community from which he had been excluded at a time and for reasons unknown to us with certainty. According to Tertullian he aspired to become bishop and seceded from the regular Church ("ecclesia authenticae regulae") on seeing a confessor of the faith preferred to himself. Whatever be the truth behind this statement, there can be no doubt that Valentinus, who had been educated at a time and in a society which knew nothing about the "regular" Church, came like Marcion to Rome, as the great Christian centre, for the purpose of carrying on religious propaganda. It is quite possible that his secession from the common Christianity was not made final until after he had left Rome, perhaps after the election of Anicetus, when he was in Cyprus, where he ended his days. In contrast to Marcion, Valentinus was far more a thinker and teacher than an organizer. The sect that he founded had not the wide expansion and long duration of Marcion's and was a less formidable rival of the Great Church.

The system of Valentinus was a salvation gnosis conveyed in a kind of metaphysical poem.[13] At the beginning of all things was Bythos, the unbegotten Abyss; with him was his female companion Sige, Silence.[14] When it was pleasing to Bythos, he begot of Silence another couple, Nous, the Intellect, and Aletheia, Truth; of these two were born Logos, the Thought-word and Zoe who is Life; from Logos and Zoe came forth Anthropos, primarily transcendent Man, and Ecclesia, the Church on high. This is the Eight-in-one, the Supreme Ogdoad, in which Basilides, the author of the fourth Gospel, the author of the second Epistle of Clement and even the good Hermas would all find themselves on very familiar ground. But the gnosis of Valentinus differs from theirs by being conceived in terms of the union of the sexes and its consequences; it unfolds in a series of syzygies, or conjunctions, after the manner of a mythology, and under the influence of the mythologies, which may or may not have been consciously followed. The great Babylonian poem of creation begins in like manner with a cosmogony. Apsu, the begetter of everything, and Tiamat, the sea which brings everything to birth, mingled their waters, etc. etc. The mythology of Valentinus is more realist and his gnosis more abstract, but some of his abstractions carry the mark of their origin, notably the Abyss and the Man.

The upper world does not comprise the Great Ogdoad only. Logos and Life gave birth to five couples of Aeons who become the Great Decade; in like manner Man and Church produced six couples, the Great Dodecade; Ogdoad, Decade and Dodecade make up together the Divine Pleroma—a valuable sidelight on the Epistle to the Colossians (i, 19) and on the Epistle to the Hebrews with its Aeons (i, 2; xi, 3). In the thoughts of Valentinus this "pleroma" was far from being the world of abstraction, the metaphysical dream that its terminology might lead us to think it; it is a world of ideas eternally alive, a world of mind and of transcendent realities. The genesis of the material world, which the rest of us call real, has still to be explained. For Valentinus this world was an appearance, accidental, corruptible and destined to perish. It was conceived as the result of a bad accident in the spiritual world, which happened as follows.

The last couple of the Great Dodecade are the figures of Theletos (Volition) and Sophia (Wisdom) not precisely moral wisdom, rather knowledge and skill. Sophia is seized with an uncontrollable desire to know the Supreme Father, the Abyss, who is knowable only by his Son, the Intellect (compare Matthew xi, 27; John i, 18); in this unappeasable desire she would have gone to pieces, had not Oros (the Limit) a kind of transcendent Saviour appointed by the Abyss on the outskirts of the Pleroma, prevented her dissolution. Sophia then recovers her sanity, but during her madness she had conceived, without intercourse with Theletos, an imperfect Aeon, Hacamoth, a debased copy of her mother; she was also called Wisdom, but this time by the Hebrew equivalent of the term. Hacamoth is then cast out by the Pleroma. To prevent the repetition of a similar calamity, Nous and Aletheia produce a seventh couple, Christos and Pneuma—Spirit is feminine in Semitic—who teach the others to take heed to the Limit by not attempting to know the unknowable; after which all the Aeons celebrate the return of peace, and combine to produce the thirty-third Aeon. This is the Saviour Jesus.

But the poor Hacamoth, turned out of the Abyss, has an important future awaiting her. The abortive creature was first visited in her abandonment by Christos who gave her a kind of form and consciousness. Then, realizing her fallen state, sorrow, fear and despair come over her. By a second visit, but this time by the Aeon Jesus, these passions are separated from her and used to constitute the elements of matter; matter is then explained as the congested or solidified form of the spiritual waste products thrown off by a mind in temporary distress—truly a strange procedure for explaining its origin and denying it an eternal existence. The Abyss, in the mythologies, is another name for Chaos, or unformed matter; but here it is the eternal fountain of transcendent ideas, and only on the rebound does it become the source of material existence and of the visible world! Hacamoth, however, thus relieved of her passions, continues to exist in herself as a psychic substance, and the mere sight of the angels who accompany the Saviour causes her to conceive and bring forth Spirit as a substantial entity. In this way the elements out of which the lower world is to be constructed are, if one may say so, brought together on the site in readiness for the building to begin.

The process is as follows. From her psychic substance Hacamoth extracts the demiurge who, in his turn, produces the materials and the psychic beings who together make up the visible world. Here in the lower world, the world of the demiurge, are comprised the seven heavens, the abodes of angels, but not of spirits, for the demiurge himself is not a spirit; knowing no other world than that of his own creation, the demiurge believes himself the master of the entire universe. His intention was to create man in two categories—material and psychic; but three categories exist in reality, because certain men happened to receive a germ of the spiritual substance that emanated from Hacamoth. Clement of Alexandria cites a passage[15] where the affair is explained. It tells how the demiurge and his angels, after creating man, were strangely surprised when they saw him putting forth ideas far beyond his natural condition; the reason is that the germ of spirit had fallen into him from on high and "formed in the name of the Man, he breathed in fear of the Man Above, who was in him" doubtless in virtue of the fiery particle he had received from Hacamoth; whereupon the astonished angels immediately changed their manner of working. Needless to say that from the standpoint of Valentinus' time, this third category, spiritual man, was the one predestined to become Valentinian; the psychic are the common run of Christians and the material are the non-Christians. The principle on which these distinctions are based is to be found in the New Testament. In 1 Corinthians ii, 14–iii, 3, we have the three-fold division "spiritual," "psychic," "carnal," the last two, however, seeming to form one category. The distinction between "spiritual" and "psychic" is also found in Jude 19.

It follows from the above that men of the third category have no immortality, that all those in the first are saved, since the spirit that has fallen into them cannot die; these, so to say, have only to know themselves by the Valentinian gnosis. Strictly speaking only the psychics have need of redemption. Valentinus also believes in the historical manifestation of Jesus, but his belief is strongly coloured by metaphysic and docetism. The figure of the Redeemer was material only in appearance; his humanity was psychic and spiritual. "He ate and drank in a manner all his own, without excrementation. So great was the force of his temperance that the food he ate did not corrupt within him, because he himself was not to know corruption." Clement of Alexandria, to whom we owe this citation, thoroughly approves the tenor of it.[16] The Saviour at his birth owed nothing to the Virgin Mary; the great Aeon Jesus descended upon him at his baptism and withdrew from him, along with the pneumatic element, to return to the Pleroma, when it was determined to bring him before Pilate; what was crucified, therefore, was the Saviour's psychic part in his semblance of a body; but his passion was no whit the less real on that account. The Valentinian Saviour carries with him the light of his doctrine and is the liturgical celebrant of his own mystery. Humanity will come to an end when the demiurge ceases to create; Hacamoth will be received into the Pleroma and become the spouse of the Aeon Jesus; spiritual men will be made one with the angels who accompany the Saviour; finally the demiurge along with the psychic men who have practised the law of the Gospel will be installed below the Pleroma in the place vacated by Hacamoth, and a general conflagration, in which all material men and worthless psychics will perish, will reduce the material world to nothing.[17]

Valentinus founded a school, of which ancient writers distinguish the Eastern from the Western disciples. Of the last the best known are Heracleon and Ptolemy, with whom Irenaeus joins a much less respectable person named Marcus. Among the Eastern school we hear of a certain Theodotus whom the extracts preserved by Clement of Alexandria show to have been a faithful disciple of the Master; and of the Syrian Bardesanes (154–223) whose activities fall outside our picture. If Bardesanes was at first a Valentinian he does not seem to have remained in the fold. His reputation for heresy came late and could only be retrospective after he had finished his career as an independent teacher connected with the Church at Edessa, in which Tatian was also able to keep his footing, but without leaving a much better reputation behind him. Bardesanes' writings came into bad odour when orthodoxy had become more strict than in his time.[18]

9. Heracleon

Heracleon (c. 155–180) who seems to have been an immediate disciple of Valentinus, added some notable retouchings to his master's system.[19] Instead of a conjunction of Aeons, or syzygye, he placed the One and Only God at the summit of the Pleroma, conceiving Him after the gnostic manner under the title "Father of Truth." Similarly he makes the Logos inspire the demiurge who himself builds the visible world, the Logos thus again becoming the world-soul; he is also the Saviour of mankind and appears for the first time on earth when John the Baptist announces him. In the substance of his teaching Heracleon stands perceptibly close to the fourth Gospel, on which he wrote a commentary valued by Origen who used it in writing his own. At Capernaum, Jesus is supposed to have descended into the lowest stratum of the cosmos, which is the realm of matter; at Jerusalem he comes into the realm of the psychic.

We know from Origen how Heracleon interpreted the meeting of Jesus with the woman of Samaria. The water of Jacob's well is the symbol of "cosmic life," a life inferior and fugitive; the water that Jesus gives is eternal life, and the Samaritan woman who thirsts for it is a pneumatic; the husband whom Jesus bids her call is the mate who is waiting for her in the Pleroma; the woman has had six husbands (instead of the five of the traditional text) because six is the number for matter or evil; Mount Gerizim represents the devil and his kingdom, matter and wickedness, and the devil-worship practised by mankind before the Law was given; Jerusalem is the headquarters of the demiurge and his Jewish worship; those cults have lapsed; the spiritual worship the Father of Truth and him alone; the Father seeks for worshippers, now sunk in matter; God is spirit and spiritual souls are of one family with him, "consubstantial" with his unbegotten nature; it is to save them from their sunken condition that the Christ came down into the lowest parts of the world; redemption works by a kind of progressive illumination, beginning as an awakened feeling for the true life, which feeling is a memory of the mate which the soul possesses in the divine Pleroma. The redemption of the psychics comes about in a different manner. The woman, who is spiritual, announces salvation to her fellow Samaritans, who are psychics, and these, abandoning their former way of life, which was according to the world, come to the Saviour by faith. It is not very clear that the final result of this conversion is an immortal condition for the converted psychics.

The fate of the "Material" men (ὑλικόι) is explained in other passages. These have, for their father, the devil, whose evil nature is derived from error and ignorance; the devil cannot possess the truth and his speech is all lying; he has no liberty but only appetites; material men are his children, incapable of good and, at least in theory, doomed to perdition; in fact, a few may have all the devil's appetites without being fundamentally ὑλικοί but psychic, and therefore open to conversion.

The mitigations applied by Heracleon to the system of Valentinus bring him nearer to orthodoxy. There is no ground for supposing that this was a tactical move made by our doctor for the purpose of bringing his doctrines more into line with Christian truth. He was not without psychological insight and a true feeling for morality. No signs are betrayed in his writings of specific influence by the Pauline Epistles. This is almost as true of Valentinus—a fact to be noted in considering the history of the Epistles.

10. Ptolemy and Marcus

Of Ptolemy's personal writings all that remains is his letter to Flora, probably written about 160 and preserved by Epiphanius. To judge by this specimen, Ptolemy was not a tiresome theologian, for the letter is written with some elegance and much clarity. The subject of the letter lies in the question "What is the authority of the Law of Moses?" Some—the majority of Christians—declare it wholly divine and derived from God the Father; others—probably the disciples of Marcion —make it out to be the work of the devil who created the present world. According to Ptolemy it cannot be the work of the Father because it is not perfect, and he notes that Jesus attributes permission for divorce not to God but to Moses; neither can it be the work of the devil, since it is distinctly not a bad Law, as it certainly would be if the devil, who is all darkness, were its author. It must therefore come from some intermediate being, who can be no other than the demiurge. Ptolemy shows very clearly that the Law contains elements of unequal value. In what way the devil and the demiurge come forth from a perfect God, if they do, is a question which Ptolemy promises to examine later on. As far as can be judged from the notice in Irenaeus there are no retouchings in Ptolemy's system of the essential points in Valentinus. He does however replace Bythos and Sige, as the first pair of the Ogdoad, by the Father and Grace (Charis)—which certainly improves the moral character of the First Principle.

If we may believe Iranaeus, who was a close observer of these proceedings, the gnostic Marcus was an impudent propagandist who turned the symbolism of the eucharistic mystery into magic and belonged to the class of licentious mystics or gnostics, which is certainly not the case with the two previously mentioned.

11. Marcion brings the Crisis to a Head

Though Marcion presents the mystery of salvation with greater sobriety than Valentinus, the main current of Christian thought found him not sober enough. He came from Sinope in Pontus where his father is said to have been bishop. He made a fortune in the shipping trade of those days, and his wealth seems to have helped him in his religious undertakings. Pliny's letter to Trajan has shown us that Christianity had taken firm root in the Pontus region. It is not impossible that his own father was the first to reprove Marcion for his heresies. He began his propaganda in Asia where he seems to have been opposed by Polycarp of Smyrna. About the year 140 he betook himself to Rome and joined the Roman congregation, to which he gave a large sum of money[20] after submitting a letter of explanation about his faith, which was considered satisfactory. It was probably at Rome that he completed his system, wrote his *Antitheses* and fixed the text of the *Gospel* and the *Apostolicon*. His mind, though well informed, was not of the speculative turn. He made no attempt to found a school on the outskirts of the Church nor to form small groups of initiates; he hoped rather to give the Church, and the whole Church, fixed doctrines and authorized Scriptures. Towards the year 144 the heads of the Roman congregation responded to his efforts by formal excommunication and the return of his money. After that he displayed astonishing energy in the founding of congregations on the same pattern as those which had cast him out, but on a foundation which he believed to be that of the pure Gospel. Marcion therefore was not the founder of a school. His object was to reform Christianity, we might even say, to institute it afresh. According to him Christianity had taken a wrong road from the very beginning.

For Christian communities existing up to Marcion's time Scripture meant the Jewish Bible taken over from hellenist Jews and interpreted in the Christian sense, the catechists making use in addition of a diversity of Gospel writings and, subordinate to them, of certain apostolic documents. Marcion professed to furnish the Church with the one true Scripture, exclusively devoted to the Gospel, purely Christian and containing only the revelation of Jesus. It was *one* Gospel, which he called *the* Gospel. It corresponded with the Gospel named Luke's in catholic tradition, save that it omitted the first two chapters concerning the birth of John the Baptist and of Jesus, and made short omissions and retouchings in the rest of the book. By the side of the Gospel Marcion placed his *Apostolicon*,[21] a collection of ten Epistles having the same authority and the same authenticity as the Gospel they accompanied. All of the ten were Epistles attributed to Paul; to wit, Galatians, Corinthians (both), Romans, Thessalonians (both), Laodiceans (=Ephesians), Colossians, Philippians, Philemon—the traditional collection, *minus* the three Pastorals—all with omissions and retouches similar to those in the Gospel. The sum of the matter was that Marcion, in his own way, edited known documents, for which he reserved an exclusive authority, repudiating not only all similar writings used by different communities but also, and chiefly, the entire body of Scripture which Christianity had taken over from Judaism.

The book *Antitheses* contained Marcion's own theology and the justification of his biblical canon.[22] His theology was sober enough. He professed to re-establish the teaching of Jesus in its original simplicity and paid no heed to the cosmological speculations in which most of his predecessors had indulged so freely; making no pretence to introduce a new doctrine, he would have nothing to do with the division of believers into two classes of which one was privileged in regard to the other. But, for all that, what he had to offer was a doctrine widely different from the Gospel of Jesus; it was the essential principle of gnosis reduced to its simplest expression in the absolute transcendence of spirit and the depreciation of matter, of nature as created. The strangest feature of this truly extraordinary enterprise is Marcion's belief that his system was backed by the authority of the pure Christian tradition, which did not contain it, and that it was deducible therefrom by unanswerable logic.

His point of departure for the restatement of Christianity is the Epistle to the Galatians. Professing to find there a radical opposition between Law and Gospel, he infers that the god who is the author of the one cannot be the author of the other. The character of the Old Testament was incompatible with the idea of the good and only God, father of Jesus Christ. But the Old Testament, in Marcion's view, was none the less a revelation, and he gave it credit so far as to allow that what it tells of its own god is true, the god of the Jews being, as it says, the real creator of our bad material world. He recognized also that the Old Testament foretold a Messiah, but the sort of Messiah whom the Jews were still expecting. Jesus had not been sent by the demiurge but by the Transcendent God, unknown to man till a manifestation revealed him in Jesus, and by Jesus, to the end that men might attain salvation by faith in the good God and be delivered from the bondage to which their creator had condemned them. Marcion's Christology was extremely simple. In framing it our reformer was as little embarrassed by questions of historical probability as by the objections to which his metaphysic stood exposed. The good God, having assumed in Jesus the semblance of humanity, but without taking a material body, because he owed nothing and was incapable of owing anything to the demiurge, whose domain matter was—this good God, of whom the world had no knowledge hitherto, became visible to human eyes at Capernaum ("descending" there, Luke iii, 1; iv, 31—the opening of Marcion's Gospel) in the fifteenth year of Tiberius, and then, in the course of his manifestation, first revealed the mystery of salvation and finally enacted it by the cross. Though Jesus, according to Marcion, did not die in a body of flesh, die nevertheless he did, and rose from the dead. By this death he released mankind, or at least the believing part of mankind, from every tittle of obligation to the god who had created them, the god of the Jews.

"Severe" is a term hardly strong enough to describe the

character of Marcion's moral code. He condemned marriage and allowed baptism only to the continent. He imposed various restrictions on diet, forbad the eating of flesh and abated nothing from the duty of martyrdom. His exaggerated asceticism was in harmony with the common temper of Christianity in his time, but was also logically involved in his system. Did not the human body, the flesh and all its works, proceed from the inferior god, and was it not he who had bidden mankind "increase and multiply"? Let the believer, then, who would be perfect, cut himself free of the flesh and its appetites. Marcion's sacraments were the same as those of the great Church: baptism with anointing and with the drinking of milk and honey,[23] the latter a practice not unknown in early Christian times; Eucharist with bread and water unmixed with wine, also a practice not then looked on as a shocking novelty. The inner organization of the communities was also on the usual pattern, except that ecclesiastical offices were not regarded as established in perpetuity. But this may not have been peculiar to Marcionism, seeing that the established Church-hierarchy was largely built up as a defence against Marcion.

Whether he was aware of it or not, Marcion was, in reality, more dependent on gnosis than on the Gospel, which, according to him, had been kept pure only by the apostle Paul. It was not the Gospel, nor the Epistles, nor even the revised version he had made of both to fit his doctrine, that suggested to him his theory of these two Gods, the one transcendent, unknowable and good, the other of a lower denomination, merely just and with a turn for cruelty in his justice. His religion might find satisfaction in the antithesis of the two gods, but it would not have furnished him with the antithesis had not certain gnostics taught and suggested it. But a simplified dualism closely related to monotheism was convenient ground for establishing the incompatibility of the Gospel with the Law and the essential difference between the God revealed in the one and he who had enacted the other. This was Marcion's fundamental dogma, and this it was that caused the Church to cast him out. When Justin couples Marcion with Simon Magus as an arch-heretic this is the point on which he fixes as the essence of the matter: "A certain Marcion, of Pontus, who is even now making disciples, teaches that there is a God greater than the Creator; helped by the demons he spreads his blasphemies among the whole human race, denying the Creator of the world and proclaiming another greater God who has done bigger things than he" (*Apology*, 26; cf. 58). For the same reason Justin reproaches Marcion for having a Christ other than the Son of God. Marcion's moral rigorism and his theological Docetism are regarded by Justin as points of secondary importance, in which he finds nothing to cause scandal. Nor does he find fault with Marcion for tampering with the Gospel text. Tertullian indeed insists on this, but the times had then changed and the canon of the New Testament had been fixed in the interval between him and Justin. The main object of the *Antitheses*, and the head of its offending, was to establish dualism by means of an artificial exegesis which professed to attach this dualism both to the Gospel and to the Apostolic writings.

Whether he invented his doctrine entire, or borrowed certain elements of it from one Cerdo, a Syrian, who is said to have come to Rome a little in advance of him, certain it is that Marcion in the plainest of terms affirmed the existence of two gods, and even of two First Principles. For the inferior god, though perishable, had no beginning, matter being regarded not as a third Principle but as a passive element employed by the demiurge in constructing the lower world.[24] Though Marcion does not take over the Persian dualism entire, he is distinctly nearer to it than were the Alexandrian gnostics. His valuation of the perceptible world and of human nature bears no trace of the Greek spirit. His higher God, creator of the invisible world, is not, as Ormuzd was, a god of Light, he is a god of Goodness, while his lower god, creator of the visible world, is not like Ahriman, essentially dark and evil; he is nothing worse than a god of strict justice with an inclination to harshness. The dualism of Marcion is not based on a naturalistic philosophy, but has its roots in a concrete and psychological morality. It is a dualism of which one side is summarily made to fit the Jewish religion with its Old Testament, and the other side to fit the Christian with its Gospel. Tertullian was not mistaken when he wrote: "The man of Pontus brings forward two gods; the one, our Creator, whom we cannot deny; the other his own, whom he cannot prove" (*Adv. Marcionem* 1, 2). Marcion's Christianity and his knowledge of Scripture have coloured his conception both of his God and of his anti-God, and though he has not borrowed the latter conception from the Persian Ahriman, he would never have arrived at it had he not been unconsciously under the influence of Persian dualism. Did he not teach that the visible creation would finally disappear, along with its creator, the demiurge? It remains to say that he does not seem to identify the demiurge formally with the Devil; whether or no he would give him a rôle as assistant to the demiurge is not clear.

A mind systematic rather than profound, more zealous than impassioned, more moralist than mystic, Marcion constructed, without great originality and somewhat hastily, a scheme for giving Christianity a firm basis and a definite form. In the process of constructing his scheme he availed himself of all the elements he found useful for the purpose, without claiming any other rôle for himself than that of a logically exact interpreter of the true Christian tradition. He was resisted and condemned in the name of the apostolic tradition, but his intentions were as truly traditionalist, if not more so, than were those of the men who resisted and condemned him.

The conditions under which he drew up his collection of Scriptures are perplexingly obscure. We can see clearly enough how he was brought to reject the Old Testament, like his contemporary, the Valentinian Ptolemy, and we can explain why he was concerned to provide Christians with a collection of Christian Scriptures to take the place of the Jewish Bible. What is not so clear are the reasons which determined his choice of the particular Scriptures which formed his collection and, in addition to that, the manner in which he understood his duty as their editor. However, if it would be quite foolish to credit Marcion with the idea of publishing a critically faultless text of the sources of Gospel revelation held by him to be authentic, it would seem equally wilful (having regard to the character of the man and the circumstances) to attribute to him any considerable part even in editing the texts presented by him as documents of the true faith. That supposition is the less acceptable because these texts, of which the main tenor is well enough known to us, do not expressly reproduce Marcion's doctrine. Marcion set out to link them and his system together. This he managed to do, but his system is not formally taught in the documents. How then did Marcion proceed?

It seems certain that, in the time when he was expelled from the Church in Rome (144), neither the Gospels, nor the Epistles, nor any other of the writings which compose the New Testament were in the forefront of Christian teaching. But neither were they private documents of which the congregations of believers knew nothing. The public reading of the Gospels, which we find customary in Justin's time, was practised before Marcion; and we may at least conjecture that it was the same with the Epistles, though reading from them is likely to have been less regular and less common. It follows that Marcion, in raising the Gospel and the letters of Paul to the rank of Scripture, did no more, so to say, than sublimate an established usage. The novelty of that achievement consisted solely in the exclusive authority conferred on these writings by the rejection of the Jewish Scriptures. His adoption of one Gospel only would afford no ground of complaint against him at the time when it was done, for there is no proof that four Gospels were then accepted throughout the congregations of the Great Church, all equally privileged to be read in public before assemblies of the faithful; on the contrary, it is far more probable, not only that it was not so everywhere, but that it was not so anywhere, each of the Gospels finally received everywhere having been used at first only in the circle where it originated, while the recognition of four normative Gospels, and no more, was later than the time of Marcion. When he found his Gospel in Luke it was not, therefore, a case of his deliberately picking Luke out from among four Gospels then current in the Church and choosing it, as easier than the others to bring into line with his system—for John's Gospel is much nearer to his system and Matthew would have given him no more trouble than Luke—it was not this, but a case simply of his canonizing the Gospel used in the Christian circle in which he lived, or at least in that in which he hoped to make converts, namely Rome. Luke had become the chief Gospel of the Roman Community, which at first had Mark and came to know Matthew, but used the fourth Gospel very little, though it knew that Gospel also.

As to the adaptation of Luke by Marcion for his own purpose which Tertullian half a century later describes outright as a massacre,[25] it is unlikely that it greatly scandalized Marcion's own contemporaries. In his time, variety in the versions of the Gospel caused no great concern to anybody; otherwise a single Gospel book, with a uniform text, would have reigned throughout. The truth is that Marcion would have no difficulty in accepting the Gospel writing most familiar to the Church in Rome, and the omissions he made would be the least possible. He made no capital out of the traditional and correct attribution of this Gospel to a disciple of Paul, which he did not bring forward, but simply called the book "The Gospel," as it had hitherto been called. Up to that time all evangelical books owed their credit not to the persons supposed to be their authors, but to their contents, the personal attributions not becoming important till later, when they were used as weapons against the gnostics, and especially against Marcion himself after his expulsion. Marcion's manipulations of the text seem to have consisted in the removal of whatever openly contradicted his doctrine and a few retouches of detail for the same purpose; but he made no explicit additions to give his doctrine formal support. His method was not the result of a design to insinuate his doctrine surreptitiously into the Church, for the Church had turned him out for his open profession of it; it arose from his belief in the substantial credibility of the text which he retained. Looking closely into the matter, we see that his method was not a whit more revolutionary than that of the editors of our canonical Gospels; in certain respects, indeed, it was much less innovating than theirs. Comparing the procedure of the editors of the first and third Gospels, who added the birth stories to the theme of the Gospel as they found it in Mark, with that of Marcion who left these stories out, which of the two shall we say represents the more audacious innovation?

The case of the Epistles is somewhat different. Marcion substantially contributed to raising their credit. As we lately remarked, there is reason to doubt that they were frequently read in all the congregations, as the Gospel unquestionably was, before Marcion's time. When Justin speaks of the readings that normally took place before the Sunday Communion, the books he mentions are the Prophets and the Memoirs of the Apostles (1 *Apology*, 67); but not a word does he say, in this connexion, of the apostolic writings, and he never mentions Paul; we might even say that, if Justin knew Paul, he deliberately abstains from making use of him, and how can he have failed to know him, seeing that he was so well acquainted with Marcion? But, though less regularly used for public reading, the ten epistles which Marcion appropriated had been for some time collected, and there is evidence that the collection enjoyed a large measure of credit in the Roman community and elsewhere, since First Corinthians is expressly quoted in the Epistle of Clement.[26] The relative antiquity of the collection has also good warrant in the fact that Marcion has the Epistle to the Ephesians under its original title of Epistle to the Laodiceans, along with Second Thessalonians, both of which are apocryphal. It seems, moreover, sufficiently clear that his method of dealing with the Epistles was the same as that he had applied to the Gospel: he took the collection as he found it in the Roman community and confined himself to systematically cutting and retouching it as required by his doctrine. Here again the liberties he took not only did not surpass, they did not even equal those taken by others before him in attributing to Paul letters he did not write and in interpolating those he did.

It is none the less true that Marcion founded the canon of the New Testament, the idea of which, it may confidently be said, had occurred to nobody before him. At this point the influence he exercised, both directly, and indirectly through the reaction he provoked, was momentous, and of greater moment than can be claimed, at that stage in the evolution of catholic Christianity, for any master of gnosis, Christian writer, or Church leader. If he failed to realize all that he aimed at, and if Marcionism did not become, as he intended it to become, the common faith of the Church, we know the reason. It lies in the fact that though with him the religious and moral interest took precedence of the speculative and theoretical, he underrated the vitality of Israel's monotheism and failed to see that the ethics of the Gospel were rooted in Judaism. The deepest tradition of Christianity was against him, nor did his more reasonable interpretation of Scripture make good the defects of his religious philosophy, so that, in the final result, his system of belief and of conduct came out less truly balanced than that of the Church. But, in spite of these disadvantages, Marcionism from the time of Marcion (about 145) to the end of the second century, continued to be the most formidable rival, and almost the only dangerous rival, that Catholicism had to encounter during the whole time it was in process of becoming organized into a system. Wherever Christianity had taken root, there was Marcionism beside it, challenging it by a greater simplicity of doctrine, by the plausible character of the argument against the Old Testament deity, and by the deadly earnestness of the Marcionite morality.[27]

Marcion had numerous disciples of whom the most noteworthy seems to be a certain Apelles who had sat at the master's feet in Rome and afterward corrected his doctrine at several points. While totally rejecting the Old Testament, his criticism of which was better reasoned than Marcion's, Apelles went back to a strict monotheism: there was one God only, the good God, creator of the invisible world and of the spiritual powers, or angels; the chief of these angels had created the visible world, making it an image of the invisible; the god of Israel was not this demiurge but a fiery angel—Old Testament texts supporting this will readily occur to mind—and this fiery angel was the author of evil, proved so by his clothing human souls in sinful flesh; the creator, who had tried to form the world for the glory of God, had become dissatisfied with his work and prayed the Father to send his Son to give the cosmos a better shape. In Christology, Apelles was no Docetist. His Christ took on a real body, but was not born of the flesh—"*solidum Christi corpus, sed sine nativitate*," says Tertullian (*De Carne Christi*, 6). He had borrowed the substance of his body from the stars, which were elements of the higher world. Thus truly incarnate, Jesus died a real death and rose alive. Redemption consists in cutting loose from sinful flesh and escaping from the rule of the fiery angel; the soul only is saved, and the Christ himself gave back his flesh to the elements as he ascended into heaven. In this way Marcion's logical offences were at least made less glaring. If we may believe a certain Rhodon who saw Apelles in his old age, he was no uncompromising sectary. He still denounced the prophecies of the Old Testament as false and contradictory, and stood firm on the unity of the First Principle, but he thought that "those questions were not meant to be discussed, and every man ought to rest quietly in the faith that he found real, and that all would be saved whose hope was in the Crucified, provided they were found doing good" (*Eusebius*, v, 13, 5).

At the time when Apelles was putting forward these wise propositions, towards the end of the second century, Marcionism had ceased to be a pressing and dangerous threat to the Church, though it had yet to linger on for many years to come. Irenaeus, Tertullian and Hippolytus give no special place to Marcion in the ranks of the gnostics, regarding them all, him included, as reckless dreamers who had tried in vain, or were still trying, to capture the holy Church of Jesus Christ.

Chapter X

BIRTH OF THE CATHOLIC CHURCH

How did the Church succeed in expelling from her territory this flood of multiform heresies which threatened to dissolve her unity in an endless ebullition of short-lived sects? This is the question we have now to answer. A summary answer lies in the fact that it was precisely this threat which determined the Church to fix her constitution and lay down the limits beyond which no Church membership could be. She concentrated her forces, built fortifications, based herself on the past, interpreting and defining her past against the turmoil of new theologies. Thus it came to pass that those who had caused her most disquiet, and Marcion before all others, at the same time incited her to define her doctrine, to regulate her organization and to put forth the energy which broke their efforts.

1. The Christian Prophets

We have already called attention to the important fact that the intense life of the first communities, their enthusiasm, and the popular appeal of the Christian movement had long sustained the new religion without the support of any literature having the authority of Scripture other than the Jewish Bible freely interpreted by catechesis to the exaltation of Jesus. Into this catechesis, in which the moral element was at first predominant, speculation soon began to infiltrate, but mainly at the beginning in the form of individual prophesyings, of which we have seen examples in the gnoses contained in Paul's Epistles, in the Epistle to the Hebrews, or, better, in the discourses of the Johannine Christ. These early gnoses tended to complete rather than to reform or supplant the common teaching. A check upon excessive audacity in prophetic outpourings was found in the control which these prophet-teachers could exercise on each other. First Corinthians, the *Didache* and Hermas all give instructions on this head, which were soon found inadequate, but were not without temporary effect.

An elementary criterion for distinguishing permissible from impermissible inspiration in a prophet is indicated in what Paul is made to say about spiritual gifts (charismata) in 1 Corinthians xii, 3:

> Also I declare to you
>   that no man, speaking by spirit of God,
>   says: "Cursed be Jesus!"
>   And that no man can say:
>   "Lord Jesus!"
>   except by holy spirit.

Any prophet, then, who in the course of his ecstasy utters a denial of Jesus, is inspired by the demon: conversely, he who gives Jesus his rightful place by proclaiming him "Lord" can only be inspired by God. In another passage (xiv, 29–31) the regulation of the outpouring is entrusted to the prophets themselves:

> As to the prophets, let two or three be the speakers,
>   And let the rest pass judgment;
> But if revelation comes to another who is seated,
>   let the first be silent;
> For you can all prophesy one after another,
>   so that all may learn,
>   and all be exhorted.

In the *Didache*, after the prayers to be used in common at the Supper, we find the following direction (x, 7): "Let the prophets make a thanksgiving at such length as they will." Thus the prophets, after Communion, have the right to improvise their thanksgiving without limit of time. But immediately afterwards the *Didache* forbids the reception of any preacher who teaches a doctrine contrary to the catechesis just developed in the book (xi, 1–2) which, be it remembered, is almost entirely moral and ritual, like the Christianity described in Pliny's letter to Trajan. The *Didache* knows moreover of travelling apostles and of prophets who remain at home in one place. Travelling apostles who stay more than two days, in order to get more board and lodging, or ask for money, are to be reckoned false (xi, 3–6), and this, not so much on account of their heresies, but on the moral ground that they are exploiting their hosts, though possibly heretical as well as rapacious. As to the sedentary prophets, their inspired outpourings are not to be lightly criticized, but conduct is to be the test for distinguishing the true prophet from the false. He alone is a true prophet who lives according to the Lord; who would not count him a false prophet who orders a sumptuous meal or demands money (xi, 7-12)? The prophets of old had certain eccentricities, and a few such, analogous to theirs, and "in harmony with the cosmic mystery of the Church," may be tolerated in Christian prophets, provided they do not require others to imitate them (xi, 11). A highly enigmatic concession, at least for us, and sufficiently disturbing in itself; it cannot have been maintained for long. (The ancient prophets are brought in only by way of a mitigating comparison.) The reference is to some symbolic proceedings representing "the mystery," which is, one can hardly doubt, the mystic union of the Christ and "the Church." According to Irenaeus the innocent "conjunctions" (syzygies) of Valentinus seem to have been mixed up by his disciple Marcus with certain rites of symbolic magic in which mysticism had degenerated into eroticism. What the *Didache* had in mind must have been something less abominable, perhaps a symbolic marriage between an inspired couple, which may have been real, or an affair of continency on both sides. But we can see that the author of the *Didache*, while not daring to prohibit these eccentricities, is not quite at ease in the matter.

2. Decline of the Prophets and Rise of the Administrators

"True prophets" and "true doctors" who regularly contribute to the edification of the community must be adequately supported, and to this end the *Didache* lays down a sort of tithe-system (xiii) which obviously calls for a measure of administration. Accordingly we find that, besides the prophets and the doctors (teachers) with their charismatic endowments, the book knows also of functionaries elected by and for the community—overseers (bishops), ministers (deacons)—charged with the general work of organization and the right ordering of the Sunday meetings.[1] The daily conduct of these functionaries must also be worthy of the Lord; they must be honest men, disinterested, sincere and well attested; and let the congregation remember that they, too, serve it in the ministry of prophecy and teaching (xv)—an injunction probably due to an early tendency to regard them as paid employees. But it was precisely to these elected administrators, who were also in charge of the arrangements for the Eucharist, that the future belonged. We shall meet them again. At the beginning of the second century, the recognized professors of prophecy, of inspired teaching, are still in the forefront of the Christian movement and pointing the way; but already it can be dimly foreseen that if ever Christian union should be disturbed these inspired doctors are likely to be the cause of disturbance and, equally, that if union is to be maintained the work of maintaining it will be done by the elected administrators.

In this connexion the *Shepherd of Hermas* is most instructive. Hermas, too, is a prophet of the congregation like those to whom the citations from First Corinthians and the *Didache* have already introduced us. Moreover he is—if one may use the the expression—a highly conservative prophet. A contemporary of Valentinus and Marcion, with whom he doubtless came into contact at meetings of the Roman Christians, our Hermas is no purveyor of novelties and hazardous speculations; he is a doctor of the old school, altogether in the style of the *Didache*, a good man living "according to the Lord," the teacher of a morality framed on the pattern of the primitive Christian catechesis—in a word, the least gnostic of prophets. But his relation to what we have called the administration of the Church is no longer that in which we find the prophets of the *Didache*. In his Third *Vision* the Church makes him sit down on her left, with the presbyters behind him, the right being reserved for the martyrs (*Vision*, iii, 1, 8–9). He himself seems to have thought, and with good reason, that the presbyter administrators might well have been seated in front of him. But the hierarchy as he conceived it, in the order of martyrs, prophets, presbyters, was not the order destined to prevail. In fact the presbyter-bishops are already in the front rank and are not going to let even the martyrs precede them. From now on, when Hermas, in his capacity of prophet, addresses his exhortations to the community, he can have them read in public only by consent of the presbyters who preside over the Church; so he has two copies made, one for Clement (doubtless a leading presbyter) and the other for the deaconess Grapté; Clement will undertake to send the book to outlying congregations—and so the prophet gets publicity, but under supervision—while Grapté will use it for the instruction of widows and orphans who are unable to attend the great meetings and belong to the department of charitable help.[2] It is clear, then, that while the Church in heaven still gives the prophet Hermas precedence over the presbyters, things are differently ordered in the Church on earth. Here the presbyters have direct control over the prophet, insomuch that without their authority and mediate action the revelations of Hermas could not have seen the light either among the Christians of Rome or elsewhere. Be it noted, these presbyters are the same men as those who examined Marcion's doctrine and stamped it with their disapproval. The next step to be taken, which we shall soon see, will be that those who preside over administration and worship will reserve to themselves the right to have their voices heard in the assemblies, especially when prophecy is raising a scandal.

Here, then, in Rome we find a body of presbyters who, almost at the same time, authorize the prophecy of the Pastor and expel Valentinus and Marcion from the community, men whom our prophet would perhaps have treated with less severity. What did Hermas think about this body, and what was it in reality? According to what seems a trustworthy tradition Hermas was own brother to the bishop Pius. But Hermas speaks only of presbyters in general and never mentions the bishop, his brother. In speaking of presbyters in general he betrays no enthusiasm and seems to make no distinction between them and the bishops whom he places side by side with the deacons.[3] The same individuals are described indifferently as "presbyters" and "heads of the church," or as "presbyters presiding over the Church."[4] But however considerable these dignitaries may be, Hermas does not hesitate to address them in pretty plain terms. It is true that the Church is here speaking as the Pastor or Angel of Penitence:

" 'Tis to you I speak, ye heads of the Church and occupants of the high places. Be not like the poisoners: poisoners carry their poison in bottles: you carry your poison and your venom in your hearts . . . Be careful, my children, or these divisions will be the end of you. How can you form the Lord's elect while you yourselves are unformed? Then set about forming one another so that I, joyously presenting you to the Father, may be able to account for you to the Lord."5

From all this the fact emerges that the presbyters, so sharply taken to task by the Church, have already assumed the disciplinary control of the community. The Church and Hermas agree, not without reason, that they would be more worthy of their headship if they were less covetous of power.

It is clear that this presbyterial body already possessed considerable authority, and highly probable that it had a presiding bishop,[6] whose authority was not exercised independently of his colleagues. Bishops and priests, who allowed Hermas to speak the truth about them, are not likely to have been more exacting than he in the matter of pure theology. For the good Hermas is far from being a dogmatist in that department, and looks upon heresy more in pity than in anger. He is ready to die for the Lord Christ; but his Christology is strangely indecisive; unshakably firm on the unity of God, he is totally ignorant of any Christological definition. The figurative language used in his book causes him to avoid mentioning Jesus and Christ by name. But clearly he has not the faintest idea of the Logos and its incarnation. His Son of God is far superior to the archangels, but is inconsistently presented as their leader and the first of them (*Parable*, ix, 4); elsewhere the Son seems to be identified with the Spirit (v, 2, 5, 6). In the fifth Parable, where the wanderings of his Christology are represented in a Parable of the Vine, imitated from the Gospel,[7] there appears a servant named "Flesh," in whom the Son-Spirit has his abode, and whose work on the Vine has been so marvellous that the Father, agreeing with the wishes of the Son and the angels, appoints him the Son's co-heir (v, 6). But let us not jump to the conclusion that Hermas here presents his Trinity composed of Eternal Father, Son-Spirit and a God-man; for the parable is so complicated and obscure that the "servant" pre-exists in the humanity of the Son, who is also active in the Vine (v, 2, 6); from which it will be seen that the Christology of Hermas is simply amorphous and incoherent. The Roman presbyters, who were not scandalized by it, cannot have been any stricter in the definition of their own. There was however one point of doctrine on which they would allow no compromise. They expelled Marcion for attacking it. This was the unity of God.

Hermas speaks of heretics, as he speaks of the presbyters, with freedom, but without a trace of passion (ix, 22). We can see clearly that the gnostics have not led him astray. He knows them well enough and could not fail to know many of them. He finds their doctors somewhat unintelligible, presumptuous, too pleased with themselves and priding themselves on being omniscient; the higher knowledge they claim seems to him mere nonsense; on the whole he judges them more fools than knaves. Many ought to be dismissed outright—which shows that the case of Marcion was not solitary, although outstanding and the best known to us. Some have repented of their follies and been taken back into the fold; those who stick to their nonsense will be destroyed by it. This seems to have been the attitude of the presbyters themselves in the excommunications of which Hermas speaks, and it would be thus that they judged Marcion and his like; gnosis was of no account and meant nothing to them, but in doctrine they held firm by the baptismal catachism, understood in the sense of the *Didache*, as Hermas also understood it. There can be no doubt that what shocked them in Marcion was his attack on the unity of God, which they would counter-attack by simply asserting against the innovator the traditional apostolic teaching of the one only God, creator of the world, and the one only Christ, Jesus the Son of God, sent by the Father to save men from their sins and to instruct them in the way of righteousness. That this tradition was an existing force is beyond question. The gnostic teachers compelled the administrators of Church discipline to exert that force with resolution against their new theologies.

It is a noteworthy fact that, except in regard to the Logos, Justin's Christology is hardly less fluid than that of Hermas. The two draw near together in the curious profession of faith in which the apologist declares that Christians believe in one only God who created the world[8] and with him worship the Son who left his Father's presence to teach true doctrine to men, having with him "the host of other good angels who resemble him, and the Spirit of Prophecy" (with which may be compared 1 Timothy v, 21, "I adjure thee before God, Jesus Christ and the elect angels"). The Roman presbyters found Justin orthodox, and after their condemnation of Marcion, Justin pronounced his, denouncing the idea of a god superior to the creator of the world as an invention of demons. In accusing Marcion of polytheism Justin speaks as a defender of Old Testament and Gospel tradition.

3. Rise of a Settled Tradition

The watchword of the Church leaders in the campaign against gnostic heresy is found in the pastoral Epistles (1 Timothy vi, 20, 21; 2 Timothy i, 14):

> O Timothy, guard the deposit,
> > shunning impious word-play
> > > and the *antitheses* of so-called *gnosis*,
> > Professed by some,
> > > who err concerning the faith.

This couplet, the closing note of the First to Timothy, is aimed directly at Marcion and must have been written under the immediate impression of his breach with the Church or, more probably, of his attempt to change the basis of Christian teaching. "Paul," and the very Paul whom Marcion exalted to so great a height, is now heard beseeching the congregations of the faithful to "guard the deposit"—against Marcion. Against Marcion also the following profession of faith (ii, 5–6) is perhaps directed:

> God is one,
> > one also the mediator between God and men,
> > > the man Christ Jesus,
> > Who gave himself a ransom for all,
> > > as witnessed in his time.

The following hymn or prophetic oracle belongs to the same class (1 Timothy iii, 16):

> He was manifested in flesh,
> > he was justified in spirit,
> > > he was seen of angels,
> > He was preached among the Gentiles,
> > > he was believed in the world,
> > > > he was taken up into glory.

Finally Marcion is probably included among the "lying spirits" (1 Timothy iv, 2-3):

> Who forbid to marry,
> prescribe abstinence from foods
> which God has made to be taken with thanksgiving
> by believers and those who know the truth.[9]

Marcion's asceticism is perhaps in the writer's mind when he advises Timothy to drink a little wine for the good of his stomach. But there is another passage (i, 4-6) where the target is not Marcion alone, but gnostics in general, with Valentinus as chief offender. Here are the instructions (1 Timothy i, 4):

> To keep clear of fables, and endless genealogies,
> which produce wranglings,
> rather than divine order in faith.
> But the goal of preaching is charity,
> coming out of pure heart, good conscience and true faith:
> Wherefrom some cut themselves off
> in their love of empty talk,
> Setting up as doctors of law,
> without knowing what they talk about,
> nor what they vouch for.[10]

These were also the views of Hermas, Polycarp and Justin. True doctrine, according to them, is a simpler affair than what these windy word-mongers have to offer; what matters above all else is life according to God.

In resisting the gnostic invasion, the defenders of the faith made continual appeal to apostolic tradition, not hesitating to represent their own denunciations of the new doctors as spoken by Paul, the "Paul," that is, of the First to Timothy (vi, 13-14):

> I charge you, before God,
> who gives life to all,
> And before Christ Jesus,
> who witnessed under Pontius Pilate
> the good confession,
> To keep intact and spotless the commandment
> until the epiphany of Lord Jesus Christ.

The "commandment" is the apostolic catechesis and the equivalent of the "deposit" of vi, 20. The mention of Pontius

Pilate is not made for the sake of historical precision; it is a formula taken from a hymn or rhythmical confession connected with the ritual recitation of the passion story.

In like strain speaks the "Paul" of the Epistle to Titus (i, 9). Let the presbyter, he says,

> Stand by the pure word according to the doctrine,
> that he may be able to exhort in the genuine teaching,
> and hurl back the rebels.

The context shows that the "rebels" against whom this was directed were not pagans, nor were they, strictly speaking, Jews. They were heretical debaters, with the turn for contentiousness characteristic of amateurs in theology. The author says that such people were extremely numerous in his time (Titus i, 10–11).

The author of the First to Timothy will have it that the apostles foretold an outbreak of gnosis. The Epistle makes Paul speak as follows (iv, 1):

> But the Spirit says expressly
> that in the last days many will desert the faith,
> Taking up with lying spirits
> and with doctrines of demons, etc."

It was not solely on account of their heterodoxy that the gnostic systems are said to be the work of "demons," but also for their mythological character, which almost turned them into pantheons. Without making distinctions among them, these heretics were credited with almost every conceivable vice and crime—see the list in 2 Timothy iii, 1–9. The accusation of immorality is the daily bread of this polemic, and hardly worth consideration, especially when formulated in general terms.

Reproducing the same diatribe against the gnostics, or commenting on it, the spurious Jude and the spurious Peter of the second Epistle recall, rather naïvely, that "the Lord's Apostles" foretold "for these last times" a crop of sectaries "who will make classifications" distinguishing two kinds of believers, the psychic and the spiritual, "psychics themselves without a trace of spirit"[11]—apparently another shot at Valentinus (Jude 17–19). Spurious Peter drops a hint that a little caution will not be out of place in reading the letters of "our dear brother Paul, in which there are certain knotty points which, to their own ruin, ignorant and unsteady souls take wrongly along with other Scriptures," namely the Old Testament and the Gospel. Who can these be but Marcion and his followers? (2 Peter iii, 15-16).

Almost contemporary with spurious Peter, we shall find Polycarp,[12] with an Epistle of John before him, attacking Marcion, as chief offender, in the following terms (Philippians 7):

"Whosoever confesses not that Jesus Christ is come in the flesh is antichrist; whosoever confesses not the witness of the cross is of the devil; whosoever twists the oracles of the Lord to suit his own desire, and denies the resurrection and the judgment is Satan's eldest son. Leave we then the futilities of that crowd and let us return to the teaching that was given us."

4. THE TRADITION ESTABLISHED

It remains only to hear Irenaeus delivering his "exposition of apostolic preaching"[13] fully assured that he is in possession of the True Faith "as traditionally taught by the elders, disciples of the apostles."[14] Immediately after him comes the *De Praescriptione Haereticorum* of Tertullian which opposes the heretics by the argument of "prescription." With that, the notion of tradition, as the Church would have it understood and as it has come down through the centuries, will be fully formed. The following passage in Chapter 19, marvellously true as a definition of Latin Christianity through the ages, gives the fundamental idea:

"Ergo non ad Scripturas provocandum est, nec in his constituendum certamen, in quibus aut nulla aut incerta victoria est, aut parum certa. Nam etsi non evaderet conlatio Scripturarum, ut utramque partem parem sisteret, ordo rerum desiderabat illud prius proponi, quod nunc solum disputandum est: quibus competat fides ipsa, cujus sint Scripturae, a quo et per quos et quando et quibus sit tradita disciplina qua fiunt Christiani. Ubi enim apparuerit esse veritatem disciplinae et fidei christianae, illic et veritas Scripturarum et expositionum et omnium traditionum Christianorum."

What Tertullian says in this passage could not have been

said as it here stands in the year 150, nor even in 180. It implies an exclusive "possession" of Scriptures, tradition and ecclesiastical authority which the church had not made good before the end of the interval between the two dates. But Tertullian's genius saw clearly the barrenness of all these disputings: saw the disadvantage the Church would suffer if she met the innovators as equals and on their own ground; saw, also, the summary procedure that was needed to put a quick end to the whole futile discussion. The one thing Tertullian did not foresee was that the system he had so clearly laid down would be turned to his own hurt, and that he would die a heretic. But the notion of "tradition," as the Church would have it understood, and as it was destined to endure through the centuries, may be counted fully born with Tertullian's assertion of the Church's prescriptive right as exclusive possessor and only competent interpreter of the sources of the faith.

This notion of tradition corresponded to a fact: the unbroken continuity of monotheistic faith, of Jewish morality taken up into the Gospel and of the worship of the Christ Jesus in the very heart of every Christian community. But, at the same time, it was and could not fail to be a somewhat fictitious assumption, an artificial but timely device of special pleading forced upon the Church by a kind of moral necessity, and onesidedly formulated in her own interest as she reacted to the pressure of a movement towards a fusion of religions on an intellectualist or pagan basis. For the idea of an absolute and unchangeable orthodoxy is in flat contradiction to the nature and history of the human mind, of human knowledge and even of Christianity itself. That which was now canonized as "the apostolic faith" was far from being the simple faith of the first believers in Jesus, nor was it that of the first apostles to the Gentile world. When Irenaeus reasons as though, between himself and the first apostles of the Christ, there was but a single generation, represented by the elders, or disciples of the apostles, he is resting upon a fiction, by then accepted, but entirely fanciful: between the second third of the first century and the time of his writing in the last third of the second, several generations of Christian believers had passed away who had not confined the expression of their belief to a repetition of the apostolic catechism. The pretended tradition, which the Church would fix for all time, was largely created in the very process of defining it. At that point in time it was nothing else than a kind of rudimentary and unformed gnosis, imperfectly coherent, in which the germ of endless disputes, nay, of heresy in many a form, lay hidden and awaiting its future development. It could not be, and never has been, anything else.

5. Birth of the Canon

We know how Marcion, cast out by the Church, had set up his own biblical canon in her face, to be used in resisting her, as need should arise. This, according to him, contained the true and authentic Gospel, the Gospel as Jesus had really preached it, which Paul alone had preserved from Jewish contamination. That is to say it contained the revelation of the good God, the true God, whereas the Jewish bible was the revelation of the Jewish god, an imperfect deity of a lower order, who was, however, the creator of the visible world, a world on the same lower level as its creator and no less imperfect than he. The idea of such a collection would never have occurred to Marcion had he not found the Church already in possession of an authorized Bible, which was judged to contain the revelation of the true God and of Christ Jesus which he, for his part, could not find there. This was the Bible of the Alexandrian Jews, in which the Church was for ever taxing her wits to find the Gospel prefigured and foretold. Marcion's acquaintance with the Jewish manner of exegesis may possibly have led him to the conclusion that this interpretation of prophecy was on the whole absolutely groundless. With these ideas in mind the arch-heretic turned to the current literature of Christianity and picked out from it the documents which he judged to give the truest account of the religion of Jesus, and then proceeded to collect them in an expurgated version in harmony with the end he had in view.

It was Marcion, then, with his belief in the unique value of the Gospel, who raised the evangelical and apostolic writings from the relative obscurity caused by the overshadowing of the ancient Scriptures, in which they had hitherto lain, more or less familiar, no doubt, to the congregation from public reading, but not yet Scripture on a footing with the books of Moses and the prophets of Israel; he it was who brought out these writings into the full light of day and endowed them with the status of Scriptures. No one doubted that they were the work of the Spirit, but, quite naturally, the prestige of the ancient Bible had hitherto outshone them. Now, if there is one thing more evident than another at this momentous juncture, it is that the Church could not effectively counter the audacity of these new theologians were it to rely solely on the existing Scriptures of Old Testament books, since these, strictly interpreted, could only be made to plead the cause of Judaism. The attack had to be met on its own ground, and this could only be done by opposing a tradition earlier to that of the innovators and by means of documents traditionally evangelical and apostolic. Certainly Marcion was under no illusion in professing that this tradition was not trustworthy. Since Irenaeus and Tertullian he is bitterly abused for rejecting or changing the apostolic writings, but neither his denial of the apostolicity of the Gospels, nor the reasons he gave for it, have been seriously discussed. When Celsus reproaches the Christians with never ceasing to make alterations in their Gospels he is perhaps only repeating something that Marcion had said after direct experience of its truth. But the cause of the Church would have been lost by admitting suspicion as to the apostolic authenticity of her texts and by making it a matter for discussion; the idea of critically examining it could not enter her mind, and did not. She boldly entrenched herself in her catechetical tradition, of which the various Gospels and the apostolic writings, or those deemed such, were also the documents; then, taking a leaf out of Marcion's book, she decided, and it would seem promptly, to canonize those of the Gospel and apostolic writings which had the usage of the congregations to recommend them or seemed likely to serve her in a situation so distressing and unforeseen.

At the time when the Church was canonizing her collection of writings she energetically went to work in assigning them to writers whose names would confer authenticity on the selected books; an assignment rather retrospective, since the question of their authenticity had been, up to that moment, of little interest. The explanations given about the New Testament books by the Canon of Muratori and the statements of Irenaeus on the origin of the Gospels are an apologia for the official collection as a whole; but already Justin had made a milder apologia for the Gospels by presenting them more discreetly under the general term "Memoirs of the Apostles," while Papias had pleaded for the ecclesiastical text of Mark and of Matthew. Both Marcion and his adversaries were eager to find assurance for texts about whose authenticity neither of them were very confident. And both sides made a virtue of necessity.

But the Church could not limit her canon as narrowly as Marcion had limited his, nor had she at the time any motive to do so. The Gospel writings to begin with were drawn up and circulated to meet the needs of the various communities, and those were selected for canonization which had been adopted for liturgical use by the most important of them. The first Gospel, as B. W. Bacon maintains, seems to have gained authority in the Syrian congregations;[15] the third held the field in Greece proper and in Rome,[16] where Mark also was in use;[17] the fourth had taken root in the congregations of Asia which were full of life at the time when the canon was made. Alexandria, at this period still a mystery to the historian, seems to have contributed nothing to the Gospel canon, although she had been fertile ground for literature of that type, but we know that she did not force the acceptance of her Gospel of the Egyptians on the canonizers and soon abandoned it herself. Perhaps she was not at first admitted to the concert of Churches, by which the Gospel canon was fixed, for Alexandria was reputed a hotbed of gnosticism, and her Gospel of the Egyptians contained more than a little of the offending article. It is possible, moreover, that the Christian groups in Alexandria were not unified early enough to speak with a single voice in the negotiations which fixed the combined canon of the Gospels and of the whole New Testament, and that this was made without consulting the Alexandrian Christians, who, however, finally accepted the decision taken by the others. It is worthy of note that when the Paschal controversy, about 180, was agitating every Christian community from Edessa to Lyons, Alexandria does not enter into direct relations with Pope Victor and sends her views on the affair, only after it was settled, to the communities in Palestine (*Eusebius*, v, 25, 23).

It is easy to explain how the three Pastoral Epistles came to be annexed to the Ten Epistles previously known as Paul's. These three letters corresponded so exactly to the needs of the hour that the correspondence cannot have been the result of chance. If not written expressly to satisfy the needs of the Church in her campaign against Marcion, they were completed and turned to such good account against him that the whole collection of thirteen Epistles may be called anti-Marcionite. We can also understand how the fourth Gospel, once accepted, would bring in the first Johannine Epistle and the two others in its train. The main difficulty of the canonists must have been that of securing acceptance, outside of Asia, for the Gospel they called John's, and first of all at Rome. Asia was its fortress. This Gospel is in keeping with the Easter usage of the Quartodecimans, which forms the background to its arrangement of the passion stories; Polycrates, with good reason, refers to this in his letter to Pope Victor (*Eusebius*, v, 24, 3); Montanism had adopted it and the Asiatic congregations made its fortune when their influence compelled the other Churches to give it recognition. Agreement on the matter was reached under the pressure of a necessity equally felt on either side and, we may be sure, not without mutual concessions and interested, perhaps concerted, adaptations of the text.[18] In establishing the canon of the four Gospels in particular there can be no doubt that a time came when the resolution was taken by all parties to establish a united front against the gnostic irruption and especially against the projects of Marcion.

Apostolicity being the quality aimed at and the order of the day, nothing came more conveniently to hand than the Acts of the Apostles, a book which had hitherto been outshone in credit by its twin brother, the third Gospel. This book of Acts was doubly to the purpose, first in its picture of Christianity as a harmless religion, loyal to the Roman empire, and then by its hostility to gnostic innovators, whom it represents Paul as denouncing in advance at Ephesus (xx, 29, 30) just as it makes him inaugurate the philosophical defence of Christianity in his speech to the Areopagus,[19] which contains the germ of Justin's apologetics—*minus* the Logos. But, notwithstanding the attractions it must have had for the canonists, the influence of this book on the evolution of Christian thought has never equalled that of the Fourth Gospel and of the Epistles attributed to Paul. Both Rome and Asia knew the first of the two Epistles called Peter's and included it in the canon as apostolic. The Apocalypse of John, declared apostolic in Asia, was received as such in Rome where, as yet, its millenarianism had raised no alarm. Justin knew and esteemed it, and the Canon of Muratori defends its reputation which had been compromised by the sudden outbreak of Montanism. But in the third century we find the catholic gnostics of Alexandria judging it unfavourably; only by the influence of the West was it saved from the discredit which overtook the Apocalypse of Peter even in Rome, where it was accepted towards the end of the second century. A strange case was that of the Epistle to the Hebrews. Although Alexandria had early attributed this Epistle to Paul; although it was read in Rome before Marcion was known there, for the Epistle of Clement puts it largely under contribution;[20] although it is cited by Tertullian as the work of Barnabas, and used by him to pour ridicule on Hermas,[21] we find nevertheless that it was not included in the canon as apostolic till the end of the fourth century. Perhaps the reason lay in the fact that Rome had begun its acquaintance with this document in full knowledge that it was not apostolic.

Whatever the truth may be about the inclusion of particular books, the fact is unquestionable that the main body of the New Testament was solidly constituted by the end of the second century. It then included the four Gospels, the Acts of the Apostles, thirteen Epistles of Paul, the first Epistle of Peter and the first Epistle of John. Needless to say this canonization of New Testament writings was not made in a day and there and then proclaimed by a council assembled *ad hoc*. But by the time of Irenaeus it appears to have been so far completed. The principle of "apostolicity" on which it was based must have been laid down at the very beginning by a kind of concert among the Churches chiefly concerned and by them made dominant. Looking closely into the matter we cannot but feel that, but for the ruling of this principle, the juxtaposition of the Fourth Gospel with the three Synoptics would not be natural in a collection intended to support the common teaching of the Church. In Rome the Fourth Gospel was long ignored and, even in the early part of the second century, Caius, a Roman presbyter, dared to launch a polemic against the Johannine writings, though this, it is true, was at a time when Asia was in bad odour at Rome over the Easter controversy. But the testimony of Irenaeus makes it clear[22] that in certain quarters opposition to the Fourth Gospel was lively enough in his time and connected with the opposition to Montanism, a movement Asiatic in origin. But, so long as these adversaries of the Fourth Gospel accepted the first three, they were not charged with heresy.

It must have been, then, by a formal agreement, arrived at after full interchange of views between Rome and the Asiatic Churches, that the principle of the fourfold or "tetramorphic" Gospel was finally adopted. When and how cannot be stated with precision and certitude. It was done before Irenaeus who defends the principle with assiduity and ardour, and certainly did not invent it, for he was in no position to lay it down for the whole Christian Church. If a conjecture may be ventured on so nice a point, as good a conjecture as any would be that agreement was reached at Rome in conversations between the bishop Anicetus and Polycarp of Smyrna. Of the reasons for Polycarp's journey to Rome we know nothing and can only say that his great age and his functions rule out the likelihood that he made the journey for pleasure. Irenaeus mentions it incidentally in his letter to Victor about the Easter controversy (*Eusebius*, v, 24 and 16). Irenaeus, then Bishop of Lyons, who may well have known more about the matter than he tells, relates how "the blessed Polycarp being come to Rome under Anicetus," the two bishops "discussed between them certain questions on which they soon came to an understanding, but avoided quarrelling on the subject" of Easter, Polycarp being immovable in the observance he held to be apostolic and Anicetus equally so in that which "the presbyters before his time" had followed. Polycarp, then, did not come to Rome to negotiate about Easter, but to examine with Anicetus "the small differences that existed between them." The gnostic crisis being then at its height and the Marcionite movement in full swing, it seems probable that Polycarp came to Rome as representing the Asiatic Churches for the purpose of concerting common measures with Anicetus for stemming the mounting flood of heresy. Obviously the first measure demanded by the situation was to fix the sources from which the true evangelical and apostolic tradition was derived. Is it not likely that among the decisions then taken one was the determination of the number of the Gospels and perhaps also the number of Paul's Epistles? The foundation of the New Testament canon would then have been built. The rest would be completed between 160 and 180, Acts obtaining official recognition by the side of the Epistles; then, finally, the anti-montanist reaction, which threw suspicion on the Apocalypse of John, would be satisfied by excluding the Apocalypse of Peter, formerly accepted by some of the Churches, along with the Pastor of Hermas, which the Roman Church piously retained till then as an authorized prophecy.[23]

6. Shaping of the Apostolic Creed

A barrier of writings declared apostolic was insufficient protection against the advancing tide of innovation. Just as Marcion was using the principles of his own doctrine to interpret the Gospel and the Apostolicon, on which he professed the principles were founded, so the Church interpreted her New Testament by the principles of her catechesis, defining them with greater amplitude and precision as she reacted against the new heresies, and especially against Marcion.

As we have seen above (pp. 332 ff.) the pastoral Epistles contain the rudiments, or the echoes, of this professedly apostolic creed. So, too, Clement when he writes (1 *Clement*, 46, 6): "Have we not one (and the same) God, one Christ, one Spirit of pardon poured out on us, one (and the same) vocation in Christ?" Justin, again, seems to be paraphrasing a formula of faith when he assures the emperors that the Christians are not atheists, but believers in the true God, venerating him with "the Son who comes from him" and with the spirit of prophecy.[24] But we have no means of knowing what the precise formula was to which the paraphrase corresponds. A little further on (i, 61) Justin explains how Christians are born anew in the baptismal immersion "in the name of God, father and lord of all things, of our saviour Jesus Christ and of the Holy Spirit." These three terms of the baptismal confession can hardly be later than the year 150. They are the main features of a formulary subsequently elaborated in opposition to gnosis and concentrate what the Church was bent on regarding as the essence of "apostolic preaching."

What Irenaeus has to say (*Heresies*, i, 10) about the faith received by the Church from the apostles and their disciples affords a glimpse of the formulary in the process of shaping. It is, he says, faith

> in one only God, the Father almighty, who created heaven, earth, sea and all they contain;
> in one only Christ, Jesus, Son of God, made flesh for our salvation;
> and in the holy Spirit, who by the prophets announced the scheme of salvation, the coming, virgin birth, passion, resurrection from the dead of Christ, Jesus our Lord, his coming again in the glory of the Father, to gather all together and raise to life the whole of mankind before passing judgment on every individual.

It is to be remarked that Irenaeus in his profession of the catholic faith introduces the Gospel history of birth, passion, etc., not into his second article (faith in the Christ) but into his third (faith in the Holy Spirit) where he presents it as a *prophesied* history, precisely as Justin conceived it and as it is conceived in the Gospels themselves. It is impossible to exaggerate the significance of this feature. It shows that the modern scholar who discovers, and truly discovers, that the Gospels are histories, not of the historical Jesus, but of the accomplishment of prophecy in the Christ, is simply discovering a fact which Irenaeus seems to have known well enough. In other respects the unity of God and the unity of the Christ are affirmed against Marcion chiefly; the same is true of the incarnation, the bodily resurrection and the last judgment. Instead of giving sole prominence to the rôle of the Father in creating the world, as was done in the catechesis before Marcion challenged it, the doctrine of salvation is now brought to the front, no doubt in accord with the Epistles of Paul and with John, but also in accord with Marcion, who is here both followed and corrected.

The title of his other writing, *The Exposition of the Apostolic Preaching*, shows by its bare announcement the dominant thought of Irenaeus and the idea he had formed of the tradition as "apostolic preaching"—a preaching whose content he himself, in his time, largely contributed to defining. In this *Exposition* he recalls how "we have all received baptism for the remission of sins in the name of God the Father, in the name of Jesus Christ, son of God, incarnate, dead and raised again, and in the holy Spirit of God" (*Exposition*, 3). A little further on (6) he explains that the whole structure of the faith and the scheme of salvation rests upon the following three articles:

> God, Father, increate, invisible, creator of all things—this is the first article of our faith.
>
> And this is the second: the Word of God, Son of God, our Lord Jesus Christ, who appeared to the prophets in the form of their prophecy and according to the power of the Father's disposition; by whom were all things created; he it was who, in the fullness of time, to accomplish all things and omit nothing, was made man among men, visible and tangible, to destroy death and reveal life, and to make effective the communion and union of God and man.
>
> Third article: the holy Spirit by whose power the prophets prophesied, the fathers were instructed in the knowledge of God, the just guided in the way of righteousness; and who, in the last days, is shed forth in a new manner on the human race throughout the world, renewing mankind for God.

The article of the holy Spirit is also the article of the Church, but given a turn which avoids the condemnation of the Montanists. In his comments on the three articles, Irenaeus develops a veritable gnosis in which soteriology is adapted to cosmology and the Old Testament harmonized with the New. This gnosis, apparently derived from the Gospels and Epistles, but better balanced than the rough outlines of doctrine to be found in the canonical writings, was plainly conceived and formulated to counter the gnosis of Marcion.

We come now to the ancient Roman Creed, the date of which is still under discussion, but probably goes back to the period 150–160:[25]

> I believe in God, the Father Almighty;
> And in Christ Jesus, his only begotten Son, our Lord,
>   who was born of the holy Spirit and the Virgin Mary,
>   who under Pontius Pilate was crucified and buried;
>   the third day, he rose from the dead,
>   ascended to the heavens, sat down at God's right hand,
>   whence he will come to judge the quick and the dead;
> And in the holy Spirit, the holy Church, the remission of sins
>   and the resurrection of the flesh.

This, in substance, is the gnosis of Irenaeus, *minus* the Word and lacking his systematic balance, but with certain points made more precise for better correspondence with the Gospels, and always with the same emphasis on the one and only God, the creator, and on Jesus his only begotten Son, incarnate, dead and risen who will come again to judge the living and those raised from the dead. Aimed at less openly, Marcion and his gnosis are here aimed at none the less in reality.

A point on no account to be overlooked is that the term here translated "one and only," which appears in the Roman Creed, is not to be found in the old baptismal formula of Rome preserved by Hippolytus. As the second question in his profession of faith the candidate was asked: "Believest thou in Christ Jesus the Son of God begotten by Holy Spirit of the virgin Mary?"[26] In this formula the divine sonship is connected with the virgin conception, as Luke also connected it (i, 35) in the passage where the virgin conception is recorded. What the meaning of the baptismal formula really was is shown by the Liturgy of Hippolytus,[27] where a paraphrase of the Creed reappears in the Eucharistic prayers:

> We thank thee, O God, by thy dear child Jesus Christ,
> > whom in the last days thou hast sent as saviour and redeemer, and angel of thy will;
> > > who is thy Word, by whom thou hast made all things;
> > > whom it pleased thee to send from heaven into a virgin's womb,
> > > and who, when conceived, became flesh and was revealed thy Son,
> > > > born of holy Spirit and a virgin, etc.[28]

Needless to say the line in the above passage concerning the Word is an addition from the personal theology of Hippolytus, a resolute defender of the Logos and of the fourth Gospel, like his master Irenaeus. But the part of the formula which presents Jesus as Son of God in virtue of his being born of God, by the instrumentality of the holy Spirit and the virgin Mary, corresponds to the baptismal formula cited immediately above which is earlier than the Roman Creed. Much older are the terms applied to Jesus, "child" of God, "angel of his will," which are nearly related to the *Didache*, while the second question of the profession looks as if its original form was only: "Believest thou in Christ Jesus, the Son of God?" The addition of "only begotten" after Son, as it is placed in the Roman Symbol, has the effect of making the sonship an eternal relation existing before the incarnation by miraculous conception. For that reason some critics hesitate to place the use of the word as far back as the second century. In any case, however, it might well have been aimed at Valentinus.

7. THE MIRACULOUS CONCEPTION

At what date the miraculous conception became an article of the faith remains a matter for conjecture. Obviously this date depends on that assigned, not precisely to the composition of the first Gospel, but to its acceptance by the Church in Rome and to the addition of the verses about the virgin conception in Luke. Not long ago some excitement was caused by a Syriac manuscript (published by W. Wright in the *Journal of Sacred Literature*, October, 1866) in which there is an account of a Council said to have been held at Rome during the reign of Hadrian in the year 119, Xystus then being bishop. At this Council the questions of the star of the Magi and of Joseph's marriage are said to have been examined. Many critics have hesitated to take this information seriously as having anything to do with the reception of the first Gospel in the Roman Church. Quite recently, however, Streeter (*The Four Gospels*, 525) and Bacon (*Studies in Matthew*, 50–59), both considerable authorities, have pronounced in favour of a connexion between the two things. They maintain that a book which, like Matthew, gave the Gospel a "beginning" other than that of Mark (see Mark i, 1) would not have been accepted in the Roman Community without further examination and testimony; but such testimony was forthcoming, and acceptance effected without much difficulty, because Ignatius of Antioch[29] had recently addressed a warm plea to Rome in favour of Matthew, highly esteemed at Antioch and by him. The second argument holds good only on the double condition of the letters of Ignatius containing the plea being authentic, and the supposed date of his martyrdom being correct, if even then. This is tantamount to saying the argument is not conclusive. The first argument, which needs very cautious handling, remains to be considered.

The authority of a witness as late as that of this Syriac manuscript (fifth century), and as isolated, is not indisputable, nor are the ancient sources on which it might possibly depend (discussed at length by Bacon) and of which, by some strange chance, it would be the only echo, anything more than a matter of more or less plausible conjecture. The discussion of its intrinsic probability would be endless. There is no proof that the canon of the New Testament was drawn up at Councils properly so called, and decided book by book, and that, as Bacon contends, the Pastor of Hermas was excluded in this way from the collection.[30] Moreover, in a case like that of Matthew, the question of its formal acceptance or rejection would have been impossible in the conditions under which a Roman Council could have taken place in the year 120. A Gospel already received in some communities, as Matthew was at Antioch, and coming to the knowledge of others, was not offered to their official examiners to be promptly accepted or rejected; it merely asked for the attention of the faithful and might be long tolerated and held in esteem without entering, to the same extent as others, into the actual usage of the congregations. It is improbable that Matthew brought anything new in the way of belief to the Eastern circles where it first appeared, its compiler merely giving Gospel form to beliefs which had already taken shape. In the same way when it arrived in Rome its contents would seem to fall in with what was already known and cannot have made the impression of bringing information hitherto unheard of. So received, its credit would increase as time went on.

It is nevertheless possible that the period indicated (119–120) corresponds to a moment of great importance in the history of the Church in Rome. When Irenaeus reminds Victor that his predecessors tolerated the Easter observance of the quartodecimans without practising it themselves, he goes back by Soter and Anicetus to Pius, Hyginus and Telesphorus, and stops at Xystus as though he has now reached the point from which the Roman tradition takes its departure. It is not impossible that the Roman observance of the Sunday Easter goes no further back; but Irenaeus may also have stopped there for lack of further information. In like manner it is not impossible that our first Gospel arrived in Rome in the time of Xystus and was there received with respect but without supplanting Mark and Luke, then in use. Nor is it impossible that the growing credit of Matthew, with its birth story, soon had the effect of introducing into Luke the addition (i, 34–35) which records the virgin conception of the Christ. Finally it is not impossible that about 145–150 the miraculous conception of the Christ was introduced into the baptismal confession of faith, against Valentinus and especially against Marcion. But all these attempts to fix the date when the miraculous conception became matter of faith remain in the realm of conjecture.

8. Remaining Articles of the Creed

The article of the remission of sins, in the ancient Roman Symbol, seems to have a special significance. Impressed by the call of Hermas and his Pastor the Roman Church may well have established the system of public penitence for Christian sinners, as a means of defending her discipline against the many continence-sects then active, and especially against the Marcionites. The express mention of "the holy Church" aims at canonizing the traditional Church, the Great Church, the Catholic Church; at establishing it in the presence, and at the expense, of the gnostic conventicles and suspected groupings, to which this true Church will henceforth refuse all claims to truth and to holiness. It is against the gnostics also, and once more against Marcion in particular, that she affirms "the resurrection of the flesh," notwithstanding the declaration of First Corinthians "that flesh and blood cannot inherit the Kingdom of God" (xv, 50).

9. Emergence of the Episcopate and the Church Fully Born

Impassioned love for the Church, and for the unity of the Church, goes back to the earliest organization of the Christian societies; beyond all question it is an inheritance from the Jewish spirit, in which the idea of a chosen people threw off its national limitations and became humanized. From the very first the community of believers in Jesus claimed to be, and was determined to remain, a spiritual homeland for the elect people of God. Spite of all divisions and, we may add, of many fallings-away, the Christian groups were kept united in the bond of their faith, of their great hope and of the fraternal practice of a truly effective charity. We have already seen how their rudimentary institutions were very naturally copied from the Synagogue. But they could not fail to undergo profound transformations of inner ordering in the course of their independent growth to maturity.

It was inevitable, even at the earliest period, that certain members would be charged with the due ordering of the meetings, chiefly of the communion supper, and with the care of the poor. The Book of Acts represents the Apostles as the first administrators of the community but soon forced to delegate the service of its material wants to seven deacons (vi, 1–6). The story is fictitious, but corresponds to one reality—that the Christian communities were organized brotherhoods from the very beginning. From the moment the groups were formed, the older men, assisted by auxiliary ministers, took the place of presidents; there were presbyters, deacons and even deaconesses. At the end of First Corinthians (xvi, 15–16) Paul mentions one Stephanas and those of his household, "first fruits of Achaia, who have taken on themselves the service of the saints," that is, the first to be converted who, ever since their conversion, have devoted themselves to the community; and he then goes on to plead that obedience should be rendered to them and to every helper who labours as they did for the common good. It would seem, then, that Stephanas and his fellow workers had already the duty of supervising as well as of serving, and were charged, as a kind of police, with the maintenance of discipline. At the end of Romans, Paul, in like manner, speaks of "the sister Phoebe," deaconess of the community at Cenchrea, who has the duty of carrying his letter, a person worthy of all respect "because she has been a help to many, including myself." With no titles or honorific badges to distinguish them from other believers, and though they had not received the indelible mark of sacramental ordination, these people were of no little consequence in the community. It is, however, true that the ordination of elders, bishop-priests and deacons, by the laying-on of hands, is of earlier date than the editing of Acts and the pastoral Epistles, perhaps even earlier than the *Didache*.

At no period of their history did the communities allow these indispensable officers to drop out. The presence of apostles, prophets and doctors may have left them at first somewhat in the shade, but did not render them less necessary. In First Corinthians (xii, 4–5) "service" is placed below "spiritual gifts." The *Didache* gives these helpers greater honour, but still finds it necessary to urge consideration for them in the community which has elected them to office. This is no longer determined by circumstances or by their own wish to serve, as it was at the beginning.

> "Choose you bishops and deacons[31] worthy of the Lord; let them be gentle men, disinterested, sincere, well-tried. For they also exercise among you the ministry of prophets and doctors; look not upon them as of low rank, for they are entitled to respect among you along with prophets and doctors." (*Didache*, 31.)

The status of elders, as Hermas describes it, is almost the same, except that they are now acquiring greater authority and are beginning to take precedence of the prophets and the doctors.

The "overseers," or bishops, were not distinguished from the elders, or priests. The elders are also the overseers; the "ministers," or deacons, are subordinate to them. In the Pastoral Epistles three orders of administrative officers are no longer recognized, but only two, the bishop-priests and the deacons.[32] Thus each community, on becoming fairly numerous, would have a *collegium* of elders presiding over its social life, meetings for worship and works of charity; the deacons would form the executive. But though, at the outset, the elders had no teaching ministry by the side of the prophets and doctors, and though even the moral discipline of the congregation did not belong to them, the force of circumstances would, nevertheless, tend to give them a leading part, not only in discipline, but in the day to day instruction of catechumens and those already baptized. The importance of their administrative function would increase with the increase of the common resources to be managed and of the alms to be distributed, with the growing sacredness of their duties in the conduct of worship and the concurrent decline and inadequacy of inspired prophecy and itinerant preaching. The *Didache* (11, 3–5) gives us a glimpse of the latter process; the wandering apostle was now becoming a burdensome charge on the localized congregations and ill-seen by the managers of their funds.[33] At Rome, in the time of Hermas, the prophet-teacher was already under the control of the presbyters, who soon set him aside altogether and themselves assumed sole charge of the day to day instruction of the congregation. The author of the Ignatian Letters speaks as though his own office were that of bishop-prophet and not as though the prophets were a separate order at the side of the bishops, priests and deacons. When Marcion tried to revive the prophets it was too late.

We can now understand why the pastoral Epistles dwell on the qualities needed in the bishop-priest and in the deacon with an insistence that seems striving to find terms strong enough. For, in reality, it is to them, not to the prophets nor to the teachers (doctors), that the "Paul" of the pastorals, through the intermediary of Timothy and Titus, commits the whole care of the congregations now menaced by a swarm of heretical doctrinaires. To Titus he writes as follows (i, 5–9):

> To this end I left thee in Crete,
> > that thou mightest complete what is unfinished,
> And appoint presbyters in every town,
> > according to the order I gave thee.
> Let each be a man above reproach,
> > the husband of one wife,[34]
> With believing children,
> > not suspected as ne'er-do-wells or disobedient.
> For the bishop must be irreproachable,
> > inasmuch as he is God's steward:
> Not arrogant, not hasty tempered, not given to drink,
> > not a man of blows, not avaricious,
> But a kindly host, a good man, having common sense,
> > just, pious, master of himself,
> Holding fast the sure word which accords with the doctrine,
> > so that he can exhort in holy teaching,
> > and send opponents to the right-about.

From this it becomes clear that the bishop-priest is now charged with the paternal government of the community and with the instruction of it according to "the doctrine" deemed apostolic. Obviously the office is not for new and untried hands, a point expressly made in the Epistles to Timothy (i, 3-4; v, 22; 2, ii, 2).

> Let the deacons likewise be worthy men,
>   not using words in a double sense,
> And not addicted to the wine cup,
>   not avaricious,
> Having the mystery of the faith
>   in purity of conscience
> But see to it also that they are first proved,
>   then let them serve, being without reproach;
> For those who do good service
>   win for themselves a position of honour
> And great assurance by faith in Christ Jesus.

When and how the bishop emerged from the general body of presbyters as sole president of the community, cannot be stated with precision. It is probable that from the very earliest time this body was not constituted without a head, that it had a president, but that his office did not exalt him very highly above his fellows and was not an appointment for life. It is noteworthy that Hermas, whose tradition makes him out to be the brother of the bishop Pius, predecessor of Anicetus, never mentions the bishop, and seems to have had dealings only with the presbyters in Rome. But a few years afterwards we find Anicetus sole bishop of the Roman community, just as his contemporary Polycarp was sole bishop in Smyrna. But Polycarp had then been bishop for a long time. It may well be that the monarchical type of episcopate existed in some regions earlier than in others. Polycarp himself, for example, writing to the Philippians makes no mention of any bishop at Philippi.[35] The community of Corinth, again, seems to have had no bishop at its head when the letter of Clement was addressed to it. This letter shows knowledge only of bishop-priests and of deacons, instituted by the apostles in the communities they had founded, and reappointed by election after the apostle's death. The letter does not speak of these functionaries as subject to recall at will or periodically, but as there for life.[36]

We may conclude, then, that the monarchical type of episcopate was at first instituted in certain communities, either because they were more prepared than the others for an autocratic regime, or through the pressure of personalities better endowed for leadership and ambitious to attain it. Have we not already heard the good Hermas rebuking the Roman presbyters for their love of place and power? On that road Asia may well have taken the lead of Greece proper, and especially of Rome, where perhaps there was some difficulty in centralizing the Christian groups under a single administration. It is likely enough that the gnostic peril brought this evolution to a sudden head; for while the unitary episcopate exists only in some places before the period 130-140, we find it existing everywhere after 150-160. Be it observed, moreover, that Marcion, who founded his communities on the pattern of the Great Church, recognized the distinction between episcopate, presbyterate and deaconate. These functions, however, were not perpetual in the Marcionite communities and did not form a true hierarchy. The tendency of the arch-heretic was, so to say, in the direction of democratizing church appointments, while the Church, on the other side, proceeded to fortify them more and more by an official conservation, which ended by separating the clergy from the lay believers.[37] In the Church, priests and deacons became united in one body, under the rule of the bishop, to guide the Christian flock in the path of apostolic doctrine. Bishops, priests, deacons, these three, while retaining their function as ministers of charity, are now to be acknowledged as masters of the truth and hierarchs of the cult.

Meanwhile the gap which divides the Church from the heresies grows deeper and more distinct. Celsus (*c*. 180) clearly distinguishes the one from the other. But, more profoundly than an outsider like Celsus could feel it, the difference between orthodox and heretical was realized within the Church, which its official representatives and apologists are now declaring to be the sole guardian of the truth. Justin, who attributes pagan idolatry to wicked demons, does not hesitate to make them the authors of all the heresies from Simon Magus to Marcion (1 *Apology*, 26, 58). "There is not a doubt," Tertullian will soon be saying, "that the spirits of perversity, from whom come the heresies, were charged with the business by the devil, nor that heresies are the same as idolatry, seeing that they come from the same author and are of the same workmanship. Either they invent another God to oppose the creator"—this for Marcion—"or, if they admit only one creator they make him out to be different from what he really is. Thus every lie they tell about God is some sort of service to idols" (*De Praescriptione*, 40).

We have already heard the author of the Ignatian Letters sounding his trumpet call to the faithful to rally round the bishop. Let us listen once more to this singer of Christian unity—unity in bishops and by bishops. For he it is who may be truly said to have created the mystery of the episcopate, that mystery of which Cyprian, in the next century, was to be the worthy exponent, and which to-day would be condemned as heresy, being now replaced by the mystery of the Pope, of which our authors had not the faintest idea.

> Since love permits me not to keep silence towards you, I am eager in exhorting you to walk in step with the thought of God. For Jesus Christ, the life we can never be parted from, is the thought of God, even as bishops, established in their seats to the end of the earth, are one with the thought of Jesus Christ. Fitting it is, then, that you walk in step with the thought of the bishop, as indeed you are doing. For your venerable presbyterium is adjusted to the bishop as cords are adjusted to the lyre. Wherefore Christ is praised by the harmony of your hearts and the symphony of your love. Join you, each one, his voice to that choir, so that, with one heart and one voice, taking up in unison the key-note of God, you may sing through Jesus Christ to the Father, who will then listen to your song and recognize by your works that you are members of his Son. Good is it for you that you keep in faultless unity, for thus will you ever be united to the very God. (Ephesians 3–4.)

10. Sudden Revival of Christian Prophecy

At the moment when this admirable symphony was about to become complete, it had a narrow escape of being broken up by the discordant cries of the Christian prophets. Christian prophecy, as we have seen, was on the way to dying a natural death in the atmosphere created by the intellectualism of gnosis and the growth of the episcopate, which was fighting gnosis and growing stronger as it fought. But all of a sudden, between 160 and 170,[38] prophecy came to life again in a region which had long been accustomed to outbreaks of mystical transport. Montanus, with his women acolytes, Maximilla and Priscilla, exalted it seems by overstudy of the Johannine writings, were persuaded that a mission had been laid upon them to revive the golden days of Christian prophecy. Great was the emotional excitement in all the congregations of God, beginning from those in Asia Minor, when news spread that astounding manifestations of the Spirit were taking place in Phrygia; an excitement which became the more confused when it was learnt at the same time that the new prophets were encountering vigorous opposition, especially from the bishops, who were actively at work in refuting the prophets and were going to the length of having them exorcised as possessed of the devil.

As with other heresies, our information about Montanus and Montanism comes mainly from those who opposed them. But Montanus was not a real heretic; at least there was nothing of the gnostic about him. He and his adepts were *illuminati* who had been carried away by the Book of Revelation and expected to see the New Jerusalem descending at an exact spot, which their visions had revealed to them, between the small Phrygian towns of Pepuza and Tymon. Far from the scene of their excesses the Montanists were looked upon with favour in 177 at Lyons where Irenaeus the bishop showed them consistent goodwill. Rome hesitated long before taking sides.39 It was while affairs were in this posture that certain Asiatics, by way of turning Montanus and his followers to mockery, rejected the whole of the Johannine books. For Montanism lasted on and was getting organized round Pepuza undeterred by the persistent delay of the heavenly Jerusalem in making its appearance. Rome, under Victor, and in the first years of Zephyrinus, took no pains to be on good terms with the Asiatic bishops, and this may explain why Caius (180–235) was able with impunity to join the Asiatic adversaries of the Paraclete, the Fourth Gospel and the Apocalypse. In this Caius was also attacking Montanism.

The violence of the agitation caused by this revival of Christian prophecy was not confined to Asia Minor. Though most of the Asiatic bishops were against the movement, it got a lasting hold in Phrygia, where the headquarters of its hopes were established. But its localization in that province did not hinder its missionaries from going far into the West. Only in Africa was Montanism able to take root, and there it won over Tertullian, the greatest of the Church's apologists in that age. Great as was the effort made by Tertullian to rally the Church to Montanism, he succeeded no further than to bring about his own secession towards the year 201,[40] taking with him a small group of followers who never counted for much in African Christianity, though they managed to hold on till the time of Saint Augustine.

The historical significance of Montanism lies in the fact that here we have a rekindling of the inner fire whose light illuminated the first believers. The medium in which that fire sprang up again was doubtless favourable to such an outbreak, but the movement is best understood as a reaction of faith against gnosis, a reaction, that is, of the mystic sense against metaphysical subtleties pretending to be a philosophy of religion. It was also a movement of rigorist morality, a continence-movement proceeding from a principle different from Marcion's but not less exacting. Montanus condemned marriage by arguments which pushed to its last consequences the reasoning by which celibacy and virginity are commended to the faithful in First Corinthians (vii, 6–8, 25–34). Both in its revival of prophecy and in its rigorist morality Montanism ran counter to tendencies manifested in the Church during the second century towards a more flexible discipline, and a more solid organization, than the first age of Christianity would have found congenial. On the one hand, the Church was building herself into a fortress by submitting to the rule of a monarchical episcopate; on the other, she was adapting herself to the conditions of human society by allowing for the wants, even the weaknesses, of human nature, and by establishing a discipline of penitence for those whose courage might fail in professing their faith when threatened with death for profession, or who might commit any other sin incompatible with the principle of Christianity. Far from yielding to the Montanist movement, the episcopate was now strong enough to deprive prophecy of any part in the direction of the Christian conscience and to set up a relatively indulgent regime for the Christian sinner, but always on condition of his penitence.

The check thus given to Montanism marks the end of primitive Christianity. From that time onwards the Christian religion is the

Christian Church under the rule of bishops accounted successors of the apostles and trustees of the apostolic tradition. This Church has her Creed, of which the essential lines are now firmly drawn. She has her Scriptures, a collection of the New Testament, supported by the Old. Her worship has evolved into a Mystery of Salvation. Her whole institution is now defined sufficiently, not indeed to render future heresy impossible, but to ensure that henceforth, and century after century, the life of the Christian communities shall be ruled with sovereign right by the principle of tradition, or seem to be ruled, when the reins of government are in able hands.

So our story concludes. A religious agitation started in Palestinian Judaism by a Galilean preacher, whose aim was the Kingdom of God, and his end to be crucified as a rebel, comes to its fruit in less than two centuries as a mighty institution established throughout the Roman empire, condemned by the law, but assured of its future and equally sure of victory over the empire which persecuted it. In the whole course of this remarkable evolution nothing happened which cannot be explained by the laws that govern human life, and this may be said with confidence in spite of the obscurity resulting from the conditions under which the movement went on its way. None the less is it true that this triumph of faith, viewed in the light of religious and moral consciousness, if not a miracle, is a human marvel, in which new life was created and a work of human progress thereby accomplished. The diffusion of Judaism had prepared the ground for Christian success, but Christianity completed a victory which Judaism, though it won the first approaches, was powerless to follow up to its conclusion, and this because it had compressed an idea, broad as humanity, into the narrow form of a nationalism, in which only a few could participate. This idea Christianity held forth, under the thin covering of a religious creed, to the disinherited multitudes of the ancient world, to the multitudes without a homeland; and round it they rallied. This element of human sympathy, born in the first preaching of the Gospel and developed in primitive Christianity, this it was that carried the Catholic Church to the very forefront of history. How she has since comported herself at that eminence, in what measure she has fulfilled or not fulfilled her programme, we know. But the history of her proceedings from the end of the second century down to our time is abundantly documented. It is the pre-history of the Christian religion that we here bring to an end, a history which the cautious inquirer may reconstruct by inference, and more or less conjecturally, from testimony whose main content is, not the history, but the mystic legend of its institution.

NOTES TO INTRODUCTION

1 *Les Livres du Nouveau Testament traduits du grec en francais avec introduction générale et notices*, 1922.

2 A complete bibliography of the subject would fill a larger volume than this present. The list below is limited to the most important of recent works dealing with the essentials, and especially to those which the present author has used or had in view when preparing his own:

E. Renan: *Histoire des origines du christianisme*, 1863-1881. A brilliant synthesis, needing correction to-day at many points but unequalled, at least in our literature, and never replaced.

L. Duchesne: *Histoire ancienne de l'Eglise*, i (1906).

B. W. Bacon: *The fourth Gospel in research and debate* (1918); *The Story of the Jews and the beginnings of the Church* (1926); *Studies in Matthew* (1930).

W. Bousset: *Kyrios Christos* (1913, 1921).

R. Bultmann: *Die Geschichte der synoptischen Tradition* (1921).

C. Clemen: *Paulus, sein Leben und Wirken* (1904); *Religionsgeschichtliche Erklärung des Neuen Testaments* (1929).

F. Cumont: *Les religions orientales dans le paganisme romain* (1929).

M. Goguel: *Introduction au Nouveau Testament* (i–v, 1923 ss.); *Jésus de Nazareth* (1925); *Jean-Baptiste* (1928); *La Vie de Jésus* (1932).

C. Guignebert: *Manuel d'histoire ancienne du Christianisme* (1906); *Le Christianisme antique* (1921); *Jésus* (1933).

A. Harnack: *Geschichte der altchristlichen Literatur* (1893, 1897, 1904); *Mission und Ausbreitung des Christentums in die drei ersten Jahrhunderten* (1906); *Beiträge zur Einleitung in das Neue Testament* (i–vi, 1906–1914).

E. Hennecke: *Handbuch zu den neutestamentlichen Apokryphen* (1904); *Neutestamentliche Apokryphen* (1923–1924).

A. Jülicher: *Einleitung in das Neue Testament* (1931); *Die Gleichnisrede Jesu* (1902).

M. J. Lagrange: *Evangile selon saint Matthieu* (1927); *Evangile selon saint Marc* (1929); *Evangile selon saint Luc* (1921); *Evangile selon saint Jean* (1925).

H. Lietzmann: *Handbuch zum Neuen Testament* (1926–1932); *Geschichte der alten Kirche. i. Die Anfänge* (1932).

E. Lohmeyer: *Das Urchristentum*, i, 1. *Johannes der Taüfer* (1932).

E. Meyer: *Ursprung und Anfänge des Christentums* (1921–1923).

E. Norden: *Agnostos Theos* (1913); *Die Geburt des Kindes* (1923).

R. Reitzenstein: *Die hellenistischen Mysterienreligionen* (1920).

A. Schweitzer: *Geschichte der Leben Jesu Forschung* (1913, 1926); *Geschichte der paulinischen Forschung* (1911).

B. H. Streeter: *The four Gospels* (1924); *The primitive Church* (1929).

J. Weiss: *Das Urchristentum* (1914, 1917).

J. Weiss, W. Bousset and W. Heitmuller: *Die Schriften des Neuen Testaments neu übersetzt und für die Gegenwart erklärt* (1917–1918).

J. Wellhausen: *Einleitung in die drei ersten Evangelien* (1911); *Das Evangelium Matthaei* (1914); *Das Evangelium Marci* (1909); *Das Evangelium Lucae* (1904); *Das Evangelium Johannis* (1908).

P. Wendland: *Die Urchristlichen Literaturformen* (1912).

NOTES TO CHAPTER I

1 R. Eisler's defence of the partial authenticity of supplements contained in the Sclavic version of *The Jewish War* is distinguished by great learning and subtlety. A criticism of the thesis may be found, by M. Goguel, in *Revue d'histoire et de philosophie religieuses*, March–April 1930, pp. 177–190.

2 ii, 1–16: Paul's self-defence against other missionaries, ending in a violent outburst against Jewish persecutors, in the spirit and style of Acts; iii, 2b–4, interpolation of the same character, presupposing a long experience of persecution (iii, 2a should be attached to 5: "we have sent Timothy, our brother and servant of God in the Gospel of the Christ, to know how you stand in the faith," etc.).

3 A fragment with a style all its own, making a violent breach in the moral precepts at the end of the Epistle. The apocalyptic description, which is a deliberate paraphrase of Gospel texts, stamps itself as later than the apostolic age (cf. iv, 15 and Mark ix, 1, xiii, 30; also v, 1–2 with Mark xiii, 31; Matthew xxiv, 43; Luke xii, 39).

4 The end of verse 3 seems to have been added to give the Epistle the character of instruction addressed to the universal Church. The words "and I am of Christ," in verse 12, are probably interpolated.

5 i, 17–ii, 8. "The princes of this world," in ii, 8, are not political rulers of human appointment, of whom there would be no need to inform us that they are not in God's confidence. Jesus is here called "the Lord of glory," in allusion to Psalm xxiv, 7–9. The quotation in verse 9 probably comes from some Apocrypha and must be a gloss.

6 Observe that, in vii, 10, the author appeals to the Gospel prohibition of divorce (cf. Mark x, 9), and then, in verse 12, takes it on himself to authorize the divorce of the Christian partners in a mixed marriage if the pagan partner takes the initiative. The case presented in verses 36–38, of the believing guardian of a virgin, who is given permission to marry her if he feels it necessary, does not belong to the earliest Christian age.

7 x, 12–13 looks like an editor's addition. The whole passage is a homily on the sacrament of the Supper as understood in xi, 23–26.

8 12b–14 may be another editorial addition. On the general theme cf. 1 Thessalonians ii, 1–12, Acts xx, 33–35.

9 17–18 again suspect as editorial.

10 Note that the passage forbidding women to speak in the assemblies

conflicts with what is presupposed by xi, 3–16. But xiv, 33b–35 is evidently interpolated.

[11] Interpolation is betrayed not only by the higher quality of the author's aim but by the forced connexions xii, 31 and xiv, 9, which are doublets. Moreover, xiii, 13, which contradicts what has gone before, seems to have been added to the song.

[12] The priority of ix is evident from the fact that, in it, the collections have not yet been made either in Macedonia or in Corinth, whereas in viii the Macedonian collection is ready and Paul has finished organizing the collection at Corinth. See Delafosse iii, 15–16.

[13] The insulting invectives against the Galilean apostles (cf. 1 Corinthians 1, 2, 6, 13) are counterblasts to those which Revelation i–iii launches against Paul and his followers.

[14] For the help which came from Macedonia, cf. Philippians iv, 15, 16 and Acts xviii, 2, 3 (where it appears that the money brought from Macedonia enabled Paul to give himself entirely to his preaching).

[15] xi, 12b–xii, 4. If this apology is not from Paul himself, it is founded on more complete and precise information than canonical Acts. But the date assigned to the great vision in xii, 2 makes a difficulty. Paul's capital vision must have been that which converted him, which cannot have taken place about the year 40. (Can there be some influence here from Galatians ii, 1?)

[16] These are dealt with by Acts xiii, 14–xiv, 23; xvi, 1–5

[17] Marcion's version lacked i, 18–20, the personal visit to Peter; also the "again" in ii, 1. But this passage, which fits so ill with the context, may well be an addition.

[18] v, 13–26; vi, 7–10, 12–16. It seems as though v, 1–12 should be attached to iv, 21–31, and that vi, 1–6 may be an addition; vi, 11 might rejoin the conclusion, 17–18.

[19] Many critics doubt whether the salutations of xvi, 3–16 (if not also xvi, 1–2, 21–22) originally belonged to Romans, and are inclined to think them addressed to the community at Ephesus. The final doxology, xvi, 25–27, is recognized as a Marcionite addition, although the entire chapters xv–xvi were at first wanting in Marcion's *Apostolicon*.

[20] To the same gnosis belongs iii, 21–26, to which iv, 15, 25 are coordinated. In the exposition of the gnosis vii, 7–25 seems of secondary origin.

[21] i, 18–iii, 20, where the indictment of the pagans, which has a rhetoric of its own, seems to have been borrowed from a Jewish source. In ii, 14, 15 we may suspect a gloss.

[22] The fragment which follows xv, 7 seems lost in this place. In the moral part, the verses in respect for established authority (xiii, 1–7) are by a later hand; 8–12 depend on the Gospel tradition. The warning against heretics, xvi, 17–20, belongs to a time when gnostic editors were at work.

[23] The essential formula is Colossians i, 15–19, which should be compared with Philippians ii, 6–10.

²⁴ Ephesus would be thought by the editors to have a better claim than Laodicea to an apostolic letter.

²⁵ Note the quotation of the baptismal hymn in v, 14. On the other hand, it results from ii, 20; iii, 5; iv, 11 that inspired prophets still stand with apostles in the first rank.

²⁶ ii, 6–11 is a short poem of Christian gnosis inserted by means of an artificial transition (verse 5).

²⁷ The rules of discipline in 1 Timothy ii–iii, 13 break into the warning against false teachers, thereafter resumed, while ii, 11–15a, forbidding women to teach (parallel to 1 Corinthians xiv, 34–35), is an evident surcharge in the rules about woman's dress, etc.

²⁸ Cf. especially 1 Clement, 36, 2; Hebrews i, 3–4.

²⁹ In ii, 3–4 the author expresses himself in much the same terms as the author of Luke i, 1–2. Similarly in xiii, 7, where the founders of the community to which the Epistle is addressed are represented as belonging to a time long passed. Assuming that the community addressed was the Roman, the founders referred to would be Peter and Paul, here associated as we find them in Clement's Epistle.

³⁰ We get a glimpse of Gospel tradition only in ii, 3–4; v, 7–10 is commonly regarded as a reference to the scene in Gethsemane; it refers in reality to Psalm xxii, on which the synoptic account was constructed.

³¹ 2 Peter i. The announcement by Jesus of Peter's death (13–14), and the appeal to a great revelation on "the holy mountain," in which the apotheosis of the Christ is completed (16–19), refer to the Apocalypse of Peter, not to John xx, 18–19, nor to the Gospel stories of the transfiguration.

³² In v, 12 the author forbids oath-taking in the terms of Matthew v, 34 but without giving any sign that he is quoting a Gospel precept.

³³ 1 John v, 6–8 appears to be an interpolation to connect with John xix, 34–35 (water and blood, after the lance-thrust), a passage equally secondary in the fourth Gospel.

³⁴ Note that the author proves by Psalm cx, 1 that Jesus was not the son of David (cf. Mark xiii, 35–37).

³⁵ 1 Clement, 5. The two apostles appear as legendary heroes, Peter taking precedence of Paul, as in canonical Acts.

³⁶ The year 155, assigned by many as the date of Polycarp's martyrdom, ill accords with what we know of his coming to Rome in the time of Anicetus. It is more probable that Polycarp died under Marcus Aurelius, in 166, as Eusebius indicates. Thus the letter to the Philippians could have been written between 150 and 160.

³⁷ Note that while Christian apocalyptic had a fixed centre in the name of Jesus, Jewish apocalyptic was always rambling loosely round the topic of the Messiah, which was not definitely crystallized round an historical name.

³⁸ The author of the Ascension proper seems to say (ix, 14) that "the god of this world" and his auxiliaries will crucify the Son of God without recognizing him; but in that he is not dependent on 1 Corinthians ii, 8.

He also seems to say that the Christ remained on the earth for eighteen months after his resurrection, an opinion held by some of the gnostics.

39 A translation of the Greek fragment and of the Ethiopian version will be found in Henneke, *Neutestamentliche Apokryphen*, 1923, pp. 314–327.

40 The Akhmim fragment has a different order. It gives the first place to the felicity of the elect, two unnamed persons among the redeemed taking the place of Moses and Elijah as types of the promised glory.

41 An obscure passage in the Ethiopian version but better preserved in the Greek fragment (cf. James in *The Journal of Theological Studies*, April 1931, pp. 270–279).

42 This can only be the Mount of Olives. Note the same designation, "holy mountain," in 2 Peter i, 18.

43 Cf. Bacon, *Studies in Matthew*, 146.

44 The Church which Hermas sees in vision is already *old*. He took her at first to be the Sibyl (*Vision*, ii, 4); and the real Church as he knew it on earth has an experience of persecution acquired after the reign of Trajan.

45 Virtues, vices, even impressions, are freely personified by Hermas. These personifications are not, with him, simple metaphors; they belong to the old Roman animism which put a god into every phenomenon. Thus he sees the Church in the form of a respectable matron. It would be difficult to understand why his shepherd, angel of penitence, should come from Arcadia, were it not that the image has been borrowed from a non-Christian type which we encounter again in the Hermetic Poimandres, in comparison with whom the Johannine Christ is acclaimed the true shepherd.

46 1 *Apology*, 66. The formula "Memoirs of the apostles" which is customary with Justin has no traditional warrant; he uses it to give distinction to this literature which he somewhat boldly assimilates to Xenophon's Memoirs about Socrates. It is not clear that Justin had the idea of a fixed canon; he appears to have made use in ordinary of the three Synoptics; also of John and perhaps of the Gospel of Peter.

47 *Heresies*, iii, 1. Note that Tatian's *Diatessaron*, about 170, is founded on the canonical Gospels and that Theophilus of Antioch, about 190, constructed a harmony of the four Gospels. The canon of four had become law at Alexandria in the time of Clement, about 200.

48 The priority of Mark results from the fact that it is to be considered as a source for Matthew and Luke. Beyond that it is impossible to assign precise dates to the stages of its revision.

49 This conclusion is wanting in the oldest manuscripts, though it is of earlier date than they. The author of it knew the three other Gospels and Acts. It has been conjectured that it replaced another conclusion either lost or suppressed. The only fact of which we can be certain is that it was intended to fill an obvious gap and bring Mark into line with the other Gospels.

50 The Meal of the Anointing (xiv, 3–9) breaks up the prelude to the arrest and betrayal and, by anticipation, doubles the last meal, where everything which concerns the Passover and the preparations for it is an interpolation in the story of an ordinary meal which took place on 13 Nisan;

of this story (where verse 24 is obviously adventitious), xiv, 23, 25 is the débris. (See my *Les Livres du N. Testament*, 273–274.)

51 Mark vi, 7–18 (Matthew x), mission of the Twelve; xii, 38–40, against the Pharisees (cf. Matthew xxiii), probably conceived in the source as the conclusion of the Jerusalem ministry.

52 Cf. B. W. Bacon, *Is Mark a Roman Gospel?* 1919, and the criticism of this book in *Revue d'histoire et littérature religieuses*, 1920, p. 627, where we read "it was perhaps for want of something better that the Roman community first accepted this Gospel text."

53 Eusebius, *History*, iv, 14, 1; v, 24, 16.

54 The collection of Logia, or discourses, was made to meet the practical needs of Christian catechesis, and there is no reason whatever to suppose that its original author was a disciple of Jesus. That hypothesis appears self-evident only to those who hold that the reason for making the collection was the desire to get a fixed and authentic version of the teaching of the Christ. But the real reason was the need to provide the catechists with an adequate repertoire of matter for their teaching.

55 The two prefaces are closely co-ordinate. On the mutilation of the preface to Acts in the editorial elaboration of that book, see my *Les Actes des Apôtres*, 133–140.

56 Duplicate of the mission of the Twelve, symbolic of the evangelization of Israel, and intended to signify the evangelization of the pagans already announced in iv, 16–30.

57 Theme resumed in Acts i, 9–11. Its connexion with the Apocalypse of Peter has been noted above, p. 37. The rôle attributed to Herod in the passion of the Christ (xxiii, 6–12) brings the third Gospel rather near to the Gospel of Peter.

58 The author effects his purpose by bringing together all the apparitions of the Risen One in a unitary perspective. There is reason to believe that the characteristic words of the mystical supper were absent in the original Luke and that the last meal was not there presented as the Passover meal. In this, its original form, the Gospel would therefore be earlier than the introduction of the Sunday Easter in the circle for which it was written, and if this circle was Roman it follows that the Gospel would be that of some Roman group which ignored or was unacquainted with the gnosis of the Epistles attributed to Paul, the harmonization of Mark and Luke having coincided with the unification of the various Roman groups.

59 In the stories of the resurrection: Luke xxiv, 12 (perhaps authentic), 24, cf. John xx, 3–10; 36–40, cf. John xx, 19–21, 27. It is probable that in Acts xii, 1–2 the original document mentioned the death of John along with that of James, conformably to Mark x, 39 and to the testimony of Papias, and that the revision of the document which brings John to the front in the first chapter suppressed the mention of his execution in deference to the Ephesian legend.

60 The hypothesis of an Aramaic original has been weightily maintained in recent times.

61 In the perspective of the first three Gospels the Galilean ministry of Jesus seems to last a few months and the Jerusalem ministry a few days; in John, the life of Jesus is crowned by a ministry of three whole years, he being regarded as forty-six when he began to teach—a symbolic trait (ii, 20). Such figures have mystical significance; but in all four Gospels chronology is only a framework for the distribution of evangelical matter.

62 So far as we can speak of last editions prior to canonization, when the last retouchings of all four Gospels may well have been made at the same time.

63 Schmidke, *Neue Fragmente und Untersuchungen zu juden-christlicen Evangelien*, 1911, boldly contests Jerome's assertion, and even refuses him all knowledge of the Gospel in question. See on this subject Waitz in Henneke 10–32 and E. Meyer i, 261; these authors doubt only that Jerome made the double translation into Greek and Latin of which he boasts (*De viris*, 2).

64 Waitz, 55, would attribute this citation to the Gospel of the Hebrews.

65 Not having the context, it is impossible to say exactly what was the Easter observance of the Nazareans, except that their fast covered the whole time of the passion from the last meal to the resurrection.

66 Waitz, 44 ff., is inclined to place it between 100 and 130, between the Synoptics and John.

67 Collected and translated in Preuschen, *Antilegomena*, 2–3, 135–136.

68 Salome comes on the scene and puts a question to Jesus about the end; Jesus insists on the disappearance from the perfect state of everything related to sex. Pretence of mystery on the subject.

69 It is not certain nor even probable that it depends on the fourth Gospel in its canonical form; its spirit and composition belong rather to the pre-canonical time.

70 Eusebius, vi, 12. Note that the bishop, without examining the book, permitted the reading of it in the community where he found it in use. On his attention being drawn afterwards to the Docetism of certain passages, he rejected it on that ground.

71 According to Clement of Alexandria, *Stromata*, vii, 17, 106. Irenaeus (*Heresies*, iii, 11, 9) says the Gospel of Truth had nothing in common with the canonical Gospels. But had he read it?

72 To these tendencies are attributed the suppression of all that concerns the earthly birth of the Christ, the non-paschal character of the last supper, etc. See Henneke, 74.

73 It is evident that the earthly epiphany of the Christ was for a long time limited to the period between his baptism and resurrection—as in Mark, John, the Gospel of the Ebionites, Basilides, etc. The idea of miraculous conception, by itself, is mythological and does not otherwise imply encratism. It is possible that the exaltation of Mary and the infant Jesus began in gnosis. On the *Genna Marias*, mentioned by Epiphanius, 26, 2, see Henneke, 82, 83, 109.

74 The brothers and sisters of Jesus are represented in this book as the

children of an earlier marriage of Joseph who has become quite an old man when he married Mary. Jerome transformed the brothers and sisters of Jesus into his cousins. Western tradition has followed Jerome.

75 The whole work of the Christian imagination in accounting for the origin of the religion is well summed up in the following quotation borrowed by Eusebius, ii, 1, 4, from the *Hypotyposes*, Book 7, of Clement of Alexandria: "The Lord, after his resurrection, transmitted the gnosis to James the Just, to John and to Peter; these passed it on to the other apostles; the other apostles to the seventy disciples, of whom was Barnabas"—a fragment of Jewish-Christian gnosis. The canonical books (Gospels and Acts) are concerned, on the other hand, to transform the teachings of Jesus from post-resurrection utterances into discourses pronounced by him during his mortal life. But the gnostic tradition may well be, in all respects, the older.

76 Observe that canonical Acts have collected a legend of Peter and a legend of Paul already considerably developed. The final edition of the book combines the two legends with facts having a surer basis, the whole forming an anti-gnostic synthesis—which brings us back to the preceding note. Henneke has good ground for saying (p. 140) that the question of spurious literature in primitive Christianity is still in need of investigation as a whole and fundamentally.

77 These Clementine apocrypha are, perhaps, too neglected at the present time, though the school of Bauer made much of them in the middle of the last century. We have to distinguish the *Kerygmata*, which belong to Jewish-Christian gnosis from the *Praxeis*, a work of anti-gnostic Christianity recounting the combats between Peter and Simon Magus from Caesarea to Antioch. On the highly complicated history of these Clementine romances, see Henneke, 212–215, and O. Culmann, *Le problème litteraire et historique du roman pseudo-clémentin*, 1930.

NOTES TO CHAPTER II

1 *Annals*, xv, 44: "Auctor hujus nominis Christus, Tiberio imperitante, per procuratorem Pontium Pilatum supplicio affectus erat. Repressaque in praesens, exitialis superstitio sursus erumpebat, non modo per Judaeam, originem ejus mali, sed per Urbem etiam, quo cuncta undique atrocia aut turpia confluunt celebranturque."

2 *Epistolae*, 96, 7. Christians under judicial interrogation told Pliny "quod essent soliti stato die ante lucem convenire carmenque Christo quasi deo dicere secum invicem." The *Carmen* is an alternating chant, hymn or liturgy. Pliny understands that the executed man, spoken of by Tacitus, is regarded as a god by his followers.

3 *Antiquities*, xviii, 21: Τὰ μὲν λοιπὰ πάντα γνώμῃ τῶν Φαρισαίων ὁμολογοῦσα, δυσκίνητος δὲ τοῦ ἐλευθέρου ἔρως ἐστὶν αὐτοῖς μόνον ἡγεμόνα καὶ δεσπότην τὸν θεὸν ὑπειληφόσιν.

4 From this we can see the meaning and importance of the question

about paying tribute to Caesar in the synoptic Gospels (Mark xii, 13–17 and parallels). The story was invented to prevent Christianity being confused with the Judaism of the extremists. It is by no means certain that Jesus and his first followers would have shown so much consideration for Caesar's authority. Observe that Mark puts the question into the mouths of Pharisees and Herodians, for whom the question was important.

5 The mistakes and exactions of the last procurators contributed to inflaming the religious passions of the Jews. As soon as revolution started in Jerusalem the friends of the Romans had to flee and, as the empire was then badly governed, rebellion was well organized before Vespasian was charged to suppress it.

6 Herod was not less hated than the Romans, but more skilful in exacting obedience. It was the Jews themselves and the Samaritans who demanded and obtained the deposition of Archelaus in the year 6 of our era. But the mass of the people never settled down under Roman rule to which the upper class had accommodated itself. The fire smouldered till the explosion of the year 66.

7 The date given in Luke iii, 1, if we take it as referring to the preaching of John the Baptist, is too late, although his activity as a preacher cannot have been of long duration; Simon Magus, whose date cannot be exactly given, was a contemporary of the apostolic age; Elchasai, founder of a baptist and judaizing sect in Transjordania, appeared about 100.

8 With the difference, that Simon, in the legend, was regarded as having been a disciple of John; which is not so with Elchasai. In spite of what we read in Acts viii, 9–24, it is unlikely that Simon ever found his way into Christianity, but he may have had some connexion with John or with his sect.

9 It reveals an effort to subordinate John to Jesus, by making John himself avow his subordination, or by drawing distinctions between the baptism of John and Christian baptism, but without success in disguising that the latter was borrowed from the former.

10 *Antiquities*, xviii, 9, 2. The notice finds credit because it seems to be independent of the Gospel tradition. But it may not be really independent.

11 Matthew xi, 11. But the end of verse 3: "Notwithstanding, he that is least in the kingdom of heaven is greater than he," is a Christian addition intended to make the preceding statement inoffensive. It seems, however, that to give a better balance both to the text and the thought we ought, with many church fathers and some moderns, to take this saying in a strictly comparative sense: "he that is smaller than John"—in the order of time, junior by age and manifestation, that is to say, Jesus—"is, in the kingdom of heaven, greater than he." This interpretation saves the pre-eminence of Jesus, and his importance in regard to the kingdom, without excluding John from the number of the elect. The messianic programme announced in Matthew xi, 2–6, might very well be applied, in its principal elements, by John's sectaries to John and by Christians to Jesus.

12 Mark i, 7–8 and parallels. As nobody can be either bathed or washed

in holy Spirit, it is obvious that baptism in spirit reposes on baptism in water, and the former has never existed apart from the latter.

13 Mark i, 5 speaks of the desert, the region round the Dead Sea, as the scene of the preaching and of the Jordan as the scene of the baptizing, followed by Matthew iii, 1, 5. Luke all the region round about the Jordan as the scene of the preaching. The indications of place in John i, 28 and iii, 23, though more precise, are far from being more trustworthy.

14 This baptism in running water was distinct from the legal ablutions. Holscher supposes it derived from the regions bordering on the Euphrates (Babylon) and from Mesopotamia. Renan thought the same. (*Vie de Jésus*, 103; *Les Disciples*, 462-465.)

15 Acts xviii, 24-28; xix, 1-6. From these notices we may conclude that Christian baptism was not originally understood as a baptism of spirit, as the editor of Acts would make out.

16 Matthew ii, 1, connected with Micah v, 1; 13-15, where Hosea xi, 1, which refers to Israel, is made into a prediction of the flight into Egypt; 16-18, massacre of the children, linked to Jeremiah xxxi, 15, which concerns the Captivity; 19-23, return to Judea and settlement at Nazareth linked to the prophecy "he shall be called a Nazorean," of which it is very difficult to find the origin, unless we may suppose the evangelist to be applying to the Christ, by a play of words, the saying about Samson in Judges xiii, 5, "he shall be a *nazir*"; iv, 12-16, Jesus at Capernaum, presented as fulfilment of Isaiah viii, 23-ix, 1, which refers to the Assyrian deportations.

17 The legend preserved in Luke, while contradicting that in Matthew, is better arranged, but not more consistent.

18 In Matthew (i, 1-17) Jesus descends from David through Solomon; in Luke (iii, 23-38), through Nathan. But both come to a common termination in Joseph, who was held to be the father of Jesus by the Jewish-Christian circles in which the genealogies were invented.

19 Ancient tradition was not unanimous on this point, as we may see from the anecdotes in Mark xii, 35-37 (and parallels) and from the so-called Epistle of Barnabas.

20 Cf. Holscher, 230, n. 10; 239, n. 5. Ed. Meyer ii, 423, n. 2, maintains the connexion of the name with Nazareth. On the other hand, the existence of Nazareth at the time of Jesus has been denied, but wrongly. Nazareth was then in existence and only because it existed could it be used for a forced explanation of the title Nazorean when the effort was made to efface the original connexion of Jesus and his sect with the baptist sect of which they were really the issue. There is no etymological relation between Nazareth and the Nazareans or Nazoreans, whose semitic names are written with a *tsadé*, and the nazirs, which is written with a *zain*. The nazirs are "men under vow" (devoted). Nazorean probably means "observer."

21 Matthew xi, 2-17 (Luke vii, 18-20, 22-25). On any interpretation the *mise en scène* and the statements attributed to the Christ reflect a polemic, courteous enough, between the sectaries of Jesus and the sectaries of John after the death of their respective leaders.

NOTES

²² It was in this character that the story (Mark i, 9–11 and parallels) occupied the first place in Gospel catechizing. The story was not conceived to show that Jesus had belonged to John's sect, but to disguise it. The intention was to show forth the messianic initiation of Jesus.

²³ The dove in the story is a mythological element somewhat time-worn. Nevertheless it is not without significance that the bird of Astarte becomes the emblem of the Spirit who, in the Gospel of the Hebrews, is expressly said to be the mother of the Christ.

²⁴ This word ($\delta\upsilon\nu\acute{\alpha}\mu\varepsilon\iota\varsigma$) is found in the saying attributed to Herod Antipas about the miracles attributed to Jesus.

²⁵ For an analysis of the miracle stories in the synoptic tradition see Bultmann, 129–150.

²⁶ They are so represented in the Acts of the Apostles and in the Epistles, especially in those to the Corinthians. Observe also what is said in Mark xvi, 17–18.

²⁷ The journey chiefly in question is that mentioned in Mark vii, 24, 31, the itinerary of which is extremely vague. Critics since Wellhausen who suppose it to have an historical basis, by connecting Luke xiii, 31–32 with Mark 14–16, have drawn the conclusion that Jesus quitted Galilee because of the Tetrarch's threatening attitude. But, in Mark, the journey to Tyre is contrived to bring in the story of the Canaanite woman, and the return through Decapolis to provide a frame for the miracles of the deaf-mute and the second multiplication of loaves, all of them stories whose symbolic meaning will hardly be contested. On the other hand, the anecdote in Luke, which floats in air without attachment, is equally without historical consistency. It may well be that the hostility of the Tetrarch had a part in determining Jesus to make for Jerusalem; but there is nothing to prove that this motive induced Jesus to take so long a journey beyond the confines of Galilee.

²⁸ Matthew iv, 25; Luke vi, 17. The *mise en scène* which in Mark iii, 7–12 is the frame for a mass of miracles is no less artificial than the arrangement of the discourse which follows them.

²⁹ For analysis of the teaching attributed to Jesus in the synoptics see especially Bultmann, 4–129.

³⁰ In the *Encyclopedia Biblica*, ii, art. "Gospels." Goguel, *La Vie du Jésus*, is more recent.

³¹ Mark xv, 34; Matthew xxvii, 46. The saying is taken from Psalm xxii, 2. For this cry of despair Luke substitutes words of confidence borrowed from Psalm xxxi, 5, "into thy hand I commit my spirit." John substitutes "it is finished" (xix, 30).

³² Mark ii, 27. The sentence is not reproduced in the parallels perhaps because its character is rather philosophic than religious.

³³ The mention of "the brothers of the Lord" in 1 Corinthians ix, 5 and in Galatians i, 19 (James) confirms the indication in Mark vi, 3 (Matthew xiii, 55, 56) concerning the brothers, enumerated by name, and the sisters of Jesus, although the scene of the preaching at Nazareth may be constructed

to make way for the aphorism "no prophet has honour in his own country.' Cf. Bultmann, 15, 29. Taken by itself the mention of the mother and brothers of Jesus in Acts i, 14 would be open to suspicion.

34 Mark i, 15; Matthew iv, 17. This feature is omitted in the parallel passage, Luke iv, 14-15; not, perhaps, without intention.

35 Granting that the reign of the Spirit began in the Christian community after the resurrection of Jesus, Christian baptism properly so-called cannot have been conferred before (cf. John xx, 22-23; Acts ii, 1-4, 37-38). But that idea is forced. In John iii, 22-26 it is stated that Jesus baptized; then, iv, 2, that he did not baptize, but that his disciples took his place in that office; finally, vii, 39, that "as yet there was no Spirit." These statements are contradictory, the result of theological embarrassment, the last two apparently glosses. Weak as is the historical authority of the fourth Gospel, it is clear that the chief author of it found nothing inconvenient in the idea that preaching and baptism went together both with Jesus and with John.

36 *Vie de Jésus*, 312-319. Renan forces the point both in the historicity he attributes to the texts and in the highly poetic commentary he passes on them. But the fundamental idea may be retained. Observe that, in regard to baptism, takes John iii, 22-23 and iv, 1 as literal history, while seeing in iv, 2 a gloss or a scruple of the editor.

37 It should never be forgotten that an ordinary meal, especially certain meals of primitive and ancient peoples, had a religious character. It was so among the Jews and in particular among the Essenes.

38 Daniel vii, 13; Parables of Enoch. In the Pauline gnosis the Heavenly Man, by contrast to the first Adam, is identical with the Son of Man of the Gospel tradition. But this transcendental idea of the Messiah is not of Jewish origin. The anointed of Jahveh was at first and remained, in essentials, a man.

39 Granting the pagan origin of the notion and the influence of Chaldeo-Iranian tradition on Jewish eschatology and apocalyptic, there is not much room for hypothesis. The thesis of a Chaldeo-Iranian origin has been developed by Reitzenstein. Holscher (192, n. 2) adopts it in the main; but the history of the myth and of its evolution is still obscure. There seems no reason to think that the myth had any influence on the preaching of Jesus, but it is far otherwise with the apostolic tradition.

40 Reitzenstein, *Das iranische Erlösungs mysterium*, 130, maintains that Jesus accepted and used "the Man?" in an eschatological sense and with a feeling of his own for union with God which can hardly have been borrowed. Obscure theology, to which Holscher, *sup. cit.*, does not adhere. This transcendent and mythical notion of "the Man" is much more easily attributed to Jesus conceived as risen from the dead than to Jesus himself in his lifetime. The latter hypothesis would make the primitive Gospel of Jesus much more gnostic than it really was.

41 Josephus, *Antiquities*, xx, 5, 1; 8, 6; *War*, ii, 13, 5.

42 Implied by the editor of Acts, v, 35-39, in the words he puts into the mouth of Gamaliel.

NOTES

43 Mark xi, 11 and xiii, 1–2 has sometimes been cited to prove that Jesus and his disciples had never previously seen Jerusalem. This is transforming the little arts of the Gospel editors into facts of history.

44 Each of the two hypotheses has supporters. They are not incompatible and each can be supported by texts. But the texts are not as consistent as they would need to be to furnish support. That the preaching of Jesus had staggering success is not probable, nor that it lasted long before alarming the Tetrarch.

45 The previsions attributed to him are conceived systematically in respect to the facts foreseen, as well as to the prophecies regarded as fulfilled by his passion. Thus the agony in Gethsemane, which the fourth Gospel is at pains to suppress, localizes a scene, deduced from Psalm xxii, but originally without specification of time and place, as we find it in Hebrews v, 7–10, where it is taken directly from the Psalm and is not, as many suppose, an echo of the Gospel story.

46 Zechariah ix, 9; Genesis xlix, 11; Psalm cxviii, 25–26. If we admit the historicity of this triumphal entry into the city it would necessarily follow that Jesus deliberately set himself to fulfil the prophecy of Zechariah ix, 9. Did he, then, intend to inaugurate the Great Event on the Mount of Olives? In that case he falls into line with "the Egyptian" who according to Josephus had the same intention. But the kind of evidence on which the tradition reposes (fulfilment of supposed prophecies) gives not the slightest support to the historicity of the facts narrated.

47 The expulsion of the traders fulfils Zechariah xiv, 20; Malachi iii, 1. If Jesus and his followers had violently taken possession of the temple court, the incident would not have terminated in an academic debate as to the authority under which Jesus claimed to act; the Roman garrison would have arrested him on the spot. Compare the case of Paul in Acts xxi, 27–34.

48 The incidents recorded of the Jerusalem ministry—academic discussion on the authority of Jesus and of John, on tribute to Caesar, on the resurrection, on the David's sonship of the Messiah, and the rating of the Pharisees—were conceived independently of each other, and then linked together by artificial transitions for the purpose of filling the Jerusalem ministry with sufficient contents.

49 The opinion recently defended by R. Eisler (*Jesus Basileus*, 1930) with great erudition but feeble proofs. The additions to Josephus' *Jewish War* in the Sclavonic version, on which Eisler chiefly relies, are probably interpolations and, even if authentic, do not contain all he would draw out of them.

50 The legend of Judas is out of harmony with the legend of the Twelve to which the attempt has been made to weld it. In reality Jesus did not choose the Twelve. They were the committee to which the first community of believers entrusted the management of their affairs after the death of Jesus. Their appointment has been antedated to the time of his ministry. On the other hand, the treachery of Judas has no sense unless we suppose him to have been one of the chief disciples. In the apostolic list Judas, the

traitor, occupying the last place, is a pendant to Peter, the renegade, occupying the first place. The legend of his death in Matthew xxvii, 3-10 and Acts i, 16-20 is wholly fictitious, and the legend of his treason, founded on some texts of the Old Testament, may have no more reality than the story of Peter's denial. Cf. Bultmann, 159, 167, 171.

51 Mark xiv, 27 (Matthew xxvi, 31), where the flight of the disciples is represented as announced in Zechariah xiii, 7. John xvi, 32 is in line with Mark, but without the reference to prophecy. In Luke there is no flight of the disciples from Jerusalem; they remain there and Jesus accordingly is made only to predict the failure of their faith (xxii, 32).

52 The dramatization of the incident goes *crescendo* in Mark, Matthew, John.

53 Mark xiv, 17-21; Matthew xxvi, 21-25; Luke xxii, 31-34; John xiii, 36-38. Bultmann, 162, thinks that the sources of Luke xxii, 31-32 knew nothing of the denial ($\dot{\epsilon}\pi\iota\sigma\tau\rho\dot{\epsilon}\psi\alpha\varsigma$ being an editorial insertion; but it may be understood in the active = "bringing back"). The fact is that the whole story of the denial has the look of a later addition.

54 Mark xiv, 22-24; Matthew xxvi, 26-28; Luke xxii, 19-20. In Luke the end of verse 19, after $\tau\dot{o}$ $\dot{v}\pi\dot{\epsilon}\rho$ $\dot{v}\mu\tilde{\omega}\nu$ $\delta\iota\delta\dot{o}\mu\epsilon\nu o\nu$, and verse 20 seem to be late additions, coming from 1 Corinthians xi, 24-25 (completed by Mark xiv, 24). The reviser of Luke and Acts knew the Eucharist as a breaking of bread and it seems that in the revision of Luke he had in mind at first its eschatological meaning (the banquets of the elect in the coming Kingdom), the author of the sources being ignorant of the mystic meaning contained in 1 Corinthians. His ignorance is not surprising if the mystic meaning did not originate with Paul.

55 The elements of this older version are embedded in Mark xiv, 23, 25. The words, "Take, this is my body," seem to have been inserted in place of the original, "Verily I say unto you I will eat no more bread," etc., a formula parallel to, "I will drink no more wine," etc., in verse 25 and in Luke xxii, 15-18. In the latter mention of the Passover has been substituted for "bread," so as to make the Last Supper into a pascal feast.

56 The scene in Gethsemane has been compressed and transported in a very curious way in John xii, 27-33, when the agony appears to dissolve into an echo of the transfiguration.

57 Dramatization is obvious in the story as given in each of the Synoptics. The object is to present the Christ as master of his destiny. See *Revue d'histoire et de litterature religieuses*, 1922, p. 445.

58 This trial, in Mark and Matthew, is composed of three elements easily distinguishable: (1) the saying about the temple which Jesus boasts he could destroy and rebuild in three days, and the testimony in relation to it—a saying which embarrassed the tradition, and which, if Jesus really pronounced it, would have been brought up in evidence before Pilate as proof of messianic pretentions; the authentic version of the saying would be in Matthew xxvi, 61, in preference to Mark xiv, 58 and John ii, 19, which expressly give it an allegorical meaning; (2) the messianic declaration made

by Jesus as Son of God, a correction in advance of the condemnation of Jesus as King of the Jews and intended to account for this condemnation by the blindness of the Jewish authorities in presence of the mystic Christ, the divine Saviour; (3) finally, the scene of the outrages inflicted on the Christ (Mark xiv, 65; Matthew xxvi, 67–68), which is a fulfilment of prophecies, especially of Isaiah i, 5 and liii, 3. The last two elements are fictitious; as to the first, there is fiction at least in the setting.

59 The morning session of the Sanhedrim (Mark and Matthew), in which Luke (xx, 66 and xxiii), who omits the night session, has lodged the trial, is a duplicate of the condemnation. In the source document this was probably the meeting at which the accusers draw up the charge to be brought before Pilate. Matthew tacks on to it the legend of the repentant Judas. In all four Gospels the story of the trial by Pilate is cut in two by the incident of Barabbas, invented less for the purpose of dramatization than to transfer, from Pilate to the Jews, the responsibility for the condemnation, which is now fixed on the Jews by the most artificial of devices. In this way Pilate is made the judge in a comic opera in which the trial loses its legal form. The intervention of Pilate's wife, in Matthew, is another attempt to whitewash the procurator. Pilate is represented as unable, in law, to refuse ratification of a sentence pronounced by the Sanhedrim according to rule. Thus arranged, the editor's version of the story defies both logic and probability.

60 Annas (Hanan) had been deposed since the year 15.

61 Jesus being regarded as a political agitator, his case would be dealt with by the Roman authority and not left to be tried by the Sanhedrim.

62 It seems certain, however, that the Sanhedrim had then the right to carry out a sentence of death pronounced in a case which came within its sphere of jurisdiction.

63 Every conceivable subtlety has been employed to reconcile the timetable of the Synoptics with that of John. They cannot be reconciled. If "traditional" be taken as meaning "historical" neither of the conflicting dates is more traditional than the other. But the synoptic date is secondary to the Johannine, the chain of stories which make up the ritual drama of the passion having been originally invented to fit what may be called the Johannine hypothesis of the Christ as the pascal lamb. While it is probable that Jesus came to Jerusalem for the Passover and was crucified on one of the days of the week before the feast, it is not impossible that he came at another time of the year, and that the coincidence of the passion with the Passover was founded solely on mystical reasons, the meaning of the feast being promptly Christianized by the hellenist Christians.

64 It would be that of the first generation if it be true that the idea of the Christ as Son of Man and Son of God was accepted at once by the earliest community. So thinks Bousset (*Kyrios Christos*, 20) supporting his view, in the first place, on 1 Corinthians xv, taken as testimony of Paul. There is no reason, however, for holding that belief in Jesus, as transfigured into the Christ by his resurrection, was at once expanded into the idea of the Man-Christ pre-existent to his appearance on earth.

65 The cohort which accompanies Judas is a happy thought for enhancing the scene of the arrest. Had Jesus been arrested by a cohort of Roman soldiers the affair would have taken a very different turn.

66 This story betrays a respect for Roman authority which can hardly have existed in the ranks of Christian believers before Hellenist Christianity had become widely spread.

67 According to the dates commonly accepted for the canonical Gospels, the Gospel of Peter would have to be in dependence upon Luke. The relation of the two Gospels is probably more complex. The Herod incident in Luke has not the air of an improvised fiction, but seems rather to be the compressed version of a story parallel to that of the trial before Pilate, which had a place in the original framework of the Gospel.

68 These facts form the background, but less as memories than as themes to exploit, explain and interpret in the ritual, that is, in the mystical poem of the passion.

69 Jerome, Ep. lviii (*Latin Patrology*, xxii, col. 581): "Ab Hadriani temporibus usque ad imperium Constantini ... in loco Resurrectionis simulacrum Jovis; in crucis rupe, statua ex marmore Veneris a gentibus posita colebatur. ... Bethleem nunc nostram, et augustissimum orbis locum ... lucus obumbrabat Thamuz, id est Adonidis, et in specu, ubi quondam Christus parvulus vagiit, Veneris amasius plangebatur." Places consecrated to pagan cults in Jerusalem may well have been requisitioned for consecration to the risen Christ just as the grotto at Bethlehem, consecrated to Adonis, was requisitioned for his birth.

70 John xix, 17 says that Jesus carried his cross; this to indicate the Christ's independence of mortal aid and his willing acceptance of death.

71 The aromatic wine is in Mark xv, 23; it may well have been the first form under which the fulfilment of Psalm lxix, 22 was indicated. It is from this Psalm that Matthew takes the gall, which he substitutes for the myrrh of Mark. The offering of vinegar, doubling in Mark and Matthew that of the wine mixed with spices, comes in all four Gospels as the last incident before the death of the Christ. The adventitious character of the incident is most perceptible in Mark (xv, 37), where we read that Jesus, having emitted a loud cry, breathed his last. This cry, which is inarticulate, was that mentioned in the original document; the previous citation of Psalm xxii, with all that follows from it, is a second version of the original, added by the evangelist.

72 Variations in the synoptics on the theme furnished by Psalm xxii, 7–9. Luke makes one of the robbers insult Jesus and converts the other, the incident of the good robber being substituted for all in Mark and Matthew that relates to the quotation from Psalm xxii, 2.

73 Fulfilment of Psalm xxii, 19, which John xix, 23–24 cites expressly, taking pains to distinguish, in spite of the text he is quoting, between the friendly division of the garments and the casting of lots for the robe. See my *Le quatrième Evangile*, 486.

74 We have seen above the meaning, in Mark and Matthew, of the

NOTES

citation of Psalm xxii, 2 and the substitution for it by Luke and John. The latter (xix, 25–27) places the mystic testament of the Christ—the sayings ot Jesus to his mother and to the beloved disciple—before the last words.

75 John suppresses this, the death of his Christ being triumphal. The prodigy seems to have been added to Mark xv, 33. Probably intended as the fulfilment of Amos viii, 9–10.

76 Also wanting in John. In the Synoptics the incident means what we read in Hebrews vi, 19–20 and x, 19–20. By the rending of the veil of his flesh the Christ enters the heavenly sanctuary, there to offer his blood, and thus open eternal life to the believer.

77 John xix, 31–37. Fulfilment of Exodus xii, 44 (Psalm xxxiv, 21) and of Zechariah xii, 10. The incident of the lance thrust may have been suggested by the last text. For the symbolic explanation connect with 1 John v, 6–7. This mystical imagery is good compensation for the centurion's profession of faith in the synoptic story and the rending of the veil. The substitution of the one symbol for the other may well have been deliberate.

NOTES TO CHAPTER III

1 The name "field of blood" is appropriate to a place of burial, but not to a cemetery "for strangers" (Matthew xxvii, 7). The idea indicated by the name is that of a burial place reserved for those who came to a bloody end in a violent or infamous death, such as suicides and executed criminals. Nothing could be more obviously artificial than the connexion of this place with "the price of blood"—the thirty pieces of silver which Judas is said to have received from the priests for betraying Jesus. The fiction contained in Matthew xxvii, 3–10, laying violent hands on certain Biblical texts (Zechariah xi, 12–13, amalgamated with Jeremiah xxxii, 6–9), has imagined a connexion between the money and the name of the place; while another fiction (Acts i, 16–20), based on other texts (Psalms lxix, 26; cix, 8), contradicts the first and connects the name with the blood of Judas, which it spills on the field bought by him with the high priests' money and where he is said, literally, to have burst. The two versions of the myth denounce each other as inventions and cancel out. "The field of blood" existed before the time of Jesus. We may conjecture that the original tradition retained some memory of a connexion between Aceldama and the crucified Jesus and that later on, when the Christ had been furnished with a befitting tomb, from which his body had miraculously disappeared to prove him risen from the dead, this connexion with Aceldama was shifted from Jesus to Judas.

2 Cf. Acts xiii, 29, and see *Le quatrième Evangile*, 496–498.

3 Matthew xxvi, 60, attributing the tomb to Joseph. Luke xxiii, 53 has "a tomb in which no man had yet been buried," followed by John who for symbolism, places the tomb in a garden.

4 Mark xv, 46; xvi, 4 insisting on the great size of the stone; Matthew xxvii, 60 does the same; Luke xxiv 2 merely mentions the presence of the stone.

5 The correspondence of this timing, in distribution, with the ritual of Adonis cannot be fortuitous.

6 John xx, 17. In the interpolated passage, 2–10, Mary of Magdala, before she yet knows that Jesus is risen, gives the information to Peter and the beloved disciple.

7 It was invented in order to conceal the real condition of the burial behind a fulfilment of prophecies.

8 These gnostic revelations are founded on instructions given by the risen Christ. So, too, are the Pauline gnosis and the Apocalypse of Peter.

9 Examples may be found in the discourses which the editor of Acts puts into the mouths of Peter and of Paul when addressing Jewish audiences. These discourses represent the apology for Christianity as presented to the Jews in the earliest Christian times.

10 John xx. The apparitions described in this chapter form the climax and bring the story to a definite end. On them the Church was founded. Chapter xxi is an addition. The Galilean apparition first described in it can by no possibility be fitted into the framework of xx. It is a parallel story, with a more limited purpose, which the author of xx, if he knew of it, decided to leave out.

11 J. Weiss, *Das Urchristentum*, 11; R. Schütz, *Apostel und Junger*, 1921, pp. 98 ff. Cf. E. Meyer, iii, 216, n. 1. But Meyer is over-hasty in deciding that a vision of Peter and study of Scripture immediately established the faith of the apostolic group; that a vision of the Twelve determined their return to Jerusalem and that Psalm cx caused them to give Jesus the title of "Lord." The requisitioning of texts did not originate this faith but followed its onward movement.

12 The word ἐκκλεσία is found again in Matthew xviii, 17, which is in the same current of tradition; but there ἐκκλεσία simply means "community."

13 Mention omitted in Matthew xxvii, 7.

14 John xxi, 15–17. The triple protestation of love, with a triple investiture in answer, seems designed to correspond with the triple denial, by way of reparation.

15 So much may be retained as historical from Acts ii, 42–46; vi, 2–3.

16 Acts iii–iv, 22. For criticism of this story see my *Les Actes des Apôtres*, 222–251. The name of John at the side of Peter is a later addition; this out of respect for the Ephesian legend and its saint. We shall see later that the same preoccupation has caused John's name to be omitted after that of James (xii, 2). In the story before us, the discourse of Peter, his arrest and appearance before the Sanhedrim appear to have been invented by the editor to fill out the picture.

17 This concludes the original story.

18 In place of these cramped conditions, which the charity of believers

could, or would, correct when they ran to extremes, the editor of Acts gives us glimpses of a fairly comfortable state of things in which pious sages live in common on a fund continually renewed, under God's blessing, by the accession of new members who bring into it all they have. Preuschen, *Die Apostelgeschichte*, 28, compares it with what we are told of Pythagoras and his disciples. But the editor is more likely to have been inspired directly by what Josephus says about the Essenes.

19 Documentation in Harnack, *Mission und Ausbreitung des Christentums*, 13, 307 ff.

20 Mark iv, 7–13, 30; cf. Matthew x. Luke ix, 1–6, 10 has the résumé of Mark's missionary discourse addressed to "the twelve apostles," and in x, 1–24 he gives the same discourse *in extenso* and makes it addressed to "seventy-two other disciples," as he found it in the source used also by Matthew. These seventy-two disciples are figures of the missionaries of the Gentiles, and the doubling is in keeping with the fiction which reserves the status of apostles to the Twelve.

21 Acts vi, 13. The elements of the text are contradictory: we are told of a legal trial before the Sanhedrim while the execution is an affair of mob violence. Many think there was no trial and that Stephen perished in a riot, stoned to death by the audience whom some discourse of his had scandalized. There is no proof whatever that the trial is a faint copy of the trial of Jesus by the high priest in the Gospels. The editor seems to have been unwilling to let Stephen be condemned on the charges brought against him before the Sanhedrim, offences against the Law of Moses. His thesis was better suited by having him massacred for reproaching the Jews for their agelong infidelity.

22 If Jesus ever uttered this saying, he did not understand it in the sense in which Stephen seems to have interpreted it.

23 Acts vii, 58, 60. All this is an interpolation in the account of the stoning.

NOTES TO CHAPTER IV

1 Cf. Heitmüller, *Zum Problem Paulus und Jesus*, Z.N.W., 1912, 320–327; Bousset, *Kyrios Christos*, 92.

2 The notice in Acts xi, 26 does not mean that the name "Christians" was bestowed on the Antioch disciples all at once, but that the pagans were not slow in so naming them. No doubt the pagans, constantly hearing the name "Christ" invoked by the new believers, took it for a proper name and thought they were calling the sect after its founder. The same would hold true of Tacitus, "Auctor hujus nominis Christus" (*Annals*, xv, 44).

3 The story about Simon in Acts viii, 5–25 is interpolated and incoherent. In certain respects Simon is the chief actor in it. But it seems that an earlier story put him in relation only with Philip from whom he wished to buy the power to work miraculous cures, which the editor of Acts turned into

a proposal to buy the Holy Spirit from Peter. In the first version Simon was denounced as a sorcerer, while in the story before us he and his sect are belittled in comparison with Christianity. The legend of Peter's relations with Simon was largely developed in later tradition and it is probable that the editor got hold of it while in process of development. It is doubtful not only whether Simon ever received Christian baptism, as the story declares, but whether he had any direct relations either with Philip or with Peter. His reputation as the father of heretical gnosis rests upon the fact that he was contemporary with the apostolic age and that his sect came into competition with nascent Christianity.

4 Acts ix, 32-35; cure of a paralytic at Lydda (on the model of the paralytic in Luke v, 18-24); raising Dorcas from the dead at Joppa (ix, 36-43, on the model of Jairus' daughter, Luke v, 21-24, 35-43, and the resurrection performed by Elijah and Elisha). These miracles are localized at Lydda and Joppa so as to bring Peter to Caesarea, the Roman political headquarters, as the right place for the conversion of a Roman centurion.

5 See *Les Mystères païens et le Mystère Chretien*, 144-146, 153-155.

6 There seems to be no doubt as to the fact of the relationship, although we are ignorant of the circumstances in which the relations of Jesus joined the group of Galilean believers. The James who is the chief figure in the first community when Paul comes to Jerusalem for the last time (Acts xxi, 18) is the brother of Jesus and he is the identical James who, in Galatians ii, 9, is counted as a "pillar" along with Peter and John. On his first journey Paul interviewed him and Cephas at the same time; but we have seen above that Galatians i, 18-20 is probably not primitive in the Epistle. The two sons of Zebedee (John and the other James) seem to have had a rather important standing by the side of Peter; but the probability is that both of them perished in 44, while Peter had to flee from the city. James, brother of the Lord, would then become the chief person in the Jerusalem community.

7 The legend was conceived in the same spirit as the great saying which appointed Peter the keeper of the keys of the kingdom (Matthew xvi, 17-19) and, like it, must have had a Syro-Palestinian origin. But the origin cannot have been narrowly Jewish-Christian. It is in point to remember that Paul, who was never chief figure at Antioch during his life, was bound to fall still further into the background there after his death. Even in the communities of Syria and Palestine that leaned towards hellenism, legend would there tend to work in Peter's favour.

8 The tale fits in with the fiction of ix, 22-26a, where Paul is made to preach at Damascus, then has him introduced to the apostles by Barnabas, and brings him back to Tarsus, whither Barnabas goes to seek him in order to bring him to Antioch. The whole story, including the commission given to Barnabas by the Jerusalem community to go to Antioch and see what has happened there is aimed at making the Twelve the prime authors of all propaganda. It is certain that Barnabas did not remain in Jerusalem after the death of Stephen.

NOTES

⁹ The mention of Barnabas as "Joseph called Barnabas, a Levite of Cyprus," in iv, 36-37, really belongs to xiii, 1 and is an anticipation. The former passage as a whole (36-37) is of a piece with the fictions indicated in the notes above and is highly suspect. If Barnabas was a Cypriot, it is not likely that he would have land to sell in Judea. See *Les Actes des Apôtres*, 262-265.

¹⁰ These statements express an ardent conviction which goes beyond the reality of the facts it brings to light. The disproportion between statement and fact may be explained either by Paul's visionary temperament or by the intervention of an editor who, at a later date, introduced into the Epistle a highly systematic interpretation of the facts in question.

¹¹ Acts xi, 26 seems to reduce the common mission of Paul and Barnabas at Antioch to one full year before their journey to Jerusalem (xi, 30) and the mission in Cyprus and Lycaonia which they are said to have accomplished together. As to the journey, it took place at the date indicated (end of 43 or beginning of 44), but the motive of it was the question of the legal observances. As to the mission, it was probably not carried out in the conditions indicated but replaces the mission to Syria and Cilicia, mentioned in Galatians i, 21-24, which must have filled the greater part of the fourteen years (according to Galatians ii, 1) between Paul's conversion and his journey to Jerusalem to discuss the question of legal observances. See *Les Actes des Apôtres*, 474-476, 506.

¹² Acts ix, 1-30. The story suppresses the mission-journey in Arabia (the Nabatean kingdom) mentioned in Galatians i, 17, and, in the face of all likelihood makes Paul begin preaching immediately in Damascus and in Jerusalem in contradiction to Galatians i, 17 and 22.

¹³ Compare 2 Corinthians xii, 14, where mention is made of a culminating vision, which is not described but may well have been, in the mind of the author, the vision which led to Paul's conversion.

¹⁴ Acts ix, 10-16: here the mission is outlined in a vision that comes to Ananias and in keeping with all that Acts will tell about Paul; Acts xxii, 1: here the mission is to the Gentiles, plainly announced in a vision Paul is said to have had in the temple at Jerusalem, after his conversion; Acts xxvi, 16-18: here the mission is laid down by Jesus himself in the original vision.

¹⁵ The fiction is not the journey into Arabia; that journey explains the intervention of the Nabatean ethnarch at Damascus (related in 2 Corinthians xi, 32-33) which determined Paul to flee the city and for which Acts ix, 23-25 substitutes a Jewish plot to kill him. See *Les Actes des Apôtres*, 414-421.

¹⁶ Cf. Acts ix, 26-30 and Galatians i, 18-20. It has been pointed out above that the editor of Acts in ix, 26-30 and xi, 22-26 manœuvres Barnabas and Paul with a view to making it appear that the foundation of the Christian groups at Antioch and elsewhere in Syria and Cilicia depend in the closest possible way on the apostles in Jerusalem, to whom in reality those foundations owed nothing at all. It will be noted that if Galatians i, 18-20 is a fiction (as it seems to be) pointing in the same direction as Acts

ix, 26–30, then the interpolator of it can have only half understood what the fiction in Acts was aimed at, for he is concerned only to subordinate Paul to Peter.

[17] On this letter, of the year 41, see Seston, *L'empereur Claude et les chrétiens* in *Revue d'histoire et de philosophie religieuses*, 1931, No. 3. The letter clearly attests the attention the Roman government is paying to Jewish affairs, the fear it has of Jewish agitations which starting at one point might have repercussions through all the empire, and its intention to suppress these disturbances. But it remains possible, even probable, that Christian preaching had something to do in the movement which Claudius intends to suppress.

[18] Acts vi, 9, where mention is made of Cyrenean and Alexandrian Jews among Stephen's audience.

[19] The story of Mark's apostolate at Alexandria belongs to legend, and the list of the first bishops of Alexandria, like that of the Roman bishops, was made up after the event.

[20] What Suetonius says (*Claud.*, 25) may easily be understood in that sense, "Judaeos impulsore Chresto assidue tumultuantes Roma expulit," if we suppose that *Chrestus* stands for Christus and that Suetonius mistook the object of the agitation for the author of it. With the same event is connected what Dio Cassius tells (lx, 6, 6) of the measures taken by Claudius against the Jews in the beginning of his reign, and many connect with it the notice about Aquila in Acts xviii, 2; at the same time they adopt the year 49, indicated by Orosius (viii, 6, 15), as the date of the edict. All that is not equally consistent; we do not know on what Orosius' date is founded; the notice in Acts, an interpolation, may be a guess of the editor. That Claudius tried to expel all the Jews is improbable and action would be taken only against disturbers of the peace. If Christians were aimed at, the date must be much earlier than the Epistle to the Romans.

[21] It would be fourteen whole years if the figure of Galatians ii, 1 has to be *added* to the three years of i, 18. But, disregarding the suspicion which falls on i, 18–20, the figure in ii, 1 seems to indicate the time elapsed since the apostle's conversion, so that we ought to *subtract* from fourteen, if not the three years, i, 18, at least the time occupied by the journey into Arabia and the stay at Damascus.

[22] Text completed as indicated in note 9 above.

[23] For example, the story about the preaching at Iconium (xiv, 1–2), to which was probably attached what is said about the stoning of Paul (19–20) which the editor has transferred to Lystra.

[24] A tale invented to furnish a reason for the journey of Barnabas and Paul, the true object of which is given further on in xv, 1–5. Paul and Barnabas were together in Jerusalem only once and it was at the date indicated by xi, 27–30, a little before the death of Agrippa I. The prophet Agabus who figures here turns up in xxi, 10–11, an interpolated passage. Our editor was not willing that Jerusalem should have no prophets when there were so many at Antioch. For the same reason he represents Jude and

Silas as prophets in xv, 32. The famine of xi, 28 is taken from Josephus, *Antiquities*, xx, 5, 2. See *Les Acts des Apôtres*, 472, 605, 785–788.

25 We have seen above how, in the editing of Acts, a common mission of Barnabas and Paul to Cyprus and Lycaonia has been substituted for their common mission to Syria–Cilicia, the former mission being placed by the editor between two journeys of Barnabas and Paul to Jerusalem (Acts xi, 30 and xv, 1–4). Of the two journeys only one took place and at the date indicated for the first; thus the substituted mission hangs in air. Other instances of one event made into two for editorial convenience will be found in the book. One might almost say that it raises this kind of amplification to the dignity of a principle. With regard to the present case see *Les Actes des Apôtres*, 474–476, 498–499, 571. Galatians (ii, 1–10) knows of only one journey of Barnabas and Paul to Jerusalem, at the date Acts assigns to the first journey, and with the object of the second.

26 Acts xv, 1–2. This preamble comes from the source document and agrees in substance with Galatians ii, 1–11, if the two texts are correctly understood. See *Les Actes des Apôtres*, 565–566.

27 The statement accords with the strange egotism with which, in this passage, Paul, or his interpreter, estimates his providential vocation.

28 This James, brother of Jesus, is certainly intended in Galatians ii, 12; cf. i, 19. At the time of the Jerusalem meeting the other James, brother of John, was still alive and is not likely to have been a dumb member of the assembly. The preponderance of James the Lord's brother would not be established till after the disappearance of the three principal disciples of Jesus.

29 Note that the theory of the double apostolate is not elsewhere formulated in the Epistle. Peter alone was the gainer by it.

30 In Acts xv, 13–21 (discourse of James) and 28–29 (apostolic letter) some special observances, abstinence from blood and the flesh of strangled animals, regulation of marriage, are substituted for the collection mentioned in Galatians ii, 10. The substitution must have been deliberate, the editor having antedated the collection in the fiction of xi, 27–30, and belittled its importance.

31 Cf. Holscher, 199, 227 n. 2.

32 E. Meyer, iii, 420. But there is no ground to conclude with Meyer (after Acts xii, 25) that the delegates from Antioch were still in Jerusalem when James and John were executed.

33 Acts xii, 1–2 mentions only the execution of James, but in hesitating language. Mark x, 39 leaves no doubt as to the martyrdom of both the sons of Zebedee and the text invites the conclusion that they perished under the same conditions. See *Les Actes des Apôtres*, 482–484. The martyrdom of John is suppressed out of regard for the Ephesian legend of his residence and death in Asia Minor towards the end of the first century.

34 According to Acts xii, 25, John-Mark left Jerusalem, after Peter's escape, in company with Barnabas and Saul; but this because the editor wants John-Mark for the companion of the two missionaries on the apostolic

journey narrated in xiii–xiv (which never took place), and also to make him the cause of the separation between Barnabas and Paul (which was caused quite otherwise). As John-Mark was really at Antioch at the time of the separation we may believe that he had fled thither with Peter.

35 Silas, after carrying to Antioch the letter of the Jerusalem elders, left with Jude (xv, 33; 34 is an interpolation co-ordinated with 40); but he returned to Antioch since we find him there after the quarrel ready to accompany Paul into Asia Minor, as John-Mark accompanies Barnabas in Cyprus. Agrippa's persecution caused Silas also to flee to Antioch and he, too, will have come there with Peter.

36 Galatians ii, 13–14. The rating administered to Peter by Paul leads to nothing definite, but continues in the general discussion of justification by faith alone without the law. This might be counted an argument against the point of view which dominates this passage. It is difficult to understand how this point of view can have been Paul's, and no less difficult to regard the story of the conflict as a pure fiction.

37 The writer of the Epistle is unwilling to confess that Paul's reprimand had the effect of embroiling him with Barnabas and making his further stay in Antioch impossible.

38 Galatians ii, 11–14 gives good ground for believing that Paul broke with Barnabas at the same time as with Peter and for the same reason or on the same pretext. The deeper motive was the growing self-importance of Paul; the pretext or occasion would be the accommodation which Barnabas and Peter wished to make with the Judaizers.

39 Acts xii, 12. In view of the general character of the story, insistence on this detail is out of place.

40 1 Peter v, 13; testimony of John the Elder in Papias. On the gratuitously unfavourable testimony which Acts gives about John-Mark see *Les Actes des Apôtres*, 519–522.

NOTES TO CHAPTER V

1 The journey and the stay at Antioch mentioned in Acts xviii, 22 in all probability never took place. See *Les Actes des Apôtres*, 706–710.

2 As the first "we" in the edited version of Acts appears in the narrative of the stay at Troas (xvi, 10), commentators have been prompt to assume that Luke first joined Paul at this place; but some critics have supposed that he was the Macedonian of the dream who, according to our story, decided Paul to pass into Macedonia. But, if we are to determine the participation of Luke in the comings and goings of Paul and other events by the alternations of "we" with impersonal forms of speech, we must assume that the editor of Acts has made no cuttings in Luke's narrative, suppressed nothing and interpolated no fictitious incidents and discourses. Now it is certain that he has done all three. The text rather invites us to think that

he who says "we" in the Troas story had been with Paul all along. There is no risk in supposing that from their starting point at Antioch he followed Paul in his haphazard journeyings, the painful stages of which are described in terms strongly suggestive of an eye-witness. The tradition which makes Luke a Christian of Antioch may well proceed from explicit testimony of the primitive book before the editor got to work on it, and is confirmed by the fact that the original author seems well informed about Antioch affairs and to have understood the birth of Christianity from his Antioch point of view. Cf. *Les Actes des Apôtres*, 627–631.

3 Acts xvi, 1 is vaguely completed by xiv, 20–21.

4 Cf. Colossians i, 1; iv, 10–11. 2 Timothy i, 5 knows both Timothy's mother and grandmother—information which the cautious critic finds rather too complete. In Acts xxi, 20–26 the nazirate of Paul is alleged as the reason for Timothy's circumcision. But Paul, when playing his part as a Jew, could practise any Jewish observance demanded by the occasion; it was not to please the Jews that he took the vows of a *nazir*, as we shall see later on. It is hardly credible that any pagan was ever circumcized by Paul merely to please the Jews.

5 At Iconium, as well as at Antioch of Pisidia, we may to some extent supplement the vague indication of Acts xvi, 4–5 by xiv, 1–3, 19, 20, and xiii, 14, 43, 50–51—employed with discernment.

6 Pressing hard on the text of Acts we might infer that the missionaries merely traversed the country without preaching in it. This is the interpretation of the text given, perhaps without warrant, by those who construe the Epistle as addressed to the communities of Lycaonia-Pisidia which belonged to the Roman province called Galatia, but were not Galatian country. The problem of the destination of the Epistle, on which critics are divided, would be non-existent if Paul, in the course of one and the same mission, founded the communities of Lycaonia and Pisidia, and then some others in Phrygia and Galatia proper, without going as far as Ancyra and Pessinonte, the Epistle to the Galatians being finally addressed to the whole of these communities.

7 The Epistle presupposes this, and the little we know about the preaching at Iconium and Antioch of Pisidia does not contradict it.

8 Acts xvi, 9–10. The "we" appears in this passage which must have been taken without alteration from the source document; 6–8 may be regarded as a highly compressed summary. There is no reason to suppose that Luke was the Macedonian, nor that he came from Philippi.

9 Acts xvi, 22, 39–40. The edited version makes Paul's captivity last for one night marked by various prodigies, in sequence to which Paul, after getting the town magistrate to exculpate him as a Roman citizen, is said to have been set free. The earthquake and its consequences are conceived on this pattern of a theme common in religious legend (cf. Euripides, *Bacchae*, 436–441, 502–503, 606–628). There is a contradiction between the proud attitude of Paul, the humble demeanour of the magistrates, and the order to quit the place without delay. The claim to be a Roman citizen is

borrowed from Paul's trial at Jerusalem and repeated. Paul was liberated without much delay, but probably by the intervention of his friends and on their bail—a trait seemingly transposed to the story that follows (xvii, 9) —on condition of his immediate departure.

¹⁰ A story cut down and changed like the one preceding. The beginning of it comes from the source document, but the riot which drives the missionaries out of the town takes place the moment after their arrival and too soon, as it did at Philippi, this time, however, provoked by Jews, as the former was by pagans. 1 Thessalonians making no reference to any occurrence of this kind, there is reason to suspect that our editor has balanced the pagan riot which put an end to Paul's ministry at Philippi by a similar charge against the Jews of Thessalonica.

¹¹ Acts xvii, 10–12. The notice about Berea seems to have a fictitious conclusion (13–14), which repeats what has been said about Thessalonica. The indications about Silas and Timothy (15) must have been changed by the editor; they are not in agreement with 1 Thessalonians iii, 1–2, nor even with Acts xviii, 5.

¹² To be inferred from 1 Thessalonians iii, 1–2.

¹³ In like manner the discourse in the synagogue at Antioch of Pisidia (xiii, 16–40) is a specimen of the teaching given to a Jewish audience, and the discourse to the elders of Ephesus (xx, 10–35) a specimen of instructions to the heads of congregations.

¹⁴ xvii, 28. The line, "for in him we live and move and have our being," is also borrowed from the poem of Epimenides, entitled *Minos*, in which we also find the saying about the Cretans in Titus i, 12. (Rendel Harris, *St. Paul and Greek Literature, Woodbrooke Essays*, 7, p. 7.)

¹⁵ Though Paul did not think that Athens might be altogether neglected, we should misconstrue his mind and the mind of the first Christian generation by concluding with E. Meyer (iii, 328–9) that Athens was the chief aim of the mission, in respect of which the preachings in the Macedonian towns was no more than rapidly completed preparation, Paul's main purpose being to overthrow hellenic philosophy on the ground where it was most at home. The editor of Acts seems to have had some such notion; but to accept the famous discourse and its *mise en scène* as authentic would be placing too much confidence in his fictions.

¹⁶ 1 Thessalonians iii, 1–2, 5–7 shows that Paul was afraid the group of Christians would not hold together after his departure; he avows his misgivings after being reassured by the good news which Silas and Timothy brought to him at Corinth.

¹⁷ Acts xviii, 1, 2, 3. His mission in Asia Minor seems to have been carried through in difficult material conditions. Later on Paul accepted help from Philippi. But on arriving at Corinth it would seem that he had to work for his living. It is possible also that his mishap at Athens induced him to test the ground before beginning his propaganda in the atmosphere of Corinth. In xviii, 2 the reference to the edict of Claudius is a later addition.

¹⁸ Cf. Philippians iv, 15–16, which shows that the Philippians helped

NOTES

Paul in his mission at Thessalonica. It is a doubtful point whether Lydia is expressly indicated, and as Paul's wife, in iv, 3, though it has been maintained by some from ancient time.

19 The story of the Corinthian mission, like the others, is mutilated and incoherent. Besides the addition in xviii, 2 (indicated in note 17), 4 should be placed after 7 and 7 attached to the beginning of 5, reading: "But, when Silas and Timothy arrived from Macedonia, Paul took up his preaching." It is then that he leaves Aquila's house and begins to preach in the synagogue. What is said in verse 6 about his quarrel with the Jews is an addition repeating the stereotyped procedure that everywhere Paul addressed himself to the pagans only after being rejected by the Jews. Paul's difficulties began after the conversion of Crispus and the others (8); between 8 and 9 there is a gap; then mention should have been made of the difficulties which no doubt compelled Paul to leave the synagogue; the vision of 9 will then encourage him to go on with his preaching in spite of everything; but there is another gap, either before or after 11, for we expect an account of the results of his ministry and get only an indication of its length.

20 To these eighteen months we must add the time spent by Paul in Aquila's house while he waited for his auxiliaries. No account need be taken of the "many days" of verse 18, which is only a bit of stitching to make a forced connexion between the mention of Paul's departure and the Gallio incident.

21 See *Les Actes des Apôtres*, 698–699.

22 See *Les Actes des Apôtres*, 508–518.

23 Acts xviii, 18–23 is a badly constructed and largely fictitious story, indicating Syria (18) as the goal of the journey, because the editor—repeating the devices he employed on the journey of Barnabas and Paul to Jerusalem at the time of the Antioch mission—cut the last approach of Paul to the mother-community into two; the vow mentioned in the same passage (18) belongs to the last journey and we shall meet it later on. The visit of Paul to the synagogue at Ephesus is wrongly timed; like the journey to Jerusalem and to Syria it is intended to disguise the true motive which determined Paul to visit the communities he had recently founded in Galatia and Phrygia. Of set purpose the editor ignores Paul's conflicts with the Judaizing Christians, just as he will know nothing of the difficulties Paul had just encountered at Corinth, in which Apollos had been involved. See *Les Actes des Apôtres*, 703–710.

24 Acts xviii, 24–28. An incoherent and touched-up story. The restriction (25), "knowing only the baptism of John," taken rigorously, contradicts the preceding statement, "he gave exact teaching about Jesus." The restriction goes with the kind of catechizing which Aquila and Priscilla are supposed to give Apollos (26). The end of the story (28), in which the preaching of Apollos is made to consist of a prolonged refutation of the Jews, throws a veil over the voluntary or involuntary part played by Apollos in the divisions at Corinth, just as what precedes is to minimize his part at Ephesus. See *Les Actes des Apôtres*, 710–717.

25 Acts xix, 1–7. The story hangs together better than that of Apollos, doubtless because the editor has put more of his own into the latter. See *Les Actes des Apôtres*, 717–723.

26 Acts viii, 14–17. Here fiction keeps to ground level and the story may serve to throw light on that of Apollos and of the twelve disciples. See *Les Actes des Apôtres*, 368–370.

27 Cf. 2 Corinthians iii, 1, where some contempt is shown for such letters which were in common use and one would think necessary.

28 Acts xix, 8–10 is a summary of the authentic story in the source document from which the editor has cut out, as he does elsewhere, the details of Paul's success and the difficulties he encountered. To make up for this he credits Paul with a parcel of miracles which form a worthy pendant to those operated by the shadow of Peter (v, 15–16), also an invention of his own. The misadventure of the Jewish exorcist has the look of being a borrowed story adapted to the history of Paul in order to bring in somehow the edifying example given by the believers of Ephesus in burning the sorcerers' books in sequence to the former incident (18–20). See *Les Actes des Apôtres*, 752–753, 756.

29 In 1 Corinthians xv, 32 there is an allusion to fighting with beasts at Ephesus, a passage whose meaning has been much discussed and the authenticity open to discussion; in xvi, 8–9 there is mention of effectual ministry in the city, but "many adversaries." The riot described in Acts xix, 23–41 fills the place of all the difficulties and setbacks Paul had to meet at Ephesus. The passage which mentions companions of Paul (29b–31) and the allusion to companions in the speech of its local magistrate (37) having the look of surcharges, and the whole story having no real attachment to Paul's Ephesian ministry, the not improbable supposition has been made that the editor of Acts found some story of an anti-Jewish riot at Ephesus and converted it into a riot against Paul. (Hypothesis of Wellhausen, taken up in *Les Actes des Apôtres*, 752–753, 756.)

30 Acts xix, 21–22, taking account of the fact that the editor deliberately omits everything that relates to the collection for the saints at Jerusalem.

31 The editor has neutralized the significance of the collection by saying nothing about it in the situations where it played a part and by representing it as a kind of symbolic act in the fictitious story where the prophet Agabus comes in (Acts xi, 27–30). See *Les Actes des Apôtres*, 471–475.

32 E. Meyer, iii, 451, would infer from 1 Corinthians i, 12; iii, 21, where Cephas is mentioned along with Paul, that Peter also came to Corinth at this time. But we may conclude with as much probability from iii, 4–9 and iv, 6 that Apollos only followed Paul to Corinth, Peter's name being merely invoked against Paul by some of his opponents. But it remains a possibility which we may regard as little probable.

33 In this passage Paul, recalling his promise, seems anxious to keep it.

34 Acts xix, 21–22. This connects with 1 Corinthians iv, 17; xvi, 1–11 where, before announcing the coming of Timothy, he says that the col-

NOTES

lection in Macedonia and Corinth is to be carried out on the lines he had laid down for Galatia.

35 Notwithstanding the somewhat cold reception Corinth had given him he had promised to return before long; later he concluded he must wait until tempers there had cooled down. Hence no doubt came the accusation of fickleness to which he replies in 2 Corinthians i, 15-20; ii, 4.

36 There seems no reason to identify this person with the incestuous man of 1 Corinthians v, 1-5, though some critics do so.

37 2 Corinthians i, 8-11, to which ii, 6 corresponds, seems to reflect such a state of mind, rather than the fear of some external danger in which Paul might have lost his life; for example, the riot described in Acts xix, 23-40 (so E. Meyer, iii, 12), in which Paul ran no danger, supposing it ever took place.

38 2 Corinthians ii, 3-4; vii, 8-12. It is this sad and severe letter which many have thought reproduced, at least in part, in 2 Corinthians x-xiii, where, rather, some fragments of it are preserved.

39 The rôle of Titus may be deduced from 2 Corinthians ii, 11-13; vii, 6-7; viii, 6, 16-17, 23, on which xii, 18 has editorial dependence. We do not know how Titus arrived in Asia at Paul's side in the nick of time to save the situation, nor how, his mission done, he disappeared from Paul's company.

40 According to 2 Corinthians xiii, 1 this was the third stay made by Paul in the city; the first, that of his mission, being much the longest; the second, certainly a short one, was that when he was checked and unable to restore order in the community; the third preceded his departure for Jerusalem and probably represents the three months which, according to Acts xx, 2-3, Paul spent "in Hellas," the editor being extremely cautious in dealing with the relations between Paul and Corinth at that time.

41 This chronology is somewhat wavering. Retaining the coincidence with Gallio's proconsulates Paul's mission to Corinth would be completed in 51 or 52, the apostle arriving at Corinth in 49 or 50, and the missions to Asia Minor and Macedonia filling the years 44-49. The mission to Ephesus cannot have been begun before 52 or 53 and ended towards 55 or 56, and Paul would then not leave Corinth for good before the spring of 56 or 57. E. Meyer (iii, 447) puts this final departure in 59; but he does this in order that he may place the death of Paul, with that of Peter, in 64, during Nero's persecution.

42 Cf. Romans xv, 26-27; xvi, 1.

43 In Acts xx, 4 Gaius is said to be "of Derbe." But the original list may have been worked over and this Gaius may be the Corinthian (mentioned in Romans xvi, 23) charged to bring the collection from Achaia. See *Les Actes des Apôtres*, 759-762.

44 The vow is antedated in xviii, 18, where the text has been retouched by the editor (see *Les Actes des Apôtres*, 704-705). This verse should be attached to xx, 16 and xxi, 23-26 as referring to the same vow. The matter in question is that of a temporary *nazirate* and a vow taken with special

reference to a pilgrimage to Jerusalem. The head was not shaved again while the vow was in force, but only on discharge from it as one of the sacrifices prescribed by the Law. The vow is antedated in the story of the fictitious journey which the editor has duplicated from the account before us. For the ordinary conditions of such vows see *Les Actes des Apôtres*, 796–798.

45 Acts xx, 5–6. The account of the sea passage is clumsily attached to the list of Paul's companions, and the "we" of the source document suddenly reappears because the editor has here picked up the thread of the original. As we know from the Epistles that Luke was not with Paul at Athens nor in the missions that followed, we may conclude that he remained at Philippi.

46 The miracle of raising Eutychus from the dead which Paul is said to have performed at Troas is on the Old Testament model, like the raising of Dorcas by Peter (ix, 36–43).

47 The editor of Acts, who says not a word about the collection, takes advantage of the stay at Miletus to lodge in this place an allocution by Paul to the elders of Ephesus on the model of a pastoral discourse to the ministers of the flock. It will be noted that the editor, whose intention is to say nothing about Paul's death, is careful to make Paul predict it (25) as a consequence of the journey he has undertaken.

48 The account of the meeting with the brethren at Tyre has, to say the least, received additions, the prophetic warning given by the brethren having a compromising likeness to what Paul himself has just said at Miletus. The seven days at Troas, the seven days at Tyre and, later on, the seven days at Puteoli (xxviii, 14) have more the look of edifying parentheses than real memoranda.

49 The conclusion of the incident (xxi, 12–14) must be nearly identical with what Luke made to follow a prediction by Philip's prophetic daughters.

50 Acts xxi, 15–16. Before the visit to James our author clumsily places a favourable reception by the brethren in general. The source document, on the contrary, represents the hospitality of Mnason as a kind of precaution against too hasty contact with the body of Judaizing Christians.

51 According to Josephus (*Antiquities*, xix, 6, 1) Agrippa I, anxious to make a show of religion, released a number of poor *nazirs* from their vows, by paying their expenses for the various sacrifices required of them by the Mosaic Law (see Numbers vi).

52 Acts xxi, 20–26. The discourse of the elders is intelligible and holds well together except for the perceptible gloss, after the words "thou seest, brother, how many thousands of Jews there are," which adds the explanation "of those who believe." Verse 22 is an artificial transition intended to make some sort of connexion between what has just been said about the disposition of believing Jews and the advice about to be given to Paul to prove his zeal for the Law before these same Jews by taking(?) a vow. The lame reference to the pseudo-apostolic decree (xv, 9) is in keeping with the false perspective.

NOTES

53 From xxi, 27 it would seem that the editor thought the nazirate lasted seven days. See *Les Actes des Apôtres*, 805.

54 The brethren mentioned in xxi, 23 had certainly been under the vow for some time.

55 In the editor's thesis, all the groups of nascent Christianity, Jewish and hellenist, keep the Law, the Jewish with the rigour of the Mosaic code, the hellenist in conformity with the prohibitions supposed to apply to all the children of Noah, and not only to the descendants of Abraham. See *Les Actes des Apôtres*, 804–807.

56 Except on this supposition the sequence of the affair is not intelligible.

57 There may be an echo of the source document in xxiii, 11. But the vision is more likely to have taken place on the night following Paul's arrest. It reveals the working of Paul's mind which suddenly led him to see that he might carry his message to Rome under Roman authority. See *Les Actes des Apôtres*, 835–837.

58 The transfer of Paul to Caesarea must have followed very soon after his arrest, but the editor has deliberately thrown the circumstances into confusion. It is certain that the Jewish authorities would not lose a moment in putting forth every possible effort to get their hands on the man whom the intervention of the Roman soldiers had saved from the fury of their people. If they thought it likely that the charge of profaning the temple would fail they could still claim Paul as a religious agitator whose revolutionary activities they had the right to suppress, especially at Jerusalem. But the tribune could not hand over to them a Roman citizen whose right to be judged only in a Roman court was incontestable. Accordingly he would at once refer the case to the procurator.

59 The resumption of the story is as easy to recognize as the interpolation which breaks it up. In xxii, 23–24 we find ourselves back at the exact point where we stand in xxi, 34–35.

60 Acts xxii, 25–29. The scene is dramatized by the editor on much the same lines as his fiction of the scourging of Paul at Philippi (xvi, 35–39), which it recalls rather too vividly.

61 xxii, 30–xxiii, 10. The editor is plainly in error in making Ananias high priest in office at the time of Paul's trial. High priest in 47, he was deposed before 52.

62 For a discussion of this and the other fictions at this point, in which the naïve audacity of the editor is indulged as freely as in the story of the sitting of the Sanhedrim, see *Les Actes des Apôtres*, 838–842.

63 xxiii, 23–30. Having invented a Jewish plot against Paul our editor has now to mobilize hundreds of soldiers to escort Paul to Caesarea, but the mention of the departure by night and the halt at Antipatris may come from the source document. The report of the tribune Lysias is no less an invention than the sitting of the Sanhedrim, of which it gives an account to Felix.

64 xxiii, 31–35. The declaration of Felix to Paul (33), "I will hear thee when thy accusers are come," has no sense unless Paul himself invoked the

jurisdiction of the procurator in order to avoid falling into the hands of the Sanhedrim which claimed him.

65 xxiv, 22–23. Two motives are alleged for the adjournment: the first, Felix knew in advance what line to take in regard to the Christian propaganda —this must come from the source document; second, that Felix wished to await the coming of Lysias—a pretext invented by the editor.

66 xxiv, 27. The editor has thought he might add that, since Felix did not release Paul before giving up office, it was to please the Jews. The fact is that Felix left Paul's case just where it was when he was relieved of office; but during the two years of its adjournment it is quite possible that an understanding, more or less tacit, was formed between the procurator and the Sanhedrim to let the matter sleep. The Jewish authority could not have much ground for complaint so long as Paul was held prisoner and the official adjournment would seem a denial of the right Paul had claimed. For the discussion of the passage, see *Les Actes des Apôtres*, 867–870.

67 xxiv, 22. See *Les Actes des Apôtres*, 862–863.

68 Aged six at the death of her father in 44, Drusilla was married in 52 to the king of Emesa, Aziz, who had himself circumcised to obtain her hand; but their union was short-lived, for the procurator Felix fell in love with her at sight and succeeded in detaching her from her husband through the good offices of a friend of his, a Jewish sorcerer from Cyprus, while Drusilla made no scruple about marrying the uncircumcised Roman in her eagerness to escape from the jealousy of Berenice, her elder sister by ten years, who envied Drusilla her greater beauty (Josephus, *Antiquities*, xx, 7, 1–2). Of Felix, Tacitus writes as follows: "Per omnem saevitiam et libidinem jus regium servili ingenio exercuit."

69 xxv, 9. The editor pretends that Festus wishes to repeat at Jerusalem the proceeding previously attributed to the tribune Lysias, that of assembling the Sanhedrim for a fuller inquiry, taking its verdict as to the guilt or innocence of the accused and getting from it a sentence which it would then be his business, as a Roman magistrate, to ratify.

70 According to the editor's point of view, Festus understood all along that the whole affair was concerned with beliefs debated among the Jews; but the procurator, faced by the demand of the Sanhedrim, is supposed unable to refuse it, just as he will be unable to refuse ratification of its sentence, if Paul elects to be tried at Jerusalem. The case is presented in the same way as the trial of Jesus in the Gospels.

71 The silly remark here attributed to the procurator is intended to corroborate the certificate of innocence he has just given to Paul in assuring Agrippa that Paul's activities in the affair were concerned only "with a certain Jesus, a dead man, whom Paul declared to be alive."

72 After all, then, the examination before Agrippa provides Festus with nothing to put into his report to Caesar!

73 "We" makes a new appearance when the sea story begins (xxvii, 1) after being in eclipse since the arrival at Jerusalem. The eclipse is partly explained by the mutilations and substitutions in the intermediate stories.

NOTES

74 The only one mentioned is Aristarchus of Thessalonica; but Timothy must also have been among them.

75 The story of the sea passage has been changed only by interpolations, easily discernible, aimed at giving greater importance to Paul's rôle in this part of the story. Examples are the following: Paul's prophetic but rejected advice to winter in Crete rather than in the place called Fair Haven; reminder of this advice and announcement, in the midst of the tempest, that no lives would be lost; probably also the intervention of Paul to denounce the sailors about to desert the ship and its passengers, and the exhortation to take food (30–38). On the substantial authenticity of the story of the tempest, which has been questioned, see *Les Actes des Apôtres*, 921–922.

76 The miracle of the harmless viper and its conclusion (3–6) remind us a little too closely of the adventure at Lystra (xiv, 8–18) in the invented story of the mission which Paul and Barnabas are said to have made into Asia Minor. The marvellous cures performed by Paul are apparently introduced to provide a filling for the three months spent at Malta.

77 From xxviii, 16, which contains the last "we," the source document must have run on to the indication in verse 30 of the two years spent by Paul in the condition known as *custodia libera*.

78 xxviii, 31. Paul devoted himself to preaching the Gospel in his own house, but it was not for the purpose of enabling him to do so that the relative liberty of which he took advantage was granted him.

79 xxviii, 22–23a. But how could the Jews of Rome at this date (62) have said to Paul that they knew of Christianity only by hearing of it as a sect that was spoken against?

80 xxviii, 25b–27. The quotation from Isaiah is found again in Mark iv, 2 (Matthew xiii, 14–15; Luke viii, 10); John xii, 39–40.

81 There is no reference to this project outside the Epistle to the Romans (xv, 24), and it would seem that Paul had renounced it even before the end of his Roman captivity. But legend has not allowed the reference to it in Romans to fall into oblivion. In any case 2 Timothy iv, 16 can be understood as a first trial at which Paul was acquitted.

82 Romans xv, 19, 23–24. Paul seems to have regarded Spain as the limit of the Western world. Circumstances may have led him to consider it impossible to reach this limit, or simply to think no more about it.

NOTES TO CHAPTER VI

1 "Exitiabilis superstitio" is to be reckoned among the "atrocia aut pudenda" which flowed into Rome from all sides. Suetonius, without connecting the persecution of the Christians with the burning of Rome, writes to the same effect (*Nero*, 16): "Afflicti suppliciis Christiani, genus hominum superstitionis novae et maleficae." The secrecy of the Christian

meetings furnished a pretext for the imputation of infamous crimes; but similar imputations had previously been brought against the Jews.

2 Tacitus writes: "Igitur primum correpti qui fatebantur." The object of *fatebantur* has to be established from the context. The first reference is to the *exitiabilis superstitio* of which *Christus* is the author and the next to the multitude condemned rather for *odium generis humani*. E. Meyer (iii, 507) says that Tacitus expressly avoided being more precise because his object was to show how the prosecution of incendiaries developed, in course of the pursuit, into the prosecution of Christians in general. In reality the first Christians laid hold of were arrested as incendiaries, and those hunted down afterwards were arrested as Christians, without the establishment of any judicial distinction between the two categories. Nevertheless the text of Tacitus can only be understood naturally as meaning a confession of incendiarism by the first of the accused. But, in view of the multitude denounced, we have still to ask what these first confessions were worth. Reitzenstein, *Die hellenistischen Mysterienreligionen*, iii, 122, maintains with some probability that the inquisition was carried out by Nero's police in the interests of the emperor and that the first to be arrested were no other than the spies employed by the police for the occasion, as happened in the trial of Octavia, when a pretended accomplice appeared to confess to adultery which had not been committed.

3 A point perfectly treated by Renan, *L'Antichrist*, 154–155.

4 Clement's evocation of the Roman martyrs comes as conclusion to a long discourse on the evil deeds, discord and jealousy recorded in the Old Testament from Cain to David. The author then comes to "examples of our generation"—to be understood as meaning the Christian age, not in the chronological sense of his contemporaries—and takes the apostles to begin with: Πέτρον, ὃς διὰ ζῆλον ἄδικον οὐχ ἕνα οὐδὲ δύο, ἀλλὰ πλείονας ὑπήνεγκεν πόνους καὶ οὕτω μαρτυρήσας ἐπορεύθη εἰς τὸν ὀφειλόμενον τόπον τῆς δόξης. διὰ ζῆλον καὶ ἔριν Παῦλος ὑπομονῆς βραβεῖον ἔδειξεν . . . δικαιοσύνην διδάξας τον κόσμον καὶ ἐπὶ τὸ τέρμα τῆς δύσεως ἐλθὼν καὶ μαρτυρήσας ἐπὶ τῶν ἡγουμένων, οὕτως ἀπηλλάγη τοῦ κόσμου καὶ εἰς τὸν ἅγιον τόπον ἐπορεύθη . . . Τούτοις τοῖς ἀνδράσιν ὁσίως πολιτευσαμένοις συνηθροίσθη πολὺ πλῆθος ἐκλεκτῶν . . . This crowd is the *multitudo ingens* of Tacitus; but we cannot be sure that the two apostles and the crowd perished on the same occasion. We have here a retrospective view of the Roman martyrs at the time of Nero. Cf. H. Lietzmann, *Petrus und Paulus in Rome*, 228–236.

5 Cf. Acts xii, 17. We have seen above why the editor of Acts omits to mention the locality to which Peter fled.

6 Account should be taken, however, of what has been said above under the Epistle to the Philippians. Peter may have been at Rome among those of whom Paul complains that they were preaching a Gospel more or less opposed to his. The fact is that the editor of Acts, who has brought the entire Roman community to pay sympathetic homage to Paul, would have been in no mind to call attention, even if he knew of them, to the divisions,

factions and contrary currents which might exist among the Roman brethren in Nero's time. At all events it is risky to suppose with E. Meyer (iii, 508) that the "jealousy and discord," of which Clement speaks in connexion with Peter and Paul, may be interpreted as playing a part in the denunciation of Christians mutually hostile. The only precise detail known in regard to the mass of the victims concerns denunciation by pagan relatives. As to the apostles, their denunciation may well have been the work of non-Christians, without any need to make the Jews responsible.

⁷ *Romans*, 4. οὐχ ὡς πέτρος καὶ παῦλος διατάσσομαι ὑμῖν. This puts the letter of Ignatius on the same level as Clement and Dionysius.

⁸ In Eusebius, *Ecclesiastical History* ii, 25. Writing to the Romans, Dionysius said that the communities of Corinth and Rome were both taught by Peter and Paul who were equally together in martyrdom at Rome. A legendary and uncritical view of primitive history.

⁹ 1 Peter v, 13. Mark is mentioned in this passage; also Sylvanus (12). We have seen that Colossians iv, 10 and Philemon 24 suppose Mark at Rome, but as one of Paul's followers, while John the Elder (in Papias) makes him the interpreter of Peter. All of which is uncertain enough.

¹⁰ John xx, 18–19 (a plain hint in xiii, 36). Martyrdom is clearly implied, and apparently by crucifixion, without indication of place. But, considering the late age of the testimony, we may believe that the author had Rome in mind. See *Le quatrième Évangile*, 524–525.

¹¹ Lietzmann, 274, concludes for the authenticity of the burial places traditionally assigned to Peter and Paul.

¹² Eusebius, iii, 5, 3, names Pella, beyond the Jordan, as the first place at which they stayed. It is noteworthy that the Judaizing Christians of those regions kept the name "Nazoreans."

¹³ Meyer, iii, 517, 554 (on the strength of Dio Cassius, 67, 14), thinks he was a Jew. But the Christian inscriptions, older than the legends Meyer sets aside, have to be reckoned with.

¹⁴ In all probability the *sacramentum* in question was the oath taken at baptism.

¹⁵ "Affirmabant autem hanc fuisse summam vel culpae suae vel erroris, quod essent soliti stato die ante lucem convenire carmenque Christo quasi deo dicere secum invicem, seque sacramento non in scelus aliquod obstringere, sed ne furta, ne latrocinia, ne adulteria committerent, ne fidem fallerent, ne depositum appellati abnegarent."

¹⁶ "Nec mediocriter haesitavi: I Sitne aliquod discrimen aetatum, an quamlibet teneri nihil a robustioribus differant; II Detur pœnitentiae venia, an ei, qui omnino Christianus fuit, desisse non prosit; III Nomen ipsum, si flagitiis careat, an flagitia cohaerentia nomini puniantur."

¹⁷ Eusebius, iv, 26 (the text quoted in iv, 13 is apocryphal).

¹⁸ Romans xiii, 1–7. A piece of padding, but introduced with a purpose.

¹⁹ This Quadratus may be the same as the person mentioned by Eusebius in iii, 37 and v, 17. As those raised from the dead are associated with those

20 Eusebius is mistaken in making the apology addressed to Hadrian. It has only recently been recovered and reconstructed. See R. Harris and A. Robinson, *The Apology of Aristides*, 1891, and Harnack, *Chronologie*, i, 271–273.

21 Cf. Colossians ii, 16–19; Acts vii, 53 (Galatians iii, 19).

22 In the *Dialogue*, 2–3, Justin himself, not, perhaps, without literary artifice, recounts the stages of his religious experience.

23 Observe that Justin here encounters Celsus, who was acquainted with the Great Church, but views Christianity as a medley of sects affecting the same name for ever quarrelling and reproaching each other with unmentionable crimes. Origen, *Contra Celsum*, iii, 12 and v, 63.

24 Justin here follows the doctrine of the Book of Enoch on the fallen angels.

25 1 *Apology*, 6. The mention of the prophetic spirit after the angels is possibly an interpolation. See Turmel, *Histoire des dogmes* (1932), 168–170.

26 Justin's imagination seems to have been occupied with a dedicatory inscription to the ancient divinity Semo Sanctus. But did he find out for himself that Simon came to Rome in the time of Claudius?

27 1 *Apology*, 26, 58. In the latter passage Justin says of Marcion: "He is still teaching. . . . Many, accepting his doctrine as the only true, make a mock of us."

28 1 *Apology*, 35, 48. The supposition has been made by some that Justin had in mind the apocryphal Acts of Pilate and that he knew them. But he speaks of official and authentic Acts, which he has not seen. The references to the registers of Quirinius and to the Acts of Pilate are conceived in identical terms.

29 2 *Apology*, 5–7. Here again Justin reproduces the Book of Enoch on the fallen angels and the bad demons.

30 Cf. Rougier, *Celse*, 361–429.

31 An authentic and contemporary account of them is contained in the letter which the Lyonnaise community addressed for the purpose to the communities of Asia and Phrygia. A copy of it was carried, with letters of the martyrs concerning the Phrygian prophets (Montanism), to the bishop of Rome by the priest Irenaeus. The story of the martyrdoms is reproduced in part in Eusebius, v, 1–4.

32 We do not know whether Pothinus also came from Asia, but the fact that the account of the trials undergone at Lyons is addressed to the communities of Asia and Phrygia points in that direction.

33 It was thus in all the persecutions, except that the accused in 64 do not seem to have been given the choice between death and apostasy.

34 The manner in which they are characterized in the letter (Eusebius, v, 1, 48) merits attention: "Those who never had a trace of faith, nor any feeling of the new marriage garment (Matthew xxii, 11–13), nor thought of the fear of God, but who by turning back brought the Way into contempt."

NOTES TO CHAPTER VII

[1] The Aramean formula is retained in 1 Corinthians xvi, 22. Revelation xxii, 20 echoes it in a translation. *Mar, marana* is the Aramean equivalent of κυρίος. This may be a title of honour and a term of politeness. In Christian usage it was a messianic title, a cult name giving divine attribute to its object.

[2] On the meaning and consequences of this see throughout Bousset, *Kyrios Christos*.

[3] *Maranatha* still appears in the Liturgy of the *Didache*. *Abba* (Father) came at some time into Christian usage (Mark xiv, 36; Romans viii, 45; Galatians iv, 6). It still retains *Amen*.

[4] Because, in synagogal reading, the divine name *Adonai*, "Lord," was usually read in place of Jahveh, which it was forbidden to pronounce.

[5] The whole chapter forms part of an instruction on the use of the flesh of animals sacrificed to idols. The position assigned to Jesus is that of a cult-lord, but the only true Lord in that category.

[6] Psalm ii, 7, quoted in Acts xiii, 32–33, where it is the equivalent of Psalm cx, 1 in the argument of Acts ii, 34–36.

[7] A strange feature is borrowed from the mystery religions in Revelation xix, 16: the title "King of Kings and Lord of Lords" is not only written on the mantle of the Christ but also tattooed on his thigh.

[8] Fragment of the Gospel of the Hebrews quoted by Jerome, *De viris*, 2.

[9] Certain cosmogonies, the Babylonian in the first instance, naturally place the creation of the world in the spring, creation being the myth of the new year.

[10] 1 *Apology*, 67, 7. The concluding remark about the instructions given by the risen Christ remind us less of Luke xxiv, 44–49 and Acts i, 2 than of the Apocalypse of Peter and of some of the gnostic gospels.

[11] Under these conditions it seems impossible to maintain that the Sunday Easter was only introduced at Rome in the time of Anicetus, otherwise we should have to place the editing of the Gospels after that date (157–168).

[12] See Dölger, *Sol salutis*, 98 ff. Evidence in Tertullian, *Apologeticum*, 16, 9 and in Clement of Alexandria, *Stromata*, vii, 7, this last inspired by 2 Corinthians iv, 6, where the symbolism is almost Justin's.

[13] Cf. Hebrews vi, 4; x, 32. In 2 Corinthians iv, 4, 6 the φωτισμός may well refer to baptismal initiation.

[14] Mark i, 8, 10; Matthew iii, 11, 16; Luke iii, 16, 22; John i, 31, 34; Acts i, 5.

[15] R. Reitzenstein, *Die Vorgeschichte der Christlichen Taufe*, would make Christian baptism depend on the baptism of the Mandeans. There may be a relationship between the two, but the alleged dependence is quite unproved, seeing that the Mandean sect is much later than the birth of Christianity. The only sacrament of the Mandeans was a repeated baptism which should

be compared, in its repeatable character, with that of the Elchasites. It is, moreover, established that the ritual of Mandean baptism owed much to the ritual of the Syrian Nestorians. A common origin is presumable; but to bring all back, including the Christian eucharist, to Mandean rites, is pure wilfulness.

[16] See the texts cited in note 15. Belief in Jesus as the Son of God passed through the following stages. In the first stage he was consecrated God's Son and Christ by his resurrection (Romans i, 4); in the second, the consecration was thrown back to his baptism (prevailing perspective of the Synoptics); in the third, it was further thrown back to his conception. The idea of the Christ as pre-existent was bound to end in proclaiming him Son of God from all eternity.

[17] The trinitarian formula in Matthew xxviii, 19 was probably added at the canonical revision and Mark xvi, 16 at the final deutero-canonical revision. In Luke xxiv, 47 baptism is implied only, as it must have originally been in the text of Matthew. John iii, 22 represents Jesus as himself baptizing. But the statement is attenuated in iv, 2 and vii, 39.

[18] If Jesus baptized he did so under the same conditions as John. Some writers would have us believe that Jesus separated from John because he attached no importance to baptism. A refinement of the imagination!

[19] Mark vi, 32–34 and parallels. In Mark viii, 1–9 and Matthew xv, 32–39 there is a second multiplication of loaves which is a duplicate of the first. Mark's reason for admitting the duplicate is to make the first a type of Jewish-Christian initiation and the second of hellenist-Christian. In John vi, 51–58 (discourse on the bread of life) the symbolism of flesh and blood is brought into relation with the multiplication of the loaves (5–14).

[20] "Gnosis" in the text.

[21] 1 Corinthians xi, 2, 17–34. This is a homogeneous instruction intended to order the Supper in keeping with the mystical conception announced in 24–25 and applied in 26–34. This instruction does not depend on the Gospels nor even on the gospel tradition, except in so far as the mystic conception of the Supper, linked to the mystic conception of redemption, is inserted into a framework, previously fixed, in which the Supper is in no sense a pascal meal but prefigures the festival of the elect in the Kingdom of God. The framework in question is also presupposed in the traditional accounts of the institution in the three Synoptics.

[22] The integrity of Justin's text is subject to caution. The last line about Jesus crucified and the Spirit as the author of the prophecies, and the earlier mention of the Christ and the Spirit, may have been added for conformity to traditional practices. Cf. Turmel, *Histoire des dogmes*, ii, 169–170.

[23] Literally "participating (incorporated) in the symbol of his death" and not "in the image of his death" as though the author were here teaching Docetism. The baptism of the Christ, not his death, is the image.

[24] The mobility of the miraculous rock in the desert is a rabbinic tradition. Philo (*Legum alleg.*, ii, 36) says that the rock is "the wisdom of God" and the manna "word of God."

25 The mention of "mingled wine" after "water" is highly suspect (ποτήριον ὕδατος καὶ κράματος). It is probable that Justin means to describe a communion with bread and water, not with bread and wine. Cf. Harnack, *Brot und Wasser, die eucharist elemente bei Justin.* On communion without wine in Christian antiquity, see Lietzmann, *Messe und Herrenmahl,* 246, 249. Tatian and the encratites, Marcion also, celebrated without wine. What has been quoted above about communion in the desert (1 Corinthians x, 1–5) may well be in accord with that practice.

26 Turmel also suspects the mention of the Spirit in this passage. See note 22.

27 But Justin shows knowledge of the rendering of thanks by the prophets which, according to *Didache,* x, 5, might be prolonged at their discretion.

28 The prayer of thanksgiving simply indicated in the Gospels. In the time of Justin the communion required only the exercise of thanksgiving over the bread and wine; the words called "the words of institution" were introduced into the liturgy at a later date. (They are artificially introduced in the liturgy of Hippolytus.)

29 The spiritual powers who ruled the visible world and without whose knowledge the coming of the Son had been effected. We have seen the place which this piece of mythology holds in diverse parts of the New Testament.

30 This confirms what has been said in note 25 of Justin's knowing the communion without wine.

31 The words, "I will raise him up at the last day," have been added to the end of verse 54.

32 For that reason probably the explanation is addressed to the disciples, not to the people who, strangers to faith, are incapable of understanding it.

33 As already said, instruction on the communion comprises 1 Corinthians xi, 2, 19–34. It is intended to authorize the mystic communion and to substitute it, as a liturgical function, for the common meal, which the primitive Supper was, and at which real abuses might occur.

34 Mark xiv, 22–25; Matthew xxvi, 26–29; Luke xxii, 14–20 (but the end of verse 19, after "given for you," and verse 20 suggest interpolation).

35 There has been much dissertation about the meaning of the preposition ἀπό (before τοῦ κυρίου in verse 23), which need not exclude intermediaries between Jesus and the author of the story. But on the hypothesis of intermediaries, as the matter concerns an act of the Christ and not a plain teaching, we should expect περί rather than ἀπό. The author places the case of the Supper among the other παραδόσεις which the Corinthians have received from him. Are all these to be transformed into Gospel traditions passed on by the Galilean apostles? Moreover, whether it be tradition or private vision, the story as here given is not in the primitive Gospel.

36 The words "till he come" are indispensable for the balance both of the phrasing and the thought. There is no ground to regard them as interpolated.

37 Because Luke xxii, 19 originally contained these words only, there is no ground for recognizing (in excluding "this is my blood") "this is my body" as an authentic saying—a metaphor employed by Jesus to indicate the fate in store for him. None of our texts has the least suspicion of this metaphor. It is highly probable that the original text of Luke referred to a supper without wine, but having the same mystic sense as the supper with bread and wine. See *L'Evangile selon Luc*, 511–512.

38 It is evident that the parallelism of the "passover," that is, the whole festival meal, with the "cup" (verses 17–18) is artificially created.

NOTES TO CHAPTER VIII

1 Romans iii, 27–iv, 24, verse 25 being the transition to the gnosis developed in the following chapters. See above, the analysis of the Epistle, p. 253.

2 Romans v, 12, 18–19. The oracular style of this gnosis attests its relatively ancient character. In 14 we read that death reigned from Adam to Moses even in those who had not sinned by imitation—$\epsilon\pi\grave{\iota}\ \tau\tilde{\omega}\ \delta\mu o\iota\acute{\omega}\mu a\tau\iota$ —of Adam's sin. We might translate, "in the manner of Adam's sin." Account must be taken of this meaning of the word for the interpretation of vi, 5, $\sigma\acute{\upsilon}\mu\phi\upsilon\tau o\iota\ \tau\tilde{\omega}\ \delta\mu o\iota\acute{\omega}\mu a\tau\iota\ \tau o\tilde{\upsilon}\ \theta a\nu\acute{a}\tau o\upsilon\ a\grave{\upsilon}\tau o\tilde{\upsilon}$, where there is no more question of an appearance of death (Docetism) than there is here question of an appearance of sin.

3 Genesis ii, 17; iii, 19. There is nothing whatever in this ancient text, taken as it stands, to suggest that death is the natural consequence of sin. Death results from the fact that, by the will of God, man has no part of the tree of life, the fruit of which nourishes the immortals.

4 *Leg. alleg.*, i, 31; *De opif. mundi*, 134. In Philo the celestial man is the ideal, divine and absolute type of humanity indicated in Genesis i, 27; the terrestrial man is the man of history, father of the human race, to which Genesis ii, 7 would refer.

5 As a slave is sold to his master.

6 The text does not mean that a non-earthly Christ has been crucified somewhere in the clouds by the "princes of the air," but that the "princes of this world" are responsible for the passion of Jesus, just as it is attributed in the Gospels to "the powers of darkness" (Luke xxii, 53), or to the "prince of this world," the devil (John xiv, 30). There is no more reason to substitute the devil for the "princes" of 1 Corinthians and to identify him with Marcion's demiurge.

7 Romans viii, 18–27. The whole of this passage differs in style from that of the context; rather ponderous prose in which there is no parallelism; viii, 28 joins on quite naturally to 17.

8 Differing in this respect from Romans v–vi, where the gnosis may borrow Biblical language here and there but not as specific quotations;

NOTES

doubtless because it is being developed on a system of its own and not as a commentary on particular texts.

9 It would be better to translate, or rather to transcribe, "by which he made even the *aeons*," but without taking this word in the full gnostic sense. The word belongs to the gnostic vocabulary, and has a meaning analogous to that of gnosis.

10 The text (Psalm viii, 6) says: "Thou hast made him but little inferior to Elohim," or "to the Elohim."

11 Hebrews vii, 1–2. "King of Righteousness" is the author's etymology of Melchisedec. The original may well have meant the god "Sedec is my King" (compare Adonizedec, "Sedec is my Lord," name of a king of Jerusalem in Joshua x, 1). Salem is understood by the author in its etymological sense. Very probably it refers to Jerusalem.

12 vii, 14. The author reasons as though Melchisedec had no real ancestors and never died. But the point of interest for us lies in the author's intention to ignore the earthly origin of Jesus.

13 ἐξ Ἰούδα ἀνατέταλκεν.

14 καθ' ὁμοιότητα helps us to understand ὁμοίωμα in Romans vi, 3–6.

15 xi, 2–40. We are even told (3) that "by faith the aeons fell into order at the word of God and the visible was not made of things that appear." This, though hardly intelligible to us, corresponds to what was said in the preamble i, 2 (see note 9 above). We would say that eternal ideas are realized in the visible world; but, to our author, the eternal ideas, as such, are just as real, if not more real, as they are when visibly externalized.

16 Cf. ix, 11–12, and the prayer *Supplices* in the Roman canon of the Mass. The Epistle to the Hebrews, which has sometimes been said to be indifferent to the Eucharist, if not to oppose it, is on the contrary full of eucharistic symbolism. We read (x, 10) that "we were sanctified by the offering" made once for all "of the body of Jesus Christ," by "the blood of the covenant" (x, 29).

17 The Peratae used the same expression—"in him all the pleroma judged good to dwell" (*Philosophoumena*, v, 2). In our next chapter the gnostics will be speaking to us again about the pleroma. The term means—God and the spiritual world as it subsists in God and forms his plenitude. The concept is founded on the idea of emanation from the source and return to it. The application of it to the Christ has never been fully and openly made by Christianity, where it has been rather compressed than developed, especially in the theology of the Latin Church. Two parallel strophes may be distinguished in the quoted passage (15–17, 18–20).

18 The conception is at once physical and theological. The στοιχεῖα are the principal parts of the cosmos and the four elements thought to constitute all bodies; but they are also the astral spirits on whom all parts of the cosmos, including humanity, were held to depend. (See Toussaint, *L'Epître de S. Paul aux Colossiens*, 137–146.)

19 The Divinity, or the divine world, being, as it were, externalized in the Christ, who is the true pleroma.

²⁰ The word πεπληρωμένοι plays with "pleroma." The literal translation would be "pleromed"—introduced into the pleroma.

²¹ We get a glimpse of what this catastrophe of the pleroma may have meant in the thought of this Christian writer; but one would like to know what the catastrophe meant—for there certainly was one—in the system which the gnosis of our Epistle opposes, while yet imitating it.

²² See above, p. 255.

²³ The meaning is that believers are parts in an invisible pleroma whose radiance is continually obstructed by the visible world in the condition to which it has come after its perversion by the "principalities" whom the Christ has conquered.

²⁴ Literally "the body." The real substance of the true mystery, which is the true salvation, is in the pleroma-Church, which is the body of the Christ.

²⁵ Unintelligible passage. Guided by verse 23 perhaps we may read verse 18 simply: ἐν ταπεινοφροσύνῃ καὶ ἐθελορησκίᾳ τῶν ἀγγέλων.

²⁶ The word ἐμβατεύων is a word of the mystery-language denoting the "first step" of initiation.

²⁷ στοιχεῖα. See note 18.

²⁸ Terms borrowed from the mystery the author is attacking.

²⁹ Prone to exaggeration as Paul was he can hardly have said that the Gospel in his time had been preached to "every creature under heaven." Cf. the spurious ending of Mark (xvi, 15), where we find the same formula.

³⁰ In some circles Jahveh Sabaoth was identified with Zeus Sabazios. On the origin of this Epistle see p. 26.

³¹ The name in question is "Lord," κύριος, a word of the Jahveh-cult. It is not the name "Jesus" which is above every name. Moreover, it is the name "Lord" that stands out in the concluding confession. The name "Jesus" corresponds to the abasement of the Christ, and "Lord" to his exaltation.

³² Verse 25 may be intended by the author in a spiritual sense and 28 a comment in terms of the common belief (see *Le quatrième Evangile*, 214). The descent into Hades is an old mythological theme which has undergone various transformations in the theologies. Ishtar in Babylonian mythology goes down to bring back Tammuz; the vegetation gods, who die and revive, also descend into Hades and return. Later the myth was sublimated. We have seen how the descent is treated in Philippians; there it becomes the descent of a celestial being into an inferior world. In some gnostic systems an aeon falls out of the pleroma and has to be ransomed. The descent of the Christ to the abode of the dead makes contact on one side with this old mythology.

³³ Romans x, 6, 7; Ephesians iv, 9–10 mention the descent only, without speaking of the Christ's activity among the dead. Matthew xxvii, 51–53 seems to imply the descent without definitely adopting it.

³⁴ *Dialogue*, 72. The Jeremiah text is quoted by Irenaeus to the same purpose, *Apostolic Preaching*, 78; *Heresies*, iv, 22. Ignatius, *Magnesians*, ix, 2,

says that Jesus went to raise the prophets because they had been his disciples in spirit. Hermas, *Parable*, ii, 16, has the dead evangelized by the apostles, not by the Christ.

35 On this point see Harnack, *Marcion*, 170.

36 It was early remarked that the Logos is called θεός not ὁ θεός. He is divine but not God absolutely.

37 To get the balance of the thought and the rhythm the words ὃ γέγονεν should be made part of verse 4, as many ancient witnesses do, instead of joining them to 3, where they have no reason to be.

38 Everything lives by the Logos and in the Logos. Recall the pleroma, note 17 above.

39 κατέλαβεν can be taken in the double sense of "understand" and "contain" (or stop).

40 Genesis i, 2. The darkness floating over the Abyss is here one of the elements in the primal chaos and has nothing of the moral meaning attached to the darkness of John i, 5, where darkness is the equivalent of evil, as in the religion of Zoroaster.

41 John xii, 31; xiv, 30; xvi, 11. The "prince of this world" has the function of the "principalities" and "powers," spoken of in the Epistles; but his character is perceptibly different. He did not originally belong to the pleroma and can never have been a part of it.

42 John viii, 44. This passage defines the nature of the devil, "a homicide from the beginning," "liar and father of lies," in whom truth is not. There is no question of his initial fall: he has always been as we find him to-day. See *Le quatrième Evangile*, 299-301.

43 John i, 9-12. All the references to John the Baptist (6-8, 15) appear to have been added to the poem of the incarnate Logos: ditto the last member of verse 13. "Those who believe in his name" explains the preceding line of the poem and the plural of the verbs in verse 13 (in the traditional text) agrees with the explaining line.

44 The reading ὅς ... ἐγεννήθη in place of οἳ ... ἐγγενήθησαν is that of Irenaeus and Tertullian and Justin seems to read it so. This verse refers quite naturally to the birth of the Logos in time, his appearance in human form, but would come in very awkwardly if understood of the birth of believers, of which, however, the divine sonship of Jesus is the prototype. See *Le quatrième Evangile*, 101-104.

45 The word "and we saw his glory, glory like that which an only begotten son might take from his father" is an irrelevant intrusion which arrests the development of the sentence and breaks the rhythm. It is in the manner of 1 John i, 1.

46 This "plenitude" is not the pleroma of gnosis—and the point is worthy of note as marking the relations of our Gospel to religious doctrines of the time—but explains what has just been said of the Logos (verse 14) as "full of grace and truth," what is now added being the direct sequel to this assertion.

47 Many interpreters, reluctant to think that the word "grace" in this

formula can be taken in its proper sense of benefit, but with two different objects—since, according to the context (14 and 17), grace is eternal life, the objective gift of salvation—deem it possible to translate not "grace (eternal life) for grace (gift of the Law)" but "grace upon grace," that is, superabundance of salvation. But the following lines, which are explanatory, favour the first interpretation, to which the Johannine language is not repugnant. It is only in the gnosis of Paul's Epistles that the Law cannot be spoken of as a "grace," or divine favour, in the ordinary sense of the word.

48 Cf. the "invisible God" of Colossians i, 15.

49 This is the meaning of i, 13–14 even if we do not admit the reading (ὅς ἐγγενήθη) of Irenaeus and Tertullian. None the less the Son, in the body of the Gospel, is conceived to pre-exist, as Son, to his incarnation in the flesh.

50 The passages in our Gospel which speak of the resurrection of the dead in the strict sense of the formula, that of rising up after death and burial, are probably the insertions of an editor. They are v, 28–29; vi, 29, 40, 44, 54.

51 The author of the Epistle has in view specially xix, 34, water and blood issuing from the side of Jesus when pierced by the soldier's lance. Misunderstanding of the spirit of both our Gospel and the Epistle reaches its limit in those who have imagined that decomposition of the blood might have produced what looked like a flow of blood and water, or that the decomposition might have been invented to prove against Marcion that the blood of Jesus was real. See *Le quatrième Evangile*, 492.

52 Cf. vii, 39.

53 In Matthew i, 16 and Luke iii, 23 we can see editorial artifice to bring the genealogies into accord with the idea of virgin conception.

54 See Bacon, *Studies in Matthew*, 151–164.

55 Cf. Bacon, 33–35.

56 Acts i, 3–11. This preamble, artificially attached to the prologue (1–2), which has been mutilated and interpolated for that purpose, gives the impression of being a résumé or extract cut out from a more complete and developed story closely analogous if not identical with what we read in the Apocalypse of Peter.

57 The scene is analogous to that of Acts in what concerns the revelation on a mountain, but the sketching more cursory.

58 The background the same as in Acts i, 3–11 but the source document is more systematically rearranged.

59 Débris of the same traditions elaborated in another way.

60 The resemblance to Acts i, 3–11 is closer, in the more developed form of the ending of Mark made known by a fifth-century manuscript recently discovered.

61 Cf. Bacon, 148–150.

62 Bacon, 151. The theme has been studied by Gressmann and Norden.

63 Bacon, 153. The theme of the star is taken up in the Ignatian Letters

(Ephesians, 19) but not in direct relation with Matthew ii, 2, 7, 9–10, as we might hastily conclude. For the first statement made is that the birth of the Christ was unknown to "the prince of this world," and that the Lord was revealed "to the worlds" (aeons) by the star which eclipsed all other stars, destroyed magic and every bond of iniquity—which can only be understood of the Christ glorified in his resurrection.

64 See *La quatrième Evangile*, 144; Bacon, 150–151. The Feast of the Epiphany was originally Dionysiac.

65 Notably Lidzbarski, *Mandäische Liturgien*, 1920, etc.

66 The chief advocate of what may be called panmandeanism was R. Reitzenstein, *Der Vorgeschichte der christlichen Taufe*, 1929, etc.

67 On the presence of this instruction in the Marcionite collection, see Harnack, 87.

68 Hermas, *Vision*, i, 2, 4; ii, 1–3, 4.

69 2 Clement, 14, 1–2 (cf. Ephesians i, 22–23); 3–5 (cf. 1 Corinthians ii, 9).

70 Revelation xxi, 9–10. Our homilist develops the metaphor into an eternal type which, spiritual in itself, comes to sensible form in the flesh of the Christ and in his followers, who themselves are his flesh.

71 *Magnesians*, 4; 6–7 (cf. Trallians, 2–3); 13; Trallians, 6–7.

NOTES TO CHAPTER IX

1 With de Faye, *Gnostiques*, 430.

2 Origin, *C. Celsum*, v, 72. Celsus says that the Helenians took the name from their master Helenos. This must be a mistake of Celsus or of the source on which he depends.

3 Origen (*C. Celsum*, i, 57; vi, 15; *In Johannem*, xiii, 27) represents Dositheus as a Samaritan Messiah who appeared after Jesus and at the same time as Simon; in like manner Hegesippus in Eusebius, iv, 22, 5. In the apocryphal Clementines (*Homilies*, ii, 23; *Recognitions*, i, 54; ii, 8) Dositheus is said to have been a disciple of John the Baptist and to have succeeded him as leader of the sect he had founded and to have soon been supplanted by Simon.

4 This results from the testimony of Origen. See the preceding note.

5 The doctrine and the practice of the Simonians here meet the gnosis of Carpocrates, which we shall consider later on, and their Docetism constitutes an affinity to Marcion. The idea that the same divinity reveals himself, and may be worshipped under different names, is met with elsewhere.

6 Hippolytus used an addition called *Apophasis megale* which he attributed to Simon. This stands in the closest affinity to the system of Valentinus and may well not come from the Simonian sect at all.

7 Justin, 1 *Apology*, 26; Irenaeus, *Heresies*, i, 23; Eusebius, iii, 26, 1–2.

8 *Epistola Apostolorum* (ed. Schmidt, 1919).

THE BIRTH OF THE CHRISTIAN RELIGION

9 Hegesippus (in Eusebius, iv, 22–27) mentions the Satornilians after the Basilideans.

10 On all these sects see de Faye, 189, 202, 349–354, 444–446.

11 See Clement of Alexandria, *Stromata*, ii, 3, 10; iii, 1, 3–4; iii, 2. Clement gives extracts from περὶ δικαιοσύνης.

12 Irenaeus, *Heresis*, i, 25.

13 On Valentinus see Irenaeus, *Heresies*, i, 1–6 and 11; *Philosophoumena*, vi, 2.

14 Ignatius, *Magnesians*, 8, 2, doubtless alludes to Sige when he says that Christ is the eternal Logos, who does *not* proceed from Silence (reading of the Greek MSS.).

15 It is not easy to find one's way through this system which has doubtless come down to us with retouchings. Inconsistence and duplication may well have existed in the original. But as there are three Saviours (Horos, Christos and the aeon Jesus) and two Wisdoms (Sophia and Hacamoth) we may suppose (invoking the résumé in Epiphanius, *Heresies*, xxxi, 4, where there seems to be only one Saviour) that the system was originally constructed on the fall of Sophia who assumed the part of Hacamoth, and on a scheme of redemption simplified to that extent (Bousset, *Gnosis*, 342). Even so the authentic quotations in Clement are enough to show that Valentinus did not construct his system with much regard to modern notions of probability.

16 *Stromata*, iii, 7, 59. Clement says elsewhere (vi, 8, 71) that Jesus was ἀπαθής. The Gospel of Peter (*Fragment*, verse 10) seems to say the same. Perhaps the Gospel of the Egyptians started this doctrine.

17 In the fragment of a homily quoted by Clement, iv, 13, 69, Valentinus addresses the initiates of his sect as follows: "You are immortal from the beginning"—that is, by nature—"you have challenged death"—in your human bodies—"that you might conquer death and that death might die in you and by you. So then, when you put the world to flight and scatter its deceitful elements without scattering the energies of your mind, you are the sovereigns of creation and masters of all perishable realities." We may see from this that Valentinus was not without eloquence nor even without philosophy. But Clement was not altogether mistaken in saying that Valentinus attributes to his "spirituals" the work of Jesus Christ himself. Between his "spiritual" mind and a stoic sage the difference is not great.

18 Cf. Burkitt, *Early Eastern Christianity* (1904), 156–192.

19 The quotations from Heracleon made by Origen in his commentary on the fourth Gospel furnish trustworthy and fairly complete information about this gnostic's doctrine. They have been collected by Brooke, *Texts and Studies*, i, 4 (1891).

20 Tertullian (*De Praescript*, 30) mentions the sum—two hundred thousand sesterces. On the letter of introduction see *Adv. Marcionem*, i, 1 and iv, 4.

21 See Harnack, *Marcion*.

22 Tertullian, *Adv. Marcionem*, i, 19: "Separatio legis et evangelii

proprium et principale opus est Marcionis, nec poterunt negare discipuli ejus quod in summo instrumento habent, quo denique initiantur et indurantur in hanc haeresim. Nam hae sunt *Antithesis* Marcionis, id est contrariae oppositiones, quae conantur discordiam evangelii cum lege committere, ut ex diversitate sententiarum utriusque instrumenti diversitatem quoque argumententur deorum."

23 Tertullian, *Adv. Marcionem*, i, 14: "Mellis et lactis societatem qua suos infantat..." The same usage among the Naassenes is attested by *Philosophoumena*, v, 8, and is found again in the liturgy of Hippolytus.

24 According to *Philosophoumena*, vii, 31, a certain disciple of Cerdo, named Prepon, made matter into a third principle beside the two gods.

25 *Adv. Marcionem*, iv, 2: "Ex iis commentatoribus quos habemus, Lucam videtur Marcion elegisse, quam caederet."

26 I Clement, 47. The reference is to I Corinthians i, 10–12: "The epistle of the blessed Paul, the apostle, which he *first* wrote to you at the beginning of the Gospel." A little further on we find a paraphrase, without reference to the hymn of charity (xiii, 1–7). To make this hymn depend on Clement is a gross misconstruction alike of the hymn and of the Clementine letter. If Clement is in nowise inspired, for his doctrine, by the salvation gnosis contained in the Epistles, there were many others like him who wrote after the formation of the canon.

27 In the third century Marcionism was still formidable enough for Origen to be at pains to refute it. At the time of Epiphanius (*obit.*, 403) there were Marcionites in Rome, in Egypt as far as the Thebaïd, in Palestine, Arabia, Syria, Cyprus, and even in Persia. Perhaps the last adepts of the sect were absorbed into Manicheism which was closely akin to their doctrine. We may indeed consider Mani, who invoked the names of Zoroaster, Buddha and Jesus, as the last of the great gnostics. His religious doctrine had the same basis as the ancient Persian religion, later penetrated by Babylonian influence (Reitzenstein, *Das iranische Erlösungsmysterium*, 94).

NOTES TO CHAPTER X

1 This results from the close connexion between *Didache*, xv and xiv The *Didache* makes no mention of presbyters (elders)—priests—just as there is no mention of them in Philippians i, 1; in I Timothy iii, 2–13; in I Clement 42, 4; in Hermas, *Vision*, iii, 5, 1.

2 *Vision*, ii, 4, 3. The difficulty of identifying the Clement of Hermas with the author of the so-called Epistle of Clement would be insurmountable if the composition of this letter is dated in the reign of Domatian (81–96), but there would be no difficulty if the letter is not earlier than 125–135. We should then conclude that neither the Clement of the Epistle and of Hermas, nor the Hermas of *The Shepherd* were disciples of the apostles, and that there is no mention of them in the New Testament.

3 See *Vision*, iii, 5, 1, a curious passage which still takes the word

"apostle" in the wide sense of an itinerant preacher, but shows the importance attached to the presbyteral episcopate by giving it prior place to the teaching apostle and to the teaching prophet.

4 *Vision*, ii, 4, 2–3; iii, 1, 8 ("presbyters"). *Vision*, ii, 2, 6; iii, 9, 7 ("the heads of the Church")—compare Hebrews xiii, 7, 17, 24 and 1 Clement i, 3; 21, 6. *Vision*, ii, 4, 3 ("the presbyters presiding over the Church").

5 *Vision*, iii, 9, 7–10. The same persons are aimed at in *Parable*, viii, 7, 4–6, as "faithful and good men but given to jealousy about preferments and honours, and all completely in bondage to the folly of striving for the first place and for honours."

6 Recall the testimony of Justin, 1 *Apology*, 65, 67, quoted above.

7 Compare "the holy vine of David" in *Didache*, 9, 2.

8 In 1 *Apology*, 8 Justin says of the only God what Marcion was saying about the demiurge: that he extracted the world "from unformed matter." If Justin did not believe that matter was eternal, he does not seem to have asked himself whence it came.

9 In contrast to the Paul of 1 Corinthians vii, the Paul of the Pastorals recommends marriage in positive terms (cf. 1 Timothy ii, 15; v, 14; Titus ii, 4).

10 Irenaeus (*Heresies*, i, preface) and Tertullian (*De Praescriptione*), without prejudice to the authenticity of the passage, apply it to Valentinus. Tertullian applies the passage recommending marriage (1 Timothy iv, 2–3) to Marcion. Cf. 2 Timothy ii, 14; iii, 7.

11 It will be noted that the distinction between spiritual and psychic is clearly laid down in 1 Corinthians ii, 10–16. In the sequel (iii, 1–3) the psychics are said to be "carnal." We have seen above that Valentinus had three classes—pneumatics, psychics and hylics (material).

12 The private meeting of Polycarp and Marcion of which Irenaeus speaks (*Heresies*, iii, 3, 4) might have taken place at Rome. If Polycarp died in 166 he might have come to Rome about 160.

13 Title of a work of Irenaeus mentioned by Eusebius, v, 26, and preserved only in an Armenian version recently (1934) discovered.

14 *Exposition*, 3 (from the Italian translation by Faldati).

15 On this point see especially Bacon, *Studies in Matthew*, 18–23.

16 See also Bacon, 32–36.

17 See Bacon, *Is Mark a Roman Gospel?* (1919); cf. *Revue d'histoire et de littérature religieuses*, 1920, 427–430.

18 There is high probability that John xxi, 15–23 (the commission to Peter) was written in Asia for the satisfaction of the Roman community (see *Le quatrième Evangile*, 69–71). Again, in the Book of Acts the forced introduction of John's name into headlines (iii, 1, 3–4, 19; viii, 6), and the apparently forced silence kept about the martyrdom of John in xii, 2, where only the martyrdom of James is mentioned, may well have been a concession made by Rome in favour of the Ephesian legend of the beloved disciple. (See *Les Actes des Apôtres*, 55, 218–223, 227, 246, 368, 481–484.)

NOTES

¹⁹ See *Les Actes des Apôtres*, 669–680, 777.

²⁰ See especially 1 Clement, 26, 2 (Hebrews i, 3–4). It is certain that Clement uses the Epistle to the Hebrews, but he does not quote it as having canonical authority. As to his other quotations, he refers to 1 Corinthians as historical evidence and not precisely as an officially sanctioned writing.

²¹ *De Pudicitia*, 20: "Et utique receptior (more widely accepted) apud ecclesias epistola Barnabae illo apocrypho (forbidden for public use) Pastore moechorum."

²² *Heresies*, iii, 11, 9; *Exposition*, 99–100 (Faldati's translation, 168–9).

²³ The canon of Muratori justifies the exclusion of *The Shepherd* on the grounds that the collection of prophets is complete in the Old Testament and that, not being apostolic, it cannot be admitted into the New.

²⁴ 1 *Apology*, 6.

²⁵ Text after Lietzmann, *Symbolstudien*, xiv, in *Zeitschrift für N.W.*, 1927, p. 91.

²⁶ Πιστεύεις εἰς Χριστὸν Ἰησοῦν, τὸν υἱὸν τοῦ θεοῦ, τον γεννηθέντα διὰ πνεύματος ἁγίου ἐκ Μαρίας τῆς παρθένου.

²⁷ Cf. Lietzmann, *art. cit.*; Hennecke, 575.

²⁸ Καὶ υἱός σου ἀπεδείχθη ἐκ πνεύματος ἁγίου καὶ παρθένου γεννηθείς. Cf. Lietzmann, *Messe*, 158.

²⁹ Streeter, *loc. cit.*; Bacon, 58.

³⁰ The interpretation given by Bacon (55) of the passage in Tertullian, *De Pudicitia*, where he says that *The Shepherd* has been judged apocryphal and spurious, "ab omni concilio ecclesiarum," seems rather forced. The reference is not to a succession of set Councils, but simply to unanimous agreement.

³¹ The word χειροτονήσατε here translated "choose" does not necessarily imply the laying on of hands, but that meaning may be supposed.

³² 1 Timothy iii, 1–13; iv, 14; v, 1, 19; 2 Timothy i, 1–6; ii, 24–26; iv, 18–20; Titus i, 5–9 (where the "presbyters" of 5 are individualized in the "bishop" of 7).

³³ The Diotrephes of 3 John 9, even if he had no personal existence, is an historical type of the bishop with no liking for wandering preachers.

³⁴ This should be taken as meaning a strict monogamy.

³⁵ Nevertheless Philippi may have had as bishop the Valens who is said by Polycarp (*Epistle*, 11) to have made himself unworthy of his office (hypothesis of Delafosse, *Lettres de Ignace d'Antioche*, 33).

³⁶ 1 Clement, 42, 44. The language of the author of these passages is clearly not that of a man who had known the apostles and was writing only thirty years after the death of Peter and Paul.

³⁷ Tertullian seems to have applied to the Marcionites in particular what he says of gnostics in general, *De Praescriptione*, 41.

Ante sunt perfecti catechumeni quam edocti. Ipsae mulieres haereticae quam procaces! . . . Ordinationes eorum temerariae, leves, inconstantes: nunc neophytos collocant, nunc saeculo obstrictos, nunc apostatas nostros . . . Itaque alius hodie episcopus, cras alius; hodie diaconus qui cras lector; hodie presbyter qui cras laicus: nam et laicis sacerdotalia numera injungunt.

38 In 172, according to the *Chronicle* of Eusebius; in 152, according to Hippolytus, *Heresies*, 48, 1. See the discussion of these dates in P. de Labriolle, *La Crise Montaniste*, 569. Maximilla died about 180, Montanus and Priscilla having previously disappeared. The date 172 may be a little too late; it is a question whether it originally referred to the outbreak of the movement or to some event which brought it to the attention of the communities.

39 Irenaeus and the martyrs of Lyons, without positively approving the saints of Phrygia, wished them not to be condemned. The attitude of Pope Eleutherus seems to have conformed to the views of Irenaeus. Tertullian, *Adv. Praxeam*, 1, speaks of a bishop of Rome who, on the point of giving express recognition to the Montanist prophesyings, was circumvented by the logician Praxeas, so that he suppressed the letter of approval which he had already written. It was probably round Zephyrinus (198–217) in the first years of his episcopate that Praxeas wove his plots.

40 Approximate date. The attitude of the bishop of Rome to Montanism seems to have contributed, at least indirectly, to the secession of Tertullian.

INDEX

Abraham, 25
Aceldama, 90, 377
Acts of the Apostles, 41, 48, 49, 340
Acts, author and editor contrasted, 129 f.
 editor of, 169, 172, 174, 176, 386–8, 390–2, 394
Akhmim fragment, 37, 365
Alexandrian Christianity, 130 f., 339
Antichrist, 20
Anti-Jewish polemic, 50
Antioch, 136 f.
Apelles, 323–4
Apocalyptic, 34
Apocalypse of John, 34, 40, 197 f., 341
 of *Peter*, 30, 35–6 f.
 the Synoptic, 34, 37
Apocryphal Acts, 58
Apollos, 158 f.
Apologists, 201 f., 208
"Apostle," 110 f.
Apostolic Creed, 343–7
Aristides, 201 f.
Ascension, the, 38
Ascension of Isaiah, 35, 37

Baptism, 40, 76, 107, 228–30, 369 f., 397
Baptism-burial, 235–6
Baptism-rebirth, 234–5
Baptismal catechism, 43, 235
Baptism of Jesus, 70, 281
Baptism, John's, 65, 66 f., 229 f.
Barabbas, 86
Barkochba, 37, 282
Barnabas, 127 f., 138, 149
Barnabas, Epistle of, 31
Basilides, 50, 56, 304
Bauer, Bruno, 9, 19
Birth-stories 46, 49, 69 f. 278–80, 282

Caesarea Philippi, 100
Canon, the New Testament, 52, 322, 337–43
Carpocras, 305 f.
Celsus, 60, 209 f., 396
Cerinthus, 300–1

Christianity, the spread of, 179
 the persecution of, 181 f., 190, 210 f.
 its legal position in the Empire, 191 f.
 in Rome, 132
 as Gnosis, 296, 345
Church, myth of, *see* Myth
Church-consciousness, 291 f.
Claudius, the Emperor, 130
Clement, First Epistle of, 31
 Second Epistle of, 32, 55, 289
Clement of Alexandria, 18, 55
Clement of Rome, 40
Colossians, Epistle to the, 26, 265–9
Communion, *see* Eucharist
Corinthians, Epistles to the, 21–4, 244–7
Couchoud, P. L., 10
Crucifixion, the, 84 f.
Cult, 11

Deacons, the Seven, 113 f.
Descent into Hades, 270 f., 402
Didache, the, 31, 33, 34, 231–4, 238, 243, 286–8, 325–8
Discourses of Jesus, 47, 51
Docetism, 31, 32, 51, 55, 58, 282
Doctrine of the "Two Ways," 31, 33
Dositheus, 298 f., 405
Drews, 10
Dujardin, E., 10
Dupuis, 9

Easter, 226 f.
Ebionites, the Gospel of the, 54
Egyptians, the Gospel of the, 32, 39, 55, 339
Empty tomb, 45, 91 f., 97
Elchasai, 64
Encratism, 55, 57, 59
Ephesians, Epistle to the, 20, 27, 289
Episcopate, development of the, 350–5
Eschatology, Jewish, 34
Esdras, Fourth Book of, 35–7 *passim*
Essenes, 64, 67, 116, 225
Eucharist, the, 82, 230–3, 238–52 *passim*, 366, 398
 the Johannine, 240–3

411

Eucharist in *First Corinthians*, 244–7
  the Synoptic account, 248–51

Faith, religious, definition of, 97
Felix, 168 f.
Festus, 170 f.
Fourth Gospel, the, 51 f., 240–3, 271–7, 340

Galatians, Epistle to the, 24, 127, 147, 160 f., 316
Gallio, 157
Gamaliel, 19
Gnosis, 25–7 passim, 28, 59, 92, 128, 232, 253, 259, 271 f., 295 f.
Gnosticism, 13, 28, 30
Goguel, 73
"Gospel," 41, 73
Gospels, the, not historical documents, 41 f., 73, 80
Gospel of Peter, see Peter

Hadrian's rescript, 196, 207
Hebrews, Epistle to the, 28 f., 260–5, 341, 401
Hebrews, the Gospel according to the, 54, 55
Hermas, 39, 328–32, 365
Hermas, Shepherd of, 35, 39, 409
Heracleon, 311 f.
Historicity of Jesus, 9–10, 69
Holy Supper, the, see Eucharist

Ignatius, Epistles of, 32, 291 f.
Initiation-rites, 228
Irenaeus, 18, 42, 52, 335, 338

James, "the brother of the Lord," 143, 380, 383
James, Epistle of, 30
Jerusalem Council, 143 f.
Jewish Dispersion, importance for spread of Christianity, 135 f.
John, Acts of, 58
John, Epistles of, 30
John, Gospel according to, see Fourth Gospel
John the Baptist, 64–8, 283
John-Mark, 146, 148 f., 177
Joseph of Arimathea, 90, 92

Josephus, 17
Judas the Galilean, 63
Justin, 42, 59, 202, 216 f., 227, 331 f.

Kingdom of God, 71, 73, 75 f., 81, 96, 133

Laodiceans, Epistle to the, see Ephesians
Last Supper, the, see Eucharist
"Logia," the, 54, 366
Logos, the, 271 f.
"Lord," 221 f.
Luke, 152, 159
Luke, Gospel according to, 44, 48, 320 f.

Marcion, 20, 27, 38, 44, 48, 50, 56, 205, 314–24, 331, 337, 396
Marcus Aurelius, 210, 212, 214
Mandeans, 68, 284, 397
Mark, Gospel according to, 45 f.
Matthew, Gospel according to, 46 f.
Melchisedec, 262, 401
Menander, 300
Messiah, 78, 96
Messianic texts, 43
Miracles, 71
Miraculous conception, 347–9
Montanism, 356 f.
Muratorian Canon, 40, 42, 338
Mystery, the Christian, 219 f.
Myth, 10, 69, 89; see also Gnosis
Myth of the Church, the, 285–91

Nazareans, the Gospel of the, 54
"Nazorean," 70, 370
Nero, 35–6, 185 f.
Nicodemus, the Gospel of, see Pilate

Ophites, 302 f.
Origen, 55, 210

Papias, 44
Parousia, see Second Advent
Passion, a liturgical drama, 85 f.
Pastoral Epistles, the, 27, 31, 332 f., 339 f.
Paul, the Acts of, 58
Paul, 151–79 passim
  his conversion, 128, 129

INDEX

Paul, his place in the Christian mission, 122, 124, 127, 179
and the collection for Jerusalem, 160, 163, 164
and Judaism, 164, 166
his Ephesian ministry, 159 f., 388
at Rome, 174 f., 177
his death, 187 f.
Peter, 99 f., 124 f., 188
Peter, Apocalypse of, see Apocalypse
Peter, First Epistle of, 29, 270
Second Epistle of, 38, 334
Gospel of, 36, 37, 55
Philip the Evangelist, 123 f., 165
Philippians, Epistle to the, 177, 269 f.
Pilate, Acts of, 57, 59
"Pleroma," 266 f., 401
Pliny the Younger, 61, 191 f.
Polycarp, 32
Polycarp, Epistle of, to the Philippians, 32
Presbyters, 328 f.
Primitive Christianity, 18, 19
Prophets, Christian, 325–7
Proto-evangel of James, 57
Ptolemy, the Gnostic, 313 f.
Purification, 67

Quadratus, 201
"Quartodeciman," 43, 53, 227, 340

Redemption theory, *see also* Gnosis
in *Colossians*, 265–9
in *Fourth Gospel*, 271–7
in *Hebrews*, 260–5
in *Philippians*, 269–71
in *Romans*, 253–60
Resurrection, 98, 224, 265, 270
Resurrection Appearances, 94 f., 223, 226
Revelation, Book of, see Apocalypse of John
Rhythmical form, 44, 52, 58
Robertson, J. M., 10
Romans, Epistle to the, 25 f., 235–40, 253–60

Sadducees, 63
Salvation, 25, 28, 41, 128, 259, 271 f.
Sanhedrim, its competency, 117 f., 171, 172, 375
Satornilians, 302
Saul, "persecutor of Christianity," 118, 129
Schmiedel, P., 73
Second Advent, 20, 74, 133, 202
Serapion, bishop of Antioch, 55
Serpent-worshippers, *see* Ophites
Seven, the, *see* Deacons
Sibylline Books, 35–6
Silas, 145, 151 f., 159
Simon Magus, 36, 64, 124, 205, 296, 369, 379 f.
Smith, W. B., 10
"Son of God," 398
"Son of Man," 78, 221, 372
Stephen, 115 f., 379
Sunday, "the Lord's Day," 225 f.
Symbolism of Fourth Gospel, 275, 276 f.

Tacitus, 61
Tatian, 56 f.
Teaching of Jesus, 72 f.
Temptation, the, 71
Tertullian, 335 f.
Thessalonians, Epistles to the, 20
Thomas, Acts of, 59
Thomas, Gospel of, 57
Timothy, 153
Timothy, Epistles to, 20, 332–4, 352–3
Titus, 23, 143, 152, 161 f.
Titus, Epistle to, 20, 352
Trajan, 191 f.
Transfiguration, the, 38, 101, 280 f.
Trial of Jesus, the, 83, 375
Twelve, the, 110, 114, 373

Van Manen, 9
Valentinus, 56, 307–11, 406

Zeus Sabazios, 26, 269, 402

413

www.ingramcontent.com/pod-product-compliance
Lightning Source LLC
Chambersburg PA
CBHW052134230426
43671CB00009B/1248